MW01700301

Gregory's

See Australia

Relax

Gregory's

See Australia

Relax

Bruce Elder

The best places to recover, recharge and unwind

Publisher Gordon Cheers

Associate Publisher Margaret Olds

Art Director Stan Lamond

Managing Editor Kate Etherington

Senior Editor Dannielle Doggett

Editor Denise Imwold

Text Editors Susan Page, Bernard Roberts

Cover Design Stan Lamond

Cartographer John Frith

Map Editors Louise Buchanan, Heather McNamara, Dee Rogers

Picture Research Gordon Cheers

Photo Library Alan Edwards

Typesetting Dee Rogers

Index Heather McNamara

Publishing Assistant Erin King

Production Rosemary Barry, Bernard Roberts

Photographers

Ken Brass, Adam Bruzzone, John Callanan, Claver Carroll, Alexander Craig, Kevin Deacon, Heather Donovan, Bruce Elder, Stuart Owen Fox, Greg French, Graham Gittins, Richard I'Anson, Ionas Kaltenbach, Judith Kempen, Colin Kerr, Mike Langford, Gary Lewis, John McCann, David McGonigal, Richard McKenna, Shane Mensforth, Ron Moon, Peter O'Reilly, Geof Prigge, Christo Reid, Jamie Robertson, Don Skirrow, Peter Solness, Phil Stanley, Steve Starling, Ken Stepnell, Warren Steptoe, Oliver Strewe, Carmen Vila, Murray White, Geoff Woods, James Young

Captions for preliminary pages and state opening spreads

Page 1: Dining outdoors at Yamba, New South Wales.
Page 2: Manly ferry on Sydney Harbour, New South Wales.
Page 3: Fishing on the Noosa River, Queensland.
Page 4: Coffee at Pellegrini's Café and Bar, Melbourne, Victoria.
Page 6: Steam train at Quorn, South Australia.
Pages 12–13: The Big Pineapple, Woombye, Queensland.
Pages 54–55: Sydney Opera House, New South Wales.
Pages 100–101: The coastline at Peterborough, Victoria.
Pages 144–145: Salamanca Place, Hobart, Tasmania.
Pages 166–167: Petaluma's Bridgewater Mill, Adelaide Hills, South Australia.
Pages 194–195: Beach and jetty at Rottnest Island, Western Australia.
Pages 230–231: The Devils Marbles, south of Tennant Creek, Northern Territory.

Photographers: Global Book Publishing would be pleased to hear from photographers interested in supplying photographs.

Published by
Gregory's Publishing Company
(A division of Universal Press Pty Ltd)
ACN 000 087 132

Marketed and distributed by Universal Press Pty Ltd
New South Wales: 1 Waterloo Road, Macquarie Park 2113
Ph: (02) 9857 3700 Fax: (02) 9888 9850
Queensland: 1 Manning Street, South Brisbane 4101
Ph: (07) 3844 1051 Fax: (07) 3844 4637
South Australia: Freecall: 1800 021 987
Victoria: 585 Burwood Road, Hawthorn 3122
Ph: (03) 9818 4455 Fax: (03) 9818 6123
Western Australia: 38a Walters Drive, Osborne Park 6017
Ph: (08) 9244 2488 Fax: (08) 9244 2554

Produced by Global Book Publishing Pty Ltd
1/181 High Street, Willoughby, NSW Australia 2068
Phone 61 2 9967 3100 fax 61 2 9967 5891

ISBN 0 7319 1444 9

National Library of Australia Cataloguing-in-Publication
Elder, Bruce.
See Australia and relax.
ISBN 0 7319 1444 9.
1. Recreation areas - Australia - Guidebooks.
2. Australia - Guidebooks. I.Title. (Series : See Australia (Sydney)).
919.4047

Printed in Hong Kong by Sing Cheong Printing Co. Ltd,
Film separation Pica Digital Pte Ltd, Singapore

Key to Road Maps

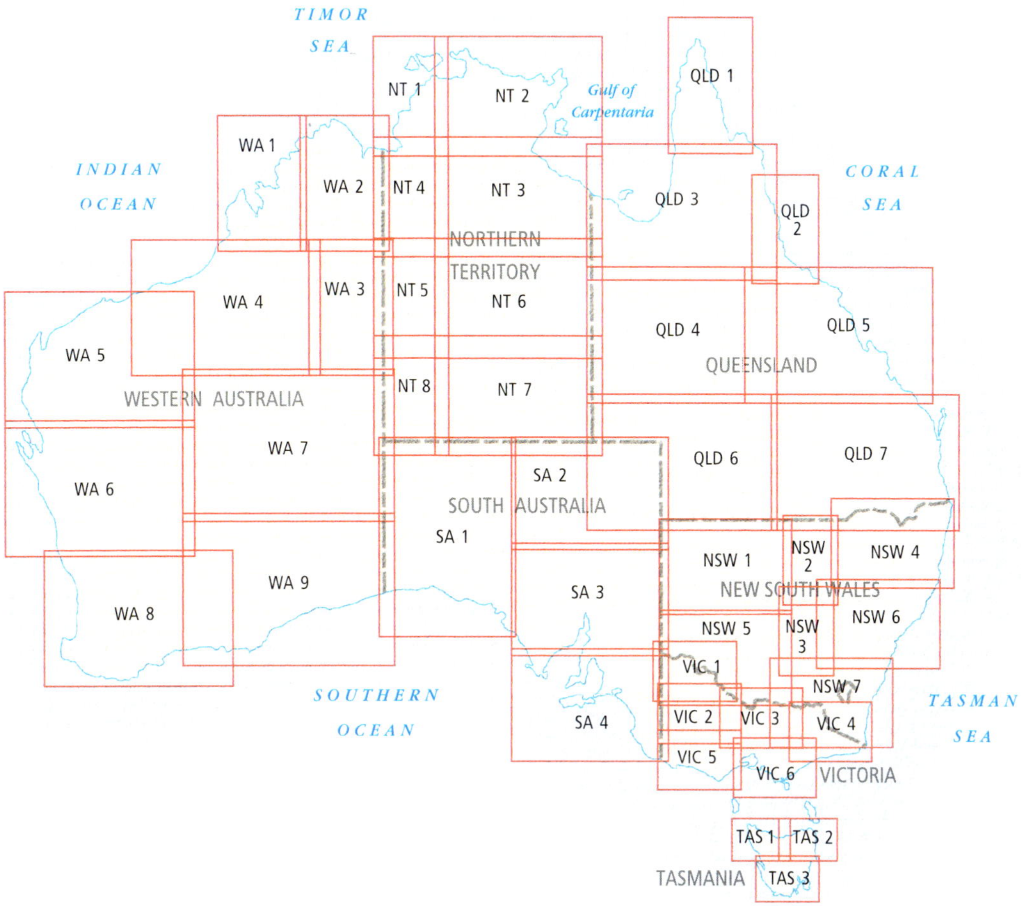

Legend to Road Maps

Freeway or motorway with national or federal route number	66 A8 1	Major linear feature (as noted)	Dog Fence
Freeway or motorway tunnel	M1	International airport	
Highway with state route numbers	69 A20	Major built up area, state or territory capital	
Major sealed road with metroad route number	5	Major city or town, other towns	
Minor sealed road, bridge		Homestead, ruin, mine,	
Major unsealed road, gate, grid		Landmark or tourist feature, mountain peak	
Minor unsealed road or track, 4WD where indicated	4WD	Bore, well or waterhole, tank or dam	
Walking track		Major river, other watercourse	
Road distances in kilometres, major and intermediate	12 18 30	Perennial lake, dry or intermittent lake	
Railway line with station	Watson	Boundary of prohibited area or military reserve	
Underground railway (city maps only)		State ot territory border	
Tramline with station (city maps only)		Marine park or reserve, coral reef	
Railway line, dismantled or abandoned (regional maps)		Aboriginal land	
Ferry route		National park, reserve, conservation area or state forest	

FLINDERS

Contents

Introduction

Just what is 'relaxing'? It is sitting on the verandah of a bed and breakfast place, a guest house or a luxury resort with an icy cocktail or a cup of tea—just enjoying the view and the atmosphere. It is going for a quiet walk on a peaceful bush track where the gum trees offer shade, the magpies and crows converse with each other in the branches and the views are constantly changing.

Above right: *Most of Australia's wineries welcome visitors, providing opportunities for tasting as well as picnic areas. This pleasant spot is at Balnaves at Coonawarra, in South Australia.*

It is about everything to do with the beach—going surfing, snorkelling, swimming, fishing, clambering around rocky headlands, cruising, sailing, water-skiing and walking along the sand. It is about exploring caves and interesting rocky formations. It is about driving to places where the air is crisp and fresh and the views are spectacular. It is about playing golf or tennis or perhaps finding a good park where the family can play a friendly game of cricket or just throw a ball to each other. It is about sitting and doing nothing.

National parks offer many beautiful places to enjoy Australia's natural wonders. Buley Rockhole at Litchfield National Park, Northern Territory, is one such place.

Australia offers unique opportunities to relax. While many of us are perfectly happy to unwind beside a beach somewhere, doing little more than sleeping and eating and reading a good book, there are those adventurous folk who think that going to the banks of the Darling or the Murrumbidgee and throwing a line in, hoping to catch a rather tasty Murray cod, is just pure heaven. There are those, anglers again, who are prepared to travel halfway across the continent to catch fresh barramundi in the waters of northern Australia. There are those—particularly city folk—who eagerly travel to farms where they can stay in simple rural accommodation, ride horses and have barbecues over open fires in the evening. And there are those whose idea of heaven is to settle themselves into chic accommodation in the Hunter Valley in New South Wales, the Clare, McLaren and Barossa Valleys in South Australia, and the Yarra Valley and Bellarine Peninsula in Victoria, and spend their days comparing the endless excellent wines at a thousand cellar doors.

Then there are those people whose idea of unwinding is getting as far away from their own kitchen, and as close to the kitchens of the country's great chefs, as possible. These people unwind with a beautiful meal served in a gracious ambience. They love the good things of life and yet, in their own way, they are no different from those people whose idea of culinary heaven is standing around a barbecue with the steaks sizzling.

Some like their holidays to be pure five-star luxury. Others, feeling part of a great Australian holiday tradition, like to find a caravan or a shack where they can barbecue the fish they caught in the morning (or some steaks and sausages) and sit around with a few beers chatting to their neighbours.

If you go on one of the Great Barrier Reef cruises and head off to Cooktown, Lizard Island, the outer reef, Hinchinbrook Channel and Dunk Island, you will immediately detect a difference between the Australian holiday-makers and the overseas visitors. The cruise is full of activities. One minute passengers will be snorkelling amidst the coral. A short time later they will be clambering through rainforest on one of the islands.

Later on they will be up and entertaining the other guests as part of a Talent Night contest. Now here's the difference. The overseas visitors participate in just about everything. They are swimming, snorkelling, running, walking and singing. But Australian passengers, for the most part, lie around

Left: *An interesting way to see the country's inland is via the rivers. The Murray River has paddleboat steamers operating from Mildura.*

Below: *Crystal-clear water for swimming and boating, plus glorious sunshine, is many people's holiday ideal, exemplified here by this beach on Rottnest Island, Western Australia.*

Left and right: *The Blue Mountains are one of the most popular destinations in New South Wales for international visitors. Australians too enjoy the beauty of the spectacular landscape and the wonderful gardens the area is famous for. Whether you want to enjoy an autumn garden at Mount Wilson or wonder at the Three Sisters, the Blue Mountains has it all*

on deck, order drinks from the bar, retreat into the air-conditioned comfort of the lounge and periodically, when the mood hits them, they drop into the deck pool for a short cooling break and then retreat back to their deck chairs to chat and snooze.

This is typical all along the Australian coast. It doesn't matter whether you are enjoying a holiday in Byron Bay, have taken a break on one of the many island resorts on the Barrier Reef, have chosen a sleepy beach for rest and relaxation—we usually take our holidays determined to take time out, not do anything too strenuous, and to 'recharge our batteries' by enjoying ourselves.

If we want a holiday full of hard exercise—just like all the people who come from other nations to our shores—we generally head overseas. We go on hiking expeditions in the Himalayas, we bicycle in southern France, we drive from one end of Great Britain to the other or we exhaust ourselves in the spectacular national parks of North America.

In this book we look at the whole of Australia and pick those places where people can really enjoy themselves and relax. From standing in awe and wonder on the edges of Shark Bay watching the dolphins being fed, to strolling around the coral shoreline of Green Island off the coast from Cairns—you can't get much more laid-back than that. If we suggest a walk—like the all-important walk to the top of Mount Kosciuszko—it will always be easy. Did you know that, with a little assistance from the snowlifts at Thredbo, a person can reach the highest point on this continent after just a couple of hours of pleasant walking along a very well-maintained pathway? That's a case of both relaxing and doing something which every Australian should do.

Australians are a group of people who love their leisure. We know how to enjoy our holidays and we know how to relax. We hope this book offers all readers a rich variety of possibilities designed to meet all requirements, from the coast to the inland, from the wealthy to the modest, from the elaborate to the simple, from the lazy to the active, and from the sports-loving to the book-reading. Remember: scientists have proved that the old line about 'all work and no play makes Jack a dull boy' is actually biologically true. We all need real rest and relaxation. Read this book and act on it.

Left: *The theme parks of Queensland's Gold Coast offer lots to see and do. These colourful characters can be seen at Movie World.*

Below: *Bushwalkers experience the scents, sounds and colours of the bush close up. Daintree National Park has some beautiful trails.*

Queensland

The Sunshine State is considered by many to be the ultimate destination in Australia for those who need to unwind and let their hair down. With warm days and balmy nights to soothe the soul year-round, Queensland offers the visitor a host of relaxing options. Take a leisurely stroll along one of the many pristine beaches, or be rocked gently to sleep on board a yacht travelling through the enchanting Whitsundays. Leave your cares at the surface as you swim among the breathtaking coral of the Great Barrier Reef, or listen to the calming bird calls and other sounds of the Daintree Rainforest. There are islands where you can join in with the crowd, and others that make you feel like you're the last person left on earth. Queensland is, in a word, paradise.

Brisbane and Environs

Brisbane is a classic subtropical city: a delightful, easy-going, modern centre situated on the Brisbane River and noted for its extensive and beautiful tropical gardens. In his book *Portrait of Brisbane* Bill Scott described the city as 'a lazy town with its sleeves rolled up, casually sprawling across its thirty-seven hills. The hills are patterned with paling fences, mango trees, high-stepping weather-board houses, and a tangle of overhead wires like the web of a demented spider.'

Above right: *As well as wandering along South Bank, taking a trip on a paddle-steamer or cruise boat is a great way to enjoy the Brisbane River.*

Of course that was long ago and today it is characterised by the gracious bridges which span the Brisbane River, the modern high-rise office blocks which rise along the river banks and, remarkably, more than 65 parks which are dotted around the city.

Attractions

The parks are the greatest attractions for many visitors. When visiting Brisbane, make sure to include a long and hugely enjoyable walk in the City Botanic Gardens which stretch in an attractive arc for over 20 hectares on the banks of the Brisbane River. The gardens occupy the gentle slopes which roll down from the elegant Old Government House (built in 1860, with many subsequent additions) and the French Renaissance-style Parliament House (erected in 1869) to the river banks.

The Botanic Gardens date back to the very earliest years of European settlement along the river. They were formally laid out by Walter Hill, the first Gardens

Brisbane's copper-domed Customs House is more than 100 years old. It has been restored and now boasts an art gallery and a licensed brasserie.

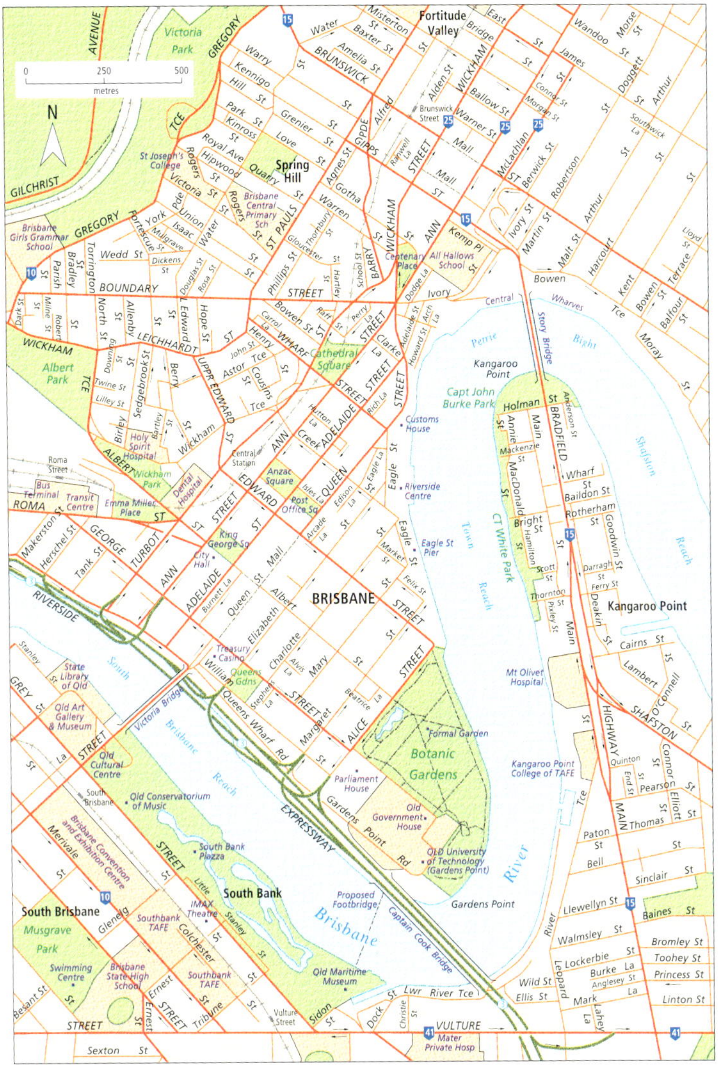

Director, who started the gardens by planting rows of indigenous bunya pines and adding plants like poinciana and jacaranda. As you wander through the gardens you will note a fountain which was constructed in 1867, and a row of weeping figs which were planted around the same time. There is no time of the year when the gardens are not spectacular. The mild climate and the rich soils of the riverbank guarantee a permanent floral display of glorious colours and wonderful tropical scents.

If you are looking for cultural activities, Brisbane is famed for its excellent Queensland Cultural Centre (located on the south bank of the river) with its complex of buildings including the Queensland Art Gallery, the Queensland Museum, the Performing Arts Complex and the State Library. It is an excellent place to see a play or a musical performance. It is also ideal for a lazy wander in the warm subtropical sun. The city has spent millions converting this into an area similar to Darling Harbour in Sydney or Fisherman's Wharf in San Francisco. The walkways, parks and restaurants give the whole area a relaxed ambience.

In the centre of the city is the City Hall Art Gallery and Museum with extensive displays of paintings, ceramics and photographs. It is part of a central business district complex based around King George Square

Below: *Colourful South Bank Markets are held on Friday nights—when they are lit by delightful lanterns—and during the day on weekends.*

which includes the clock tower, a neo-Italian renaissance edifice which rises 91 m above the City Plaza and offers panoramic views of the city.

In recent years the Queen Street Mall has become the shopping centre of the city. Boasting more than 1200 specialty shops, about 100 cafés and restaurants, 20 cinemas and five shopping malls, it is where shoppers and holiday-makers in the city inevitably head if they want to feel the pulse of the city. Like malls around the world, Queen Street is proud of its wide range of free entertainment.

Brisbane Forest Park has 28 500 hectares of lush rainforest to explore. There are scenic picnic areas plus an information centre at The Gap.

For people looking to spend at least some of their money on the gambling tables, the Treasury Casino in George Street is a magnet. Located in the city's old Treasury Building, it is open 24 hours a day, has more than 1100 poker and gaming machines, five restaurants, seven bars and over 100 tables where roulette, craps and blackjack are played.

Plan to spend at least half a day at Mount Coot-tha Botanic Gardens and Reserve, which cover an area of 57 ha. Of particular interest are the Japanese Gardens, the Tropical Dome indoor display and the Exotic Rainforest. Relax at the restaurant in the gardens which overlooks one of the many lakes or enjoy a picnic under the trees.

Map: Qld 7 N7

Beyond the City

Like all Australian cities, much of the appeal of Brisbane lies just beyond the city boundaries. To the east and around Moreton Bay lie the peaceful daytripper islands—Bribie in the north, North and South Stradbroke Islands in the south, and Moreton Island in the middle. Each has its own appeal.

Bribie Island

Bribie Island, located only 70 km north of Brisbane, is quite commercialised, being easily accessible across a bridge from the mainland. It has a wide range of accommodation, from camping sites to good quality motels. There is an emphasis on caravan parks (the island has five) and self-catering accommodation.

Bribie Island is separated from the Queensland mainland by Pumicestone Passage, which at times can be home to dugongs, dolphins and turtles. The island's northern end is a national park.

The Blue Lake is North Stradbroke Island's most famous natural attraction. It was created when fresh water filled an indentation in the landscape that lay below the level of the water table.

It is a haven for those people looking for relaxing activities, with an excellent golf course as well as outstanding fishing. The angler can expect to catch flathead, whiting and tailor. The channel which lies to the south and west of the island is also ideal for sailing, canoeing and sailboarding. Here is a destination where people can choose the appropriate environment: some areas of the island are developed while others are quiet and undisturbed.

Map: Qld 7 N6

North & South Stradbroke Islands

Located only 30 km south-east of Brisbane, North and South Stradbroke Islands were separated from each other by a storm in 1896. They are popular daytripper destinations for Brisbane residents, being only 13 km by ferry from the seaside suburbs of Cleveland and Redland Bay. Again the primary appeal of both islands is their unspoiled beauty.

North Stradbroke Island is famous for its beautiful white beaches which are ideal for walking, swimming and fishing. The island's premier attraction is Blue Lake National Park which is centred on the intensely coloured 'Blue Lake'. Here bushwalkers and visitors can expect to see a range of animals including swamp wallabies, skinks, ospreys, the mottled tree frog and, if you are very lucky, golden wallabies. The island's Brown Lake, which is only a short walk from the port of Dunwich, offers freshwater swimming as well as excellent picnic and barbecue facilities. Those interested in the island's

Anglers in southern Moreton Bay will find an abundance of bream in winter and flathead in spring. Whiting can be caught all year, but the best fishing for this species is in summer.

Right: *Australia's largest Japanese Garden is at the Toowoomba campus of the University of Southern Queensland. It features both ancient and medieval influences.*

history should stop at the fascinating Dunwich Historical Museum which has a good display of local artefacts and tells the island's history.

South Stradbroke Island, at 22 km in length, is the smaller of the two islands. It is popular with anglers and people who want to explore a destination which, although so close to the state capital, can seem to be far removed from any hints of civilisation.

Map: Qld 7 N7

Moreton Island

Moreton Island can be reached by ferry, which takes two hours from the mainland. It is a vast 192 600-ha wilderness and, as such, is ideal for people wanting to experience the peacefulness of nature. Here the visitor can see perched lakes (these are freshwater lakes nestled in between sand dunes), wetlands, and Mount Tempest which is reputed to be the highest permanent sand dune in the world. It is also claimed that the sand dunes are the steepest in the world. The visitor should remember that there are no established roads on the island, so the choices are really 4WD vehicles or walking. Of particular interest are the endless kilometres of unspoiled beaches, the Blue Lagoon (a beautiful perched lake) and the excellent opportunities for fishing. This is a destination for people who love the environment and want to be 'far from the madding crowd'.

Map: Qld 7 N6

don't miss

Situated in Purga, just a short drive south-west of Ipswich, is Ironbark Ridge Winery. Sample some of their award-winning wines, including the 1998 Chardonnay, and take a walk around the vineyard.

Ipswich has many classic examples of the timber Queenslander, as well as restored historic buildings like the Town Hall, which is now a cultural centre.

Ipswich

To the west of Brisbane is one of the most beautiful and interesting cities in Queensland. Ipswich is not usually thought of as a holiday destination, but there are many who believe it has some of the finest domestic architecture of any city in Australia. Located on the Bremer River only 40 km from Brisbane (it is now considered an outer suburb of the sprawling city), Ipswich has a staggering 78 buildings listed on its City Heritage Trail. But

ignore the public buildings—apart, obviously, from the charming and unusual local incinerator which was designed by Walter Burley Griffin (the man who designed Canberra) and which is now used as a local theatre—and concentrate instead on the beautiful houses, particularly those on the hill which overlooks the centre of the city. The houses on Denmark Hill have delightful names like 'The Foxes', 'The Palms' and 'Lakemba' and are stunning turn-of-the-century buildings. It is equally true that the view over the town from the Denmark Hill Environmental Park is exceptional, as are the parklands of Queens Park which lies near the gracious Ipswich Girls Grammar School.

Map: Qld 7 M7

Toowoomba

Toowoomba is located 128 km from Brisbane. Perched on the escarpment, the drive to the city from the east is spectacular as the visitor keeps rising up to the edge of the plateau which is 600–800 m above sea level. Toowoomba spreads from the edge of the escarpment to the west and south. The poet Bruce Dawe, who lived and worked here, wrote about the experience in a poem titled 'Provincial City': 'Climbing the range, your ears pop like champagne ...'.

It is very relaxing to ponder the reflections from the bridge that crosses the lake in Toowoomba's Japanese Gardens. The Dry Garden is also popular for meditation.

The appeal of the city, which is one of the largest in inland Australia, lies in its gardens and parks. The visitor should try and visit Toowoomba in September when it celebrates its beauty with the Carnival of Flowers.

Where does the visitor start? There is no substitute for Picnic Point Lookout which is set in parkland on the way into the city. The lookout offers excellent views across the Lockyer Valley and towards Tabletop Mountain. The park surrounding the lookout is part of more than 1000 ha of parkland in the city. No visit to Toowoomba is complete without a quiet wander through the Queen's Park Gardens (formerly known as the Botanical Gardens) which, apart from having a wide array of floral displays, are one of the highlights of the city's annual Carnival of Flowers festivities. While in Toowoomba the visitor should also have a look at the Cobb and Co Museum at 27 Lindsay Street which has the country's best display of Cobb and Co memorabilia.

Map: Qld 7 L7

Toowoomba is known as Queensland's 'Garden City'. Laurel Bank Park is one of the prettiest, with exotic trees, scented gardens, a pleasant gazebo and croquet greens.

The Gold Coast

If there is a region of Australia which is recognised as the fun park of the entire country then it is the Gold Coast. The reason for this glamorous reputation is based on the simple fact that, as early as the 1940s, Surfers Paradise and the Gold Coast started to be known, particularly in the cities of Melbourne and Sydney, as the places where smart people went to lie in the sun, enjoy themselves and partake of a lifestyle which was more like that enjoyed on the French Riviera than on a piece of Australian coastline.

Consequently the Gold Coast has been growing and developing for over half a century. It has become a famous and very diverse holiday and relaxation destination. It is now widely recognised, for example, that many people from New South Wales and Victoria retire to the Gold Coast where they enjoy the casual, subtropical lifestyle and patronise the huge sports and social clubs which are an integral part of the coast's culture. So whether you want to go and see your favourite 1960s band perform in one of the many clubs in the area (The Seekers are known to have played five sold-out nights in a row at a large club in Tweed Heads across the border in NSW), or to go and enjoy the numerous family fun parks dotted across the Gold Coast, or to sit and enjoy a coffee in a chic brasserie, or to go surfing or swimming, or to try your luck at the famous Jupiter's Casino or whether you want to enjoy the hundreds of other attractions the region has to offer, there is always something to suit every budget and every taste on this holiday coast.

Dreamworld features 12 different areas including Kennyland, which has colourful characters and rides in miniature cars, helicopters and planes.

Theme Parks and Attractions

By far the largest and most popular places to visit are the family entertainment theme parks. There is Warner Bros Movie World, Dreamworld, Wet 'n' Wild Water World and Sea World, and nearby is the smaller attraction of Koala World. Each of these 'worlds' is designed to keep the family entertained for at least half the day. Dreamworld, for example, is an Australianised version of Disneyland. Instead of the famous Disney characters the owners have created characters with a distinctively Australian feel to them: Coo-ee the Gumnut Fairy and Kenny Koala entertain the younger family members. Then there is a Main Street full of gift and food shops, a roller-coaster ride, a section called Goldrush Country and a paddle-steamer known as the *Captain Sturt*, which recalls the times of the great steamers on the Murray River. The complex also includes an Imax Theatre where visitors have an opportunity to see movies shot for the largest conventional movie screens in the world.

Warner Bros Movie World is similar to Universal Studios in Hollywood. It is both a theme park and a working studio. The Main Street is home to well-known and much-loved Warner Bros characters such as Yosemite Sam, Sylvester, Daffy Duck, Tweety Bird and Bugs Bunny. The major attractions include a marvellous re-enactment of a scene from the film *Police Academy* complete with exploding cars, people falling from high buildings and a dramatic shootout between the police and the baddies. Both are shown regularly through the day to audiences of up to 500 people. There is also an opportunity to inspect the studios and to see how many of the great special effects are achieved.

For families looking for aquatic fun away from the excellent beaches of the Gold Coast there is Wet 'n' Wild Water World, which boasts that it is one of the best and most comprehensive water-fun playgrounds in the world. This boast is backed up by more than 10 ha of park, where visitors can experience dramatic and hair-raising water slides, where they can swim in a fabulous freshwater wave pool, and where activities are pitched at all members of the family. There is also plenty of room for the family to enjoy a picnic, and the whole area is well catered for with takeaway food outlets.

Just as interesting is Sea World, a 25-ha marine park where visitors can see dolphins, whales, sea lions and penguins perform, as well as take heart-stopping rides on the infamous Three Loop Corkscrew. There is also an unusual experience known as Lasseter's Lost Mine. So popular has Sea World become that it now has its own hotel—the Nara Sea World Resort—attached to it.

Sea World has a number of marine-themed rides and attractions, plus the only polar bear exhibit in Australia.

Surfers Paradise beach is ideal for swimming, surfing, beach volleyball—or just lying in the sun.

As well as rainbow lorikeet feeding, Currumbin Wildlife Sanctuary has a fantastic free-flight bird show and a marvellous night tour by torch light.

In a similar vein to Sea World is Koala World where visitors, particularly those from overseas, can experience many of Australia's unique animals.

A more sedate family activity is visiting the marvellous bird sanctuary located on the Gold Coast Highway at Currumbin. Spread over an area of 27 ha, the sanctuary is famous for its rainbow lorikeets which descend at feeding time. The sanctuary is also home to kangaroos, wallabies, snakes, koalas and emus, and it boasts the largest subtropical rainforest aviary in the Southern Hemisphere. Other attractions include glass-blowing and a miniature railway, and there are regular re-enactments of Aboriginal myths and legends through performances of songs, dances and fire-making skills.

While the Gold Coast is dominated by these attractions and theme parks (many of which can take up a full day in a visitor's schedule), these are only some of the many reasons people visit the region. Those with alcohol on their minds can head towards Brisbane. Only 35 km south of the state capital is the centre of Beenleigh where the famous Beenleigh Rum Distillery, which reputedly houses the oldest-surviving still in Australia (built in 1864), offers visitors an opportunity to inspect the rum-making process and taste the results.

The Currumbin Wildlife Sanctuary has 27 ha of grounds, some of which has been set aside to showcase local indigenous culture.

Mountains in the hinterland afford views of Hinze Dam, which has picnic and barbecue areas, as well as the Gold Coast in the distance.

The Hinterland

If you are more inclined towards a cup of tea than a beaker of rum, then you should head for the peaceful hinterland which lies behind the Gold Coast. Here you will find an abundance of delightful villages—Tamborine Mountain, Nerang, Mudgeeraba—ideal for those people wanting to escape the excitement of the coast. Here are gift shops and tea-houses scattered along the escarpment. Here are views with the high-rise apartment blocks of the Gold Coast off in the distance and here are beautiful parks like Lamington National Park.

The World Heritage-listed Lamington National Park is famous for its outstanding ecological accommodation options. Only 45 minutes from the Gold Coast is the famous Binna Burra Mountain Lodge at Beechmont (07 5533 3622), located right on the edge of the National Park. The lodge is noted for its walking trails through the coastal rainforest and around the mountain. You can't help but relax here, as there are no phones, newspapers, radios or televisions. Children of all ages will enjoy a wide range of activities. It is also possible to camp at Binna Burra.

O'Reilly's Tree Top Walk takes visitors 15 m above the rainforest floor; birdwatchers may spot native species such as the king parrot, noisy pitta, regent bowerbird, sooty owl and rose-crowned fruit dove.

don't miss

Natural Bridge, in the Gold Coast hinterland's Numinbah Valley, is a breathtaking grotto with a waterfall that showers through a gap in the roof. The cave also has the biggest glow-worm colony in Australia.

Below: *Bushwalkers making their way through the mist-shrouded valleys of Lamington National Park may come across grey kangaroos, long-nosed bandicoots or red-necked pademelons.*

Nearby is the equally famous O'Reilly's Rainforest Guesthouse which also boasts a number of particularly cool and beautiful rainforest walks. This long-time destination for eco-travellers is set on the edge of the Lamington National Park at Green Mountain. The guesthouse has been owned by the O'Reilly family for over 80 years; members of the family still enjoy sharing their enduring love of this unique area and its wildlife with their guests. If you are not up to bush-walking, a 4WD bus can take you to some truly wonderful scenic lookouts. Contact (07) 5544 0644.

Above: *The shops and fast-food outlets of the Esplanade at Surfers Paradise are a drawcard. On Friday nights there is also a market here.*

Another great hinterland attraction is the Golden Door Health Retreat which is located 30 minutes from the Gold Coast behind the thriving township of Nerang. This famous resort (the first ones started in California decades ago) is designed, as the promotion says, for 'you to take time out from the everyday, to relax, re-focus and revitalise the senses. To retreat to a place where tired spirits can be re-newed, fresh vigour gathered and life's balance restored. A place which will truly make a difference to your health and well-being.' It mixes healthy yet delicious food with plenty of exercise and some of the most marvellous ways to pamper yourself—facials, holistic body treatments, oxygen therapy, massage, hydrotherapy, hair care, waxing and tinting. Contact (07) 5546 6855.

Other Places of Interest

Back on the coast, people who see gambling as a form of relaxation will enjoy a visit to the $185 million Jupiter's

Casino which lies behind the beachfront at Surfers Paradise. Visitors hoping to enjoy the local surf can try any of the beaches from Coolangatta to Southport.

Lying to the extreme south of the Gold Coast is Coolangatta. It is the oldest of all the holiday settlements and, as such, has a quieter and more relaxed feeling. The beaches around Coolangatta are less hurried and the accommodation seems to be less overtly Miami-style high-rise. There are some particularly attractive beach and headland walks around Coolangatta (notably around the lighthouse on Point Danger). A little further up the coast is the Burleigh Heads National Park, one of the few remnants of natural bushland on the Gold Coast. This small park—it is only 24 ha—lies between Tallebudgera Creek and Burleigh Heads. It is a remnant of a huge volcano which was centred at Mount Warning 22 million years ago. The park offers visitors the opportunity to walk along a well-maintained 3-km track through coastal rainforest and heathlands. It is possible from this track to enjoy excellent views of the ocean. There is also the possibility of seeing a variety of native animals including wallabies, koalas and bandicoots in one of Australia's most densely urbanised areas.

There's nothing more relaxing in Surfers Paradise than leaving the crowds behind to fish from the beach. Charter boats take anglers out to the waters off the Gold Coast.

Captain Cook Memorial Park in Coolangatta is dedicated to the British explorer who charted this part of the coast in 1770. Point Danger, named by Cook, is now protected by a lighthouse.

did you know?

Tamborine Mountains National Park is made up of seven smaller parks in the Gold Coast hinterland. One of these parks, Witches Falls, was gazetted in 1908 and is Queensland's oldest national park.

The Sunshine Coast

The region known as the Sunshine Coast stretches from Caloundra in the south to Noosa Heads and the Great Sandy National Park in the north—and is little more than an hour's drive north of Brisbane. The Sunshine Coast has around 150 km of perfect surfing beaches, tropical fruit plantations, delightful hinterland towns and larger-than-life tourist attractions. Noosa Heads has a cosmopolitan air, while Maroochydore and Caloundra both boast excellent swimming beaches.

Buderim, located on a plateau between the Blackall Range and the coast, is noted for its beautiful homes and gardens, and the markets at Eumundi are a must for those looking for a bargain.

The Coastal Attractions

How good is the Sunshine Coast? Well, like all areas of Australia it has enough egalitarian flexibility to be ideal for just about everyone who comes to visit it. If what you want is coffee of a high quality, cuisine like that found in the major cities and fine wines then there are plenty of restaurants on Hastings Street which cater for such tastes. It is equally true that a milkshake and a chiko roll or a hamburger are possible all the way along the coast and particularly in the major centres of Maroochydore and Caloundra. If you want to lie on the veranda of a very expensive apartment overlooking Noosa Beach that is possible. It is also possible to stay in a caravan park in Maroochydore (there are six) or Caloundra where there are four. This is an area where the family can happily spend quite a few hours at The Big Pineapple gorging themselves on pineapples and macadamia nuts, or a couple, looking for a quiet evening, can drink a bottle of Grange Hermitage wine while paying hundreds of dollars for a haute cuisine meal.

Noosa Heads

The heart of the Sunshine Coast is definitely Noosa Heads. It is an affluent coastal town located 146 km north of Brisbane. The town has always attracted those wanting to escape. In fact its first known European inhabitant was the convict 'Wandi' (David Bracefell) who managed to escape four times from the penal colony

Right: *Located north of Maroochydore, Coolum is a popular holiday town—but there are still places where you feel like you can escape the crowd.*

Caloundra's Dicky Beach is an outstanding surf beach, which makes it an ideal location for surf-lifesaving competitions throughout the year.

at Moreton Bay between 1828 and 1839. Each time he went to Noosa and lived with the local Australian Aboriginals. It could be argued that he was the first person who really understood what going to Noosa to relax and unwind was all about.

Noosa Sound is a great place to stay while in this resort town, as it is tranquil and green yet still remains within walking distance of Main Beach, busy Hastings Street and Noosa National Park.

It wasn't until the 1940s that Noosa began to develop as a major tourist destination. Today it is a place where most people come just to enjoy the beach and to get a suntan—particularly in winter. There is a popular joke that says that Noosa Heads—known to its admirers simply as 'Noosa', the chic and unofficial capital of the Sunshine Coast—is really nothing more than Double Bay or Toorak on holidays. The suggestion is that the main street of Noosa—Hastings Street—with its very expensive clothing shops, its brasseries, its fashionable gift shops and its inner city-style coffee lounges is not a typical Australian beachside main street. This is true. Today this stretch of the Queensland coastline is one of the most exclusive holiday destinations found on the whole of the Australian coast.

However sunshine and shopping are not the town's only attractions. There is excellent bushwalking in the small Noosa National Park (382 ha) which covers most of the headland to the east of the town. There are five delightful tracks through the park, all leading to vantage points and beaches where the walker can escape from the crowded main beach. Fishing is also popular in the area. Other pleasant holiday options include tours and cruises (particularly to Fraser Island which lies to the north of the town), and there is handy advice and services for anglers, divers and surfers. Both surf skis and catamarans are available from the main beach, and other centres around the town will furnish enthusiasts with a wide variety of watercraft including jet skis, canoes and dinghies.

Native to the rainforests of Queensland, macadamia nuts are now cultivated throughout the Sunshine Coast. As well as being delicious, they provide high energy and are cholesterol-free.

Along the shore between Noosa and Tewantin there are many excellent and well-catered picnic spots where it is possible to enjoy a barbecue while watching boats cruise by.

At Teewah, located to the north of Noosa, there is a fantastic beach with 200-m high cliffs which is ideal to visit. It is noted for its beautifully coloured sands, with scientists identifying over 72 distinct colourings.

Map: Qld 7 N5

South of Noosa

The large centre of Maroochydore is, in many ways, the quintessence of the Australian beach scene. Seemingly endless golden beaches are patronised by surfers, swimmers and anglers. Behind the beach, large blocks of units and apartments cater for those seeking rest and recreation. The seafront is characterised by outlets where cans of soft drink, milkshakes and fast food are sold to people eager to eat quickly before getting back onto the beach and into the water. Located only 96 km from Brisbane, Maroochydore is both an easy daytrip and an ideal holiday destination for that city's residents. Apart from the attractions of the sea, the surrounding area is also well known for

The serene Maroochy River at sunset is a feast for the eyes. Anglers who drop a line in the river from Chambers Island or the Bli Bli Bridge are sure to catch bream, whiting, flathead or tailor.

Early morning is the perfect time to enjoy Noosa's natural environment. Take in the fresh sea air with a walk along the beach or a gentle cruise.

Bli Bli Castle, a theme park encompassing a re-created medieval castle; some of its attractions include dungeons and suits of armour. It is perched on a hill near the ocean between Noosa and Maroochydore and further beyond it lies Gingertown, an unusual theme park built around a ginger factory. Over the years it has developed from a small shop selling the products of the factory (it is reputedly the largest producer of ginger confectionery in the world) to a theme park where visitors can take a river cruise on the *PS Ginger Belle*, see a short but interesting video on the Australian ginger industry, check out a doll's museum or board the Ginger Bus for a tour of a ginger farm.

In turn this leads to the area's most famous attraction—The Big Pineapple. This started as little more than a big fibreglass pineapple (and, at 16 m high, it is very convincing) on a hill overlooking a pineapple plantation. Over the years, as the popularity of the attraction has grown, it has offered not only tropical fruits and gifts, but also a ride on a cane train through a tropical plantation, a visit by nutmobile of 'Nutcountry', and an opportunity to see a variety of native animals in the animal nursery. It has a licensed restaurant (with both macadamias and pineapples on the menu), a macadamia display, and a large greenhouse.

The Hinterland

Many people visit the popular beach resorts along the Sunshine Coast without realising that the inland towns, particularly the towns on the foothills of the escarpment, have a radically different ambience. If the coast is about hot beach activity, the inland is about cool relaxation and sleepy little towns. This is almost always true, with one notable exception: Woodford. The Woodford Folk Festival is an annual celebration of world music and culture held from 27 December to New Year's Day. The festival has been known to attract crowds, predominantly alternative lifestylers, of up to 100 000 people.

Left: *The subtropical climate of Buderim is ideal for growing plants like the native hibiscus, which can have mauve, lilac, cream or yellow flowers.*

If you want to enjoy tea and scones at a quiet and cool tearoom; if you want to see waterfalls and walk through subtropical national parks; if you want to stroll around attractive villages and enjoy spectacular views across to the coast, then the Sunshine Coast hinterland is ideal for your needs.

At the town of Buderim, just up the hill from Maroochydore, you can gasp at the beautiful gardens with their displays of bougainvillea, poincianas and frangipani. You can visit the interesting local art galleries and antique shops. And you can spend a pleasant couple of hours at the Pioneer Cottage (more a gracious home than a cottage) which was built of pit-sawn cedar and beech

don't miss

Buderim Forest Park has a delightful boardwalk through the peaceful rainforest setting that is easy enough for young children and people in wheelchairs. There is a barbecue area and a swimming hole.

Four small parks make up Glass House Mountains National Park—Beerwah, Coonowrin, Tibrogargan and Ngungun—and are popular for bushwalking and scenic drives.

and is surrounded by tall palm trees in pleasant subtropical gardens which offer great views across the hinterland.

Equally interesting is the tiny township of Mapleton. Just behind Mapleton's main shopping centre are some attractive lily ponds which make an ideal place for a picnic, but it is the Mapleton Falls in the Mapleton National Park which are the area's main attraction. The Mapleton National Park is quite small (25.9 ha) but the lookout from the falls offers interesting views over the valley, which is covered with dense rainforest. The park also has a number of relatively easy rainforest walks.

The trip to Buderim and Mapleton also takes in the small towns of Maleny, Flaxton and Montville, all of which are reminders that there are many people who prefer to seek the relative coolness of the hinterland and turn away from the heat of the coastal beaches.

No visit to the Sunshine Coast is complete without going to see the amazing Glass House Mountains, a series of spectacular volcanic plugs rising dramatically from the flat coastal plain. This is strictly a 'look and see' exercise—yes it is possible to climb them, but this can be relatively taxing and is certainly not what most people would call a 'relaxing' activity. The excellent main lookout offers views across all the plugs, and places them in a larger context by providing stunning views across to the Pacific Ocean. If you are wondering how the Glass House Mountains got their name: it was Captain James Cook who, seeing them from aboard his ship, wrote 'These hills lie but a little way inland, and not far from each other: they are remarkable for the singular form of their elevation, which very much resembles a glass house, and for this reason I called them the Glass Houses.'

Markets

It is not surprising that the Sunshine Coast, particularly with its large number of alternative lifestylers living in the hinterland, has quite a few excellent markets. No matter where you are staying you will find a market quite close by which offers a wide range of local arts and crafts, seasonal plants and produce, fashion, bric-a-brac and a healthy variety of local fresh food. There can be few more pleasant ways of spending a day on the Sunshine Coast than visiting the markets and soaking up the colourful atmosphere.

don't miss

North of Beerwah on the Glass House Mountains Tourist Route is Australia Zoo, home of Steve Irwin (famous as the Crocodile Hunter). It has over 550 animals on 8 ha of land, including the world's oldest Galapagos tortoise.

Markets throughout the Sunshine Coast offer visitors the chance to sample fresh tropical produce that they might not be able to buy at home, such as coconuts, pineapples, mangoes and jackfruit.

Most of the markets occur on Sunday mornings. There is the excellent Caboolture Show Society Flea Market at the Caboolture Show Ground; the Caloundra Markets which are held in the grounds of the local hospital; the Cotton Tree Markets in King Street, Cotton Tree; the interesting Maleny Handcrafts Market located outside the Maleny RSL Hall in the Sunshine Coast hinterland; and the Mooloolaba Markets which are held in Venning Street, Mooloolaba.

The biggest markets of all are held at Parklyn Circuit, Tewantin, 7 km from Noosa, but are known as the Noosa Harbour Markets. They attract craftspeople from the local district and are a delightful way of spending Sunday morning. There is often live entertainment. There is always a range of interesting foodstuffs (there are five restaurants in the market, including a seafood restaurant) and the enterprising can always pick up a few decent bargains (there are excellent stalls with goods from both Indonesia and Thailand) from the huge number of stalls and exhibitions.

If you are in the area on Wednesdays and Saturdays then a trip to the impressive and popular Eumundi Markets in Eumundi is strongly recommended. They are recognised as one of the best markets in the region, partly because of their strict policy that stallholders can only exhibit goods if they 'make it, bake it, grow it or sew it'.

The markets are a great place to pick up a unique souvenir of your trip to the Sunshine Coast. There is handmade pottery, jewellery, hand-painted silk, woodwork, leatherwork and much more.

The Islands

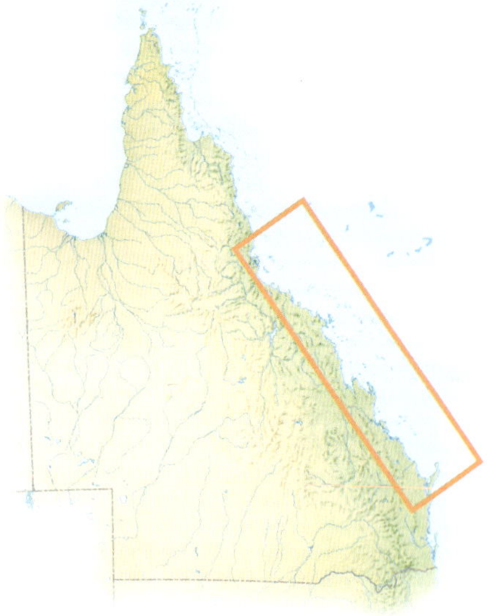

There has always been a sense of romance about tropical islands. Beautiful sunsets, white sandy beaches edged by clear aquamarine waters, gentle palm trees rustling and swaying in the lazy tropical breezes. It is one of the most potent images of perfection ever created by humans. Too often, particularly in Australia, this image is associated with the islands of the South Pacific and the Caribbean. We rarely acknowledge that just off the Queensland coast we have dozens of islands with those romantic attributes.

Dunk Island, 7 km off Mission Beach, is known by the local Aboriginal people as coonanglebah, *which means 'the island of peace and abundance'.*

If you really want to rest and unwind by lying beside a perfect white beach, there is nothing as beautiful as, say, Lizard Island or Heron Island.

In total there are about 20 islands off the coast of Queensland which feature resorts or at least some sort of guest accommodation. They range from the five-star resort at Lizard Island which lies to the north of Cooktown and is, by general consensus, the best of all the island destinations, through to Fraser Island in the south, the largest sand island in the world. In between there are the small coral atolls (Green Island, Lady Elliot Island and Heron Island); the Whitsunday Islands (Bedarra Island, Daydream Island, Dent Island, Hamilton Island, Hayman Island, Hook Island, Lindeman Island, Long Island, and South Molle); and a variety of islands which are dotted throughout the Great Barrier Reef and which, for a number of different reasons, are neither atolls nor part of the Whitsunday cluster (Dunk Island, Magnetic Island, Orpheus Island, Brampton Island, Fitzroy Island, Hinchinbrook Island, Great Keppel Island, and Double Island).

There are certain 'relax' truisms about all of these islands. If you want to go snorkelling and experience the true beauties of the Great Barrier Reef then only the coral atolls (Green Island, Lady Elliot Island and Heron Island) offer that experience from their shores. All other islands, with the exception of Lizard Island, can only offer the Great Barrier Reef to people prepared to take a boat out to the reef.

All the islands offer a wide range of activities and, as a general principle, the holiday-maker is able to enjoy the non-motorised activities (sailing, snorkelling, swimming, sunbathing, fishing) as part of the resort's total cost but has to pay for motorised activities such as parasailing, deep-sea fishing, scuba diving, jet-ski riding and water-skiing.

Left: *Rainforest reaches right to the edge of the beach on Fitzroy Island. The island is surrounded by crystal-clear water and fringing coral reefs.*

Certain resorts specialise in particular activities and certain kinds of lifestyles. Smart holiday-makers will determine what they want to do (have a family holiday, be left alone on a quiet beach, have great food, participate in group activities, do lots of bushwalking) and then go looking for the resort island which most accurately caters for their needs. For example, Bedarra Island Resort (07 4068 8233) is very expensive but it caters for only a small number of guests, has excellent food and the bar (even down to French champagne and the very best spirits) is open and free 24 hours a day. South Long Island specialises in eco-tourism and is proud of its record as an environmentally friendly destination. It even has weekend stays when visitors are expected to help clean up the local environment. The resort at Lindeman Island (07 3229 3155) is owned by Club Med and therefore, while the mass-produced food is exceptional, there is an expectation that you will be happy to join in with the many activities which are going on all the time. Hayman Island (which, when it was being refurbished, actually purchased a marble mine in North Queensland because it was using so much marble) is a typical five-star resort with five-star prices, rooms and services (07 4940 1234). And Lady Elliot Island is a budget destination with simple accommodation, simple food but excellent reef activities because, being a coral atoll, the reef edges every beach on the island (07 4124 9943).

All resorts offer relaxing seaside activities such as fishing, swimming, snorkelling, lying on the beach and the usual array of beachside entertainment. These are Australia's glamorous equivalents of the famed holiday destinations in the Mediterranean, along the Florida coast and in the Caribbean.

Above: *Hayman Island is the most northerly island in the Whitsunday Group. Sailing to nearby deserted islands is popular here.*

Bedarra Island Resort has just 15 villas, concealed within the lush rainforest. Visitors can easily find a secluded beach on which to enjoy a private picnic.

did you know?

Magnetic Island was named by Captain James Cook in June 1770 when his 'compass would not travis well when near it'. Two-thirds of Magnetic Island is now protected from development by national park status.

Fraser Island's eastern beach is a popular 4WD site, but only drive on it within two hours either side of low tide when the sand is firm.

Fraser Island

Located some 300 km north of Brisbane and 37 km east of Maryborough, Fraser Island is renowned as the largest sand island in the world. It is 123 km long and covers an area of 184 000 sq km; its sand dunes rise to a height of 240 m. It is estimated that the sands that make up Fraser Island reach over 600 m below the sea. Visitors to Fraser Island can camp on the island; they can also stay in modest accommodation or try the excellent, and environmentally friendly, Kingfisher Bay Resort and Village (1800 072 555). The resort offers an interesting variety of restaurants and tours around the island.

Visitors come to the island for a variety of different reasons. Some come to camp and experience nature, and they find the facilities on the island—barbecues and well-maintained camp sites—are ideal as they explore the great dunes and the perched lakes. Campers should be aware that dingoes can often be aggressive, particularly towards children. Some visitors come to drive their 4WD vehicles along the hard, sandy beaches. Some come to visit the famous sites—the 'painted' cliffs, the wreck of the *Maheno*, the beautiful creeks which run across the island, and the superb perched lakes: Lake Bowarrady (situated 120 m above sea level), Lake McKenzie, Lake Boemingen (reputedly the largest perched lake in the world), Ocean Lake, Hidden Lake, and Coomboo Lake (all freshwater lakes and set in attractive bushland surroundings). Some people come for the excellent fishing and some come for the bushwalking trails. Fortunately Fraser Island is large enough to encompass all these activities, and it caters quite well for all the differing visitor requirements.

Map: Qld 6 N2

The Maheno*, a Japanese-owned ocean liner, was blown ashore on Fraser Island in 1935 during a cyclone. It is now one of the island's most visited attractions, and anglers fish for tailor here.*

Magnetic Island

This large island has a pleasant country-town feel about it. You can go to the local pub and enjoy the Cane Toad Races just as easily as you can find a good spot and do a little fishing. Located only 8 km from Townsville and visible from the city, Magnetic Island is a small, rugged and wooded island covering 49 sq km and rising to 497 m at Mount Cook. It is 11 km at its widest point, and has more than 40 km of coastline which includes 23 bays and beaches. The island also has 24 km of walking tracks.

One of the most popular modes of transportation used on Magnetic Island is the mini-mokes which can be hired and are an ideal way of getting around (you can even get a ferry and moke combined ticket from Townsville). The island is too large for all but the most enthusiastic bushwalkers and on a hot day, even keen bushwalkers will find that the hike up to The Forts—a series of old gun emplacements—is arduous, although the path is well maintained.

Magnetic Island is a great economical destination. There is a wide range of budget accommodation, and eating on the island—where the pub and the local café are the popular options—is usually inexpensive and reasonable. Access to the island is by ferry, which is fast and quite reasonably priced.

Map: Qld 2 D8

Magnetic Island is just a scenic 20-minute ride by fast catamaran ferry from the city of Townsville. The island has much to tempt the visitor, including 16 beaches and over 20 km of walking trails.

Hinchinbrook Island

Further north from Townsville is the beautifully isolated Hinchinbrook Island. For people wanting to relax, the famed Hinchinbrook Island Resort—known for its environmentally discreet accommodation and its away-from-it-all feel—is ideal. Contact (07) 4066 8585. Camping sites and permits are also available (07 4066 8601) and need to be arranged in advance. The island also boasts some very extensive walks.

Map: Qld 2 C6

Sunset is a particularly magical time of day in the Whitsundays. There are more than 70 islands in the Whitsunday Group; only eight are inhabited.

Green Island

Another interesting and very different experience is Green Island which lies only 27 km east of Cairns. It is a popular daytripper destination. The ferries arrive around 10.00 a.m. and depart around 4.00 p.m. During the day visitors can go snorkelling off the beaches (being a coral atoll, the displays are spectacular close to shore), can visit the historic underwater observatory, can eat at a range of interesting restaurants which are all located behind the palm trees and only a few metres from the jetty and the main beach area, can go swimming and windsurfing, and can enjoy sunbathing on the beach. It is not so good for bushwalkers (although, in fairness, those interested in tropical plants will be impressed by the way all the flora has been carefully labelled), being a 15-ha coral cay which can be effortlessly walked around in 20 minutes. In fact its circumference is almost exactly 1.5 km. It is only about 300 m wide and 650 m long. Still this should not dissuade those who want to stay on the island. There is a five-star hotel hidden in the centre of the island. After 4.00 p.m., when all the daytrippers leave, only the hotel residents are left on the island. The contrast makes you feel as though you are part of a very exclusive little group as you lie on the beach watching the gorgeous sunset and enjoying a delicious cocktail (or two!).
Map: Qld 2 B2

don't miss

Cook's Look on Lizard Island is the 359-m high hill from which Captain Cook observed a route through the Great Barrier Reef. While you're there, keep an eye out for monitor lizards, after which the island was named.

A trip to Green Island should include a visit to the underwater observatory—the oldest one in the world—to see turtles, eels and giant clams.

Lizard Island

This is regarded by many as the pick of the resort islands off the Queensland coast. It is located 240 km north of Cairns (the usual access is by aeroplane) and, because it is a rocky outcrop of a mainland mountain range which is 27 km offshore, it is surrounded by beautiful coral. The food on the island is also exceptional. The activities range from snorkelling to deep-sea fishing and scuba diving. In 1939 the island was declared a national park. It is as close to paradise as any island could ever be. However be warned: it is expensive and exclusive.
Map: Qld 3 N1

Sailing Around The Whitsundays

One of the most pleasant and the safest options for holiday-makers travelling in the Whitsundays is to either hire a boat and sail it yourself (this is not nearly as frightening as you might think—the islands and the coral reef form a natural protection against bad weather and huge waves) or to go sailing with an experienced crew. There are a number of operators in the region offering a wide variety of sailing options. Sailaway Whitsunday Cruises have excellent three-day and two-night cruises around the Whitsundays on *Mollo*, their 40-foot catamaran, and *Ambition*, their 40-foot cruising yacht. These stress-free trips include all meals, and all the sailing is undertaken by knowledgeable crews. Contact (07) 4786 5018.

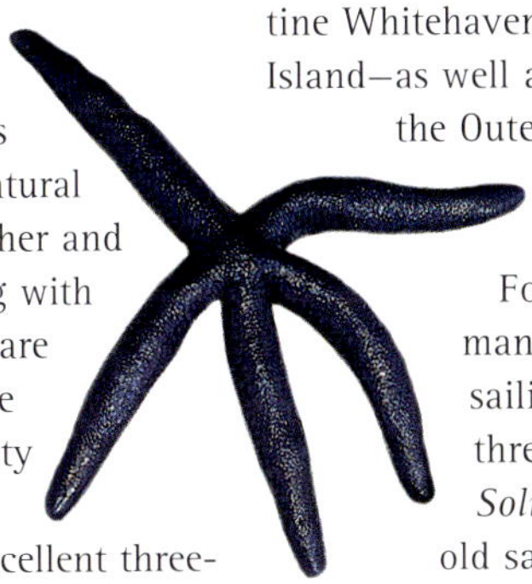

Fantasea are the major daily cruise operators in the Whitsundays. They operate out of Shute Harbour with cruises to many of the islands—including the pristine Whitehaven Beach on Whitsunday Island—as well as excellent day trips to the Outer Reef where people can snorkel and swim. Contact (07) 4946 5111.

For those with a more romantic, old-world vision of sailing there are three-day, three-night cruises on the *Solway Lass*, a delightful old sailing ship built in 1902 and totally remodelled recently. Contact 1800 675 790.

The options for sailing around the Whitsundays are extensive, and all the cruises specialise in taking passengers to the quieter beaches to enjoy the relaxing ambience of this beautiful island group.

Left: *The warm waters of the Whitsunday Islands are home to 1500 species of fish, 350 varieties of coral and 350 types of echinoderms, like starfish.*

The North Coast

For many visitors the North Coast of Queensland—the area between Cairns and Cooktown and including the Atherton Tablelands—is what Australia is really all about. This is the tropics, where the days, even in winter, are warm and sunny. Here it is possible to go and visit the Great Barrier Reef and snorkel, scuba dive and go deep-sea fishing. Here, once you cross the Daintree River, you are in true tropical jungle with huge trees, dense undergrowth and savage creatures like crocodiles waiting in the rivers.

Here it is possible to experience the tropics in a 'first world' country, where the motel and hotel rooms are all air-conditioned, where the meals from the hundreds of cafés and restaurants are of superior quality, and where there is a vibrancy and range of activities produced as a result of the huge influx of visitors. The best time to visit the tropical North is between May and October, when the weather is warm, there is less rain and humidity, and the ocean is relatively free of sea-wasps.

The Daintree Valley is home to over 250 different species of birds. The estuarine crocodile is also frequently sighted along the Daintree River.

Cairns

Cairns is a large and bustling port. It was a wild and reckless place on the edge of the world but in the 1970s the airport was upgraded to accept international flights and soon it became a first stop-over for visitors from both Japan and North America. Overnight Cairns was converted into a destination characterised by shopping malls, efficient transport, sophisticated hotels, restaurants and nightclubs and a lifestyle that was appropriate for a modern Western city.

Tour operators began offering deep-sea fishing, trips to the outer reef, 4WD adventures into the tropical rainforest, scuba diving on uninhabited coral atolls, helicopter joy rides over the reef, inland trips to the remarkable Undara lava tubes and even coastal adventures up beyond Cape Tribulation.

No trip to Cairns is complete without experiencing some of these activities because they are very, very good and well worth the effort.

Map: Qld 3 P5

Aboriginal culture

The Tjapukai Aboriginal Cultural Park at Smithfield, for example, is one of the nation's best Aboriginal experiences: a highly successful attempt to explain Aboriginal culture (specifically the life and society of the local Djabugay and Yirrgandyji peoples) in a broad thematic way. This is a remarkable experience and

Right: *At Tjapukai's outdoor camp, visitors can learn about traditional Aboriginal hunting methods, weapons, bush foods, medicine and music.*

is recommended to anyone who cares for or is interested in indigenous culture.

Skyway

Next to the Cultural Park is the Skyrail Rainforest Cableway—an outstanding 7.5-km journey over rainforest which rises to the top of the escarpment, crosses across a tropical river, and runs beside a huge waterfall before reaching the village of Kuranda, where the visitor is tempted by dozens of charming gift shops and a large market.

Reef cruises

Another popular activity in both Cairns and Port Douglas is to catch one of the many day cruises which make their way to the platforms on the outer reef. This is the best way to experience the wonders of the Great Barrier Reef—apart, of course, from staying on one of the coral atolls—because passengers on the cruises get to snorkel, scuba and swim on the edge of the reef. At the same time underwater vessels, an underwater viewing station and helicopter rides are also available.

The ultimate experience of the reef is to take a three-, four- or seven-day cruise with Captain Cook Cruises. Their vessel leaves Cairns and travels north to Cooktown and Lizard Island before returning to Cairns and heading out to Fitzroy Island, Hinchinbrook Channel and Dunk Island.

The Great Barrier Reef measures 2000 km in length. It encompasses over 1000 islands—either coral atolls or the tops of submerged continental mountains—and more than 2900 single reefs.

The lively marina of Port Douglas inspires some of the amazing architecture seen in the town. Simple market stalls selling arts and crafts also abound.

Port Douglas

Further north from Cairns is the tourist town of Port Douglas, which became famous in the 1980s when Christopher Skase built the huge Sheraton Mirage Resort. Today the resort has been joined by others, all offering five-star luxury.

Still, Port Douglas has more to offer than just the large resorts. It has become an important centre for people planning day trips out to the outer reef and the main street has become a haven of interesting gift shops and classy cafés, brasseries and restaurants.

The Port Douglas markets, which provide a wide range of interesting items, are a particular attraction of the area. Many of the products for sale are handmade, and the fruit and vegetables are often cultivated locally.

Another one of the town's highlights is Ben Cropp's Shipwreck Museum on the wharf at Port Douglas. This collection of material from historic shipwrecks includes everything from ballast to coins, and there is a continuous video featuring Cropp's remarkable underwater photography.

Of equal interest is the truly unusual Rainforest Habitat, an artificial rainforest environment near the Daintree Rainforest. There are plenty of butterflies and birds on display as well as koalas, kangaroos and crocodiles.

Map: Qld 3 N4

did you know?

The Daintree Rainforest is home to some 3000 plant species from 210 different families—17 per cent of all of Australia's plant species. Over 700 of these plants are found only in this region and are millions of years old.

Right: *Cane toads were introduced to control the cane beetle, but are now considered a pest—locals in Port Douglas have found a use for them.*

Daintree

In recent years the 'Daintree experience' has become an integral and vital part of any visit to North Queensland. There are now a large number of moderately priced lodges nestled in the Daintree Forest. There is also delightful treehouse accommodation within the Daintree Rainforest at the Silky Oaks Lodge and Healing Waters Spa (1800 737 678), which offers remarkably elegant accommodation that is of a top-class standard. Wherever you stay in the region you can still enjoy excellent rainforest experiences, with trips to Cape Tribulation and plenty of opportunities to explore this beautiful, untouched stretch of rainforest.

Part of the appeal also lies in the way the tiny village of Daintree has managed to protect itself from the excesses of tourism and over-development. Today it still has little more than a general store, the Bushman's Lodge, a couple of restaurants, a butterfly farm, a caravan park, a school, a number of river and rainforest tour operators and the timber museum. This is a far cry from the glamour of Cairns and Port Douglas.

Map: Qld 3 N4

Atherton

Atherton (population 10,200) is located 1727 km north of Brisbane. It sits on the Atherton Tableland between Cairns and Innisfail and is 760 m above sea level. It is the service centre for a rich agricultural district, where maize is the main crop.

The town was named after John Atherton, who settled in the area around 1877. The town's beginnings were as a camp for timbergetters seeking elusive cedar trees. Later, the European and Chinese pioneers arrived, drawn to the area by the promise of gold and tin. They stayed, and laid the foundations of the wealthy agricultural industry; they also established the beef and dairy herds.

The Chinese built a joss house in 1900 which has since been classified by the National Trust. Flying Fortresses from the USA were based in the area during World War II. Atherton's old post office houses an art gallery, museum, visitor's centre and tearooms. Crystal Caves, located in Main Street, houses a unique underground cave museum with some quite fascinating giant crystal formations, fossils and fluorescent minerals from around the world.

The Chinese temple—or joss house—in Atherton is dedicated to the emperor Ho Wong. It features a unique combination of traditional Chinese architecture and Australian corrugated iron.

There is a walking track to the top of Hallorans Hill, where there are splendid views of the town and surrounding area. To the north-east of the town is the Tinnaroo Falls Dam, where you can swim or fish. Millaa Millaa Falls, which is in the south, is also attractive. For a different experience, take a steam train ride to Herberton. The Railco Steam Railways is a non-profit organisation, staffed mainly by volunteers, and operates the only full-sized steam locomotives in North Queensland. Two major festivals are held in the Atherton area each year: the Maize Festival is on in September and the Tablelands Folk Festival is held on the last weekend in October.

Map: Qld 3 N6

don't miss

Approximately 150 km south-west of Atherton, the Undara Lava Tubes are strange geological formations created over 190 000 years ago. Stay in a converted railway carriage and enjoy a genuine bush breakfast.

Located just south of the town of Atherton, a picturesque 9-km circuit drive passes lush rainforests, scenic rivers and breathtaking waterfalls such as the well-known Millaa Millaa Falls.

Map 1

0 20 40 60 80
kilometres
NORTH
A B C D E F G
1 2 3 4 5 6 7 8 9 10
10° 12° 14° 142° 144°
TORRES STRAIT
ARAFURA SEA
CORAL SEA
GREAT BARRIER REEF
CAPE YORK PENINSULA
Great Barrier Reef Marine Park (Far Northern Section)
Mabuiag Island
Badu Island
Sassie Island
Great North East Channel
Moa Island
Cook Reef
Bramble Channel
West Island
Hawkesbury Island
Long Reef
North Torres Reef
South Torres Reef
North West Reef
Wednesday Island
Hammond Island
Thursday Island
Friday I
Horn I
Prince of Wales Island
Possession I Nat Park
Cape Cornwall
Dayman I
Endeavour Strait
Simpson Bay
Mt Adolphus Island
Cape York
Albany I
Somerset
Newcastle Bay
Injinoo Aboriginal Community
Bamaga
Van Spoult Head
Crab Island
Turtle Head Island
Sharp Point
Shadwell Peak
Furze Point
Womer Cay
Jardine
Vehicular Ferry
Left Hill
Ussher Point
Jardine River National Park
Orford Bay
Orford Ness
Vrilya Point
Parsons Reef
Maclennan Cay
Onslow Reef
Yule Entrance
Olinda Entrance
Pandora Entrance
Ashmore Reef
False Orford Ness
Bosanquet Hill
McHenry River
Helby Hill
Boydong Cays
Wizard Reef
Dougbboy R
Macdonald R
Jackson R
Skardon R
Port Musgrave
Captain Billy Landing
Great Detached Reef
Thrush Reef
Forwood Reef
North Channel
Three Reefs
Messum Hill
Heathlands
Red Cliffs
Dulhunty
Shelburne Bay
Round Point
Cockburn Reef
Five Reefs
Star Reef
Yule Detached Reef
Middle Peak
Conical Hill
Cape Grenville
Home Islands
Job Reef
Cullen Point
Mapoon Aboriginal Community
Ducie River
Mason Reef
Martha Ridgeway Reef
Nomad Reef
Laurel Reef
Agnew
Bramwell
Batavia Outstation
Pennefather River
Bertiehaugh
Olive R
Black Rocks
Bolt Head
Temple Bay
Mosquito Point
Fair Cape
Huxley Hill
Carron Hill
Quoin Island
Lagoon Reef
Wenlock
Stone Crossing
Grove Ck
Moreton Telegraph Station
Weymouth Bay
Long sandy Reef
Andoom
Duyfken Pt
Mission River
Jackson Channel
Weipa
Napranum
Portland Roads
Cape Weymouth
Joyce Hill
Second Small Reef
Albatross Bay
Hey River
Sudley
Batavia Downs
North Pap
Pascoe R
Cape Griffith
Iron Range NP
Lloyd I
Iron Range
Lockhart River Aboriginal Community
Cape Direction
Bligh Reef
Boyd Point
Pera Head
Thud Point
Wenlock R
Tor Hill
Peninsula
False Pera Head
Merluna
Iguana Mtn
Jacks Knob
Osborne Reef
Franklin Reef
New Reef
Watson River
Wenlock (ruins)
Dev
Night Island
Bobardt Point
Tijou Reef
Worbody Point
Wallaby Island
Aurukun Aboriginal Community
Geikie
Wolverton
Celebration Reef
Mungkan Kandju National Park
Coen River
Archer River Roadhouse
Cone Peak
Range
Friendly Point
First 3 Mile Opening
Cape Sidmouth
Whale Hill
Birthday Mtn
Campbell Pt
Ogilvie Reef
Round Mtn
Creech Reef
Archer
Mcllwraith
Hay I
Noddy Reef
Rokeby
Merapah
Double Hill
Colmer Point
Magpie Reef
Coen Aerodrome
Mt Croll
Rooda Reef
Wilson Reef
Melville Passage
Kirke R
Roberts Point
The Twin Humps
Coen
Hedge Reef
Corbett Reef
Knox Ck
Sinclair Ck
Mt White
Silver Plains
Claremont Point
Davie Reef
Tydeman Reef
Old Silver Plains
Eden Reef
Stewart R
Kendall
Pretender
Flinders Group Nat Park
Stanley I
Flinders I
Cape Melville
Bathurst Bay
Twin Peaks
Foxs Lookout
Great Dividing Range
Bathurst Head
South Warden Reef
Holroyd
Yarraden
Pollappa
Princess Charlotte Bay
Beabey Hill
Bathurst Head
Barrow Point
Annie R
Strathburn
Fox Ck
Lily Vale
Wakooka Outstation
Cape Bowen
Howick Island
Howick Group Nat Park
Salt Ck
Edward River
Marina Plains
Cape Melville National Park
Old Strathgordon
New Strathgordon
New Bamboo
Lakefield National Park
Brown Peak
Saddle Hill
Musgrave
Breeza Plains Outstation
Flat Top Hill
Black Hill
Glen Garland
Strathaven
Strathmay
Kalpowar
Jack Lakes
Jack R
Munburra
Mt Norkwa
Starcke Nat Park
Pormpuraaw Aboriginal Community
Coleman River
Lakefield
Dixie Outstation
Starcke
33 24 23 63 44 36 11 56 30 11 329 49 70 40 48 31 43 88 31 116 20 65 46 304 60 94 59 68 23 33 38

QLD 3

Map 2

0 20 40 60 80
kilometres

QLD 5

Map 3

A
B
C
D
E
F
G
1
2
3
4
5
6
7
8
9
10
138°
140°
16°
18°
NORTH
GULF OF
CARPENTARIA
NT 3
QLD 4
NORTHERN TERRITORY
QUEENSLAND
Pormpuraaw
Aboriginal Community
Wallaby Island
Kowanyama
Aboriginal Community
Edward
Lochnagar
Inkerman
Galbraith
Macaroni
Delta Downs
Lotus Vale
Myra Vale
Stirling
Double Lagoon
Maggieville
Karumba
Mutton Hole
Normanton
Shady Lagoon
Timora
May Vale
Haydon
Gum Creek
Coralie
Claraville
Iffley
Myola
Taldora
Dora Vale
Arizona
Numil Downs
Vanrook
Mornington
Island
Thabugan Point
Lingnoonganee Island
Halls Point
Gumbannge Point
Bilmagun Point
Gee Wee Point
Gununa
Billmahgun Point
Wellesley
Islands
Bountiful Island
Denham Island
Midbagar Point
Sydney I
Tulburrerr Island
Forsyth Island
Forsyth Islands
Pains I
Bayley I
Horseshoe I
Allen I
Oaktree Point
Bentinck Island
Sweers Island
South Wellesley
Islands
Tarrant Point
Pascoe Inlet
Kangaroo Point
Gore Point
Disaster Inlet
Cadell Landing
Point Burrowes
Point Austin
Accident Inlet
Fitzmaurice Point
Alligator Point
Massacre
Inlet
Wollogorang
Westmoreland
Hells Gate Roadhouse
Buck Hill
Kingfisher
Camp
Doomadgee
Bowthorn
Lawn Hill
Nat Park
Mt Oscar
Mt Caroline
Lawn Hill
Adels Grove
Lawn Hill
National
Park
Mended Hill Mine
Silver Star Mine
Mt Kay
Riversleigh
Herbert Vale
Norfolk
Morstone
Undilla
Thorntonia
Escott
Burketown
Yarrum
Tirranna
Roadhouse
Beames Brook
Brookdale
Brinawa
Punjaub
Almora
Armraynald
Wernadinga
New Armraynald
Leichhardt Falls
Floraville
Planet Downs
Gregory Downs
Augustus
Downs
Talawanta
Nardoo
Lorraine
Jacks
Waterhole
Dinner Camp WH
Gum
Waterhole
Inverleigh
Magowra
Burke and
Wills Cairn
Milgarra
Macalister
Two Tree Hill
Mt Victoria
Poverty Knob
Neumayer Valley
Warren Vale
Bang Bang
Wondoola
Uralla WH
Vena Park
Donors Hill
Donors Hill
Cowan Downs
Burke and Wills
Roadhouse
Wurung
Earles Camp WH
Lyrian
WH
Lyrian
Canobie
Monstraven
Violet Vale
Alcala
Black Mtn
Kamileroi
Mistake Bore
Gleeson
Alsace
Mt Gordon Mine
Chidna
Mt Oxide Mine
Mt Gordon
Mt Oxide
Mammoth Mines
Gunpowder
Gregory
Downs
Camooweal
Road
Wills
Developmental
(Matilda Hwy)
Burketown
Road
Devel
Burke
Gulflander
Blackbull
225
219
117
144
228
186
151
83
1

0 20 40 60 80
kilometres

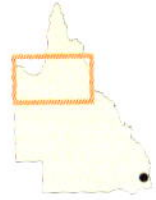

QLD 1

QLD 4

QLD 2

Map 4

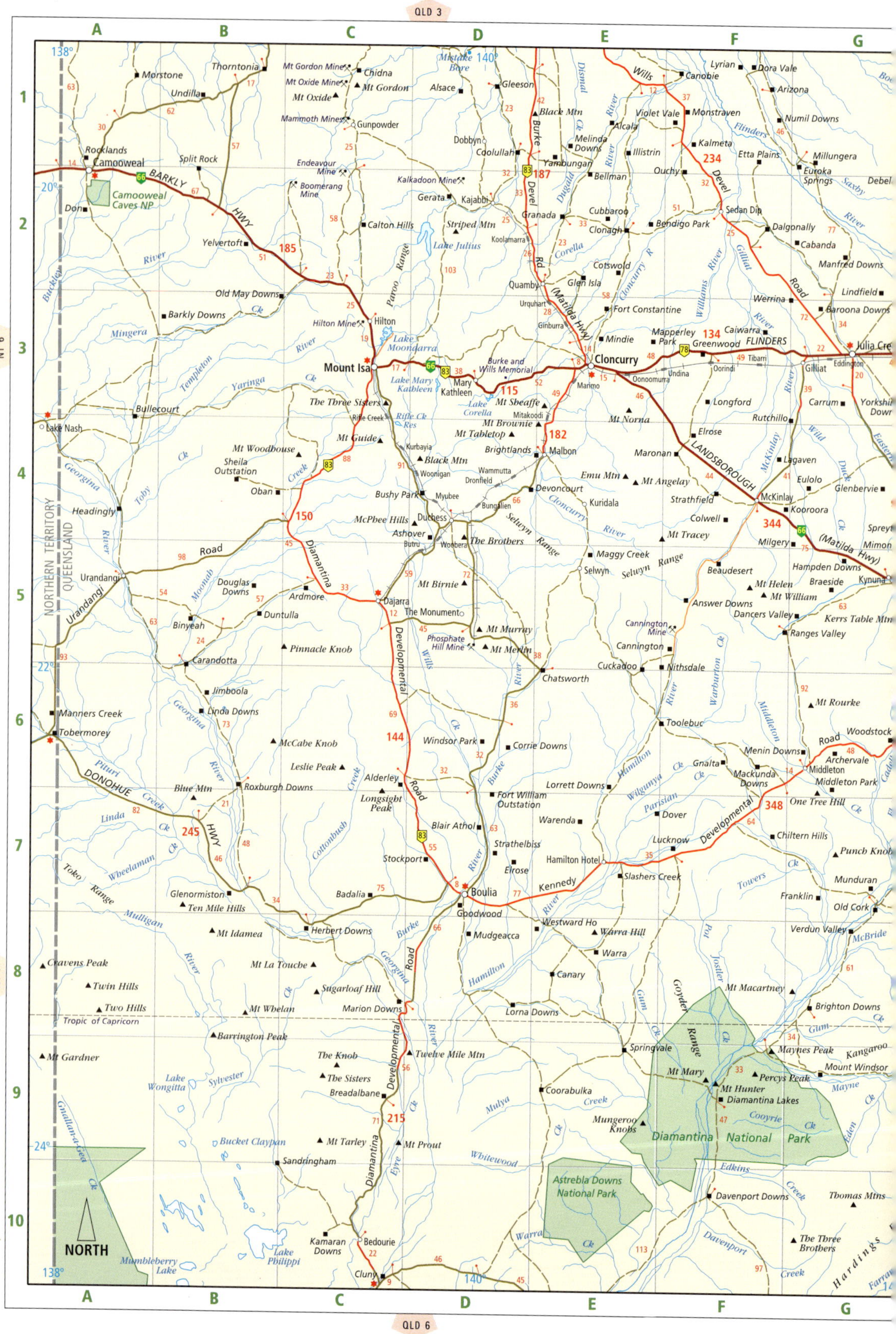
QLD 3
A
B
C
D
E
F
G
1
2
3
4
5
6
7
8
9
10
NT 6
NT 7
QLD 6
138°
140°
20°
22°
24°
NORTHERN TERRITORY
QUEENSLAND
NORTH
Morstone
Thorntonia
Mt Gordon Mine
Chidna
Mt Oxide Mine
Mt Gordon
Mt Oxide
Mistake Bore
Alsace
Gleeson
Wills
Canobie
Lyrian
Dora Vale
Arizona
Undilla
Mammoth Mines
Gunpowder
Dobbyn
Coolullah
Black Mtn
Burke
Dismal
River
Alcala
Violet Vale
Monstraven
Numil Downs
Flinders
Rocklands
Camooweal
Split Rock
Endeavour Mine
Boomerang Mine
Kalkadoon Mine
Melinda Downs
Yambungan
Bellman
Illistrin
Kalmeta
Etta Plains
Millungera
Euroka Springs
Saxby
Debel
BARKLY
HWY
Camooweal Caves NP
Don
Gerata
Kajabbi
Devel
Rd
Granada
Dugald
Cubbaroo
Clonagh
Ouchy
Sedan Dip
Bendigo Park
Dalgonally
Cabanda
Manfred Downs
Calton Hills
Striped Mtn
Koolamarra
Yelvertoft
Lake Julius
Corella
Cotswold
Cloncurry R
Gilliat
Buckley
Paroo
Range
Quamby
Glen Isla
Williams
Werrina
Lindfield
Old May Downs
Urquhart
(Matilda Hwy)
Fort Constantine
Baroona Downs
Barkly Downs
Mingera
Hilton Mine
Hilton
Ginburra
Mindie
Mapperley Park
Caiwarra
Greenwood
FLINDERS
Julia Creek
Lake Moondarra
Mount Isa
Lake Mary Kathleen
Mary Kathleen
Burke and Wills Memorial
Cloncurry
Oonoomurra
Undina
Oorindi
Tibarri
Gilliat
Eddington
Templeton
Yaringa
Ck
The Three Sisters
Rifle Creek
Rifle Ck Res
Lake Corella
Mt Sheaffe
Marimo
Mitakoodi
Mt Norna
Longford
Carrum
Yorkshire Downs
Rutchillo
Bullecourt
Lake Nash
Mt Guide
Mt Brownie
Mt Tabletop
Brightlands
Malbon
Maronan
Elrose
Wild
Kurbayia
Black Mtn
Woonigan
LANDSBOROUGH
McKinlay
Lagaven
Eastern
Mt Woodhouse
Sheila Outstation
Oban
Wammutta
Dronfield
Emu Mtn
Mt Angelay
Eulolo
Duck
Glenbervie
Georgina
Toby
Creek
Bushy Park
Myubee
Devoncourt
Kuridala
Strathfield
Headingly
McPhee Hills
Duchess
Bungalien
Colwell
Kooroora
Spreyton
Ashover
Butru
Woobera
The Brothers
Selwyn
Range
Mt Tracey
Milgery
Mimong
Road
Diamantina
Maggy Creek
Urandangi
Douglas Downs
Moonah
Selwyn
Beaudesert
Hampden Downs
Kynuna
Ardmore
Dajarra
Mt Birnie
Mt Helen
Mt William
Braeside
Duntulla
The Monument
Answer Downs
Dancers Valley
Kerrs Table Mtn
Binyeah
Mt Murray
Cannington Mine
Ranges Valley
Phosphate Hill Mine
Mt Merlin
Cannington
Pinnacle Knob
Cuckadoo
Nithsdale
Carandotta
Developmental
Chatsworth
Warburton
Jimboola
Middleton
Mt Rourke
Manners Creek
Linda Downs
Toolebuc
Tobermorey
Woodstock
Archervale
Middleton
Middleton Park
McCabe Knob
Windsor Park
Corrie Downs
Menin Downs
Gnalta
Mackunda Downs
One Tree Hill
DONOHUE
Pituri
Creek
Leslie Peak
Alderley
Hamilton
Wilgunya
Roxburgh Downs
Lorrett Downs
Fort William Outstation
Blue Mtn
Longsight Peak
Parisian
Dover
Linda
Warenda
Chiltern Hills
HWY
Cottonbush
Blair Athol
Strathelbiss
Lucknow
Punch Knob
Wheeleman
Toko
Range
Stockport
Hamilton Hotel
Slashers Creek
Elrose
Towers
Glenormiston
Ten Mile Hills
Badalia
Boulia
Kennedy
Munduran
Franklin
Old Cork
Mulligan
Goodwood
Westward Ho
Herbert Downs
Mt Idamea
Mudgeacca
Warra Hill
Verdun Valley
McBride
Warra
Pot
Jostler
Cravens Peak
Mt La Touche
Canary
Twin Hills
Sugarloaf Hill
Mt Macartney
Two Hills
Mt Whelan
Marion Downs
Lorna Downs
Brighton Downs
Tropic of Capricorn
Gum
Goyder
Barrington Peak
Springvale
Maynes Peak
Kangaroo
Mt Gardner
The Knob
Twelve Mile Mtn
Mt Mary
Percys Peak
Mount Windsor
Lake Wongitta
Sylvester
The Sisters
Breadalbane
Coorabulka
Mt Hunter
Diamantina Lakes
Mayne
Mulya
Mungeroo Knobs
Cooyrie
Gnallan-a-Gea
Bucket Claypan
Mt Tarley
Mt Prout
Diamantina National Park
Sandringham
Whitewood
Edkins
Eyre
Astrebla Downs National Park
Davenport Downs
Thomas Mtns
Kamaran Downs
Bedourie
Lake Philippi
Warra
Davenport
The Three Brothers
Mumbleberry Lake
Cluny
Hardings
Farrars

QLD 3

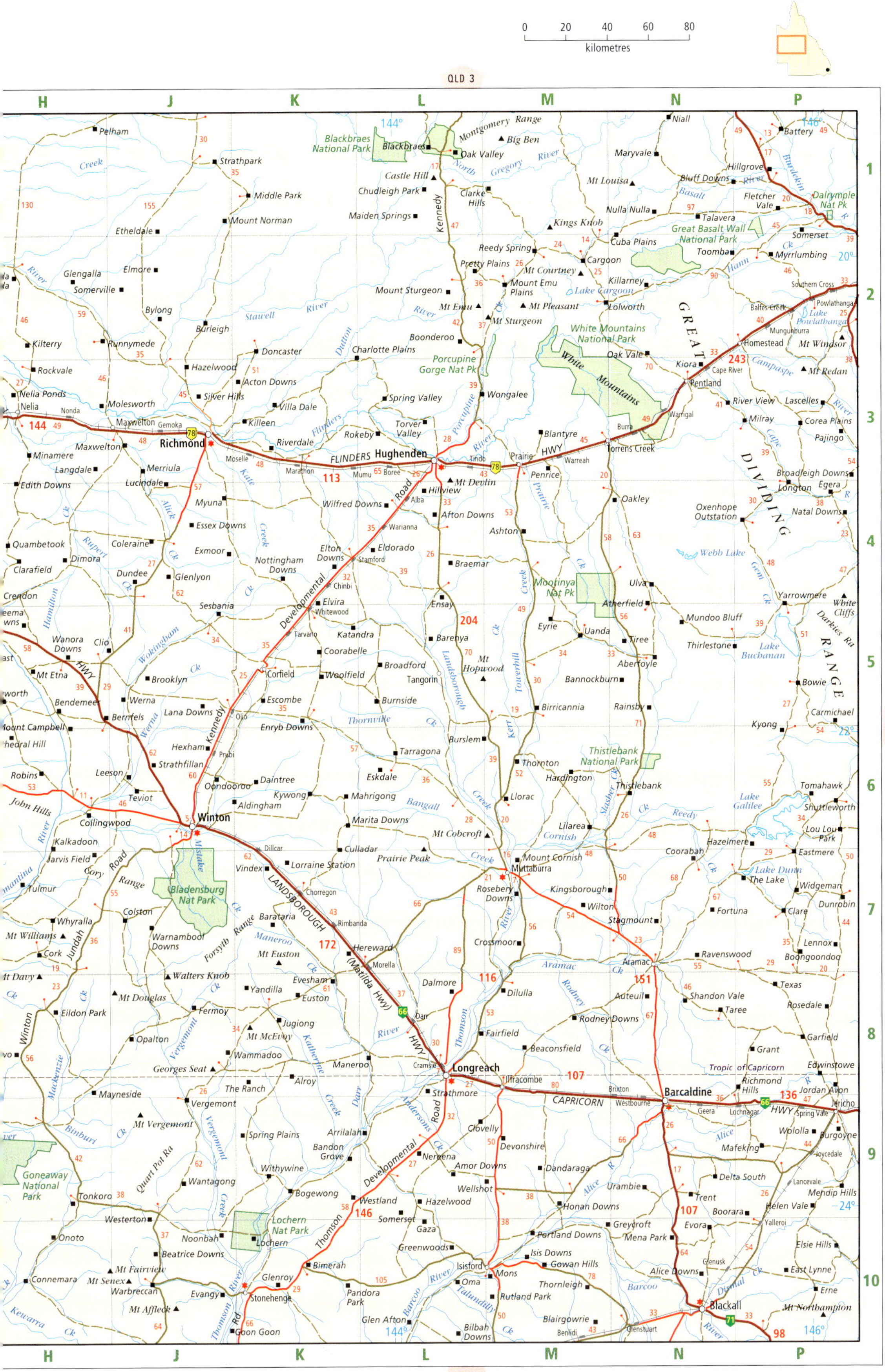

QLD 5

QLD 6

Map 5

QLD 2

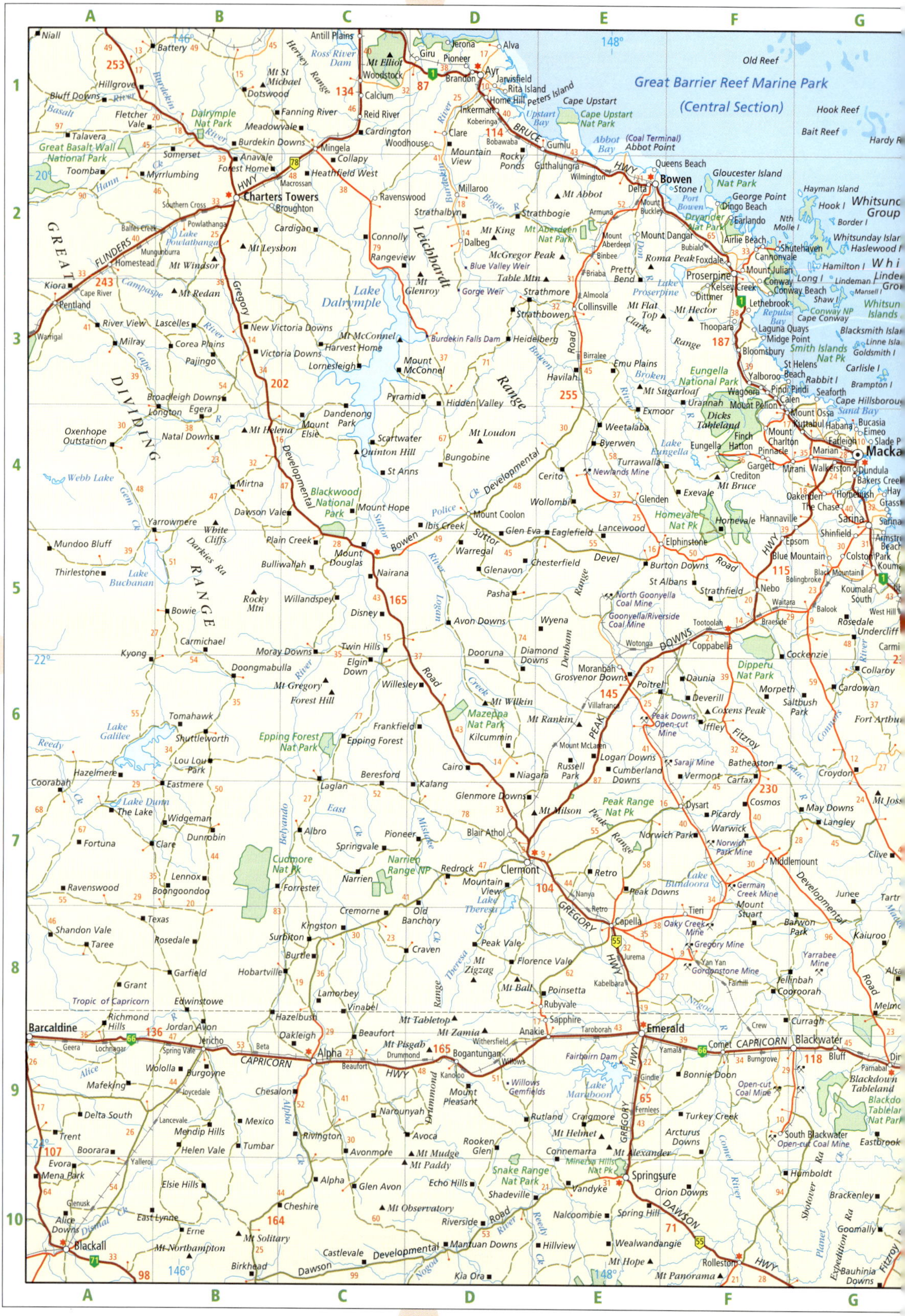

QLD 4

QLD 7

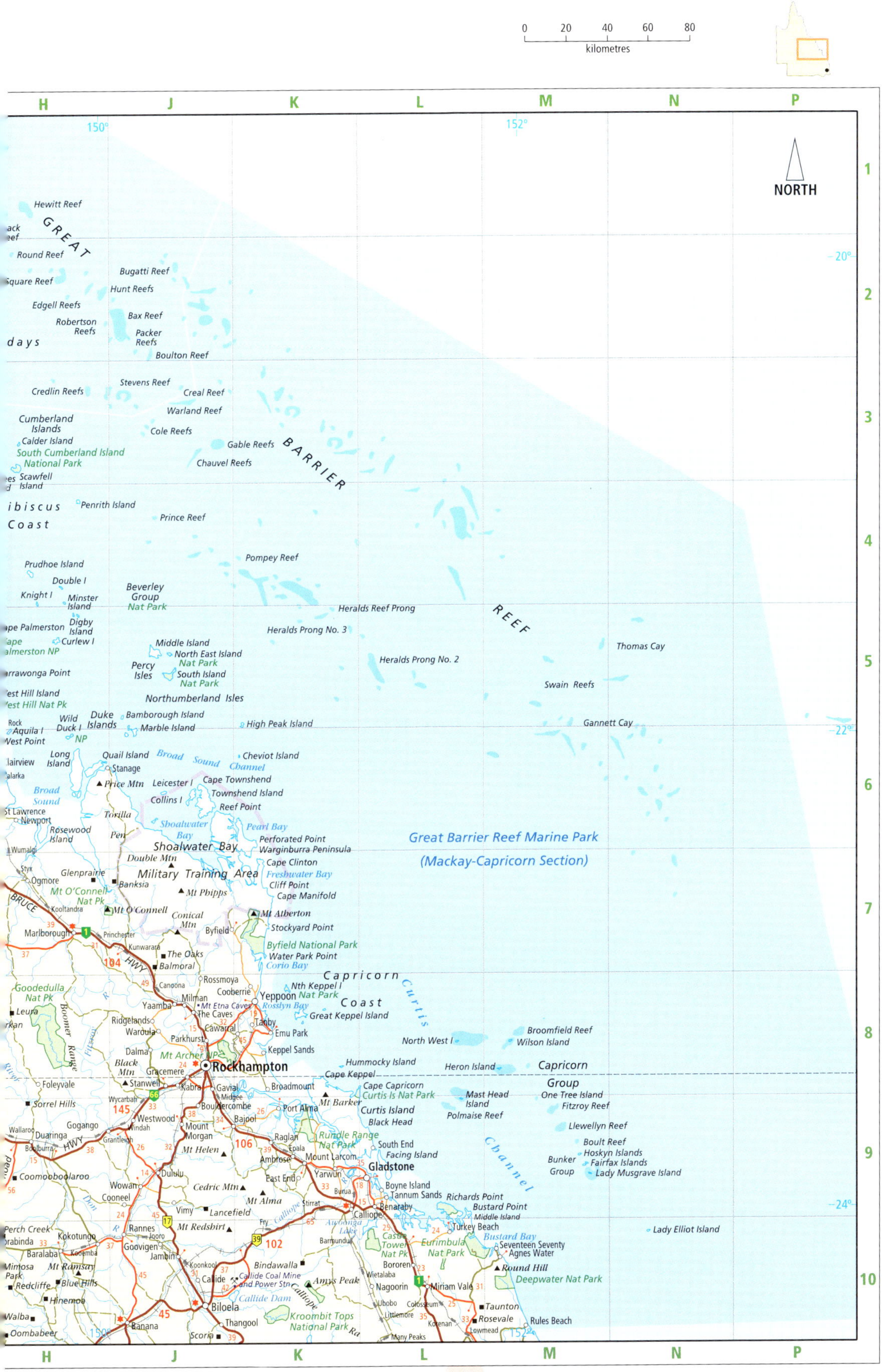
0 20 40 60 80
kilometres
NORTH
H J K L M N P
1 2 3 4 5 6 7 8 9 10
150° 152° 20° 22° 24°
Hewitt Reef
GREAT BARRIER REEF
Round Reef
Square Reef
Bugatti Reef
Hunt Reefs
Edgell Reefs
Robertson Reefs
Bax Reef
Packer Reefs
Boulton Reef
Stevens Reef
Credlin Reefs
Creal Reef
Warland Reef
Cumberland Islands
Cole Reefs
Calder Island
South Cumberland Island National Park
Gable Reefs
Chauvel Reefs
Scawfell Island
Penrith Island
Coast
Prince Reef
Pompey Reef
Prudhoe Island
Double I
Knight I
Minster Island
Beverley Group Nat Park
Heralds Reef Prong
Digby Island
Heralds Prong No. 3
Curlew I
Middle Island
North East Island Nat Park
Thomas Cay
Heralds Prong No. 2
Percy Isles
South Island Nat Park
Swain Reefs
Northumberland Isles
Duke Islands
Bamborough Island
Wild Duck I NP
Marble Island
High Peak Island
Gannett Cay
Quail Island
Broad Sound Channel
Cheviot Island
Long Island
Stanage
Price Mtn
Leicester I
Cape Townshend
Collins I
Townshend Island
Reef Point
Broad Sound
St Lawrence
Newport
Torilla
Shoalwater Bay
Pearl Bay
Rosewood Island
Pen
Perforated Point
Great Barrier Reef Marine Park
(Mackay-Capricorn Section)
Shoalwater Bay
Warginburra Peninsula
Double Mtn
Military Training Area
Cape Clinton
Glenprairie
Freshwater Bay
Styx
Ogmore
Banksia
Cliff Point
Mt O'Connell Nat Pk
Mt Phipps
Cape Manifold
BRUCE HWY
Kooltandra
Mt O'Connell
Mt Alberton
Conical Mtn
Stockyard Point
Marlborough
Princhester
Byfield
Byfield National Park
Kunwarara
The Oaks
Water Park Point
Balmoral
Corio Bay
Capricorn Coast
Curtis Channel
Goodedulla Nat Pk
Canoona
Rossmoya
Nth Keppel I Nat Park
Cooberrie
Boomer Range
Yaamba
Milman
Yeppoon
Mt Etna Caves
Rosslyn Bay
Ridgelands
The Caves
Great Keppel Island
Tanby
Waroula
Cawarral
Emu Park
Parkhurst
Broomfield Reef
North West I
Wilson Island
Mt Archer NP
Dalma
Keppel Sands
Hummocky Island
Black Mtn
Heron Island
Capricorn Group
Gracemere
Rockhampton
Cape Keppel
Foleyvale
Stanwell
Kabra
Gavial
Broadmount
Cape Capricorn
Mast Head Island
One Tree Island
Midgee
Curtis Is Nat Park
Mt Barker
Fitzroy Reef
Sorrel Hills
Boulder
Bouldercombe
Port Alma
Curtis Island
Polmaise Reef
Westwood
Bajool
Black Head
Llewellyn Reef
Gogango
Mount Morgan
Wallaroo
Duaringa
Windah
Rundle Range Nat Park
Raglan
Boult Reef
Grantleigh
South End
Bunker Group
Hoskyn Islands
Mt Helen
Epala
Fairfax Islands
Mount Larcom
Facing Island
Lady Musgrave Island
Ambrose
Gladstone
Coomooboolaroo
Dululu
Yarwun
Boyne Island
East End
Tannum Sands
Richards Point
Wowan
Cedric Mtn
Burua
Cooneel
Mt Alma
Benaraby
Bustard Point
Vimy
Lancefield
Stirrat
Calliope
Middle Island
Fry
Turkey Beach
Lady Elliot Island
Perch Creek
Rannes
Mt Redshirt
Awoonga Lake
Bustard Bay
Kokotungo
Seventeen Seventy
Castle Tower Nat Pk
Eurimbula Nat Park
Agnes Water
Goovigen
Jooro
Barmundu
Baralaba
Koorngoo
Jambin
Round Hill
Bindawalla
Boronen
Deepwater Nat Park
Mimosa Park
Mt Ramsay
Koonkool
Wietalaba
Blue Hills
Callide
Callide Coal Mine and Power Stn
Amys Peak
Miriam Vale
Redcliffe
Nagoorin
Callide Dam
Hinemoa
Ubobo
Colosseum
Taunton
Walba
Biloela
Kroombit Tops National Park
Littlemore
Rosevale
Rules Beach
Thangool
Banana
Kolonan
Lowmead
Oombabeer
Scoria
Many Peaks
Calliope Ra
1 17 24 25 31 32 33 35 37 38 39 42 45 49 56 65 66 102 104 106 145

Map 6

QLD 4
A
B
C
D
E
F
G
1
2
3
4
5
6
7
8
9
10
NT 7
SA 2
NORTH
138°
140°
141°
28°
NORTHERN TERRITORY
QUEENSLAND
SOUTH AUSTRALIA
Simpson Desert National Park
Simpson Desert Conservation Reserve
(Desert Parks Pass required prior to entry)
SIMPSON DESERT
STRZELECKI DESERT
Innamincka Regional Reserve
(Desert Parks Pass required prior to entry)
Strzelecki Regional Reserve
Lake Eyre Nat Park
Sturt National Park
QAA Line
K1
Rig Road
Inside Track
Outside Track
Birdsville Track
Strzelecki Track
Pipeline Track
Developmental Road
Mumbleberry Lake
Kamaran Downs
Bedourie
Cluny
Lake Philippi
Bedkira Water Facility
Glengyle
Lake Machattie
Lake Mipia
Lake Koolivoo
Mulligan River
Eyre Creek
Muncoonie Lakes
Oasis Bore
Carcoory
Bilpa Morea Claypan
Diamantina River
Umpadiboo Ck
Whitulania Ck
Warra Ck
Monkira
Davenport Creek
The Three Brothers
Hardings Ra
Farrar
Carbine Creek
Palparara
Round Mtn
Currawilla
Mooraberree
Farrars Creek
Blue
Flat Top
JC Hotel
Morney
Road
Canterbury
Cuddapan
Lake Cuddapan
Old Roseberth
Durrie
Betoota
Mount Leonard
Mt Hal
Roseberth
Mt Lewis
Birdsville
Lake Nappanerica
Poeppel Corner
Shallow Lake
Moonda Lake
Planet Downs Outstation
Lake Thomas
Dickeree Waterhole
Pandie Pandie
Lake Cooninnie
Frew Hill
Cadelga Outstation
Haddon Corner
Karrathunka Waterhole
Lake Short
Lake Etamunbanie
The Sisters
Lake Yamma Yamma
Nullah Outstation
Lake Uloowaranie
New Alton Downs
Andrewilla Waterhole
Goyder Lagoon
Koonchera Waterhole
Geake Hill
Cordillo Downs
Arrabury
MacGregor Hill
Cooks Well Outstation
Cooper
Clifton Hills
Warburton Crossing
Warburton Creek
Tippipilla Ck
Lake Goyder
Leap Year Bore
Durham Downs
Coongie
Coongie Lake
Mt Gason
Mt Gason Bore
Sturt Stony Desert
Lake John
Lake Koodnanie
Kudriemitchie Outstation
Cooper Creek
Walkers Crossing
Patchawara Bore
Karmona
Lake Howitt
Cowarie
Kalamurina
Mirra Mitta Bore
Nappa Merrie
Burke and Wills Dig Tree
Innamincka
Gidgealpa
Cullyamurra Waterhole
Lake Perigundi
Mt Hogarth
Mungeranie Gap
Uwinya Hill
Lake Andree
Kalamurra Lake
Gidgealpa Gas Field
Tennappera
Mungeranie
Mungeranie Roadhouse
Lake Kittakittaooloo
Moomba
Moomba Gas Field
Della Gas Field
Big Lake Gas Field
Burke-Dullingari Oil and Gas Field
Orientos
Lake Warrakalanna
Lake Ngapakaldi
Lake Hope or Panda
Epsilon
Bransby
Mulka
Lake Moomba
Toolache Gas Field
Santos
Lake Puntawolona
Tickalara Oil Field
Lake Murteree
Merty Merty
Naryilco
Lake Killamperpunna
Etadunna
Lake Kopperekoppinna
Lake Florence
Lake Gregory
Omicron
Bollards Lagoon
Yaningurie Waterhole
Strzelecki Crossing
Strzelecki Creek
Lake Eyre North
Dulkaninna
Conical Hill
Cameron Corner
Fort Grey
Warri Warri Gate
Grey
Coonyanna Ck
Clayton River
Waka
Lake Blanche
Muloorina
Clayton
Montecollina Bore
Lake Stewart
4WD
167
280
278
308
351
239
174
203
106
SA 2

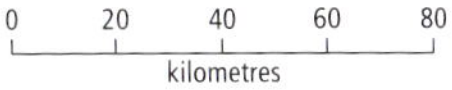
0 20 40 60 80
kilometres

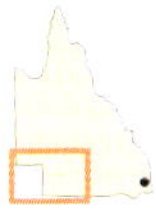

QLD

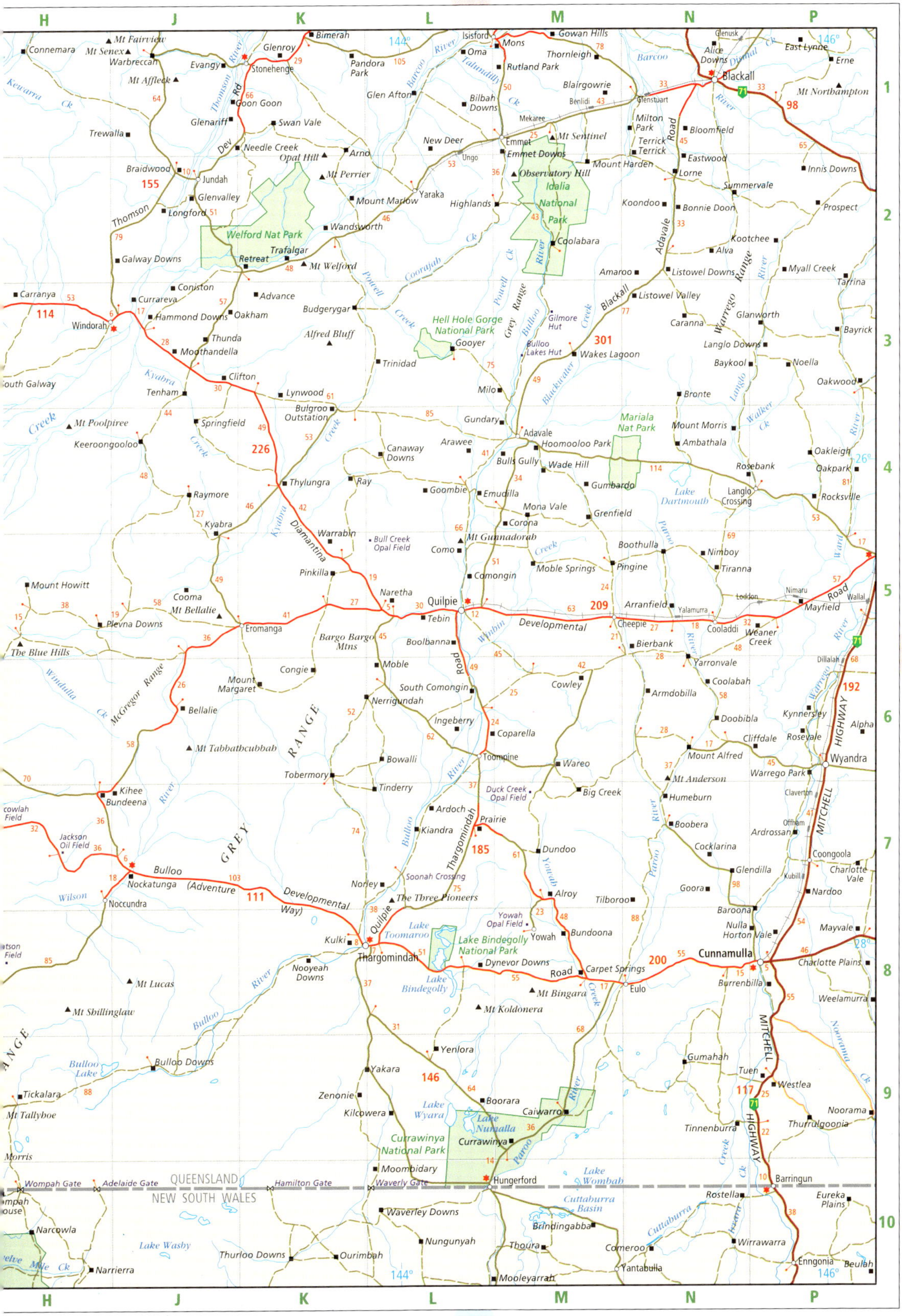
H J K L M N P
1 2 3 4 5 6 7 8 9 10
144° 146° 26° 28°
QLD 7
Connemara
Mt Fairview
Mt Senex
Warbreccan
Mt Affleck
Evangy
Glenroy
Stonehenge
Bimerah
Pandora Park
Glen Afton
Isisford
Oma
Mons
Talundilly
Rutland Park
Gowan Hills
Thornleigh
Blairgowrie
Benlidi
Glenusk
Alice Downs
Blackall
East Lynne
Erne
Mt Northampton
Kewarra Ck
Thomson
River
Goon Goon
Glenariff
Swan Vale
Trewalla
Dev Rd
Needle Creek
Opal Hill
Arno
New Deer
Emmet
Emmet Downs
Ungo
Bilbah Downs
Mekaree
Mt Sentinel
Glenstuart
Milton Park
Terrick Terrick
Road
Bloomfield
Eastwood
Barcoo
River
Mount Harden
Lorne
Innis Downs
Braidwood
Jundah
155
Mt Perrier
Yaraka
Mount Marlow
Highlands
Observatory Hill
Idalia National Park
Koondoo
Bonnie Doon
Summervale
Prospect
Glenvalley
Longford
Thomson
Welford Nat Park
Wandsworth
Coolabara
Adavale
Kootchee
Alva
Galway Downs
Retreat
Trafalgar
Mt Welford
Amaroo
Listowel Downs
Range
Myall Creek
Tarrina
Carranya
114
Windorah
Currareva
Coniston
Advance
Hammond Downs
Oakham
Budgerygar
Powell
Creek
Cooraiah
Hell Hole Gorge National Park
Gooyer
Grey Range
Bulloo
Gilmore Hut
Bulloo Lakes Hut
Blackall
Listowel Valley
Caranna
Warrego
Glanworth
Bayrick
Thunda
Moothandella
Alfred Bluff
Trinidad
Wakes Lagoon
301
Langlo Downs
Baykool
Noella
Oakwood
South Galway
Kyabra
Tenham
Clifton
Lynwood
Bulgroo Outstation
Milo
Blackwater
Bronte
Langlo
Walker Ck
Gundary
Mariala Nat Park
Mount Morris
Ambathala
Creek
Mt Poolpiree
Keeroongooloo
Springfield
226
Canaway Downs
Arawee
Adavale
Hoomooloo Park
Bulls Gully
Wade Hill
Rosebank
Oakleigh
Oakpark
Raymore
Thylungra
Ray
Goombie
Emudilla
Gumbardo
Lake Dartmouth
Langlo Crossing
Rocksville
Kyabra
Diamantina
Warrabin
Bull Creek Opal Field
Mt Gunnadorah
Mona Vale
Corona
Grenfield
Como
Moble Springs
Boothulla
Pingine
Nimboy
Tiranna
Ward
Mount Howitt
Cooma
Mt Bellalie
Pinkilla
Naretha
Quilpie
Comongin
Paroo
Arranfield
Yalamurra
Cheepie
Cooladdi
Loddon
Nimaru
Wallal
Road
Mayfield
Plevna Downs
Eromanga
Tebin
209
Developmental
Weaner Creek
The Blue Hills
Bargo Bargo Mtns
Boolbanna
Bierbank
Yarronvale
Dillalah
Windulla
McGregor Range
Moble
Congie
Mount Margaret
Road
Cowley
Coolabah
Armdobilla
192
Alpha
Bellalie
South Comongin
Nerrigundah
Ingeberry
Coparella
Doobibla
Kynnersley
HIGHWAY
Rosevale
Mt Tabbabtcubbah
RANGE
Toompine
Wareo
Cliffdale
Mount Alfred
Wyandra
Bowalli
Tobermory
Warrego Park
Mt Anderson
Kihee
Bundeena
Tinderry
Duck Creek Opal Field
Big Creek
Claverton
Humeburn
Jackson Oil Field
GREY
Ardoch
Kiandra
Thargomindah
Prairie
185
Boobera
Offham
Ardrossan
MITCHELL
Cockslarina
Coongoola
Bulloo
Nockatunga
(Adventure
111
Developmental Way)
Norley
Soonah Crossing
Dundoo
Yowah
Glendilla
Charlotte Vale
Kubill
Wilson
Noccundra
The Three Pioneers
Alroy
Tilboroo
Goora
Nardoo
Quilpie
Lake Toomaroo
Yowah Opal Field
Baroona
Kulki
Thargomindah
Lake Bindegolly National Park
Bundoona
Nulla Horton Vale
Mayvale
Nooyeah Downs
Dynevor Downs
Road
Carpet Springs
200
Cunnamulla
Charlotte Plains
Lake Bindegolly
Eulo
Burrenbilla
Mt Lucas
Mt Bingara
Weelamurra
Mt Shillinglaw
Mt Koldonera
Bulloo
Yenlora
Nebine
Gumahah
Bulloo Lake
Bulloo Downs
Yakara
146
Tuen
Westlea
Tickalara
Zenonie
Lake Wyara
Boorara
117
Noorama
Mt Tallyboe
Kilcowera
Lake Numalla
Caiwarro
Tinnenburra
Thurrulgoonia
Currawinya National Park
Currawinya
HIGHWAY
Morris
Moombidary
Paroo
Lake Wombah
Barringun
Wompah Gate
Adelaide Gate
QUEENSLAND
Hamilton Gate
Waverly Gate
Hungerford
Cuttaburra Basin
Rostella
Eureka Plains
Wompah House
NEW SOUTH WALES
Waverley Downs
Brindingabba
Cuttaburra
Narcowla
Lake Wasby
Nungunyah
Wirrawarra
Thurloo Downs
Ourimbah
Thoura
Comeroo
Yantabulla
Enngonia
Beulah
Narrierra
Mooleyarrah
Warrego
River
Ck

Map 7

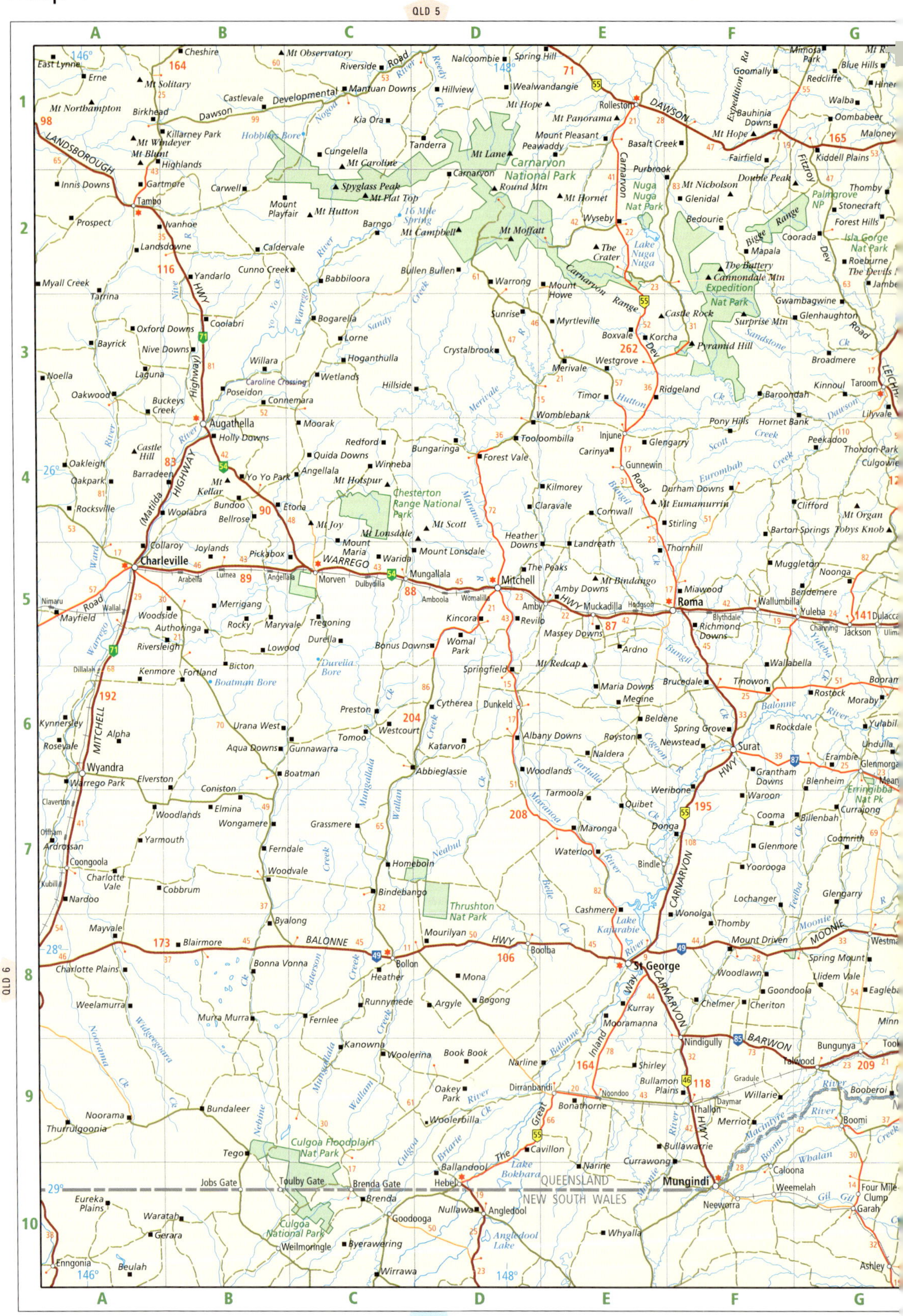
QLD 5
A
B
C
D
E
F
G
East Lynne
Erne
Cheshire
164
Mt Solitary
Mt Observatory
Riverside
Road
Nalcoombie
Spring Hill
71
Mimosa Park
Blue Hills
Redcliffe
Goomally
Walba
Oombabeer
Mt Northampton
Castlevale
Developmental
Mantuan Downs
Hillview
Wealwandangie
Rolleston
Dawson
Mt Hope
Mt Panorama
Bauhinia Downs
Maloney
98
Birkhead
Dawson
Kia Ora
Killarney Park
Hobblers Bore
Mt Windeyer
Mt Blunt
Tanderra
Mount Pleasant
Peawaddy
Basalt Creek
165
Fairfield
Kiddell Plains
Landsborough
Highlands
Cungelella
Mt Caroline
Mt Lane
Carnarvon National Park
Purbrook
Carnarvon
Double Peak
Innis Downs
Gartmore
Carwell
Spyglass Peak
Mt Flat Top
Round Mtn
Nuga Nuga Nat Park
Mt Nicholson
Glenidal
Palmgrove NP
Thomby
Stonecraft
Tambo
Mount Playfair
Mt Hutton
16 Mile Spring
Mt Hornet
Wyseby
Bedourie
Forest Hills
Prospect
Ivanhoe
Barngo
Mt Campbell
Mt Moffatt
The Crater
Lake Nuga Nuga
Bigge Range
Mapala
Coorada
Isla Gorge Nat Park
Landsdowne
Caldervale
Roeburne
The Devils
116
Yandarlo
Cunno Creek
Bullen Bullen
The Battery
Cannondale Mtn
Myall Creek
Tarrina
Babbiloora
Warrong
Mount Howe
Carnarvon Range
Expedition Nat Park
Gwambagwine
Jambe
Coolabri
Bogarella
Sunrise
Myrtleville
Castle Rock
Surprise Mtn
Glenhaughton
Oxford Downs
Sandy
Lorne
Boxvale
Korcha
Sandstone
Bayrick
Nive Downs
Crystalbrook
262
Pyramid Hill
Broadmere
Willara
Hoganthulla
Merivale
Westgrove
Noella
Laguna
Caroline Crossing
Wetlands
Hillside
Kinnoul
Taroom
Oakwood
Buckeys Creek
Poseidon
Connemara
Timor
Ridgeland
Baroondah
Lilyvale
Augathella
Moorak
Womblebank
Pony Hills
Hornet Bank
Holly Downs
Redford
Tooloombilla
Injune
Glengarry
Peekadoo
Castle Hill
Quida Downs
Bungaringa
Forest Vale
Carinya
Thordon Park
Oakleigh
Winneba
Gunnewin
Culgowie
Oakpark
Barradeen
Yo Yo Park
Angellala
Mt Hotspur
Chesterton Range National Park
Eurombah
Mt Kellar
Kilmorey
Durham Downs
Rocksville
Woolabra
Bundoo
Etona
Claravale
Cornwall
Mt Eumamurrin
Clifford
Mt Organ
Bellrose
Mt Joy
Mt Scott
Stirling
Barton Springs
Tobys Knob
Collaroy
Joylands
Pickabox
Mount Maria
Mt Lonsdale
Heather Downs
Landreath
Thornhill
Charleville
Warida
Mount Lonsdale
Muggleton
Noonga
Warrego
Mungallala
The Peaks
Mt Bindango
Bendemere
Arabella
Lurnea
Angellala
Morven
Dulbydilla
Mitchell
Amby Downs
Miawood
Nimaru
Road
Wallal
Amboola
Womalilla
Amby
Muckadilla
Hodgson
Roma
Wallumbilla
Yuleba
Dulacca
Mayfield
Merrigang
Hwy
Blythdale
Jackson
Woodside
Rocky
Maryvale
Tregoning
Kincora
Revilo
Richmond Downs
Channing
Authoringa
Womal Park
Massey Downs
Ardno
Riversleigh
Lowood
Durella
Bonus Downs
Bungil
Dillalah
Kenmore
Fortland
Bicton
Durella Bore
Boatman Bore
Springfield
Mt Redcap
Wallabella
Brucedale
Tinowon
Booram
Maria Downs
Megine
Rostock
Moraby
192
Cytherea
Dunkeld
Beldene
Balonne
Preston
Kynnersley
Alpha
Urana West
Westcourt
Spring Grove
Rockdale
Yulabil
Rosevale
Mitchell
Aqua Downs
Tomoo
Katarvon
Albany Downs
Royston
Newstead
Surat
Undulla
Wyandra
Gunnawarra
Naldera
Glenmorgan
Erambie
Warrego Park
Elverston
Boatman
Abbieglassie
Woodlands
Grantham Downs
Blenheim
Meandarra
Coniston
Tarmoola
Weribone
Waroon
Erringibba Nat Pk
Claverton
Woodlands
Elmina
Quibet
Currajong
Wongamere
Grassmere
Maranoa
Maronga
Donga
Cooma
Billenbah
Offham
Ardrossan
Yarmouth
Ferndale
Homeboin
Neabul
Waterloo
Glenmore
Coomrith
Coongoola
Charlotte Vale
Woodvale
Bindle
Yoorooga
Kubill
Nardoo
Cobbrum
Bindebango
Thrushton Nat Park
Cashmere
Lochanger
Glengarry
Byalong
Wonolga
Lake Kajarabie
Thomby
Mayvale
Mourilyan
Mount Driven
Moonie
Westmar
173
Blairmore
Balonne
Hwy
Boolba
106
St George
Spring Mount
Charlotte Plains
Bonna Vonna
Bollon
Heather
Mona
Woodlawn
Llidem Vale
Weelamurra
Runnymede
Argyle
Bogong
Chelmer
Goondoola
Cheriton
Eagleba
Murra Murra
Fernlee
Kurray
Mooramanna
Widgeegoara
Noorama
Kanowna
Woolerina
Book Book
Narline
Nindigully
Barwon
Bungunya
Talwood
209
Shirley
Bullamon Plains
118
Gradule
Booberoi
Oakey Park
Dirranbandi
Noondoo
Bonathorne
Thallon
Willarie
Daymar
Noorama
Bundaleer
Wooleribilla
Merriot
Boomi
Thurrulgoonia
Culgoa Floodplain Nat Park
Tego
Cavillon
Bullawarrie
The Great
Narine
Currawong
Caloona
Jobs Gate
Toulby Gate
Brenda Gate
Ballandool
Lake Bokhara
Hebel
Queensland
Mungindi
Weemelah
Four Mile Clump
Eureka Plains
Brenda
New South Wales
Garah
Neeworra
Waratah
Culgoa National Park
Goodooga
Nullawa
Angledool
Angledool Lake
Whyalla
Gerara
Byerawering
Weilmoringle
Enngonia
Beulah
Wirrawa
Ashley
146°
148°
26°
28°
29°
QLD 6
NSW 2

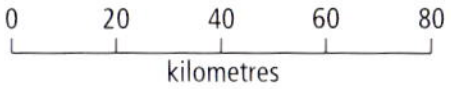
0 20 40 60 80
kilometres

H J K L M N P
1 2 3 4 5 6 7 8 9 10
NORTH
152°
154°
26°
28°
Great Barrier Reef Marine Park
(Mackay-Capricorn Section)
Hervey Bay
Marine Park
SOUTH
PACIFIC
OCEAN
Sunshine
Coast
Gold
Coast
Bindawalla
Callide
Callide Coal Mine
and Power Stn
Amys Peak
Callide Dam
Biloela
Banana
Thangool
Kroombit Tops
National Park
Callide Ra
Scoria
Dawes
Barfield
Lake Cania
Cania Gorge
Nat Park
Kurrajong
Coominglah
Harrami
Lonesome Creek
Lone Hand
Gold Mine
Moonford
Glandore
Rawbelle
Wingfield
Monto
Theodore
Mt Kandoonan
Camboon
Barram
Glencoe
Isla Plains
Multi
Lake Wuruma
Tireen
Euroka
Cracow
Precipice
National Park
Cloncose
Fairyland
Dawson Vale
Redbank
Widbury
Yerilla
Cockatoo
Auburn
Tabletop Hill
Hawkwood
Auburn
River Nat Pk
Mt Misery
Mt Saul
Collingwood
Monogorilby
Coondarra
Pinedale
Lismore
Turkey Mtn
Durah
Guluguba
Glenrowan
Barakula
Kentucky
Miles
WARREGO
Columboola
Rywung
Chinchilla
Brigalow
Gunbarwood
Boonarga
Jandowae
Wilga Downs
Condamine
Barramornie
Dunkerry
Alkira
Woolfield
Kogan
Govana
Daandine
Tara
Goranba
Weranga
Gulera
South Glen
Kumbarilla
The Gums
LEICHHARDT
Waar Waar
New Dunmore
Moonie
Saint Hilliers
Southwood
Nat Park
Boondandilla
Allawah
Kindon
GORE
Bendidee
Nat Pk
Commoron
Boggabilla
Goondiwindi
CUNNINGHAM
North Star
Yallaroi
Painters Bore
Camp
Coolatai
Ironbark Dam
Rocky Dam
Wallangra
Ashford
Yetman
Texas
Bonshaw
Maidenhead
Mt Bowman
Torrington
SRA
Torrington
Stannum
Boroorren
Wietalaba
Nagoorin
Ubobo
Littlemore
Many Peaks
Kalpower
Burnett Range
Mt Takilberan
Black Mtn
Abercorn
Rosslyn
Eidsvold
BURNETT
Mundubbera
Binjour
Gayndah
Ban Ban Springs
Scrubby Mtn
Mt Barbara
Allies Creek
Lake Boondooma
Proston
Hivesville
Windera
Durong South
Dangore Mtn
Tingoora
Wondai
Kingaroy
Ironpot
Kumbia
Coolabunia
Nanango
Cooranga North
Bunya Mtns
Nat Pk
Mt Kiangarow
Bell
Jimbour
Macalister
Warra
Kaimkillenbun
Dalby
Bowenville
Jondaryan
Oakey
Cecil Plains
Mount Tyson
Springside
Yarranlea
Pittsworth
Brookstead
Millmerran
Captains Mtn
Clontarf
Pine Hill
Koorongara
Mt Bodumba
Inglewood
Yuraraba
Whetstone
Yelarbon
Glenarbon
Beebo
Smithfield
Browns Mtn
Limevale
Silver Spur
Texas
Lake Coolmunda
Lake Glenlyon
Glenlyon
Mingoola
Mole River
Riverton
Round Hill
Miriam Vale
Taunton
Rosevale
Lowmead
Colosseum
Deepwater Nat Park
Rules Beach
Rosedale
Eurimbula
Lake Monduran
Yandaran
Moore Park
Moorland
Bundaberg Harbour
Bargara
Bundaberg
Elliott Heads
Kinkuna NP
Gin Gin
BRUCE
Mount Perry
Goodnight
Scrub Nat Pk
Booyal
Childers
Woodgate
Woodgate NP
Burrum Pt
Burrum Heads
Howard
Torbanlea
Dallarnil
Biggenden
Coalstoun Lakes
Mt Walsh
Mt Walsh Nat Pk
ISIS
Coast Ra
Urah Range
Maryborough
Tiaro
Bauple
Glenwood
Gunalda
Tansey
Woolooga
WIDE BAY
Kilkivan
Cloyna
Murgon
Goomeri
Mt Coora
Glastonbury
Widgee Mtn
Gympie
Amamoor
Kandanga
Manumbar
Elgin Vale
Lake Borumba
Mt Gibbarnee
Imbil
Memerambi
Lake Barambah
Kenilworth
Conondale Nat Pk
Conondale
Conondale Range
Jimna
Yarraman
D'AGUILAR
Linville
Moore
Yednia
Blackbutt
Wengenville
Cooyar
Wutul
Quinalow
Peranga
Kulpi
Haden
Crows Nest
NEW ENGLAND
Toogoolawah
Goombungee
Acland
Esk
Lake Wivenhoe
Meringandan
Murphys Creek
Toowoomba
Cooyar
Helidon
Gatton
Grantham
Laidley
Hatton Vale
Marburg
Rosewood
Cambooya
Greenmount
Felton East
Fordsdale
Mulgowie
Mt Cooper
Mt Lowe
Mt Mistake
Nat Pk
Towoomba
Clifton
Tummaville
Ryeford
Spring Creek
Allora
Goomburra
Leyburn
Pratten
Thane
Maryvale
Main Range
Nat Pk
Mt Huntley
Rockbrae
Warwick
Karara
Lake Leslie
Allan
Killarney
Koreelah
Nat Pk
Mt Barney
Mt Burrabaranga
Tank Mtn
The Summit
Stanthorpe
Dalveen
Wylie Creek
Pikedale
Liston
Amosfield
Rivertree Peak
Tooloom
Glen Aplin
Sundown
Nat Pk
Ballandean
Girraween
Nat Pk
Boonoo Boonoo
Nat Pk
Bald Rock
Nat Pk
Wallangarra
Bryans Gap
Leechs Gully
Tarban
Tenterfield
Sandy Flat
Sprabo
Nat Pk
Washpool
Nat Pk
Timbarra
Dalman
Legume
Woodenbong
Tooloom NP
Urbenville
Old Grevillia
Rosebery
Toonumbar
Nat Pk
Old Bonalbo
Paddys Flat
Bonalbo
Richmond Range NP
Mummulgum
Tabulam
Mallanganee
Leeville
Coombell
Wyan
Alice
Mt Pikapene
Nat Park
Mt Neville
Nat Res
Baryulgil
Banyabba
Nat Res
Camira Creek
Rappville
Whiporie
Chatsworth
Tabbimoble
Bundjalung
National Park
Mororo
Tiaro
Poona
Nat Pk
Tuan
Hervey Bay
River Heads
Moon Pt
Rooney Point
Platypus Bay
Marloo Bay
Sandy Cape
Orchid Beach
Waddy Point
Fraser Island
Great Sandy
National Park
Seventy Five Mile Beach
Happy Valley
Eurong
Hook Point
Wide Bay
Rainbow Beach
Double Island Point
Tin Can Bay
Goomboorian
Wolvi
Great Sandy
National Park
Kin Kin
Cooran
Boreen
Lake Cootharaba
Lake Cooroibah
Pomona
Tewantin
Noosa Heads
Noosa Nat Park
Lake Weyba
Cooroy
Eumundi
Coolum Beach
Yandina
Brooloo
Nambour
Mapleton
Montville
Palmwoods
Maroochydore
Mooloolaba
Buderim
Maleny
Landsborough
Caloundra
Beerwah
Woodford
Kilcoy
Bribie Island
Bribie Island Nat Park
Beerburrum
Lake Somerset
Mount Mee
Wamuran
Caboolture
Bongaree
Cape Moreton
Moreton Island
Somerset Dam
Dayboro
Beachmere
Deception Bay
Tangalooma
Moreton Island
National Park
Lake Samsonvale
Petrie
Redcliffe
Strathpine
Sandgate
Moreton Bay
Mud I
Samford
Cominya
Fernvale
Mount Nebo
BRISBANE
Amity Point
Point Lookout
Dunwich
North Stradbroke Island
Capalaba
Cleveland
Victoria Point
Ipswich
Browns Plains
Loganholme
Beenleigh
Purga
Mt Elliott
Park Ridge
Harrisville
Warrill View
Wolffdene
Pimpama
Oxenford
Woongoolba
Eden Island
Jacobs Well
South Stradbroke Island
Paradise Point
Milbong
Kalbar
Mt Castle
Tarome
Tamborine
Tamborine NP
Boonah
Coulson
Bromelton
Beaudesert
Nerang
Southport
Surfers Paradise
Laravale
Maroon
Lake Moogerah
Mudgeeraba
Numinbah Valley
Lamington
Nat Pk
Springbrook NP
Burleigh Heads
Coolangatta
Tweed Heads
Banora Point
Kingscliff
Rathdowney
Bald Mtn
Border Ranges NP
Numinbah
Tumbulgum
Murwillumbah
Uki
Burringbar
Mt Jerusalem
Nat Park
Wooyung
Brunswick Heads
Mullumbimby
Nimbin
Nightcap NP
Byron Bay
Blue Knob
Bangalow
Suffolk Park
Kyogle
Dunoon
Cedar Point
Wiangaree
Eden Creek
Ettrick
Fairy Hill
Goolmangar
Lismore
Lennox Head
Casino
Alstonville
Ballina
Empire Vale
Coraki
Wardell
Dungarubba
Yorklea
Ellangowan
Broadwater NP
Evans Head
Woodburn
Snapper Point
Tabbimoble Swamp NP
HWY
WARREGO
BURNETT
BRUCE
WIDE BAY
D'AGUILAR
NEW ENGLAND
CUNNINGHAM
GORE
LEICHHARDT

New South Wales

Nature-lovers and history buffs alike find New South Wales a fabulous place to get away from it all. The beauty of the Blue Mountains beckons visitors with a bushwalking bent, while those looking for something less taxing will enjoy sitting in a café and watching the world go by. For a little fun on the water, sail Sydney Harbour or hire a houseboat on the Hawkesbury River. Reminiscent of the English countryside, the Southern Highlands is a mecca for antiques aficionados, and the wineries of the Hunter Valley welcome weary travellers with a drop or two of their finest. Enjoy Sydney's galleries, museums, parks and shopping, or find a quiet beach to relax in the sun. All in all, New South Wales is the premier state for recharging the batteries.

Sydney and Environs

It is generally agreed that Sydney is one of the most beautiful cities on Earth. The Harbour, the exquisite foreshores mixing luxurious housing with elegant bushland parks, the internationally famous Harbour Bridge and Opera House, the ferries criss-crossing the Harbour, the easy-going nature of the locals who, as some wit once observed, 'look as they are on holiday all the time', and the cleanliness and modernity of the central business district all add up to a city which is very special and which is ideal for those looking for relaxation and comfort.

Above: *The* Crystal Harmony *is just one of many luxury liners bringing visitors to Sydney. Circular Quay can be seen in the background.*

In spite of cosmopolitan Sydney's large size and population, the Pacific Ocean and abundance of waterways in and around the city create a relaxed ambience.

But the visitor doesn't have to rely on Sydneysiders for glowing descriptions of this remarkable city. English writer Anthony Trollope, when he visited Australia, wrote of Sydney: 'I despair of being able to convey to any reader my own idea of the beauty of Sydney Harbour. I have seen nothing to equal it in the way of land-locked sea scenery.'

Some of the architecture of Sydney's early days remains, particularly in The Rocks, the famous historic area near Circular Quay, and in Macquarie Street.
Map: NSW 6 J8

Shopping

If shopping is the way you relax then where do you start in Sydney? The

cularly the Aboriginal Art and Tribal Centre and the S. H. Ervin Gallery), and shops specialising in opals and Australian memorabilia. Part of the appeal is to simply wander and explore.

Beyond The Rocks, Sydney's central business district is a mixture of office blocks, hotels, restaurants, cafés, and shopping areas ranging from large department stores to small specialist boutiques selling everything from haute couture to classic wines.

Perhaps the city's most famous shopping destination is the QVB (Queen Victoria Building) which Pierre Cardin, the famous French couturier, once

don't miss

For an exhilarating, once-in-a-lifetime experience try the night or day Harbour Bridge Climb. Climbers are led and harnessed for safety; the pace is steady and at the top of the bridge you are rewarded with the most spectacular panoramic view—a fairytale of lights at night and scenery stretching to the Blue Mountains by day.

Below: *The Hero of Waterloo, at Millers Point, was built by convict labour in 1843. There are still iron shackles on the cellar walls.*

Above: *The coast from Queenscliff to Manly. As well as beautiful beaches, the Manly area offers surf carnivals, weekend markets and Oceanworld.*

Right: Magnolia and Palm *is one of the contemporary artworks in the Sydney Sculpture Walk among the trees near Farm Cove.*

blocks, hotels, restaurants, cafés, and shopping areas ranging from large department stores to small specialist boutiques selling everything from haute couture to classic wines.

Perhaps the city's most famous shopping destination is the QVB (Queen Victoria Building) which Pierre Cardin, the famous French couturier, once described as 'the most beautiful shopping centre in the world'. The building is a centre of high-class fashion boutiques (as well as more affordable fashion). It also has a fast-food takeaway area, a selection of restaurants, and a large number of high turnover tourist gift shops, and is designed to meet a diverse range of shopping needs.

Nearby is one of the city's major attractions—Centrepoint Tower—which offers unsurpassed views of the city as well as plenty of good shopping and the Sydney Tower Restaurant.

Darling Harbour is another venue with much to offer, including waterfront walkways, a multitude of shops, restaurants and bars, open park areas and children's playgrounds, and many interesting attractions. Among these are the Sydney Aquarium, with its underwater viewing stations, the tranquil Chinese Garden, the giant screen of the IMAX theatre, the Casino, and the fascinating Powerhouse Museum and Australian National Maritime Museum.

People eager to inspect contemporary art should head for Paddington,

on the outskirts of the city centre, which has become Sydney's commercial gallery centre.

Eating

Where to eat in Sydney? Well, everywhere is the simple answer. Sydney is widely regarded, by international experts, as having some of the cheapest and best food of any major city in the world. If you are happy with tourist fare, and want a good view, you could do worse than find a restaurant in The Rocks. The restaurants there offer seafood, Italian and Chinese cuisine and contemporary Australian meals.

If you are looking for Asian food you can have fun in and around Dixon Street, the heart of the city's Chinatown. There are excellent yum cha restaurants, as well as places noted for excellent seafood and regional specialities.

People keen to find an interesting restaurant but undecided about the style of cuisine will find that Oxford Street in Paddington, King Street in Newtown, and Glebe Point Road in Glebe all offer an excellent range of cuisines including Nepalese, Indian, Thai, Italian, Modern Australian and Vietnamese.

Tetsuya's, in Kent Street, is widely regarded as the city's greatest restaurant. In fact many overseas experts have rated it as one of top ten greatest restaurants in the world. This restaurant is pure 'theatre of food' and the experience is unforgettable. So, by Sydney and Australian standards, is the bill.

The Ferries

Is there anything more relaxing than sitting on a ferry and watching the world go by? Today Sydney's ferries are a mixture of fast JetCat services and the more sedate older ferries. The best trip of all is the one from Circular Quay to Manly which crosses the Harbour and offers excellent views of the Heads and the gracious homes which line the foreshores. Another enjoyable trip is the leisurely ride up the Parramatta River from the Quay to Parramatta. There are other north-shore services at Mosman, Neutral Bay, the world-class Taronga Park Zoo, Cremorne and McMahon's Point, and there is a service which runs along the eastern suburbs shoreline from Circular Quay to Watson's Bay. In many instances it is easy to see the possible walks and vantage points which are available if you decide to alight from the ferry and go harbourside walking.

The Harbour Parks

How would you best enjoy the natural beauty of Sydney? Go bushwalking, swim in a harbourside pool, or just sit and admire the scenery? Sydney's harbour parks, now grouped together as the Sydney Harbour National Park, are perfect for all these activities. You can find out all about them and get excellent maps of the parks at Cadman's Cottage in George Street at The Rocks.

If you have the time to go for a 3–4 hour walk there is nowhere better than walking from Manly to the Spit Bridge. It is the most spectacular of all the harbour walks. The walk starts at the Manly

An authentic Chinese dining experience, savouring such delights as barbecued duck, can be followed by a stroll through Sydney's Chinese Garden of Friendship.

Sydney Harbour is notable for the large number of ferries that constantly ply its waterways. There is no more relaxing way to take in the sights and sounds of the Harbour.

Wisdom, *one of the artworks adorning the Chief Secretary's Building in Macquarie Street, where there are several fine examples of Victorian architecture.*

ferry terminal, so all you have to do is take the ferry from the city across to Manly, pick up the map at the wharf, and start walking.

If you want a shorter, but no less interesting journey, try the walk around Bradley's Head. Catch the ferry across the harbour from Circular Quay to Taronga Zoo, walk a short distance up Athol Wharf Road, take the path which winds around the foreshore, and marvel at the carefully signposted remnants of the original bushland which has remained untouched since the arrival of Europeans in 1788. Continue on to the fortifications which were first constructed by convicts in 1839; this is an ideal spot to enjoy a picnic.

Don't forget the parks near the city centre. The Botanic Gardens, and the nearby Domain, are popular retreats for the city's office workers. The diversity of plants in the Botanic Gardens is remarkable. The gardens have over 4000 trees and plants from all over the world. There are specialist collections in the herbarium and in the pyramid glasshouse where the heat and humidity support an outstanding mixture of tropical and subtropical plants.

The setting and location of the gardens is ideal. Visitors can wander through The Rocks, around the Opera House and enter the Gardens before walking to Mrs Macquarie's Chair, the Art Gallery and the historic buildings of Macquarie Street.

The Baha'i House of Worship at Ingleside near Sydney's northern beaches is a quiet place for contemplation and reflection where all are welcome.

The Northern Beaches

From Manly in the south to Palm Beach in the north, the northern beaches offer some of the finest beaches in Australia. They can be reached by both private vehicle and bus (take the ferry from Circular Quay to Manly or get the buses from Wynyard in the city). The opportunity to simply relax on a beach is the area's greatest appeal. Some people enjoy bodysurfing. Some people just walk along the beach or the foreshore. Some people go to test their skills on bodyboards and surfboards. This is really what Sydney is all about. Sun, sand and surf.

For those who prefer still waters, Pittwater offers many opportunities to relax. Sailing, taking a ferry from Palm Beach over to The Basin, or having a drink at the Newport Arms Hotel are some of the favourite local pastimes.

Bondi

No trip to Sydney can be complete without a visit to Bondi. Apart from the obvious pleasure of swimming and surfing at one of Australia's most famous beaches, this is an ideal location to stroll along the esplanade and to pick and choose from the dozens of excellent restaurants, brasseries and cafés which line the beachfront. There are also delightful walks both north and south of Bondi along the cliffs and foreshores. Just south of Bondi is Tamarama which is a beach famous for perfect bodies, and is particularly popular with Sydney's trendsetters.

Parramatta

Located just 24 km from Sydney, the area that is now called Parramatta was settled just one year after the arrival of the First Fleet in 1788. Many historical buildings from the colonial era still stand, including Elizabeth Farm (1793)—the oldest surviving house in Australia—and Hambledon Cottage (1824). Old Government House (1799) in Parramatta

Bondi Beach has a well-deserved reputation as one of Sydney's best. Whether you swim, surf, sunbathe, stroll along the Esplanade, or sit at one of the many outdoor cafés or restaurants and watch the world go by, you are guaranteed an enjoyable experience.

Park is Australia's oldest public building, and the park also offers a lush green setting for picnickers in the heart of the city. For those who find shopping a relaxing way to spend a day, Westfield Parramatta is the largest shopping centre in the Southern Hemisphere.

Some Special Treats

It is probably true to say that Sydney caters for absolutely every imaginable taste and enthusiasm. There are many interesting possibilities.

If you want to enjoy the great outdoors, contact the NSW Confederation of Bushwalking Clubs for suggestions (02 9548 1228), or hire a bicycle and enjoy cycling around Centennial Park, the city's largest and most relaxing civic park (02 9398 5027), or hire a horse and go riding there (02 9339 6699), or learn to sail across Sydney Harbour (02 9327 1166), or try parasailing—one of the most exciting ways of experiencing Sydney Harbour (02 9977 6781).

You can go fishing—Balmoral Boat Shed hires small boats (02 9969 6006)—or learn to cook some of Sydney's maritime delicacies at the Sydney Seafood School (02 9552 2180).

To see what Sydney was like before Europeans arrived, contact Sydney Aboriginal Discoveries (02 9568 3226).

Other relaxing alternatives include watching the horseracing at Royal Randwick Racecourse (02 9663 8400), or visiting one of the city's excellent day spas for a great massage.

Old Government House in Parramatta Park was built in 1799 by Governor Hunter. It is open every day, and twice a month offers a great candlelit ghost tour followed by a light supper.

The North Coast

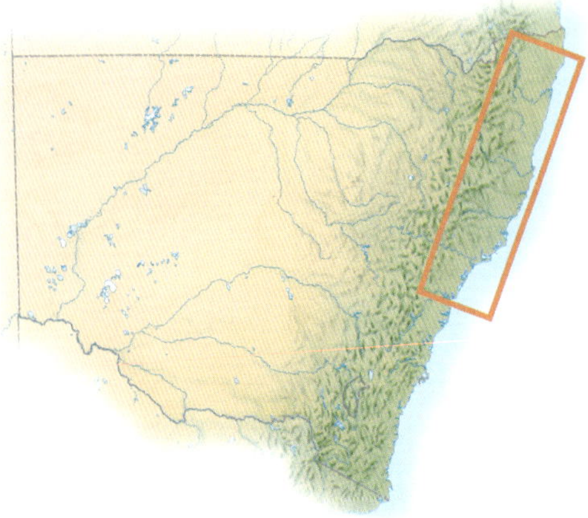

The North Coast of New South Wales has much to offer the visitor in search of relaxation: fine surf beaches and a sunny but not too humid climate on the coast, and a fertile hinterland with many other attractions. The Hunter Valley, for example, is Australia's most visited wine region, while in other regions quiet country towns, fast-flowing rivers and unspoiled mountain wilderness areas provide attractive alternatives to the beauty of the coast.

Port Stephens

For some strange reason, probably because they have always driven past it at great speed, many Sydneysiders don't know a lot about Port Stephens. Some of them don't even know where it is. Like so many attractive coastal destinations on the New South Wales North Coast, Port Stephens is not well known because drivers heading north have to make a conscious effort to visit it. In many instances, they can only return to their journey north if they then make the long trip back to the Pacific Highway.

The appeal of Port Stephens lies in the ease with which it provides the visitor with special experiences. At Corlette, for example, there is delightful five-star accommodation at Merretts at Peppers. This classy establishment boasts the best restaurant in the area, where sensational food is served. As an additional and indulgent luxury, it is possible to stay on one of the boats moored at the Corlette Marina (contact Anchorage Marina 02 6574 7118).

The jetty at Tea Gardens, on Port Stephens' northern shore. Anglers can catch flounder, garfish, sand whiting, blackfish and tailor in these waters.

To experience the full joy of the quiet bay, all a visitor has to do is catch the ferry from Nelson Bay (a thriving and attractive seaside resort town with a number of good restaurants and excellent accommodation options) over to Tea Gardens. The chances are very high that dolphins will come alongside the ferry. If they don't there are a number of excellent tours from the wharf at Nelson Bay which offer dolphin- and, in season, whale-watching.

The journey across to Tea Gardens is delightful. The ferry makes its way through the shoals and reaches the sleepy settlement, where a number of cafés and restaurants (including some very good ones, such as Tillermans) have sprung up beside the wharf. People eager for some walking can cross the Singing Bridge and make their way to Hawks Nest (once the holiday haunt of Prime Minister John Howard and his family), where the beach is long, beautiful and unspoilt. This is a perfect, old-fashioned retreat where visitors can go boating, swimming, surfing, windsurfing, waterskiing, diving, fishing, canoeing, bushwalking, birdwatching, camping and pursuing the 4WD tracks both north and south of town.

Of particular interest is the walk across to Yacaaba Head, the enormous headland which stands at the northeastern tip of Port Stephens. Dolphins frequent an area just offshore from here and can be seen, usually on a daily basis, rubbing their bodies on the smooth pebbles. The area is known as Dolphin Hole. The walk to the top of Yacaaba Head is tough, but the views are spectacular and well worth the effort.

It is also possible, if you have driven to Hawks Nest (the drive from Port Stephens is long because you have to return to the Pacific Highway and then make your way back to the coast), to access the Myall Lakes National Park, a 31 562-ha reserve comprising fresh- and salt-water lakes, swamps, high dunes, rugged headlands and 40 km of beaches which stretch all the way from Hawks Nest north to Seal Rocks.

Map: NSW 6 M5

Hunter Valley

The accommodation and attractions in the Hunter Valley are centred around the region's rich and outstanding grape and wine production. This is where wine connoisseurs go to taste the latest vintages and to load up the boots of their cars with boxes of fine whites and reds. Some of the more famous wineries include McWilliams Mount Pleasant Winery, Hungerford Hill, Brokenwood, and McGuigan Bros Winery and Cellars. Every visit to the region should start at The Wine Country Visitors Centre at Cessnock (02 4990 4477).

The local tourist authorities have recognised that moving from one cellar to the next can be arduous and so they have provided entertaining diversions such as the annual 'Jazz in the Vines' festival for music lovers, and horse-drawn carriages for those who feel confident that their tastings will be consumed rather than expelled.

Although relaxing in the Hunter Valley usually involves a lot of wine tasting, there are many other

Above: *In Myall Lakes National Park high sand dunes separate rocky headlands and long stretches of stunning ocean beach from the lakes.*

Below: *Briar Ridge Vineyard, in the Hunter Valley, is a delightful setting for wine tasting, and also offers picnic and playground facilities.*

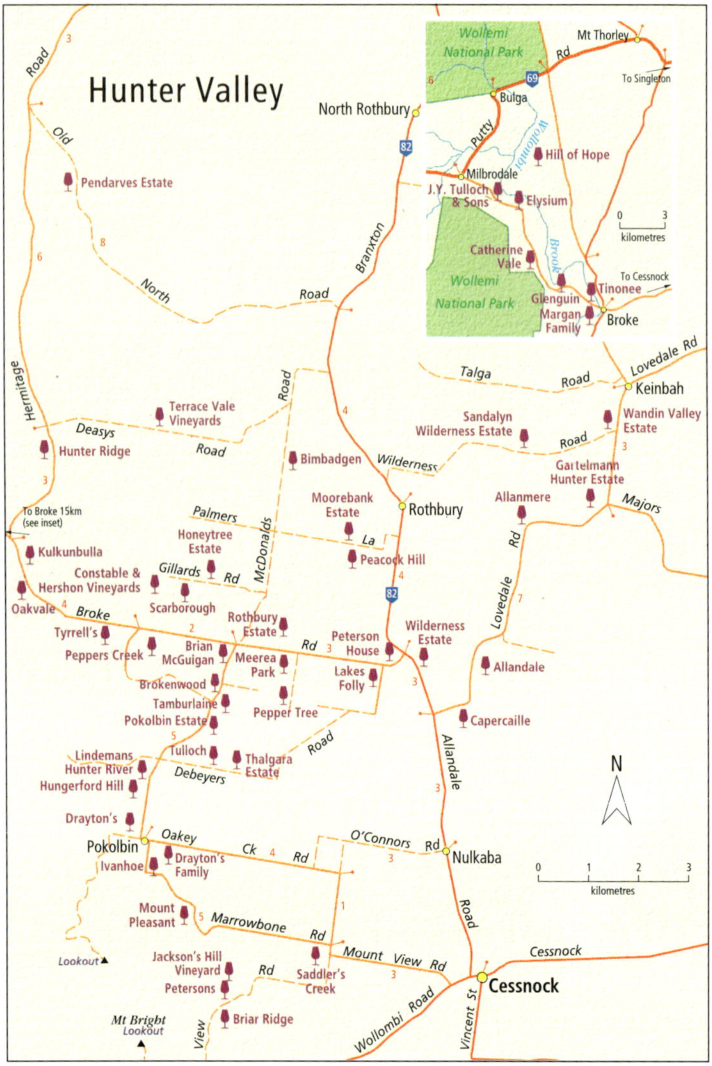

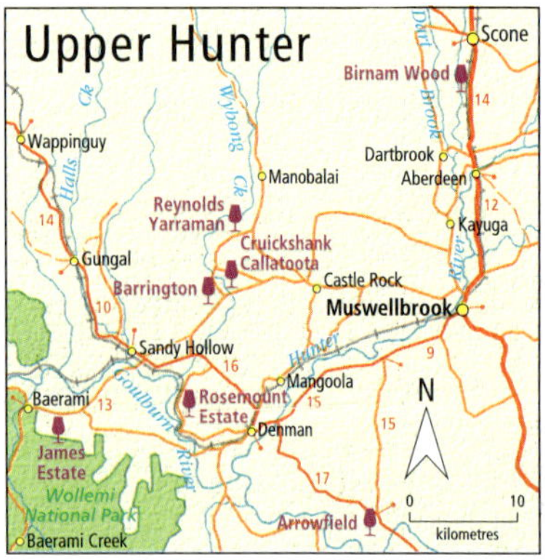

Below: *The Upper and Lower Hunter Valley, which produce world-class red and white wines, welcome more visitors than any other other wine region in the country.*

things to see and do in the region. The superbly appointed Cypress Lakes Resort (02 4993 1822) includes the excellent Cypress Lakes Golf and Country Club.

If you really want to pamper yourself, head off to the sensational Golden Door Health Retreat in the resort. It is the New South Wales counterpart to the famous Gold Coast health spa.

For those unfamiliar with the Golden Door, the spa offers people eager to look and feel great an opportunity to be dipped in mud baths, annointed with essential oils (in scents of cinnamon, vanilla, ginger, patchouli, marjoram, clove and jasmine), massaged and pummelled, exfoliated, moisturised with a rose-water toner and given an all-over body treatment. No one should be surprised if they come away radiating beauty and health.

There are other, quieter, enjoyable retreats in the valley. Splinters Guest House in Hermitage Road (02 6574 7118) has a golf practice green, easy walks around the grounds and a pleasant and substantial swimming

pool. It's the kind of place where you can stay and never let a drop of wine pass your lips.

For something different, you could visit the historic coalmining towns of Kurri Kurri, Cessnock and Maitland, and from Maitland take a scenic drive along the New England Highway, passing through some of Australia's best horse and cattle country.

Map: NSW 6 K5

Port Macquarie

One of the North Coast's most popular family destinations is Port Macquarie, located at the mouth of the Hastings River and 420 km north of Sydney. There is a simple reason for this: it is large enough to cater for virtually every need. It has a range of good restaurants, a huge variety of accommodation (from self-catering to motels, apartments and B&Bs) and excellent shopping.

In terms of activities, the local tourist information centre has brochures and information on everything from scuba diving to yachting, boat hire, fishing charters, local fishing locations, sail-boarding, windsurfing, houseboats, jet-skis, canoe safaris, scenic and charter aeroplane flights, river cruises, parasailing and skydiving, 4WD and motorcycle tours, hang-gliding, horseriding, golf and eco-tours. Contact 1800 025 935 for more information.

Of particular interest in the Port Macquarie area are the adventure holidays, including abseiling and bushwalking, around Comboyne. The Timbertown Heritage Theme Park at Wauchope has dozens of houses recreating an old timber town of the 1880s and is open daily from 9.30 a.m. to 3.30 p.m. There is a blacksmith, a leather-worker and other crafts-people, a steam train, a railway station, a steam

Above: *Port Macquarie has an excellent climate and idyllic setting on the coast. The area is becoming busier, but there are still some peaceful spots.*

Below: *Timbertown's steam train chugs slowly through the forest.*

South West Rocks, a watersport haven, where you can charter a fishing boat and be assured of a good catch. Beach and estuary fishing are also good in this area.

sawmill, shops, a bakery, a pub, and barbecue facilities if you want to picnic.

In the town of Port Macquarie you will find the Kooloonbung Creek Nature Park with its colourful flower beds, expansive lawns and shady trees, 3 km of walking trails and several bird-watching platforms. Peppermint Park is an amusement park with attractions to please all the family, while animal-lovers will enjoy the Kingfisher Conservation Park and the Billabong Koala and Wildlife Park. The Koala Hospital and Port Macquarie Nature Reserve is situated in a 12-ha section of forest which is used as a treatment and relocation centre for injured koalas.

Map: NSW 4 M10

did you know?

The Sea Acres Rainforest Centre at Port Macquarie comprises 76 ha of four different types of rare coastal rainforest, with a 1.3 km boardwalk. The centre, a joint state and federal government project, was established in 1989 to protect the unique flora of the area.

South West Rocks

South West Rocks is another of those special places which holiday-makers have to make a conscious decision to visit. Turn off at Kempsey and drive 25 km to the coast and you will come to a sleepy and hugely attractive holiday destination which attracts many television personalities because they are left alone by the local community. The appeal of South West Rocks is obvious. The bay is ideal for fishing, swimming and lazy recreation activities. The nearby Trial Bay Gaol is a truly fascinating ruin. It is under the control of the National Parks and Wildlife Service, who have maintained it in superb condition. There is a self-guiding brochure which leads the visitor through the main points of interest. It is open daily from 9.00 a.m. to 5.00 p.m. For more information contact (02) 6566 6168.

Further down the coast there are a number of excellent and interesting walks in Hat Head National Park. There are also camping facilities at Smoky Cape and Hungry Head. Off the coast is Fish Rock Cave, recognised as one of the largest ocean caverns in the Southern Hemisphere. This cave is 120 m long and is noted for its coral, live cowry shells, trumpetfish, wobbegong sharks, black cod and stingrays.

Map: NSW 4 M9

Byron Bay

What can be said about Byron Bay? Ever since people started migrating from Sydney in the 1970s (the most famous being Paul Hogan and John Cornell) this town has become a symbol of everything that is good and wonderful about coastal life. Located 790 km north of Sydney, it is the spiritual heart of an area where many people have chosen to seek relief from the city. This section of the North Coast has long been a magnet for artists, writers and musicians. Since the 1970s, Nimbin has had the distinction of being the most alternative

Right: *The Nimbin Hotel, like most shops and cafés in town, is colourfully decorated. This interesting town near Byron Bay is the alternative-lifestyle capital of Australia.*

enclave, and also close by is Lismore, a thriving township which is the hub of much of the region's activities.

Over the past decade, the citizens of Byron Bay have prevented both Club Med and McDonald's from moving in. They have banned drive-through takeaways. They have restricted buildings to three storeys and they have ensured that the accommodation is diverse and interesting. No visit to Byron Bay is complete without eating at Fins—which is regarded by many as the finest restaurant in rural New South Wales—and it is fun to stay at such award-winning destinations as Crystal Creek Rainforest Retreat (02 6679 1591), the superb Ewingsdale Country Guest House (02 6684 7047), and Treetops, where you literally gaze out across the tops of the trees (02 6685 7390). Interesting galleries and craft shops abound, and there are plenty of places to go if you are in the mood for a massage, tarot reading or yoga class. The East Coast Blues and Roots Festival held every Easter weekend is a major event.

But for those who really want to experience the magic of this interesting coastal town a visit to the lighthouse is an absolute must. Arakwal National Park, which includes the headland, has several walking tracks. The track which heads both north and south from the lighthouse is ideal for easy walking, and there are superb views over the Pacific and back into the hinterland. Watego's Beach is directly below the lighthouse and is popular with surfers.

Map: NSW 4 P2

Above: *Main Beach and other beaches in Byron Bay offer clean, warm waters (average 21° C in winter) for swimming and surfing.*

Below: *Cape Byron Lighthouse is Australia's most powerful lighthouse, and is on the country's most easterly point.*

The Riverina

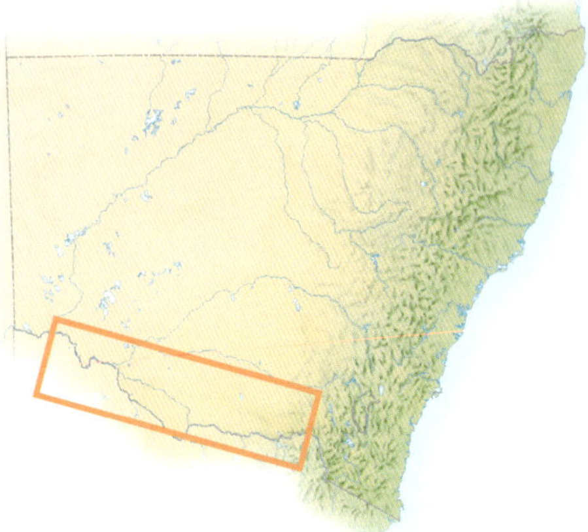

The Riverina covers a vast area of south-western New South Wales from Wagga Wagga and Albury in the east to the edges of the outback and the Murray–Darling Basin in the west. It is, for people looking for an interesting and unusual holiday, an ideal location for two activities: farmstays and riverboat adventures. Both of these activities can be accomplished in luxury or they can be true tests of adventure.

Riverboat trips can last for just a few hours, or visitors can hire a boat for an extended holiday and explore the river more fully, stopping by the banks at night and slowly cruising up or down the river during the day.

Farmstays (basically a B&B on a farm) give visitors the chance to enjoy country hospitality and wide open spaces, participate in farm activities and see the animals close up. The Riverina is an interesting mixture of agriculture. At some points it is purely sheep country. At other points, particularly around Griffith and the Murrumbidgee Irrigation Area, it is ideal citrus- and fruit-growing country. This is a part of Australia where visitors should ensure, no matter where they are, that they go and marvel at the vast clear skies during both the day and the night.

Albury

Located 567 km south-west of Sydney via the Hume Highway, Albury is a major rural centre. There were plans in the 1970s to make it one of the country's large regional developments by combining Albury with the Victorian township of Wodonga. That plan was shelved long ago but Albury, because of its location on the Hume Highway (567 km south-west of Sydney), has continued to grow and prosper. It is a town of great parks. On the northern side of the Murray River are a series of parklands—Oddies

Panoramic views of Albury and beyond are obtained from Monument Hill lookout, which is 214 m above the city. Albury has a pleasant mix of modern and late-1800s buildings.

Creek Park, Noreuil Park, Hovell Tree Park, the Sportsground, the Botanic Gardens, Mates Park and Padman Park—all of which are well catered for with barbecue and picnic facilities, swimming spots and walking tracks.

At Noreuil Park you will find the PS *Cumberoona*, a replica of an 1886 paddle-steamer which once used to visit Albury. It offers one-hour tours of the Murray every day in summer—phone (02) 6041 5558.

Travellers looking for a cool, and remarkably attractive, spot to visit should consider the city's exceptional Botanic Gardens (established in 1871) which boast a 30-m high Queensland kauri, some river red gums grown from seeds of a tree marked by Hume and Hovell and known as the Hovell Tree, and a pine which has been grown from a seed taken at Lone Pine in Gallipoli.

Being an important stopover, the town boasts a huge number of good quality motels. For those looking for something more adventurous the Lake Hume Resort, set on 21 ha beside Lake Hume, has facilities for all the family. Contact (02) 6026 4444.

Map: NSW 7 C6

PS Cumberoona *offers old-world charm and a sedate tour of the Murray River. The tour evokes images of the days when paddle-steamers laden with wheat, wool and wine plied the river.*

Griffith

Griffith lies in the heart of the Murrumbidgee Irrigation Area. It is an Australian town with an Italian flavour: 60 per cent of the town's population are descended from Italian migrants. This is one of the most agriculturally productive areas in the state producing 80 per cent of New South Wales' and 20 per cent of Australia's wine grapes—the Riverina's productivity is among the world's highest. The same applies to the local rice industry which was founded in 1924. Citrus fruit is the other major local product although, increasingly, stone fruits, vegetables, wheat, cotton, sheep, wool, eggs and canola are becoming important. Visitors to Griffith should definitely experience the local Italian food which is outstanding, and call into a few of the wineries—De Bortoli and Miranda are among the most popular.

Map: NSW 5 N5

Below: *McWilliam's Hanwood winery near Griffith has a statue of John McWilliam—son of founder Samuel McWilliam—with an old wine press, outside the cellar door.*

Wagga Wagga

There was a time when Wagga Wagga was just another country service centre. Today it is the economic centre of the eastern Riverina and a good base for exploring the area. It is an inland city boasting a thriving university, a number of attractive parklands (particularly around the Murrumbidgee River) and the delightful 30-km long Wiradjuri Walking Track. The Victory Memorial Gardens and the beautiful Botanic Gardens are well worth visiting.

Only twenty minutes south of Wagga is the small township of The

Below: *Mustering sheep is just one of the many farm activities you can experience on a farmstay holiday, where the pressures of city living disappear in the wide open spaces.*

Rock. Just south of The Rock is one of Australia's most famous farmstay destinations. As the website explains (http://www.hanericka.com.au): 'Owned and operated by the Male family, "Hanericka Farmstay" offers the finest in country hospitality combined with the unique opportunity to see and experience this magnificent working wheat, sheep and cattle property.'

Whether it is spotlighting for kangaroos in their natural surrounds, assisting with a calf being born, visiting a working shearing shed or just discussing the way of farming over scones and a cup of tea—a visit to Hanericka offers a great opportunity to see the real Australia. You can also choose to relax and take it easy alongside the swimming pool, play tennis, enjoy a gentle horseride or just soak up and appreciate the fresh air and tranquillity of the surrounding countryside.

Hanericka has become famous in Japan since the arrival of a Japanese student who came to work there—when the Japanese discovered there was a real Japanese jackeroo they rushed to experience the Australian bush.

Map: NSW 7 D3

Above: *Golden fields of barley waving in the wind—a wonderful setting for quiet contemplation or to picnic by and appreciate the changing colours of the landscape.*

Left: *A calf waits to be fed—the opportunity to see young animals up close is part of the attraction of farmstay holidays.*

The South Coast and Southern Highlands

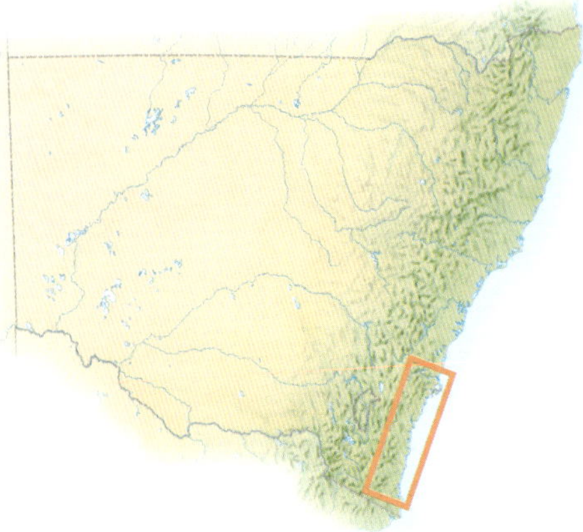

Over the past ten years both the South Coast and the Southern Highlands of New South Wales have become very desirable holiday, weekend and relaxation destinations for over-worked Sydneysiders. Realising that Sydney residents wanted luxury, fine dining and often healthy farm breaks, the hoteliers and restaurant owners have risen to meet these demands.

Right: *Bradman Oval, located in a peaceful setting in the heart of Bowral, is where 'The Don' began his cricketing career. The Bradman Museum is also here.*

Places like Bowral in the Southern Highlands are known for their fine cuisine and excellent accommodation. So too are a number of popular haunts—Berry, Jamberoo and Tilba Tilba—on the South Coast.

The Southern Highlands

After the railway line came through the Southern Highlands in the 1850s and 1860s, the district quickly acquired a reputation as an ideal retreat from the summer heat and increasing urbanisation of Sydney. By the 1880s and 1890s wealthy Sydney families were building gracious homes in the area. Other Sydneysiders would take the train to the highlands and stay for the summer.

The Southern Highlands are a garden lover's paradise and the many events held here in springtime include Tulip Time, a spectacular festival of flowering bulbs.

Bowral

Bowral is a classic 'mountain retreat' destination. One of the most famous houses was built in 1910 by the noted livestock breeder, Anthony Hordern, grandson of the Anthony Hordern of Sydney-department-store fame. Known as Milton Park, it is now an ideal retreat from the city and boasts a fine restaurant, large and elegant rooms and beautiful gardens (for decades tended with much love by Mrs Hordern), where the visitor can wander in peaceful tranquillity.

Garden lovers throng to Bowral in September for the Tulip Festival—Corbett Gardens is the focal point of this annual event, but there are also many private gardens open to the public at this time.

No visit to the Bowral area is ever complete without spending some time at the famous Donald Bradman Museum—a huge, state-of-the-art edifice which celebrates the great man's career. Called 'A Museum of Australian Cricketing History', it has an interesting section on cricket's origins. There is a large room in which the development of cricket in Australia (complete with lots of clever television technology) is on display. Then there is a re-creation of a cricket change room and a workman's bench where a cricket bat is being shaped.

As well there's 'The Bradman Walk'. A single sheet of paper lists no fewer than ten 'Bradman' locations (with brief explanations and descriptions) and 'takes you on a self-guided tour of Bradman's Bowral'. Cricket fans will be interested in the huge makeover that the old Bradman Oval has experienced.

Map: NSW 6 G10

Above: *The lovely old Surveyor General Inn at Berrima is the oldest continually licensed inn (since 1836) in Australia.*

Other places of interest

The Southern Highlands also offers excellent walks and superb views from the numerous falls which tumble over the escarpment. Morton National Park's Fitzroy Falls and Belmore Falls have outstanding views to the south and there are some interesting bushwalks.

People looking for more relaxed and less energetic activities in the Southern Highlands should head for small villages like Berrima where the gift shops abound and the historic stone buildings give the entire township an old-world charm. In Berrima, the gaol—on which construction commenced in the 1830s—and the Court House—the site of the colony's first trial by jury in 1841—are particularly impressive.

No less interesting are the small townships dotted along the railway line—each has its own appeal. There's Exeter, Bundanoon, Penrose and Wingello as well, of course, as Moss

Below: *A walking track leads to the summit of Pigeon House Mountain, in Morton National Park. The view from the top is spectacular.*

don't miss

On the first Saturday of April, Bundanoon hosts 'Brigadoon' one the finest Highland Games in Australia. A stirring, massed bagpipe and drum display, tartan kilts swinging, is a highlight of the gathering.

Vale, Mittagong and Bowral. Exeter is a quiet highlands settlement which is known as 'Little England' because of its trees, private gardens and climate. It is a beautiful village to wander around.

Bundanoon

Bundanoon, with its stands of English trees and its overtly Scottish name (although it may be a corruption of a local Aboriginal word), is known for its impressive hotel and its excellent bush-walking in the Morton National Park. The park's rugged sandstone cliffs, deep valleys, and the Clyde, Shoalhaven, Endrick, and Kangaroo Rivers are home to flora ranging from sedgeland through woodland to heath and rainforests.

The town of Bundanoon began to attract tourists in the late 1880s. Guest-houses began to appear, and pathways to the scenic sights. Today Bundanoon has became a peaceful holiday resort in the Southern Highlands. It is popular with bushwalkers because there are no fewer than 14 walks from the town to points within the national park. These include Echo Point, Mount Carnarvon, Bonnie View, Beauchamps Cliffs, Grand Canyon, Tooths Lookout, Fairy Bower Falls and the famous Glow-Worm Glen. Most of these vantage points offer spectacular views across the valley.

Map: NSW 7 M2

The South Coast

The primary appeal of the South Coast is that it is unspoilt. It is still a series of

coastal retreats and hillside hideaways where people can avoid large resorts and high-rise apartment blocks.

Kiama

A perfect example of this relatively low-key development is Kiama, located only 119 km from Sydney. This town is a classic daytripper destination. People come to watch the famous blowhole (although it now blows very infrequently—a smaller blowhole south of the town is always much more impressive), to enjoy the beaches and the parks, to explore the hinterland around the attractive village of Jamberoo, to go bushwalking in the Minnamurra Rainforest (this is an ideal daytrip with well-maintained paths leading through dense rainforest to a series of waterfalls high on the escarpment) or to go birdwatching at the famous Barren Grounds Bird Observatory and Nature Reserve. There is an excellent and comfortable lodge—the

Bass fishing on the upper reaches of the Kangaroo River. The upper Shoalhaven, too, has been stocked with hatchery-bred bass to improve the fishing.

Left: *Rolling green farm pastures meet the sea at Kiama, a pretty south coast town bordered by the sea on one side and Minnamurra Rainforest on the other.*

Below: *Much of the coastline of Jervis Bay is protected by national park. Part of Jervis Bay belongs to the Federal Government, so that Canberra will always have access to the sea.*

Jamberoo Valley Lodge (02 4236 0269)—and good quality B&B accommodation options are available throughout the area. Two local restaurants—Esse and Zumos—offer fine dining.

Map: NSW 7 N2

Berry to Batemans Bay

The traveller continuing down the coast will find a variety of different and unusual attractions. Each town has its own charm, each beach its own appeal.

Berry, just some 20 km south of Kiama, is now known as a popular 'get away from it all' destination with literally dozens of excellent B&Bs and self-catering facilities hidden in the hills behind the town, nestling in the peace and tranquillity of Kangaroo Valley.

Just south of Berry is Silos Winery and Restaurant, where both the food and the wines are memorable.

Similarly, the attractions around Jervis Bay are so diverse as to ensure

don't miss

The Lady Denman Heritage Complex in Huskisson has a broad range of attractions including wetlands, a walking trail and mangrove boardwalk. The Lady Denman Museum, housed in the old Sydney ferry of the same name, profiles the history of wooden shipbuilding at Huskisson.

that the visitor will stay for an extended period. There is the interesting and unusual Paperbark Lodge (with African-style tents and a classy restaurant in the bush) at Huskisson (02 4441 6066) and further around Jervis Bay is Booderee National Park, where bushwalking, camping, dolphin-watching and sightseeing attract large numbers of holiday-makers eager to experience a seaside holiday in natural bushland. Nearby is the Australian National Botanic Gardens Annexe, an area of about 80 hectares characterised by sandstone outcrops, swamplands and wet gullies. It is an unusual botanic garden in that it only has native Australian species, notably frost-tender species that will not grow in the main Gardens in Canberra.

Batemans Bay to Tathra

The extended community of Batemans Bay is one of the larger townships on the South Coast. This fishing and tourist town is now effectively 'Canberra by the Sea'—only two hours by good road from Canberra, it has become a popular seaside escape for the national capital's residents.

At nearby Durras and South Durras it is possible to see kangaroos enjoying themselves on the beaches. The ideal destination in this area is the Murramarang Resort (02 4478 6355), an extraordinary place which caters for everyone from campers to people seeking good-quality resort accommodation on the edge of Murramarang National Park. The park itself covers about 27 km of coastline stretching from Kioloa south to Batemans Bay. No more than 2 km across at its widest point it features sandy and shingle beaches, rugged headlands, tombolos, cliffs, rock stacks, wave-cut platforms, fossil-bearing rocks and four offshore islands.

The wildlife is fairly typical of the coast: eastern grey kangaroos, swamp wallabies, red-necked wallabies and other mammals. The birdlife is varied, and includes parrots, finches, honeyeaters, eagles, hawks, terns, thrushes, oystercatchers, wrens, muttonbirds, albatrosses and fantails. Kangaroos are commonly seen feeding near the beaches.

Batemans Bay has a number of good-quality restaurants, some of which are scenically located on the edges of the Clyde River. Further south is the 'modern historic' township of Mogo (many of the buildings look old but are very new)

The view across Batemans Bay to the Clyde River estuary. Clyde River oysters are of first-class quality, and the local restaurants serve them with locally caught, fresh, succulent seafood.

NSW

which boasts an interesting zoo specialising in endangered species—snow leopards, red pandas, Bengal and Siberian tigers, ringtailed lemurs, cottontop tamarins, lar gibbons—and offers horseriding as a pleasant option. It is the first of a series of attractive smaller townships. The next are Central Tilba and Tilba Tilba, two historic dairy towns which are almost entirely built from timber, where it is possible to get good food and interesting accommodation before heading on to Tathra—a quiet and unspoiled fishing port seen extensively in the popular movie *The Man Who Sued God*.

Eden

At the very end of the coast (before entering Victoria) is the beautiful fishing port of Eden. This is a wonderland of surprises. The town itself has three outstanding fish restaurants where the produce caught by the local fleet can be eaten the same day.

Nearby is Boydtown, a historic whaling village, and beyond is Green Cape where a lighthouse stands alone on a headland surrounded by interesting walking tracks, quiet beaches and extensive camp sites. If you are seeking real relaxation, book a stay at the lighthouse. Here you can sit, feeling as though you are on the edge of the world, without another person in sight, and enjoy the wildness of the Pacific Ocean as it beats relentlessly against the rocks far below.

Map: NSW 7 N2

Above: *The coastline around Murramarang National Park boasts some of the state's most spectacular scenery.*

Below: *Wild eastern grey kangaroos* (Macropus giganteus) *can be seen feeding near some south coast beaches.*

The Mountains and Beyond

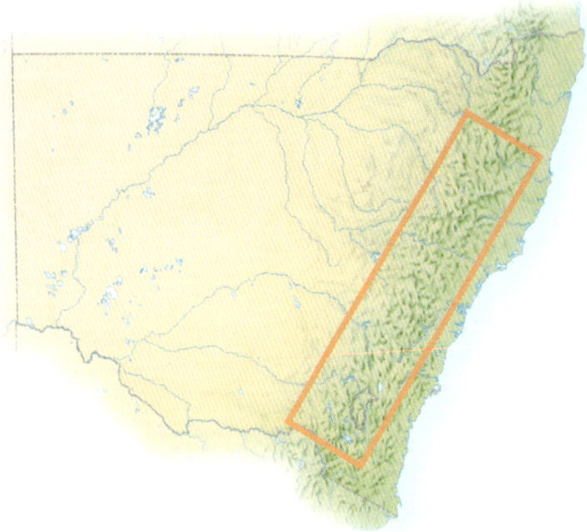

The rugged escarpments and wooded foothills of the mountains of the Great Dividing Range divide the more densely populated coastal areas of New South Wales from the rural inland. West of the mountains the landscape changes to vast plains, where large areas of agricultural land are broken up by national parks and country towns.

The Blue Mountains

The Blue Mountains have always been a welcome retreat for Sydneysiders. The coolness in the summer months, the delightful bushwalks, the large and gracious guesthouses and hotels, the elegant homes built by the city's wealthy families, the outstanding gardens and parklands all add up to an area which sharply contrasts with the city, just less than an hour away.

And there is always something new to do and see in this vibrant region.

Katoomba

The heart of the Blue Mountains is Katoomba which is located 106 km west of Sydney and is 1017 m above sea level. This historic town has a near-monopoly on the major attractions of the Blue Mountains. It is here that the famous Three Sisters stand beyond Echo Point which, in turn, offers outstanding views across the Jamison Valley. It is here that both the Scenic Skyway and Scenic Railway depart, offering exceptional experiences of the Jamison

The Three Sisters, the most recognisable scenic highlight of the Blue Mountains, are known in Australian Aboriginal mythology as Mennhi, Wimlah and Gunnedoo.

Valley. The Skyway floats across the valley, suspended some 275 m above the valley floor, and offers views of the Katoomba Falls and Orphan Rock. In the case of the Railway, it drops 230 m in its very steep descent into the Jamison Valley in a cable car that was once used by coalminers.

Katoomba is also an ideal destination for people wanting to experience the magic of the Mountains through bushwalking. There are tracks along the Jamison Valley floor starting from the base of the Scenic Railway, and there are outstanding scenic walks around the cliffs. The walks range from an easy 1-km walk to the Three Sisters to a strenuous 8-km walk to the Ruined Castle from the Golden Stairs.

Like many of the towns in the Blue Mountains, Katoomba is famous for its old and gracious hotels. The most famous of these is the Carrington Hotel (02 4782 1111). It is a companion to the famous Hydro Majestic Hotel at Medlow Bath (02 4788 1022) which has recently been revitalised and modernised. Or you can enjoy a 'healthy high' at Crystal Lodge Health Retreat, a beautifully restored guesthouse (02) 4782 5122).

Map: NSW 6 G8

Interesting places and events

On the way up to the Mountains from the east it is always worthwhile to visit Norman Lindsay's House and Gallery at Faulconbridge. The property is now owned by the National Trust who have preserved the gardens (in spring the wisteria is heady and beautiful) and presented an interesting exhibition of Lindsay's model ships, paintings and illustrations. The Blue Mountains Folk Festival, held in Katoomba in March, attracts highly acclaimed musicians from around the globe, and Yulefest in July is popular all through the area.

The township of Leura, with its small cafés and chic restaurants, is popular with people wanting to escape the city. People visiting this area often stay at Peppers Fairmont Resort (02 4782 5222), which has spectacular views over the valley and easy access to lots of good walking trails. It also has four all-weather tennis courts, two squash courts, a gymnasium, games room, indoor swimming pool and a wide range of suitably up-market eating places. It is also adjacent to a golf course. There are two pleasant bushwalks to Gladstone Lookout and Cathedral Point.

No trip to the Blue Mountains is complete without experiencing the superb Rhododendron Garden in Bacchante Street, Blackheath. At the peak of the season in November, Blackheath boasts more than 1500 rhododendrons in gardens spread throughout the township. Equally impressive are the falls at Govett's Leap and the beautiful botanic gardens at Mount Tomah, on the Bells Line of Road.

The Mountains are famed for their excel-

Above: *The village atmosphere of Leura invites visitors to slow down, relax and breathe in the mountain air. There is a good selection of antique shops and art galleries to browse in.*

Below: *Flowers add colour to Leura's main street, where interesting small shops sell anything from candles to cappuccinos.*

Right: *This old post informs passersby that it is only another 2 miles (3.2 km) to the summit of Mount Kosciuszko, the country's highest point.*

lent restaurants. Vulcans at Blackheath, Silk's Brasserie at Leura and the restaurant at the Mount Tomah Botanic Gardens are all acclaimed and well worth patronising. A grand old Katoomba institution is the National Trust listed Paragon Café, which is loved as much for its Art Deco ambience as for its delicious hand-dipped chocolates.

did you know?

In 1860, an audacious Italian crossed the magnificent Dangars Gorge and Falls on a tightrope. Oxley Wild Rivers National Park includes ten separate river gorges.

Those wanting to reach beyond the main mountains area are well advised to go to both the Jenolan Caves (the caves are excellent, and beyond them the famous Kanangra Walls offer the most spectacular views in the whole Blue Mountains) and to Mount Wilson, a glorious village characterised by some of the most delightful English-style gardens in the area. It is particularly impressive in spring and autumn.

For further information, contact Blue Mountains Tourism on 1300 653 408.

The Snowy Mountains

It is a common perception that the only reason people go to the Snowy Mountains is to ski. This is not the case. In summertime there are excellent walks through the mountains and, in season, the trout fishing is unequalled anywhere on mainland Australia.

The starting point for most explorations of the Snowy Mountains is Jindabyne where, at the Visitor Information Centre (02 6450 5600), it is possible to organise special trout fishing expeditions as well as whitewater rafting, mountain biking, horseriding, canoeing, and walking treks.

From Jindabyne there are two roads into the mountains. One heads towards Thredbo, the other towards Perisher Village and Charlottes Pass. Both routes lead to paths which will take the adventurous traveller to the top of Mount Kosciuszko. This unassuming mountain stands a very modest 2228 m above sea level. It can be reached either by walking from Charlottes Pass on the Summit Walk (a healthy 9 km each way) or from Thredbo. The Thredbo route is the easiest. All that is required is to buy a ticket on the ski lift. It is 12 km from Crackenback Terminal (1930 m above sea level) to Kosciuszko and back. The trip is worth making because it is a very pleasant walk on well-maintained pathways and because, at the end of the walk, you can say you have been to the highest place on the whole continent.

Thredbo, a fine resort with excellent skiing conditions, is part of Kosciuszko National Park. This park has the most extensive snowfields in the country.

In recent times both accommodation and dining have improved hugely in the mountains. Restaurants like Altitude 1380 and Credo in Thredbo Village offer fine food, and resorts such as the huge and beautiful Lake Crackenback Resort at Lake Crackenback near Thredbo (it is open all year and offers horseriding and canoeing as well as excellent bushwalks) can make a holiday in the Snowy Mountains a very special experience. Phone (02) 6456 2960.

Map: NSW 7 G7

Armidale

The New England region to the north-west of Sydney has a special charm due to its outstanding national parks and delightful bushwalking. It is hard to imagine a more beautiful inland city than Armidale (located 525 km north of Sydney) in autumn. The city has an easy elegance with large parks, beautiful historic buildings and the University of New England. The city centre and the area around Central Park (where the city's Catholic and Anglican cathedrals vie for prominence) are perfect examples of the city's graciousness. Visitors should make sure to visit the New England Regional Art Gallery which has an impressive collection of Australian paintings, including works by Tom Roberts, Norman Lindsay and Arthur Streeton.

There are a number of fine national parks in the Armidale area including the 120 393-ha Oxley Wild Rivers National Park which boasts 13 major waterfalls, and plant habitats that include open forest, gorge woodland, dry rainforest and shrublands (it is possible to camp here—and the bushwalking is excellent). Dangars Falls has camping and picnic facilities and 20 km of walking tracks around and down to the Macleay River. The Wollomombi Falls, which cascade down more than 220 m, are Australia's longest single drop falls; there are gorge rim walks (including a wheelchair track). The Styx River State Forest also has good camping and picnic areas.

There is also the World Heritage listed New England National Park which varies so dramatically that its ecosystems range from snow gum woodland and Antarctic beech rainforest to subtropical rainforest, including wet and dry eucalypt forest,

Dangars Falls in Oxley Wild Rivers National Park. Easy walking tracks lead to the edge of the gorge and onto lookout platforms with superb views.

The Uralla Hotel. This charming little town was founded in the gold rush era and is now a centre for agriculture and tourism.

subalpine heath and wetlands. Clearly marked bushwalks lead through mossy beech forests and fern gullies. Near the park entrance is the Thungatti Camping Area where there are picnic, barbecue and toilet facilities. There are a number of outstanding walks in the park ranging from short 3-km easy jaunts to Point Lookout and Eagle's Nest Lookout to treks involving many days of walking. Cabins and chalets are available in the park. Phone (02) 6657 2309 for bookings.

The rivers around Armidale are noted for their rainbow and brown trout which can be fished in season, from the October long weekend to the end of the Queen's Birthday long weekend in June. The river at Wollomombi, the Oaky River, Barwick Creek, Dumaresq Dam, Dumaresq Creek and Guy Fawkes River at Ebor are all recognised as excellent fishing spots.

If you are staying in Armidale it is hard to beat the Moore Park Inn (built around an historic homestead) which boasts the outstanding Archie's on the Park Restaurant. For bookings phone (02) 6772 2538.

Either side of Armidale are the interesting townships of Uralla (which has a monument to the exploits of its most famous bushranger, Captain Thunderbolt) and Guyra.

Map: NSW 4 J8

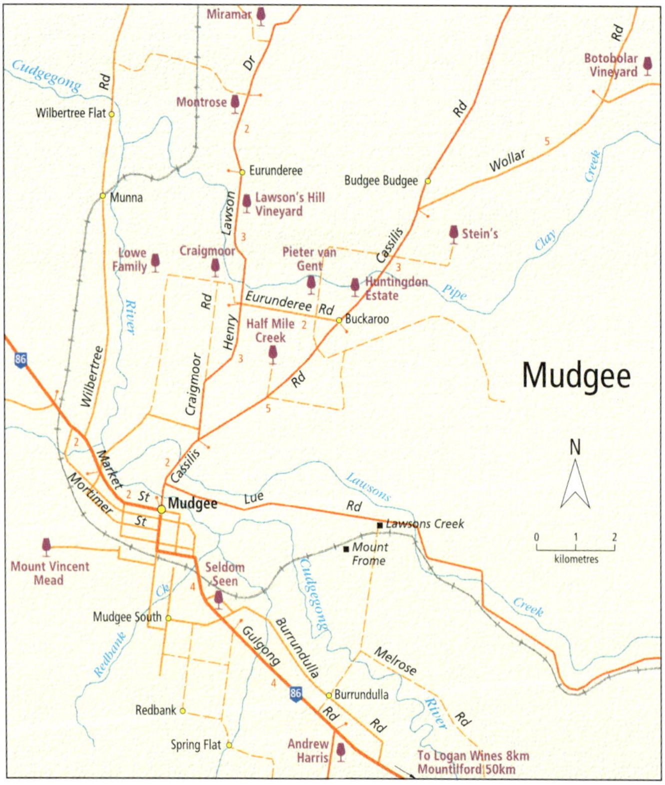

Mudgee

In recent times Mudgee has become a serious competitor with the Hunter Valley as a destination for people seeking respite from the city who want to visit wineries, eat well and do a little sightseeing. Located 265 km north-west of Sydney, it is a town with a large number of interesting heritage buildings including the widely acclaimed Lauralla Historic Guest House (a classic Victorian mansion built in 1882) on the corner of Lewis and Mortimer Streets. Contact (02) 6372 3320. There are also a number of excellent rural accommodation options available outside the town offering farmstays and hospitality.

Although Mudgee is better known for wool- and wheat-growing and wine, the pastures around Mudgee are also home to Havallah Stud, seen here, and the Melrose Park Deer Farm.

German settlers planted the first grapevines here in 1858, and now there are over 20 wineries in the area, mostly to the north and north-east of town. These include the Pieter van Gent Winery, Mansfield Wines, Huntington Estate Wines, Steins Wines, Craigmoor Winery, Mudgee Wines, Montrose Wines and Burnbrae Vineyard.

Apart from wineries, the area is also noted for its honey. Mudgee Honey Haven has royal jelly and other honey products for sale. The Fragrant Farm herb nursery is a pleasant diversion, as is Mudgee Valley Violets—an indoor nursery with over 250 varieties of African violets.

Nearby Windamere Dam, Wollemi National Park and Munghorn Gap Nature Reserve are all worth visiting.

Map: NSW 6 E5

Mudgee vineyards produce rich full-flavoured reds and good chardonnays. Wine, restaurants, guesthouses and galleries—Mudgee has it all.

Canberra

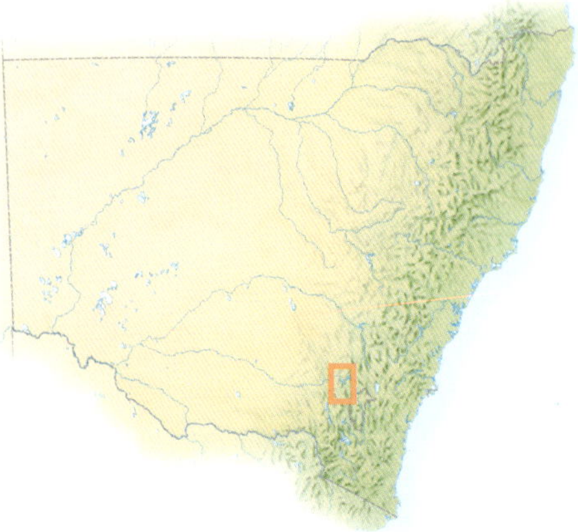

The national capital is within easy access of both Sydney and Melbourne, and is a fully planned, modern, stylish city. It enjoys four distinct seasons, and is at its most beautiful in spring and autumn. The city offers many attractions—museums, art galleries, restaurants, wineries, parklands, national monuments, shopping and family amusements. This relatively small area provides just about every possible opportunity to relax and enjoy yourself.

Above: *Part of the National Museum of Australia's* Garden of Australian Dreams, *a stylised representation of the country's north.*

Did you realise, for example, that there are over 300 restaurants to choose from? The cuisines range from Asian, Mediterranean, Turkish and Russian to contemporary Australian. Canberra is really a food lover's paradise. Did you realise that for lovers of museums and art galleries Canberra is superb? And did you realise that, in terms of both cycling and walking, Canberra has some of the best-designed routes of any city in Australia?

Map: NSW 7 J4

Museums

Camberra's wealth of wonderful museums includes special-interest museums such as the National Dinosaur Museum and the Canberra Railway Museum as well as the better known, more general ones.

The Australian War Memorial is, at least in theory, a war memorial rather than a museum. However it does include excellent displays of memorabilia, paintings and models from all Australian conflicts, as well as an interactive centre. For more details contact (02) 6243 4211.

The National Film and Sound Archive stores an extensive collection of old films and sound recordings. Contact (02) 6248 2000, as they often show old films and run guided tours as well.

Located on Acton Peninsula, about 5 km from the city centre, the superb National Museum of Australia is designed to tell the story of Australia in an interesting and modern way. The

Below: *The impressive Australian War Memorial building, at the foot of Mount Ainslie, is a moving tribute to all Australians who served in war.*

subject matter ranges widely: from the arrival of Aborigines through to the country's modern inventions. It is particularly interesting to children. Contact (02) 6208 5000 for more information.

Art Galleries

The National Gallery is the home of the national collection of paintings. Opened by Queen Elizabeth II in 1982, it regularly hosts major international art exhibitions. Its famous paintings include Jackson Pollock's *Blue Poles*, David Hockney's huge *Grand Canyon* and Lucien Freud's *After Cézanne*. The main galleries are free. For more details contact (02) 6240 6411.

Old Parliament House has partially been turned into a portrait gallery. It now includes an excellent exhibition of portraits of prominent Australians—both contemporary and historic. If this sounds a little dull, it is not. It is much more interesting than you would expect. For more

Left: *One of the figures in Auguste Rodin's* Burghers of Calais. *This is one of a number of fine sculptures that can be viewed in the enchanting Sculpture Garden at the National Gallery of Australia.*

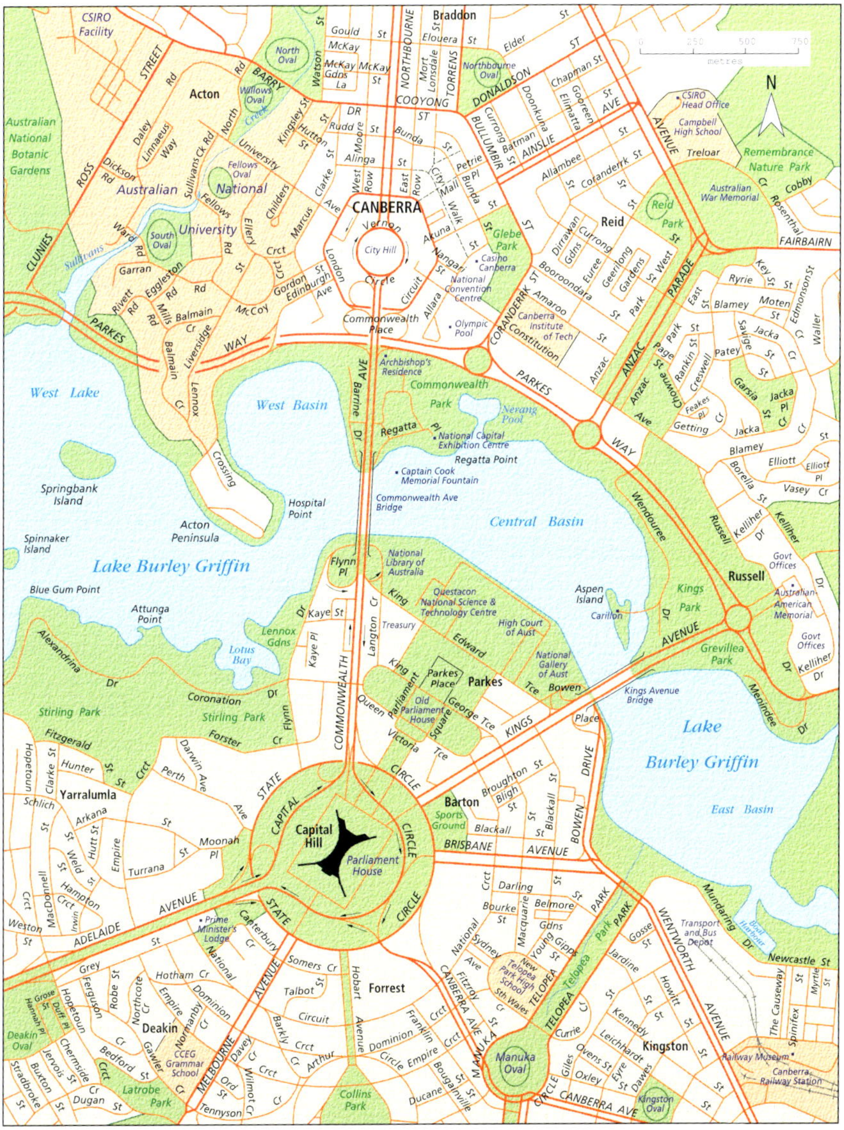

The design for Parliament House was chosen from 329 entries from around the world. It has several outstanding features, including the 48 marble-clad columns of the Foyer which represent a eucalyptus forest.

detailed information and opening times, contact (02) 6273 5130.

A gallery devoted to the works of Australian artist, Sidney Nolan, The Nolan Gallery is located at Tharwa, 30 km south of Canberra. It houses a range of Nolan's works including some of his famous Ned Kelly paintings. Contact (02) 6237 5192 for details.

Special Places

Parliament House was built on Capital Hill overlooking Lake Burley Griffin, and it dominates Canberra. In democratic fashion you can walk on top of the politicians by climbing up the grassy hill which covers the building. It has portraits of all the Prime Ministers, an interesting art gallery, and exceptional facilities. There are guided tours every 30 minutes. For details of opening times (usually 9.00 a.m.–5.00 p.m.) contact the Sergeant-at-Arms on (02) 6277 4889.

Balloons at Lake Burley Griffin. Canberra holds a Balloon Fiesta in March, but hot-air balloon flights are available to visitors all year round.

The National Library might not sound promising. What do you look at in a library? But there are regular exhibitions of paintings, letters, photographs, etc, which range widely across interesting literary to historical subjects.

The National Science and Technology Centre (Questacon) is a delightful opportunity to learn about science in a fun-filled, hands-on environment. It is hugely popular with children. For general information phone 1800 020 603. As the publicity says: 'Questacon shows how science and technology are relevant and important to our everyday lives. Whether you're making a telephone call, cooking a meal or throwing a ball, with the use of everyday examples science becomes easier to understand.'

The Australian Institute of Sport is now known as one of the world's most successful sports academies. There are public tours at 11.00 a.m. and 2.00 p.m. which explain and explore the nation's passion for sport. For bookings contact (02) 6252 1444.

Activities

Canberra, as the national capital, has excellent facilities for almost any activity. Some of the more relaxing options follow.

There are numerous walking trails around Canberra. For easy walking there is nothing to compare to the path around Lake Burley Griffin. If you want to go bushwalking and not disappear from the city centre, the walks around Black Mountain, Mount Ainslie or Mount Taylor—collectively known as the Canberra Nature Park—are great fun. It is common to see kangaroos on the walks, and the birdlife is exceptional.

Canberra has over 300 km of cycleways, which means that the most enthusiastic cyclist can explore the capital without having to deal with traffic. Of particular appeal are the cycleways around Lake Burley Griffin. It is possible to hire bicycles in Canberra. The most well known place is the Lake Burley Griffin Bicycle Hire at the Acton Ferry Terminal. Phone (02) 6249 6861.

There are a number of operations offering a range of boating options on Lake Burley Griffin. One of the best is

Above: *The National Library of Australia, a superb example of 1960s architecture, contains the best collection of the country's documentary and literary heritage.*

Lake Burley Griffin Boat Hire at the Acton Ferry Terminal. Contact them on (02) 6249 6861. Southern Cross Cruises, on (02) 6273 1784, can arrange a cruise.

Several vantage points are strategically located on the hills around Canberra, and all of these lookouts afford outstanding views of the city.

Canberra comes alive in a burst of spring colour each September during Floriade, a four-week flower festival.

Left: *A sample of Floriade—a huge, flamboyant, themed display of flowers. This spectacularly successful spring festival is held in Commonwealth Park.*

Canberra's Eating

Where do you want to eat? If you want to sit on the edge of Lake Burley Griffin try The Boat House by the Lake. If you want to sit in the gardens of the National Gallery try Juniperberry. If you want the city's best Chinese you can't beat The Chairman and Yip and if, by general consensus, you want the best eating available in Canberra, then Atlantic in cosmopolitan Manuka will tickle your tastebuds. There are many more choices—Greek, Japanese, Italian ...

Canberra's Accommodation

There is a huge range of accommodation available, suitable for every budget. Towards the upper end of the market is the Hyatt Hotel, across the road from the Old Parliament House. Apart from the history (so many political plots were brewed up in this environment), it is a perfectly preserved hotel from the 1930s which captures the spirit of the times. The Canberra YHA is recognised as one of the best backpacker destinations in Australia and there are some B&Bs in the suburbs which offer exceptional food and accommodation.

Map 1

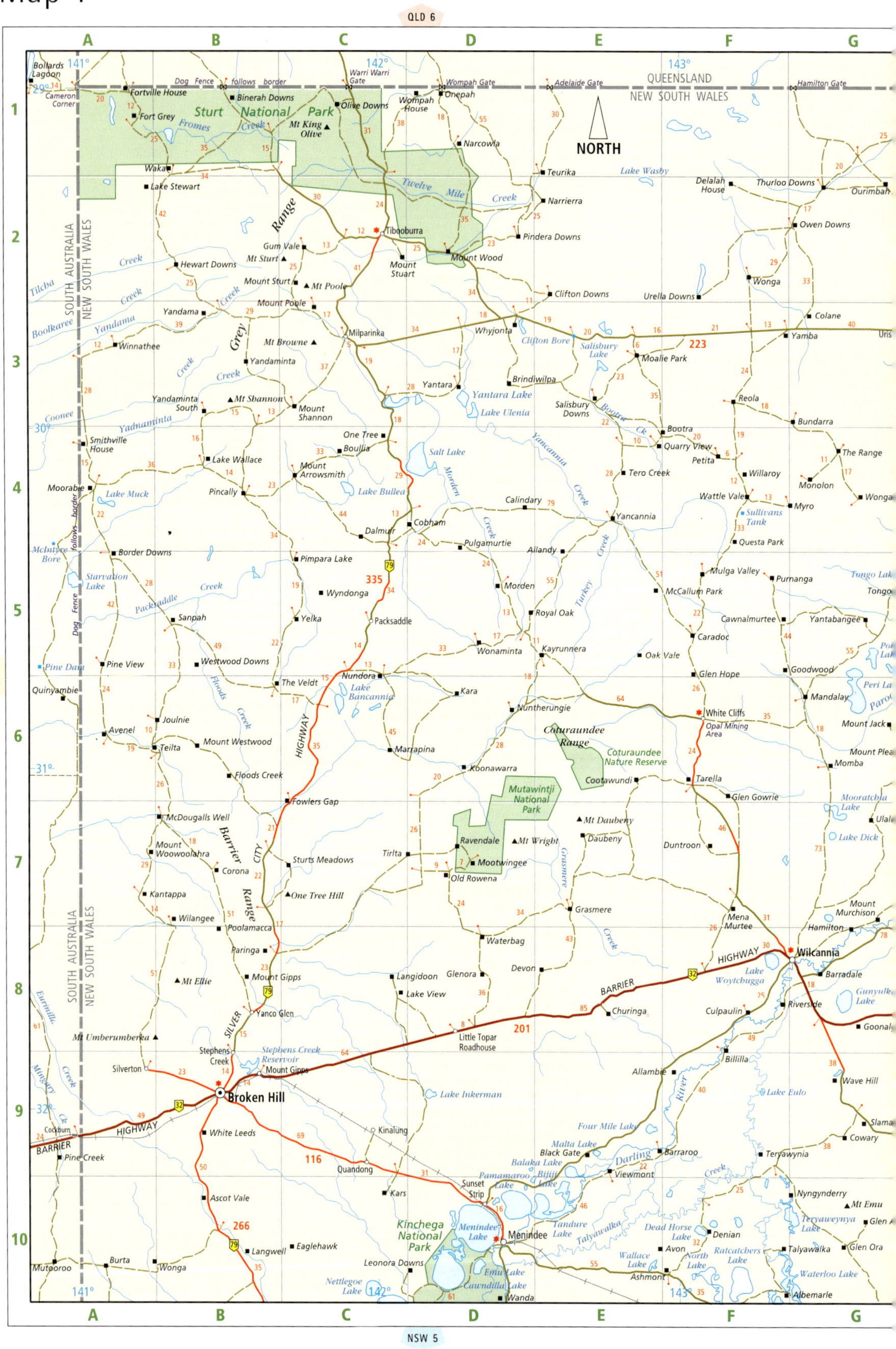
QLD 6
NSW 5
SA 3
A
B
C
D
E
F
G
1
2
3
4
5
6
7
8
9
10
141°
142°
143°
29°
30°
31°
32°
NORTH
QUEENSLAND
NEW SOUTH WALES
SOUTH AUSTRALIA
Dog Fence follows border
Bollards Lagoon
Cameron Corner
Fortville House
Fort Grey
Binerah Downs
Sturt National Park
Frome Creek
Olive Downs
Mt King Olive
Warri Warri Gate
Wompah Gate
Onepah
Wompah House
Adelaide Gate
Hamilton Gate
Narcowla
Teurika
Lake Wasby
Delalah House
Thurloo Downs
Ourimbah
Waka
Lake Stewart
Twelve Mile Creek
Narrierra
Owen Downs
Grey Range
Tibooburra
Pindera Downs
Gum Vale
Mt Sturt
Mount Wood
Mount Stuart
Hewart Downs
Tilcha Creek
Mount Sturt
Mt Poole
Mount Poole
Clifton Downs
Urella Downs
Wonga
Bookaree Creek
Yandama Creek
Yandama
Colane
Milparinka
Whyjonta
Clifton Bore
Salisbury Lake
Yamba
Winnathee
Mt Browne
Moalie Park
Yandaminta
Creek
Brindiwilpa
Yantara
Yantara Lake
Lake Ulenia
Salisbury Downs
Bootra Ck
Reola
Bundarra
Yandaminta South
Mt Shannon
Mount Shannon
Coonee Creek
Yadnamnta
One Tree
Bootra
Quarry View
Petita
The Range
Smithville House
Boullia
Salt Lake
Yancannia Creek
Lake Wallace
Mount Arrowsmith
Tero Creek
Willaroy
Monolon
Moorabie
Lake Muck
Pincally
Lake Bullea
Morden Creek
Wattle Vale
Wonga
Calindary
Myro
Sullivans Tank
Cobham
Yancannia
Dalmuir
Pulgamurtie
Questa Park
McIntyre Bore
Border Downs
Pimpara Lake
Allandy
Starvation Lake
Creek
Mulga Valley
Purnanga
Tongo Lake
Tongo
335
Wyndonga
Morden
Turkey Creek
McCallum Park
Packsaddle Creek
Sanpah
Yelka
Packsaddle
Royal Oak
Cawnalmurtee
Yantabangee
Caradoc
Wonaminta
Kayrunnera
Oak Vale
Pine Dam
Pine View
Westwood Downs
Goodwood
Floods Creek
The Veldt
Nundora
Lake Bancannia
Kara
Glen Hope
Peri Lake
Paroo
Quinyambie
Mandalay
Nuntherungie
White Cliffs
Opal Mining Area
Mount Jack
Joulnie
Avenel
Mount Westwood
Marrapina
Coturaundee Range
Coturaundee Nature Reserve
Mount Pleasant
Momba
Teilta
Koonawarra
SILVER CITY HIGHWAY
Floods Creek
Cootawundi
Tarella
Glen Gowrie
Mutawintji National Park
Fowlers Gap
Mooratchia Lake
Ulalie
McDougalls Well
Mt Daubeny
Daubeny
Lake Dick
Barrier Range
Ravendale
Mt Wright
Duntroon
Mount Woowoolahra
Tirlta
Mootwingee
Sturts Meadows
Corona
Old Rowena
Grasmere Creek
Kantappa
One Tree Hill
Mount Murchison
Grasmere
Mena Murtee
Wilangee
Poolamacca
Hamilton
Waterbag
Paringa
BARRIER HIGHWAY
Wilcannia
Devon
Mt Ellie
Mount Gipps
Langidoon
Glenora
Barradale
Lake Woytchugga
Lake View
Gunyulka Lake
Churinga
Yanco Glen
Culpaulin
Riverside
Eurinilla Creek
201
Goonalga
Mt Umberumberka
Little Topar Roadhouse
Stephens Creek Reservoir
Stephens Creek
Billilla
Mingary Creek
Silverton
Mount Gipps
Allambie
Wave Hill
Lake Inkerman
Lake Eulo
Broken Hill
River
Cockburn
White Leeds
Kinalung
Four Mile Lake
Slama
Cowary
Malta Lake
Black Gate
Barraroo
Pine Creek
Balaka Lake
Darling
Teryawynia
116
Quandong
Pamamaroo Lake
Bijiji Lake
Viewmont
Creek
Sunset Strip
Kars
Nyngynderry
Mt Emu
Ascot Vale
Menindee Lake
Tandure Lake
Talyawalka
Dead Horse Lake
Denian
Teryaweynya Lake
Glen
266
Kinchega National Park
Menindee
Avon
Talyawalka
Glen Ora
Langwell
Eaglehawk
Wallace Lake
North Lake
Ratcatchers Lake
Mutooroo
Burta
Wonga
Leonora Downs
Emu Lake
Ashmont
Waterloo Lake
Nettlegoe Lake
Cawndilla Lake
Wanda
Albemarle
223
79
32
Uris

QLD 6

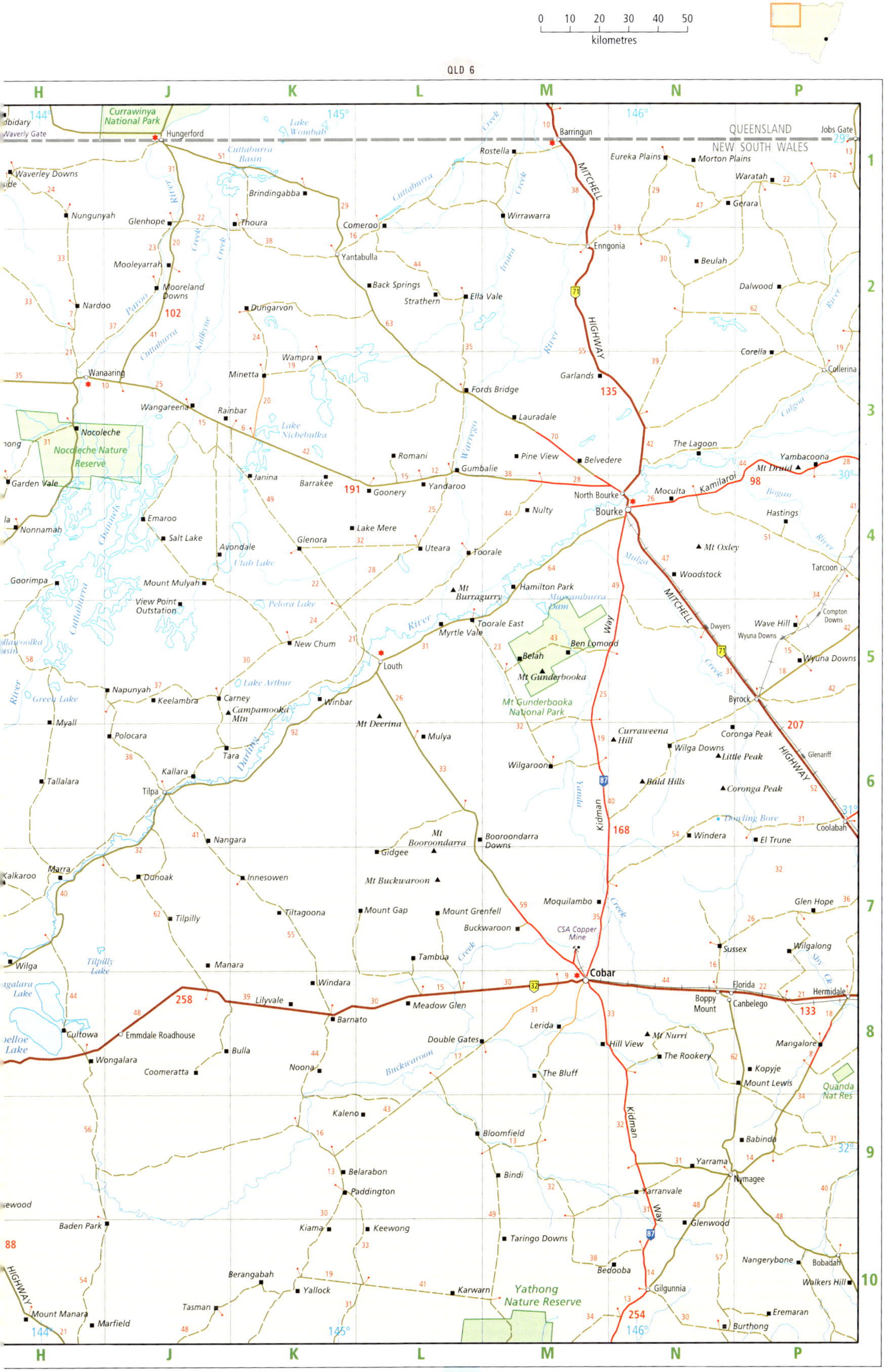
0 10 20 30 40 50
kilometres
H
J
K
L
M
N
P
1
2
3
4
5
6
7
8
9
10
144°
145°
146°
29°
30°
31°
32°
QUEENSLAND
NEW SOUTH WALES
Currawinya National Park
Hungerford
Waverly Gate
Lake Wombah
Cuttaburra Basin
Barringun
Rostella
Jobs Gate
Eureka Plains
Morton Plains
Waverley Downs
Brindingabba
Waratah
Gerara
Nungunyah
Glenhope
Thoura
Comeroo
Wirrawarra
Yantabulla
Enngonia
Beulah
Mooleyarrah
Mooreland Downs
Back Springs
Strathern
Ella Vale
Dalwood
Nardoo
Dungarvon
MITCHELL
HIGHWAY
Corella
Wampra
Wanaaring
Minetta
Garlands
Collerina
Wangareena
Rainbar
Fords Bridge
Lauradale
Nocoleche
Nocoleche Nature Reserve
Lake Nichebulka
The Lagoon
Romani
Pine View
Belvedere
Yambacoona
Mt Druid
Garden Vale
Janina
Barrakee
Gumbalie
Goonery
Yandaroo
North Bourke
Moculta
Kamilaroi
Bourke
Nulty
Hastings
Emaroo
Nonnamah
Salt Lake
Lake Mere
Glenora
Avondale
Utah Lake
Uteara
Toorale
Mt Oxley
Woodstock
Tarcoon
Goorimpa
Mount Mulyah
View Point Outstation
Pelora Lake
Mt Burragurry
Hamilton Park
Mulwamburra Dam
Compton Downs
Dwyers
Wave Hill
Wyuna Downs
New Chum
Toorale East
Myrtle Vale
Ben Lomond
Louth
Belah
Mt Gunderbooka
Mt Gunderbooka National Park
Lake Arthur
Napunyah
Green Lake
Keelambra
Carney
Campamooka Mtn
Winbar
Byrock
Myall
Mt Deerina
Mulya
Currraweena Hill
Coronga Peak
Polocara
Tara
Wilga Downs
Little Peak
Glenariff
Wilgaroon
Tallalara
Kallara
Tilpa
Bald Hills
Coronga Peak
Darling
Yanda
Kidman
Way
Booroondarra Downs
Mt Booroondarra
Nangara
Gidgee
Darling Bore
Windera
El Trune
Coolabah
Kalkaroo
Marra
Dunoak
Innesowen
Mt Buckwaroon
Moquilambo
Glen Hope
Tilpilly
Tiltagoona
Mount Gap
Mount Grenfell
Buckwaroon
CSA Copper Mine
Sussex
Wilgalong
Wilga
Tilpilly Lake
Manara
Tambua
Cobar
Windara
Florida
Hermidale
Lilyvale
Meadow Glen
Boppy Mount
Canbelego
Emmdale Roadhouse
Cultowa
Barnato
Lerida
Mt Nurri
Wongalara
Bulla
Double Gates
Hill View
The Rookery
Mangalore
Coomeratta
Noona
The Bluff
Kopyje
Mount Lewis
Quanda Nat Res
Kaleno
Bloomfield
Babinda
Belarabon
Bindi
Yarrama
Nymagee
Paddington
Yarranvale
Baden Park
Kiama
Keewong
Glenwood
Taringo Downs
Nangerybone
Bobadah
Bedooba
Walkers Hill
Berangabah
Yallock
Karwarn
Yathong Nature Reserve
Gilgunnia
Mount Manara
Marfield
Tasman
Eremaran
Burthong
HIGHWAY
Way
102
135
98
191
207
168
258
254
88
71
87
32

NSW 2

Map 2

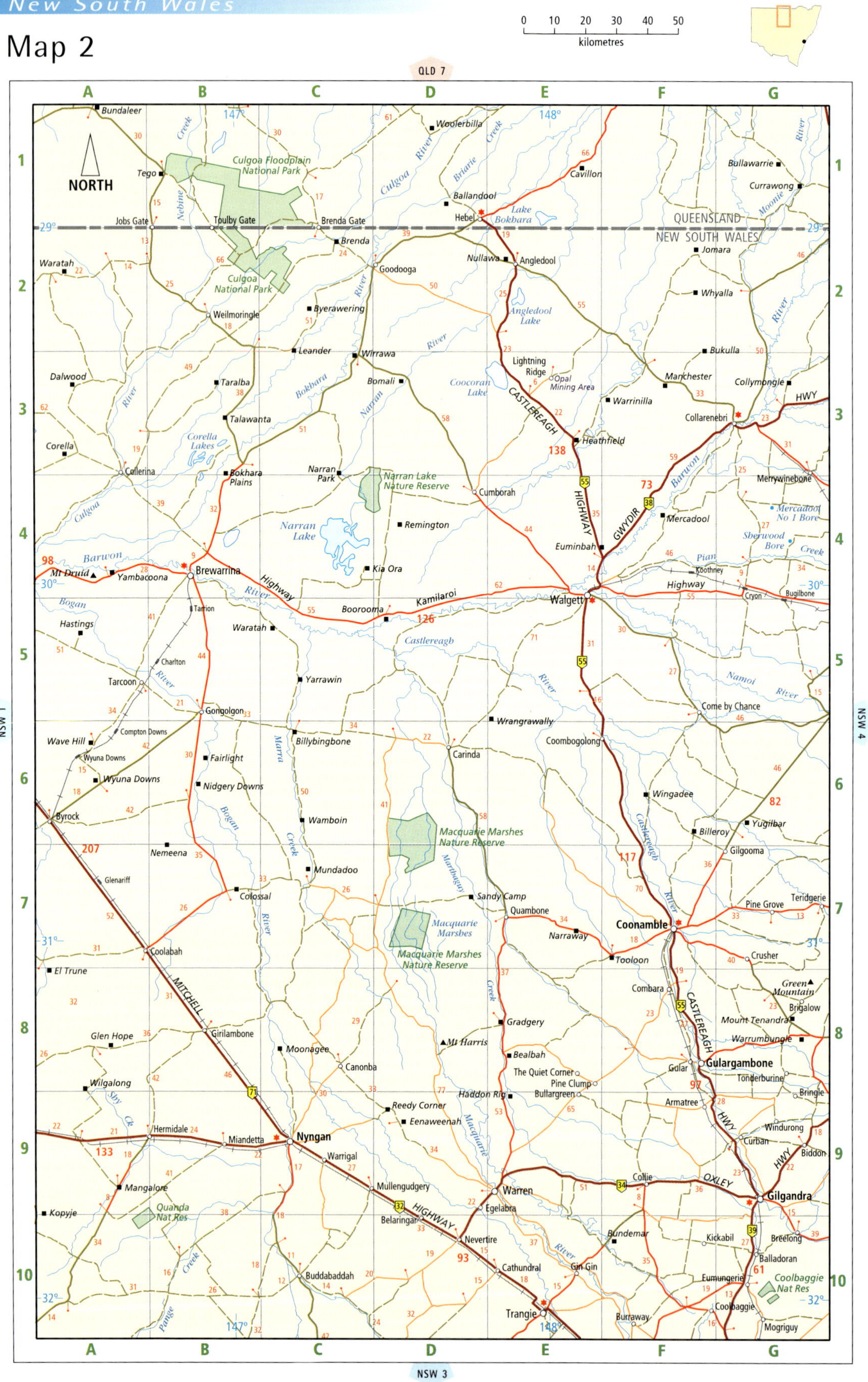
QLD 7
NSW 1
NSW 4
NSW 3
NORTH
0 10 20 30 40 50
kilometres
QUEENSLAND
NEW SOUTH WALES
Bundaleer
Tego
Culgoa Floodplain National Park
Jobs Gate
Toulby Gate
Brenda Gate
Brenda
Woolerbilla
Ballandool
Hebel
Lake Bokhara
Cavillon
Bullawarrie
Currawong
Jomara
Nullawa
Angledool
Goodooga
Waratah
Culgoa National Park
Weilmoringle
Byerawering
Angledool Lake
Whyalla
Leander
Wirrawa
Bukulla
Dalwood
Taralba
Bomali
Lightning Ridge
Opal Mining Area
Coocoran Lake
Manchester
Collymongle
Warrinilla
Talawanta
Collarenebri
Corella Lakes
Corella
Heathfield
Collerina
Bokhara Plains
Narran Park
Narran Lake Nature Reserve
Cumborah
Merrywinebone
Mercadool No 1 Bore
Mercadool
Remington
Narran Lake
Sherwood Bore
Euminbah
Mt Druid
Yambacoona
Brewarrina
Kia Ora
Koothney
Walgett
Cryon
Bugilbone
Tarrion
Boorooma
Hastings
Waratah
Charlton
Tarcoon
Yarrawin
Come by Chance
Gongolgon
Wrangrawally
Compton Downs
Wave Hill
Billybingbone
Coombogolong
Carinda
Fairlight
Wyuna Downs
Nidgery Downs
Wingadee
Byrock
Wamboin
Macquarie Marshes Nature Reserve
Yugilbar
Billeroy
Nemeena
Gilgooma
Mundadoo
Glenariff
Colossal
Sandy Camp
Pine Grove
Teridgerie
Quambone
Narraway
Coonamble
Macquarie Marshes
Coolabah
Tooloon
El Trune
Crusher
Combara
Green Mountain
Brigalow
Gradgery
Mount Tenandra
Glen Hope
Girilambone
Mt Harris
Warrumbungle
Moonagee
Bealbah
Gularganbone
Gular
Canonba
The Quiet Corner
Pine Clump
Bullargreen
Tonderburine
Wilgalong
Haddon Rig
Bringle
Reedy Corner
Armatree
Eenaweenah
Windurong
Hermidale
Miandetta
Nyngan
Curban
Biddon
Warrigal
Mangalore
Mullengudgery
Warren
Collie
Gilgandra
Kopyje
Quanda Nat Res
Egelabra
Belaringar
Bundemar
Kickabil
Breelong
Nevertire
Balladoran
Cathundral
Gin Gin
Eumungerie
Coolbaggie Nat Res
Buddabaddah
Coolbaggie
Trangie
Burraway
Mogriguy
MITCHELL HIGHWAY
CASTLEREAGH HIGHWAY
Kamilaroi Highway
GWYDIR
OXLEY HWY
Culgoa River
Nebine Creek
Briarie Creek
Bokhara River
Narran River
Barwon River
Bogan River
Castlereagh River
Namoi River
Pian Creek
Marra Creek
Macquarie River
Marthaguy Creek
Moonie River
Mole River
Sly Ck
Pangee Creek

Map 3

0 10 20 30 40 50
kilometres

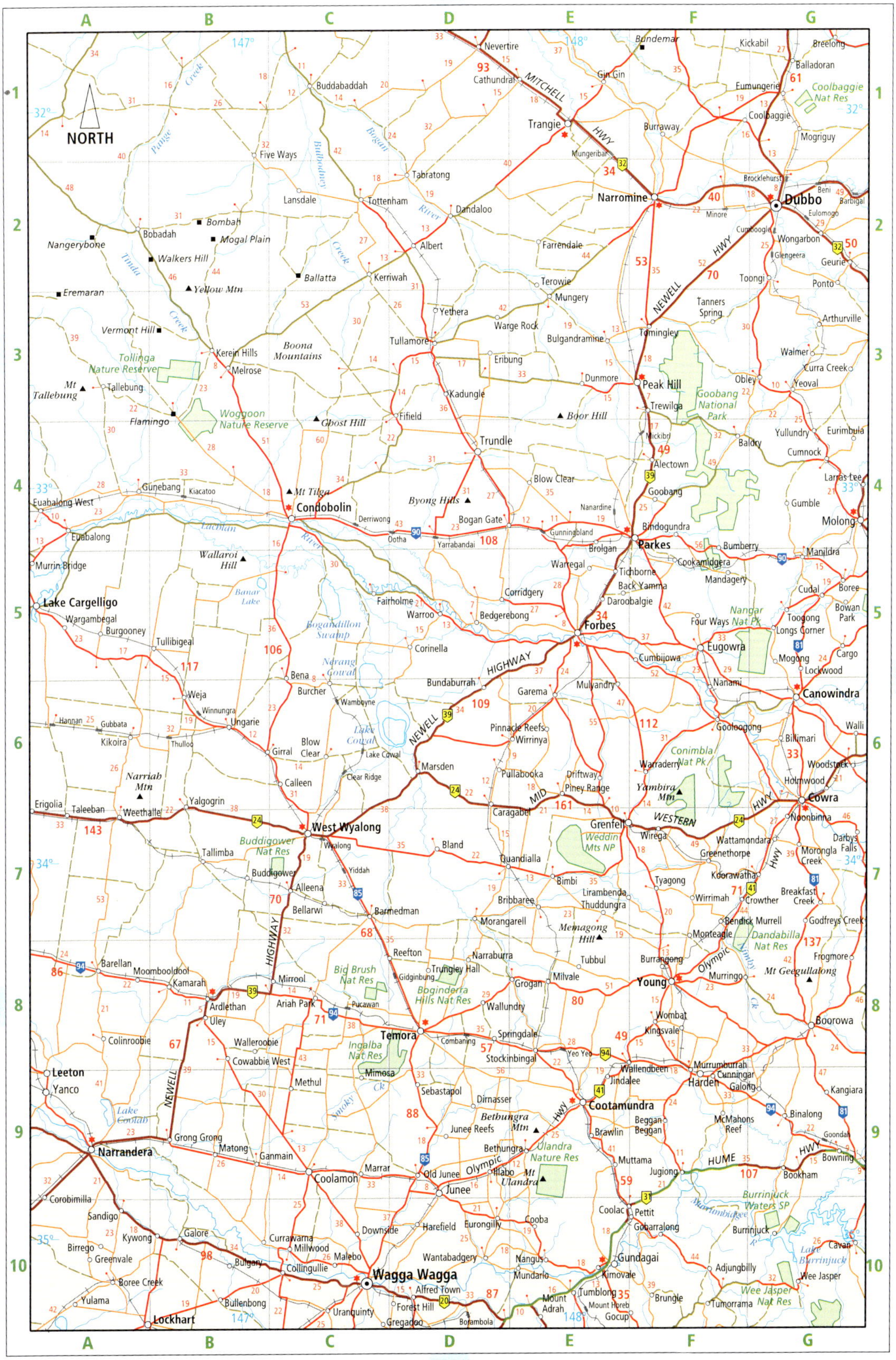

Map 4

QLD 7

NSW 2

NSW 6

0 10 20 30 40 50
kilometres

QLD 7

NSW 6

Map 5

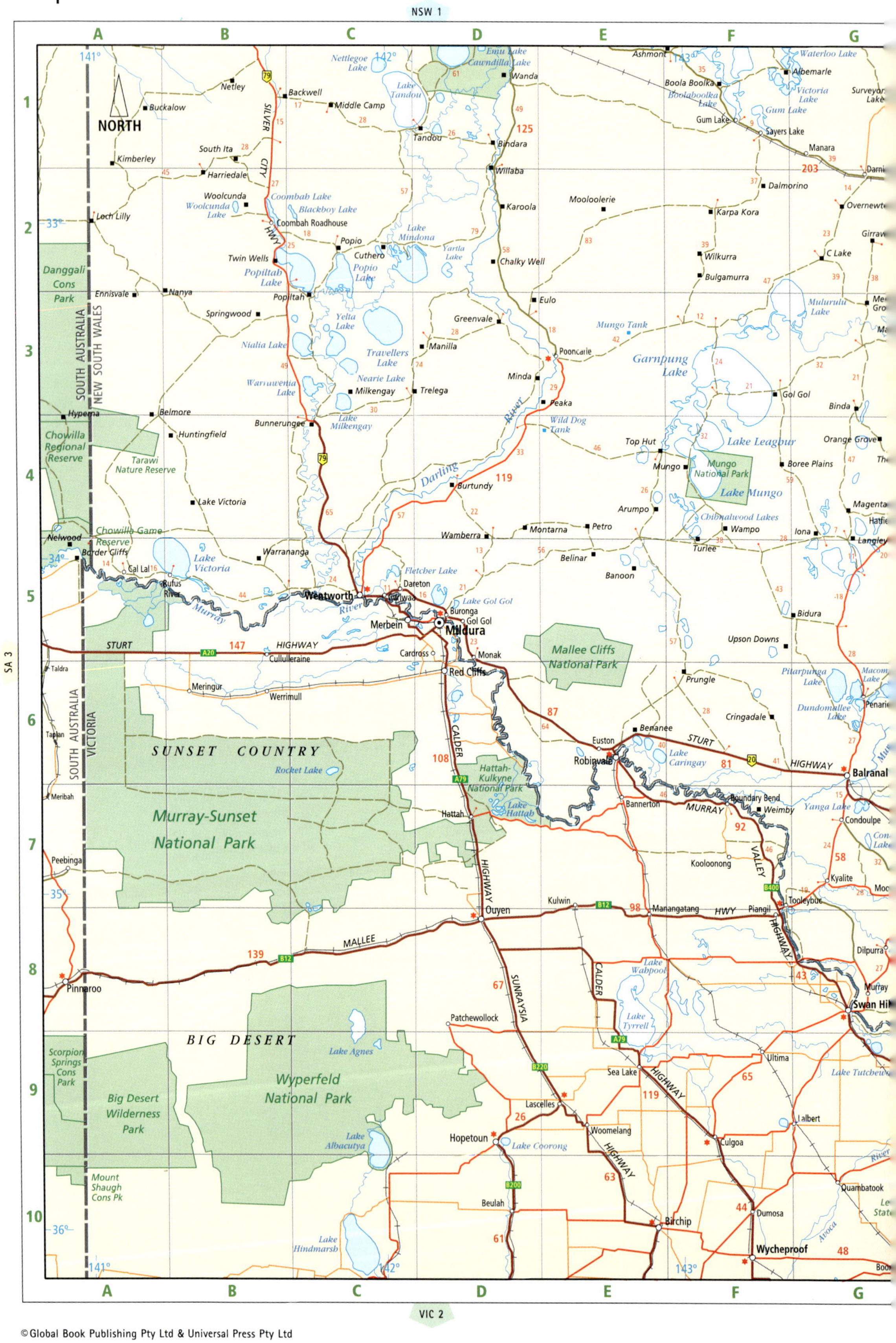
NSW 1
VIC 2
SA 3
A B C D E F G
1 2 3 4 5 6 7 8 9 10
141°
142°
143°
33°
34°
35°
36°
NORTH
Netley
Buckalow
Backwell
Middle Camp
SILVER CITY HWY
Nettlegoe Lake
Lake Tandou
Tandou
Emu Lake
Cawndilla Lake
Wanda
Bindara
Willaba
Karoola
Chalky Well
Eulo
South Ita
Kimberley
Harriedale
Woolcunda
Woolcunda Lake
Coombah Lake
Blackboy Lake
Coombah Roadhouse
Loch Lilly
Popio
Cuthero
Lake Mindona
Yartla Lake
Twin Wells
Popiltah Lake
Popio Lake
Popiltah
Danggali Cons Park
Ennisvale
Nanya
Springwood
Yelta Lake
Greenvale
Manilla
Travellers Lake
Nialia Lake
Warrawenia Lake
Nearie Lake
Milkengay
Trelega
Minda
Peaka
Pooncarie
Mungo Tank
Garnpung Lake
Mooloolerie
Ashmont
Boola Boolka
Boolaboolka Lake
Gum Lake
Victoria Lake
Gum Lake
Sayers Lake
Albemarle
Waterloo Lake
Surveyor Lake
Manara
Dalmorino
Karpa Kora
Overnewton
Wilkurra
Bulgamurra
C Lake
Girraween
Mulurulu Lake
SOUTH AUSTRALIA
NEW SOUTH WALES
Hypema
Belmore
Huntingfield
Bunnerungee
Lake Milkengay
Chowilla Regional Reserve
Tarawi Nature Reserve
Lake Victoria
Chowilla Game Reserve
Darling River
Wild Dog Tank
Burtundy
Top Hut
Mungo
Mungo National Park
Lake Leaghur
Lake Mungo
Gol Gol
Binda
Orange Grove
Boree Plains
Magenta
Arumpo
Chibnalwood Lakes
Wampo
Turlee
Iona
Langley
Hatfield
Wamberra
Montarna
Petro
Belinar
Banoon
Nelwood
Border Cliffs
Cal Lal
Rufus River
Murray River
Warrananga
Fletcher Lake
Dareton
Wentworth
Gol Gol
Lake Gol Gol
Buronga
Mildura
Merbein
Curlwaa
Mallee Cliffs National Park
Upson Downs
Bidura
STURT HIGHWAY
A20
Taldra
Cullulleraine
Cardross
Red Cliffs
Monak
Meringur
Werrimull
Prungle
Pitarpunga Lake
Macommon Lake
Penarie
Dundomallee Lake
Cringadale
SOUTH AUSTRALIA
VICTORIA
Taplan
SUNSET COUNTRY
Rocket Lake
CALDER
Hattah-Kulkyne National Park
Lake Hattah
Hattah
Euston
Benanee
Robinvale
Lake Caringay
Balranald
Meribah
Murray-Sunset National Park
Bannerton
Boundary Bend
Weimby
Yanga Lake
Condoulpe
MURRAY VALLEY HIGHWAY
Kooloonong
Kyalite
Peebinga
Ouyen
Kulwin
Manangatang
Piangil
Tooleybuc
MALLEE
B12
HWY
Dilpurra
Pinnaroo
Lake Wahpool
Lake Tyrrell
Murray
Swan Hill
SUNRAYSIA
Patchewollock
BIG DESERT
Lake Agnes
Scorpion Springs Cons Park
Big Desert Wilderness Park
Wyperfeld National Park
Ultima
Sea Lake
HIGHWAY
Lake Tutchewop
Lascelles
Hopetoun
Lake Coorong
Woomelang
Culgoa
Lalbert
Lake Albacutya
B220
B200
Mount Shaugh Cons Pk
Beulah
Birchip
Dumosa
Quambatook
Lake Hindmarsh
Wycheproof
Avoca

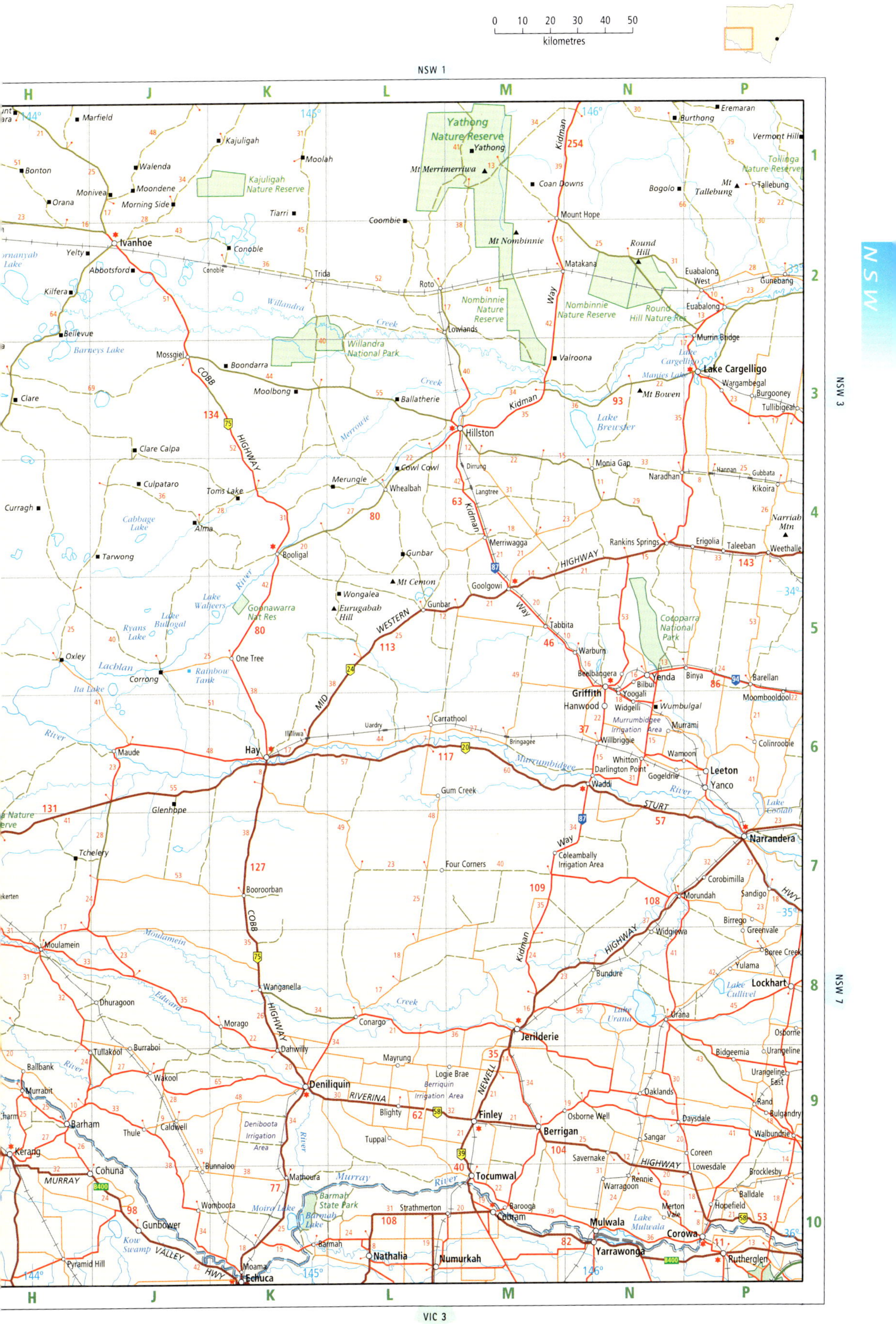
0 10 20 30 40 50
kilometres
NSW 1
VIC 3
NSW 3
NSW 7
NSW
H J K L M N P
1 2 3 4 5 6 7 8 9 10
Marfield
Kajuligah
Moolah
Yathong Nature Reserve
Yathong
Mt Merrimerriwa
Kidman
Eremaran
Burthong
Vermont Hill
Tollinga Nature Reserve
Bonton
Walenda
Kajuligah Nature Reserve
Moondene
Monivea
Orana
Morning Side
Coan Downs
Bogolo
Mt Tallebung
Tallebung
Tiarri
Coombie
Mount Hope
Mt Nombinnie
Ivanhoe
Yelty
Conoble
Abbotsford
Trida
Roto
Matakana
Round Hill
Euabalong West
Gunebang
Euabalong
Kilfera
Willandra
Creek
Nombinnie Nature Reserve
Nombinnie Nature Reserve
Round Hill Nature Res
Lowlands
Bellevue
Barneys Lake
Willandra National Park
Murrin Bridge
Mossgiel
Boondarra
Valroona
Lake Cargelligo
Lake Cargelligo
Manies Lake
Wargambegal
Burgooney
Tullibigeal
COBB
Moolbong
Ballatherie
Mt Bowen
Clare
Kidman
Lake Brewster
HIGHWAY
Hillston
Merrowie
Clare Calpa
Dirrung
Monia Gap
Naradhan
Hannan
Gubbata
Kikoira
Cowl Cowl
Culpataro
Merungle
Langtree
Whealbah
Toms Lake
Curragh
Cabbage Lake
Alma
Narriah Mtn
Merriwagga
Rankins Springs
Erigolia
Taleeban
Weethalle
Booligal
Gunbar
Tarwong
HIGHWAY
Mt Cemon
Goolgowi
Wongalea
Lake Waljeers
River
Gonnawarra Nat Res
Eurugabah Hill
Gunbar
WESTERN
Way
Tabbita
Cocoparra National Park
Lake Bullogal
Ryans Lake
Warburn
Beelbangera
Yenda
Binya
Barellan
Oxley
Lachlan
One Tree
Rainbow Tank
Corrong
Bilbul
Griffith
Yoogali
Moombooldool
Ita Lake
MID
Hanwood
Widgelli
Wumbulgal
Murrumbidgee Irrigation Area
Murrami
River
Maude
Uardry
Carrathool
Illilliwa
Hay
Bringagee
Willbriggie
Colinroobie
Whitton
Wamoon
Murrumbidgee
Darlington Point
Gogeldrie
Leeton
Waddi
River
Yanco
Gum Creek
Glenhope
STURT
Lake Coolah
Nature Reserve
Way
Narrandera
Coleambally Irrigation Area
Tchelery
Four Corners
Corobimilla
Booroorban
Morundah
Sandigo
HWY
Birrego
Widgiewa
Greenvale
Moulamein
Moulamein
COBB
Kidman
HIGHWAY
Boree Creek
Yulama
Lake Cullivel
Lockhart
Wanganella
Bundure
Edward
Dhuragoon
Creek
Lake Urana
Urana
HIGHWAY
Conargo
Morago
Jerilderie
Osborne
Burraboi
Tullakool
Dahwilly
Mayrung
Bidgeemia
Urangeline
Ballbank
River
Wakool
Logie Brae
Urangeline East
Berriquin Irrigation Area
Murrabit
Deniliquin
RIVERINA
NEWELL
Oaklands
Rand
Barham
Thule
Caldwell
Blighty
Finley
Osborne Well
Daysdale
Bulgandry
Deniboota Irrigation Area
River
Tuppal
Berrigan
Sangar
Walbundrie
Kerang
Bunnaloo
Savernake
Coreen
Cohuna
Mathoura
Murray
River
HIGHWAY
Lowesdale
Brocklesby
MURRAY
Tocumwal
Rennie
Warragoon
Barmah State Park
Barmah Lake
Strathmerton
Balldale
Wombooota
Moira Lake
Barooga
Merton Vale
Hopefield
Cobram
Mulwala
Gunbower
Kow Swamp
VALLEY
Barmah
Lake Mulwala
Corowa
Nathalia
Numurkah
Yarrawonga
Rutherglen
Pyramid Hill
HWY
Moama
Echuca
144°
145°
146°
33°
34°
35°
36°

Map 6

NSW 4

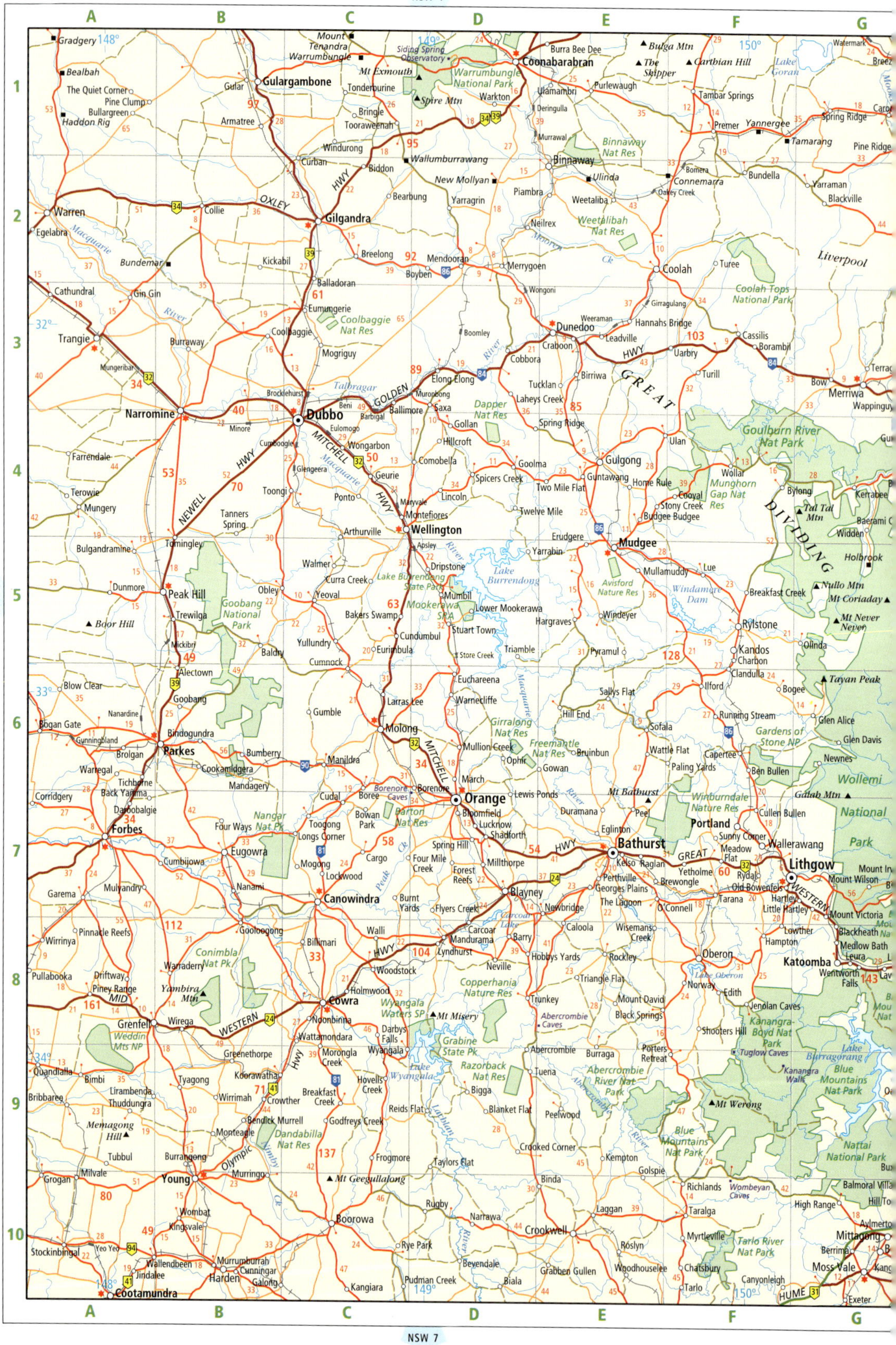

NSW 3

NSW 7

0 10 20 30 40 50
kilometres

NSW 4

Map 7

NSW 3
A
B
C
D
E
F
G
1
2
3
4
5
6
7
8
9
10
NSW 5
VIC 3
VIC 3
Griffith
Hanwood
Yenda
Bilbul
Yoogali
Widgelli
Wumbulgal
Murrumbidgee Irrigation Area
Murrami
Willbriggie
Whitton
Darlington Point
Wamoon
Gogeldrie
Leeton
Yanco
Waddi
Murrumbidgee
STURT
Way
Coleambally Irrigation Area
Narrandera
HIGHWAY
Corobimilla
Morundah
NEWELL
Widgiewa
Bundure
Lake Urana
Urana
Barellan
Moombooldool
Kamarah
Ardlethan
Uley
Colinroobie
Lake Coolah
NEWELL
Grong Grong
Matong
Ganmain
Sandigo
Kywong
Galore
Birrego
Greenvale
Boree Creek
Yulama
Lake Cullivel
Lockhart
Milbrulong
French Park
Tootool
Osborne
Bidgeemia
Urangeline
Pleasant Hills
Urangeline East
Oaklands
Osborne Well
Daysdale
Rand
Bulgandry
Alma Park
RIVERINA
Sangar
Coreen
Lowesdale
Savernake
HIGHWAY
Rennie
Warragoon
Merton Vale
Walbundrie
Wiesners Swamp Nat Res
Walla Walla
Brocklesby
Balldale
Burrumbuttock
Gerogery
Hopefield
Jindera
Mulwala
Lake Mulwala
Yarrawonga
Corowa
Rutherglen
Bungowannah
Lavington
Table Top
Albury
Wodonga
Mirrool
Ariah Park
Walleroobie
Cowabbie West
Methul
Coolamon
Currawarna
Millwood
Malebo
Bulgary
Collingullie
Bullenbong
The Rock
The Rock Nat Res
Yerong Creek
Mangoplah
Henty
Olympic
Culcairn
Cookardinia
Ralvona
Big Brush Nat Res
Pucawan
Ingalba Nat Res
Mimosa
Smoky
Temora
Reefton
Trungley Hall
Narraburra
Gidginbung
Bogindera Hills Nat Res
Wallundry
Combaning
Springdale
Stockinbingal
Sebastapol
Dirnasser
Bethungra Mtn
Junee Reefs
Bethungra
Ulandra Nature Res
Mt Ulandra
Illabo
Marrar
Old Junee
Olympic
Junee
Downside
Harefield
Eurongilly
Cooba
Wagga Wagga
Alfred Town
Forest Hill
Uranquinty
Gregadoo
Wantabadgery
Nangus
Mundarlo
Borambola
Tarcutta
Umbango
Kyeamba
Humula
Burrandana
Pulletop
Westby
Little Billabong
Carabost
HUME
Holbrook
Woomargama
Mt Jergyle
Lankeys Creek
Mullengandra
Bowna
Lake Hume
Wymah
Talmalmo
Jingellic
Walwa
Burrowye
Hume Weir
Mt Granya State Pk
Mt Granya
Mt Lawson State Park
Burrowa-Pine Mtn Nat Park
Bullioh
Koetong
Berringama
Tallangatta
Corryong
Thurgoona
Tubbul
Burrangong
Young
Murringo
Grogan
Milvale
Wombat
Kingsvale
Yeo Yeo
Wallendbeen
Jindalee
Murrumburrah
Harden
Cunningar
Galong
Cootamundra
Beggan Beggan
Brawlin
McMahons Reef
Muttama
Jugiong
Coolac
Pettit
Gobarralong
Murrumbidgee
Gundagai
Adjungbilly
Wee Jasper
Kimovale
Tumblong
Mount Horeb
Gocup
Brungle
Tumorrama
Mount Adrah
Tumut
Adelong
Lacmalac
Gilmore
Mt Hugel
Blowering Reservoir
Batlow
Westbrook
Talbingo
Talbingo Reservoir
Laurel Hill
Rosewood
Wolseley Park
Granite Mtn
Yarrangobilly
Rules Point
Tumbarumba
Mannus
Munderoo
Elliot
Way
Sue City Camp
Pilot Reef Mtn
Ournie
Mt Hay
Cabramurra
Tooma
Welaregang
Tintaldra
Jagumba Mtn
Mt Selwyn Snowfields
Towong
Mt Toolong
Big Boy Mtn
Khancoban
Khancoban Pondage
Grey Mare
SNOWY
MOUNTAINS
Island Bend
Guthega
Geehi
Charlottes Pass
Smiggin Holes
Perisher Valley
Mt Kosciuszko
Thredbo Village
Tom Groggin
Dead Horse Gap
Kosciuszko National Park
Bogong
Goobarragandra
Kosciuszko National Park
SNOWY
Mtns
Ovens River
FREEWAY
M31
Chiltern Box-Ironbark NP
Warby Range State Park
Lake Mokoan
Wangaratta
OVENS
Beechworth
Beechworth Park
Oxley
Benalla
HUME
A300
B500
Moyhu
Myrtleford
KIEWA
VALLEY
HWY
C531
Wabba Wilderness Park
Bucheen Creek
OMEO
Mitta Mitta
Dartmouth
Lake Dartmouth
C543
HIGHWAY
Mt Buffalo National Park
Bright
Mount Beauty
Bogong
Falls Creek
Whitfield
Dandongadale
Alpine National Park
Alpine National Park
Hotham Heights
Mt Cobberas
Alpine National Park
Suggan Buggan
Barry
Way
NSW
Vic
Lake Nillahcootie
Mount Samaria State Park
Mansfield
Alpine National Park
Mount Buller Alpine Village
Omeo
C608
Snowy River National Park
Lake Eildon
Tambo
Tambo River
Snowy River
Buchan
Mitchell River National Park
146°
147°
148°
35°
36°
37°

0 10 20 30 40 50
kilometres

NSW 6

VIC 4

Victoria

Victoria may be one of the smallest states in Australia, but it is brimming with bountiful places to relax and unwind—whether that means getting out and about or staying indoors and doing nothing at all. The capital city, Melbourne, has become a popular haven for shopaholics looking for a little retail therapy, and there is a mouth-watering array of restaurants and cafés to tempt the tastebuds. Pamper yourself at one of the health spas in Daylesford and Hepburn Springs, or meditate on the grand majesty of the natural formations along the Great Ocean Road. Snow bunnies can forgo the physical exertion of skiing and head straight for the après-ski festivities at resorts throughout the High Country. As you can see, Victoria is the queen of relaxation.

Melbourne and Environs

Like all major urban centres, Melbourne offers the visitor a rich mixture of interesting museums, art galleries and historic buildings, combined with excellent shopping both within the city itself and out in the suburbs. Beyond these attractions there are lots of outdoor activities and plenty of interesting daytrip locations which can relax or stimulate you, depending on your mood.

Melbourne is a sophisticated modern city. It is still regarded as the most cultured city in the country, being known for its elegant boutiques, its fine restaurants and its splendid parks and gardens. The city is located on the shores of Port Phillip Bay and Western Port.

Although in recent times a number of overtly modern buildings (both the South Bank complex and the Crown Casino skyscraper are examples) have changed the city, it is still true that the central business district sensitively tries to blend the Victorian architecture of the latter half of the nineteenth century (Melbourne's boom period) with more modern high-rise buildings. The result is that there is a good balance between colonial elegance and urban modernity.

There are many ways of experiencing the joys of Melbourne. An obvious starting point is to find a building which gives views across the city. The view from West Gate Bridge, which rises 54 m above the Yarra River, offers an excellent panorama of the city. There is also a superb view from the restaurant on the 35th floor of the Regent Hotel in Collins Street.

Built in 1854, Flinders Street Railway Station is Australia's oldest city station and is, arguably, its most impressive. This grand station remains a major link in Melbourne's rail system.

Opened as a permanent venue in 1996, the Crown Casino provides entertainment, gambling opportunities and shopping.

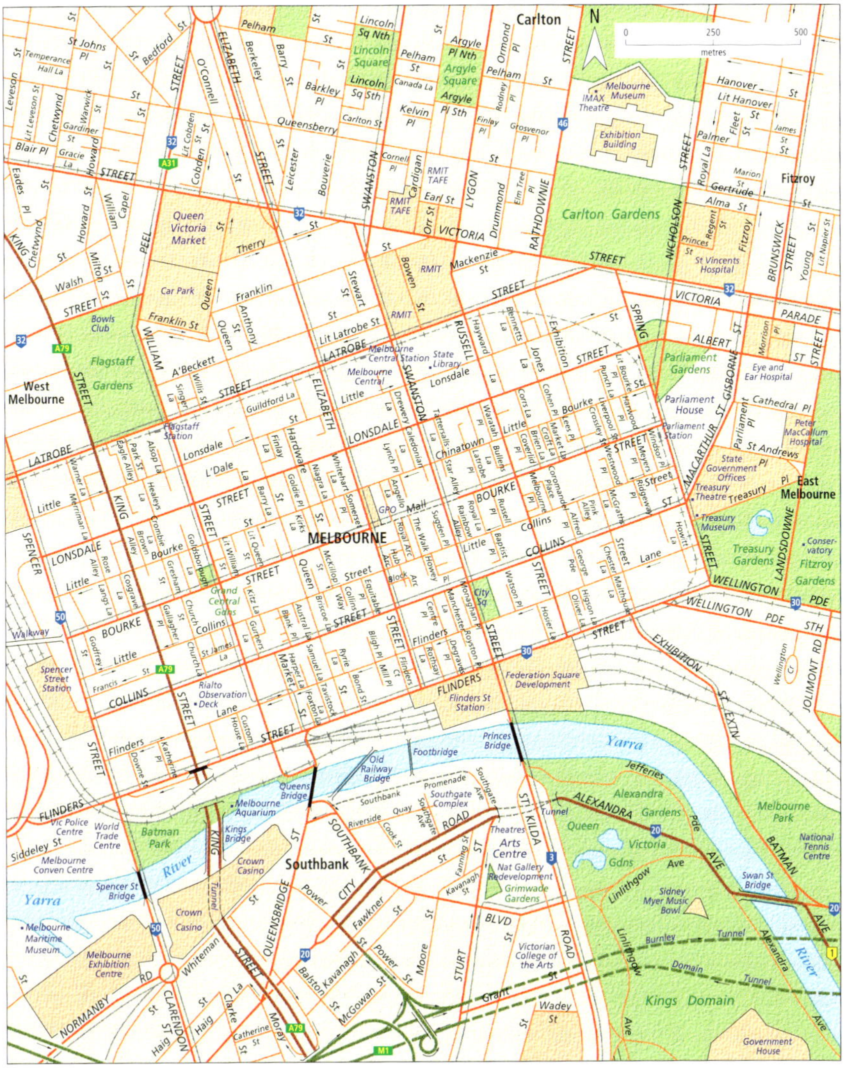

If you are looking for something a little more active there are great ways of seeing the city which include historic walking tours, hot air ballooning, travelling down the Yarra River by ferry or a cruise vessel, canoeing on Albert Park Lake, taking a daytrip across Port Phillip Bay or hiring a bicycle and cycling along the Yarra River Cycle Track.

The Shopping

One of the huge attractions of the city centre is the number of elegant Victorian shopping arcades which offer delightful ways to spend a day. The Block Arcade (1892) located at 282 Collins Street is a glorious Victorian shopping arcade full of interesting shops. The Rialto Building at 497 Collins Street is built in an Italian Gothic style and is characteristic of the time when Melbourne was prosperous with money coming from the goldfields. The Royal Arcade (1869) at 331 Bourke Street is another shopping arcade full of quite charming and elegant boutiques. Arcades like these have led Melburnians to believe that they have the best shopping in Australia. You can test this theory by window shopping in both Bourke and Collins Street.

Beyond the city centre the shopping experiences are no less attractive. Visitors should ensure, particularly around lunchtime, that they walk down Lygon Street, Melbourne's famous Little Italy

Mural at Melbourne's Queen Victoria Market. Established in 1878, this is the world's largest outdoor market.

which offers food shops, cafés and restaurants. The Queen Victoria Market is the largest outdoor market in the world. It has an amazing selection of fresh produce and clothing. If you want to experience true luxury a walk down Toorak Road will find you passing some of the city's most exclusive boutiques and clothing shops. Chapel Street also is known for its attractive specialist boutiques.

The Yarra

Right: *Melbourne's café society is renowned—relax with a frothy cappuccino at one of the many coffee shops or brasseries in the city.*

No visit to Melbourne is truly complete without experiencing the Yarra River. The muddy river, often seen as dirty by outsiders—although in recent times it has looked particularly attractive—runs through the heart of the city and offers visitors and residents a huge range of interesting activities. It is possible to enjoy picnics on the river banks and, at certain points along the river, the local councils have constructed excellent barbecues. It is also possible to hire canoes and row along the river. There are a number of floating restaurants moored along the banks which serve fine food and wine to travellers who can eat and watch the world go by. And there is still no better way of experiencing the Yarra than walking along its banks from the South Bank Complex around to the National Tennis Centre at Melbourne Park and on to the parklands which lie beyond.

Parklands and gardens edge the Yarra River, providing vantage points to watch the water traffic pass by or to take in stunning views of the city.

Special Places

Melbourne is a special sporting centre. Visitors curious about the city's love of sport who arrive either in summer or winter should try to go to the Australian Open tennis, an international cricket match or an Australian Rules football match. They are integral parts of the city's popular culture and offer an insight into the psyche of Melburnians.

Melbourne is justifiably proud of its restaurants, particularly in the inner suburbs. The variety of destinations—ranging from cafés through brasseries to high-quality restaurants—is remarkable. Still, there is nothing to compare with the concentration of Italian restaurants on Lygon Street.

The city has a number of substantial and gracious parks. The Royal Botanic Gardens and King's Domain Gardens with La Trobe's Cottage (1839) and the Shrine of Remembrance—a memorial to those who died during World War II—are a pleasant respite on the south side of the Yarra River. Nearby is the Arts Centre of Victoria, with the excellent National Gallery of Victoria on St Kilda Road. This recently redeveloped art gallery features a permanent exhibition of international art from ancient Greek, Roman and Egyptian antiquities and European masterpieces to contemporary photography and new media. This building's facade is notable for its attractive waterwall. The National

Gallery of Victoria's Australian art is now housed at Federation Square. This gallery is well worth inspecting, as it contains one of the country's most comprehensive collections of Australian paintings, drawings, photographs as well as Aboriginal and Torres Strait Islander art.

Fitzroy Gardens with Cook's Cottage (1775), which was painstakingly transported from its original location in Yorkshire in 1933, is worth visiting. It is conveniently located only a few tram stops away from Spencer Street Station on the north side of the Yarra River.

Another aspect of Melbourne which is worth experiencing is its wonderful trams. It is now the only Australian city with a comprehensive tram service. This charming and highly efficient form of transportation is an integral part of city life. The smart visitor should buy a day ticket which allows you to take as many tram trips as you like on that day and to explore some of the city's more interesting suburbs, such as bohemian St Kilda.

Map: Vic 6 D3

The Dandenong Ranges

The time to really enjoy the Dandenong Ranges is in spring when the numerous gardens are in full bloom. Located east of the centre of Melbourne, the attractions in the Dandenongs include the National Rhododendron Gardens—a 43-hectare complex of outstanding botanic gardens which is home to 15 000 rhododendrons, 12 000 azaleas, 250 000 daffodils, cherry tree groves and laburnums, all of which blossom in spring. The R. J. Hamer Forest Arboretum (100 hectares in area) has an outstanding collection of maples, liquidambars, ash, elms, birch, conifers and oaks. The award-winning formal gardens of Cloudehill, inspired by the Art and Craft style of design, are surrounded by woodlands of maples, beeches, magnolias and rhododendrons and feature fields of bluebells, daffodils,

Above: *St Kilda, a seaside suburb of Melbourne, boasts a delightful pier plus Australia's oldest theme park—Luna Park.*

Below: *Spring is the best time to visit the National Rhododendron Gardens, when the grounds are awash with colour.*

Set in a lush fern-filled forest, the William Ricketts Sanctuary features a wealth of clay sculptures inspired by the artist's experience of living with Aboriginal people in central Australia.

nerines and grape hyacinths. The trees date back to the earliest days of the Woolrich Nursery and are now considered quite historic. Pirianda Garden is known for its rare, exotic and native plant species.

The ranges are also noted for their tea-houses, lovely guesthouses and the extraordinary William Ricketts Sanctuary which features a large number of delightful clay sculptures. There are organised tours of most of the larger gardens in the area.

Map: Vic 6 E3

Yarra Valley

These days the magnificent Yarra Valley is to Melbourne what the Hunter Valley is to Sydney and the Barossa Valley is to Adelaide. It is the home of fine wines, excellent restaurants and interesting accommodation options. The wineries in the area include the Yarra Glen Vineyard, Yarra Ridge Winery, Tarrawarra Estate, Fergusson Winery and Restaurant, Hinkell Vineyard and Café, Lovey's Estate and Restaurant, De Bortoli Winery and Restaurant, Yering Station Winery, Diamond Valley Vineyard and St Huberts Vineyard. For those interested in cheeses, the Yarra Valley Dairy is a glorious eatery. There is a wide range of organised tours which include visits to the wineries and lunch at one of the region's well-known restaurants.

Nearby is the Healesville Sanctuary, which boasts over 200 species of native mammals, reptiles and birds in a natural bushland setting. The sanctuary's fauna includes Tasmanian devils, lyrebirds, an 800-strong ibis colony, kangaroos, emus, wallabies, dingoes, echidnas, cockatoos, owls, flying foxes, lorikeets, bats, lizards and many others.

Map: Vic 6 E2

Mornington Peninsula

For those looking for a beachside holiday (both on the Port Phillip Bay side

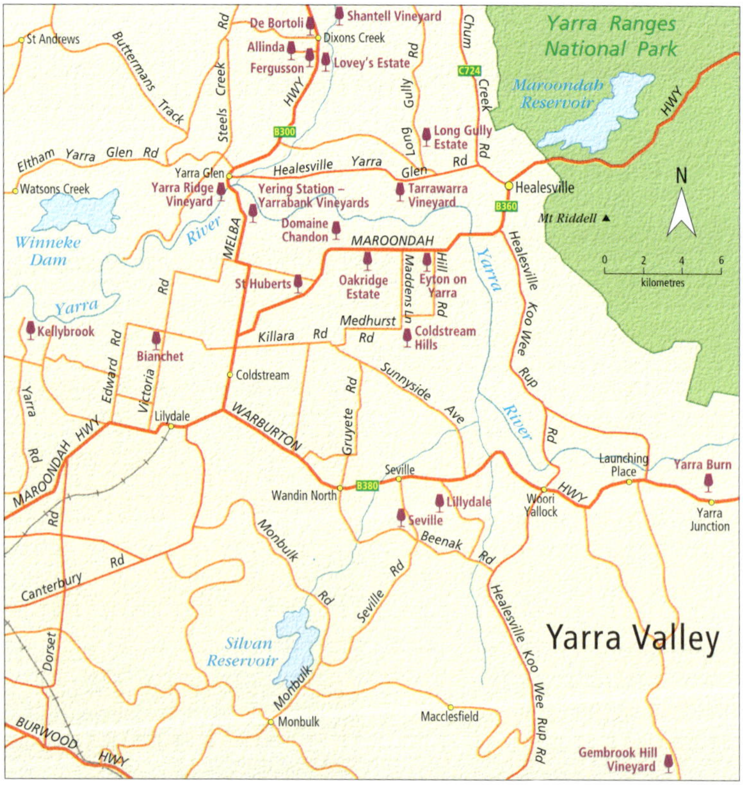

and the ocean side) the Mornington Peninsula offers the usual bewildering collection of Australian beachside attractions. Sorrento, one of the main townships on the Peninsula, offers good beaches, some excellent scenic walks along the coast, a range of accommodation from motels to B&Bs and guesthouses, a number of interesting historic buildings and sites, dolphin-watching cruises (the area is famous for the boat trips which allow passengers to don a snorkel and goggles and swim with the friendly dolphins—if these creatures can be found) and ferry trips across to Queenscliff on the other side of Port Phillip.

Similarly Portsea, a popular but rather exclusive seaside holiday resort located 93 km south of Melbourne, mixes rugged cliffs and interesting bushwalks (on the ocean side of the narrow peninsula) with bayside activities that include family picnics on the beach, angling from the long wooden pier and guided fishing tours. Portsea is also the perfect place to hire boats, windsurfing equipment, aqua bikes and canoes which will allow you to explore the shallow waters of the bay.

Map: Vic 6 C5

Above: *Mornington Beach boasts clean white sand and safe swimming in the waters of Port Phillip Bay.*

Below: *The soil and climate of the Yarra Valley are perfect for the production of wine grapes.*

The South-East Coast

Victoria's south-east coast, which starts at Mornington Peninsula (really part of the outer suburban sprawl of Melbourne) and stretches all the way around to Ninety Mile Beach and beyond to the New South Wales border, is characterised by great diversity. Here is Phillip Island, a popular daytrip destination from Melbourne which, incongruously, combines fairy penguin watching with summer holidays and motorcycle racing.

Here is Wilsons Promontory, a glorious area of windswept coastline that is ideal for bushwalking and getting-away-from-it-all holidays. And here is the attractive region around Lakes Entrance and Mallacoota which has, at various times, been a dairy farming area, a haunt for artists and a popular holiday resort area for campers and bushwalkers.

Beyond the coast are the great coal and gas townships of Moe, Yallourn and Leongatha. The contrast is quite surprising. Still, the coast is isolated and ideal for those people seeking a peaceful retreat or wanting to enjoy a simple, economic and uncomplicated holiday.

Phillip Island, famed for its fairy penguin population, is home to koalas, fur seals and varied bird life. The island also hosts a famous sporting event: the Australian 500cc Motorcycle Grand Prix.

Phillip Island

Most people visit Phillip Island to see the fairy penguins. This, however, undersells the rest of the island and its appealing attractions. Located only 124 km south of Melbourne, at the entrance to Westernport, Phillip Island is hardly an island at all. It is actually connected to the mainland by a 640-m long bridge and therefore it feels like it is part of the mainland. The island itself is 26 km in length and 9 km in width and consists largely of open and flat countryside. Its large fairy penguin colony and other natural features (such as Churchill Island, Seal Rocks and the fantastic Koala Conservation Centre) are the major attractions. Cowes and Newhaven are substantial towns on the island.

Visitors should make sure they visit the Phillip Island Penguin Parade, go for a walk around Churchill Island, go birdwatching on Cape Woolamai, check out the local fauna at the Koala Conservation Centre and the Phillip Island Wildlife Park, take a look at the Nobbies and Seal Rocks, and ponder over the power of Bass Strait.

Map: Vic 6 D6

Penguin Parade

The Phillip Island Penguin Parade is a major tourist attraction. Located 22 km from the Newhaven bridge, the large and carefully controlled area is more like a theatre than an informal viewing place. Visitors are organised by rangers who insist on no flash photography and no physical contact between people and penguins. The appeal is that each evening, around dusk, thousands of fairy penguins make their way back to their burrows in the sand dunes behind Summerland Beach. There is no doubt that these creatures are cute. The fairy penguins, native to southern coastal areas of both Australia and New Zealand, are the smallest of their species, and they grow to a mere 33 cm in height. Each day they go out to sea to catch food (mostly small fish) for themselves and their young. They return to the beach in 'rafts' and quickly make their way across the sand to their burrows. People sit in the grandstand and watch in awe.

Other Attractions

Bushwalkers will find Churchill Island very enjoyable. The Churchill Island Loop Track is an easy stroll which takes about 2 hours. There is also the North Point Loop Track (1 hour); the Bass Rock Loop (30 minutes); Grant's Monument Loop (30 minutes) and the Mangrove Loop (45 minutes). These walks offer some fine views and opportunities to see the island's flora and fauna. The northernmost tip of the island is a particularly good place to see a range of migratory birdlife, including pied oystercatchers, royal spoonbills, ibis, herons and gulls.

Birdwatchers will love Cape Woolamai (located at the very tip of Phillip Island's south-eastern peninsula) where, every

Left: *The fairy penguin* (Eudyptula minor)*—the most popular attraction on Phillip Island—commonly nests in burrows, caves, crevices or under coastal houses.*

Below: *The picturesque coastline around Cape Woolamai, which is the highest point on Phillip Island, is highly regarded by surfers. Lifesavers patrol Woolamai Beach in summer.*

The Nobbies, an unusual formation created by volcanic eruptions long ago, is now part of the Sea Life Centre on the westernmost tip of Phillip Island.

September, more than one million short-tailed shearwaters, otherwise known as muttonbirds, arrive from as far away as Japan, Alaska and Siberia, to breed.

Nature-lovers will probably want to visit both the Koala Conservation Centre and the Phillip Island Wildlife Park. The latter boasts 900 animals and birds in all, including emus, echidnas, crocodiles, dingoes, goannas, wedge-tailed eagles, pelicans, koalas, a wide variety of snakes, kangaroos, wallabies, rosellas, lorikeets, black swans, kookaburras, native owls, Tasmanian devils and wombats. There is also a nocturnal animals centre.

After the delightful fairy penguins, the most popular attraction on Phillip Island is definitely the Seal Rocks Sea Life Centre, an important part of any visit to the Nobbies and Seal Rocks. This is an excellent place for people wanting to walk around the edge of the island to see nesting seabirds and, in the appropriate season, colonies of Australian fur seals. At their peak during the breeding season, between 5000 and 9000 seals can be found on Seal Rocks. The males arrive in November to claim a site, and the females arrive later in the month. A series of boardwalks has been built on the slopes below the kiosk. It is a short walk around to The Blowhole which can be very impressive during the high tide and when heavy seas pound the coast. Silver gulls nest here, and the chicks can be seen in spring and early summer.

Seemingly unperturbed by humans, the emus of Wilsons Promontory National Park can often be seen boldly crossing roads in the park.

Wilsons Promontory

If you want a real wilderness experience on the coast of Victoria, it is hard to beat the sheer beauty and wildness of Wilsons Promontory, which lies 230 km south-east of Melbourne. With its interesting blend of mountainous forests, lush fern gullies, heaths, salt marshes, grey granite ranges and 130 km of truly spectacular coastal scenery, Wilsons Promontory—the most southerly point of mainland Australia—is one of the country's largest and most popular national parks.

Joined to the mainland by the narrow Yanakie Isthmus, Wilsons Promontory National Park is surrounded by water on three sides. The park was preserved in 1898 and has since been expanded.

People visiting the area usually go for the bushwalking, as there are 22 walking tracks in the park. Some are enjoyable strolls, while others are overnight treks. The Lilly Pilly Gully nature walk is 5 km return, and the Mount Oberon walk is 3.2 km return. It takes about one hour to climb the 562-m high mountain, which offers excellent views of Tidal River, Norman Bay and the headlands to the north. Pillar Point is 6 km return and looks out over Tidal River. Longer walks take you to Sealers Cove (20 km return) and the granite lighthouse (40 km return). There are camp sites throughout the park, along the walking tracks.

Map: Vic 6 J8

Lakes Entrance

Lakes Entrance is an ideal holiday destination for the whole family because it offers a wide variety of different activities, ranging from walking along Ninety Mile Beach (a walk that could keep the family going for a week) to fishing and

Tidal River, lying on Norman Bay in Wilsons Promontory National Park, is a popular family destination as it has safe, shallow swimming waters and camping facilities.

Running south from Lakes Entrance, Ninety Mile Beach is a narrow stretch of sand dunes which separates the ocean and the shallow Gippsland Lakes, Australia's most extensive coastal lake system.

hiring paddleboats, catamarans, paddle-skis, aquabikes, canoes and body boards. There is also an antique car museum, a recreation park featuring water slides and mini-golf, and a seashell museum with over 80 000 shells and corals.

Lakes Entrance is located 319 km east of Melbourne and, as its name suggests, it is the gateway to the Gippsland Lakes which cover 400 sq km and extend for 90 km down the coast. Two areas, covering 17 880 hectares, have been classified as national parkland—The Lakes National Park and the Gippsland Lakes Coastal Park—and both offer excellent bushwalking for those people wanting to enjoy a coastal adventure. The region, known as the Victorian Riviera, is noted for its minimal variation in temperature the year round, being relatively warm in winter and cool in summer.

Fishing from the jetty is one of the relaxing activities on Raymond Island, in Lake King—one of the three main lagoons that make up Gippsland Lakes.

The most popular activity around the lakes is fishing. For those without a boat, fishing trips and boating tours of the lakes and rivers are available, and small fishing boats can also be hired from the jetties located on Marine Parade. Black bream are especially plentiful in the waters of the Gippsland Lakes.

Map: Vic 4 E9

Mallacoota

There are three very good reasons for visiting Mallacoota: it is quite famous for its connections with an unusual literary colony, it is the perfect starting point for several bushwalks into the Croajingalong National Park, and it just about the ideal place for fishing.

Located 521 km east of Melbourne, Mallacoota is a peaceful and quiet seaside holiday village which is perfectly suited for families and anglers who arrive and set themselves up beside the water. The most common forms of accommodation are either rented premises or camping and caravans. There is a sign on the outskirts of town which claims that Mallacoota is 'Victoria's Best Kept Secret'. Certainly it is a great place for a relaxing family holiday.

Adjacent to Mallacoota is Croajingalong National Park, a superb wilderness region which claims to be the home to more than 70 native orchards and wildflower species as well as at least 250 different species of birds. It is a perfect destination for bushwalkers and birdwatchers. Croajingalong stretches along more than 100 km of coastline and is home to kangaroos, possums, tree goannas, sea eagles, lyrebirds and kingfishers.

Much of the park is accessible by either boat or vehicle, although some areas can only be reached on foot. There are a number of informative brochures available on Croajingalong National Park. Contact either the Information Centre at Cann River (03 5158 6351) or the Park Office located on Genoa Road, Mallacoota (03 5158 0263).

One of the most interesting developments in the town's history was the arrival of the journalist E. J. Brady, who established a writers' and artists' camp at Captain's Point in 1909. Brady lived in the area until his death in 1952. During that time he was visited by Henry Lawson, Katharine Susannah Prichard and the playwright Louis Esson. All wrote passionately and romantically about their time in Mallacoota. Brady once wrote: 'I have never seen anything in Australia to equal some sunsets that have held me spellbound in Mallacoota.' This is just one of the magical experiences awaiting you when you visit this tiny town to relax.

Map: Vic 4 M8

don't miss

The cave system at Buchan Caves Reserve, 50 km north of Lakes Entrance, was formed by underground rivers cutting through the limestone. Guided tours of Fairy Cave and Royal Cave are operated daily.

VIC

Mallacoota, surrounded by Croajingalong National Park and edged by Mallacoota Inlet and the ocean, is the ideal spot for fishing, bushwalking, 4WD touring or simply getting away from it all.

The North-East

The North-East of Victoria is a region which has been dubbed a place of skiing, wine, gold and bushrangers. It is a strange and unusual combination that includes some of the best snowfields in the Australian alps, some of the most famous vineyards and wineries in the country, some of the most important goldmining towns from the boom days of the Victorian goldfields as well as the home territory of Ned Kelly.

This diversity inevitably means that visitors look towards the North-East with mixed expectations. There are those who start off in Bright and move on to Falls Creek and Mount Buller for the snow and the exercise and excitement of skiing. There are those who come to Rutherglen knowing that they can spend a week wandering through the region, tasting and buying a wealth of excellent wines. Then there are those who look towards historic Beechworth, seeking attractive restaurants and cafés in the midst of one of the country's most perfectly preserved goldmining towns. And, not to ignore them, there are the lovers of the Ned Kelly legend who come to visit Euroa and Glenrowan, knowing that Australia's most famous outlaw lived and committed his crimes in this area.

did you know?

Originally called Morse's Creek, after explorer Hamilton Hume's brother-in-law F. H. Morse, the small town of Bright officially changed its name in 1862 to honour British political reformer John Bright.

Bright and the Snow Country

In autumn, Bright is one of Australia's most beautiful towns. The foliage of the deciduous trees in the area turns a spectacular red and yellow, and the ground is absolutely covered by fallen leaves. There are oaks, chestnuts, poplars, elms and Japanese maples, surrounded by the pines and eucalypts of the mountains. Willows, wattles, plum trees and apple orchards can be seen to best advantage in the spring, when the mountains are carpeted with wildflowers.

The town has become a popular haunt for people wanting something relaxed and charming (good cafés, restaurants and accommodation) before heading off to the Snow Country. The award-winning Bright Chalet (03 5755 1833) offers visitors an Austrian-style ambience.

Named by Hume and Hovell in 1824, Mount Buffalo is one of Australia's oldest ski resorts and lays claim to the first ski lifts in the country.

Bright's magnificent trees provide attractive flowers in spring, welcome shade in summer and brilliant hues in autumn. When they are bare in winter, the scenery of the Victorian Alps can be enjoyed.

Situated a little over 300 km north-east of Melbourne, Bright has good quality off-the-mountain accommodation for those wishing to ski at the nearby resorts of Mount Buffalo, Mount Hotham and Falls Creek. It is also a centre for people looking for activities other than skiing. In the area it is possible to play sports such as golf, mini-golf, bowls, croquet, tennis and squash. It is also possible to go roller-skating, flying, gliding, hang-gliding, horseriding, panning for gold, as well as bushwalking in the mountains and foothills. Water sports such as swimming, canoeing, boating and water-skiing are popular in warmer months. Fishing in the region is also excellent. Good blackfish can be found in the Ovens River, and trout are also plentiful in the lakes and streams of the area and at the Stony Creek Trout Farm, Harrietville.

Mount Buffalo, which is located 320 km north-east of Melbourne, is considered to be the ideal resort for families. It offers good beginners slopes, as well as more advanced tracks. There are also cross-country trails and toboggan courses, ski schools and ski hire. Hang-gliding, abseiling and horse-riding are also possible within the area.

Colourful leaves carpet the streets of Bright during autumn—many of the town's deciduous trees were planted more than a century ago.

Though more famous for its snowfields, Mount Hotham is an attractive location to visit during the warmer months of spring and summer, when bushwalking and rock climbing are popular.

If you are looking for a more exclusive and testing holiday destination then Falls Creek, located 363 km north-east of Melbourne, is considered to be one of the best ski fields in Australia. In winter there are up to 23 chairlifts operating. Seventeen per cent of the slopes are for beginners, 54 per cent are intermediate and 29 per cent are for advanced skiers. The surrounding terrain is also ideal for cross-country skiing.

Mount Hotham is 373 km north-east of Melbourne. At 1840 m, the resort is the most elevated in Australia. In the winter months it has reliable snow and consequently is highly regarded by the skiing community, who claim it has both excellent powder snow and high-quality downhill skiing slopes.

In the summer months all of these mountain locations are ideal for bushwalking and enjoying the invigorating, pollution-free air.

Map: Vic 3 N7

The historic courthouse in Beechworth was the site of the hearing that saw Ned Kelly committed to stand trial in Melbourne for the murders of two constables in 1880.

Beechworth

Quite close to Bright is the delightful township of Beechworth. In a state where many towns came into existence because of the gold rushes in the latter half of the nineteenth century, Beechworth holds a very special place in historians' hearts as it is considered to be Victoria's best-preserved nineteenth-century gold town. Over 30 buildings have been listed with the National Trust and, for the most part, they are substantial and often elegant buildings in excellent condition. The whole main street of the town, particularly when the old horse-drawn carriage (a popular tourist attraction) trundles down it, seems unchanged and timeless. People come to Beechworth to explore the town's historic past. No visit is complete without spending time wandering around the town and simply soaking up the atmosphere of a charming town made prosperous by the hard work and good fortune of goldminers.

The best place to begin your tour of the town is the Beechworth Visitor Information Centre (03 5728 3233). Apart from providing information about the town, it is located in the old Town Hall (1858) and around the back is a small dark cell with a dirt floor where for six months Ned Kelly (then aged 15) was imprisoned following his first conviction.

Just across the road from the Visitor Information Centre is the former courthouse (1858) and the Beechworth Gaol (1859). Both have strong associations with Ned Kelly, his family and his associates. The courthouse is now a museum with items relating to the Kellys and their crimes. The gaol is still being used and therefore is not open to the public—unless, of course, you commit a crime. The courthouse is part of an excellent collection of public buildings which were built between 1857 and 1859. There is the old sub-treasury, the offices of the Chinese Protector and Warden of the Goldfields and the former telegraph office. They all stand prominently at the end of Ford Street. Nearby there are a number of bank buildings which have been converted for a variety of modern uses ranging from restaurants to B&Bs. There are also interesting old churches in town. All the buildings have been beautifully preserved to reflect their former glory.

Chinese Burning Towers at Beechworth Cemetery mark a dark time in the town's history, when racial tension provoked a riot in 1857. During this time many Chinese prospectors were slain.

Of particular interest to history buffs is the Burke Museum (1856) which was established in 1863 in honour of Robert O'Hara Burke, who served as the Superintendent of Police at Beechworth from 1854 to 1858. The museum houses one of the country's largest collections relating to Ned Kelly, his bushranging gang and his family. It includes a revolver used by Joe Byrne; Steve Hart's surcingle; the dock from the courthouse in which Ned Kelly once stood; a replica of the famous armour worn by Ned at Glenrowan; his death mask; and the steps of Aaron Sheritt's hut, where Ned stood while watching Sheritt being gunned down by Byrne.

There are walking tracks, horseriding trails, gold-panning, gem-fossicking, abseiling, 4WD possibilities and trail-bike riding for those who want to go beyond Beechworth's history. The town also has a wide range of accommodation, such as the historic Old Priory (03 5728 1024) and Rose Cottage (03 5728 1069).

Map: Vic 3 M5

VIC

For a relaxing way to see many of the fascinating historic sites in the town of Beechworth, travel as they did in the gold rush era—take a ride down the main street in a restored horse-drawn carriage.

The great tasting room at Stanton & Killeen Wines, established 1875. Many of the vineyards in the Rutherglen area date back to the 1860s, and have been handed down through the generations.

Rutherglen

Rutherglen is located 275 km north-east of Melbourne and only 10 km from the Murray River. Once a rich goldmining town, in recent times it has become the centre of one of Victoria's most important wine-producing areas. People come to Rutherglen to visit the local wineries. They drift from cellar door to cellar door hoping to find a wine which will surprise both their palate and their friends. Robust fortified wines as well as dry reds matured in oak casks are a specialty of the region.

Not surprisingly, over the years the town has acquired a certain old-world charm which attracts visitors. The main street is now an historic precinct with old timber buildings, veranda-fronted pubs, antique and bric-a-brac shops and tearooms.

Those wishing to explore the wineries should ensure that they see at least some of the following: Chambers Rosewood Winery, Campbells Winery, Stanton & Killeen Wines, Bullers Calliope Vineyard, Lake Moodemere Vineyards, Jones Winery, Fairfield Vineyard, Sutherland Smith Wines, Anderson Winery, Mount Prior Vineyard, Warrabilla Wines, Morris Wines and Gehrig Estate.

Tours of the wineries, by bus or by chauffeur-driven service, can be organised here, and there are mountain bikes for hire. Of particular interest for people looking for interesting accommodation is the Mount Ophir Estate which offers bed-and-breakfast accommodation in the homestead, gatehouse, tower and yeast house. For more information, phone (03) 6032 8920.

Map: Vic 3 L4

don't miss

Yackandandah, located south-east of Rutherglen, has so many preserved buildings from the goldmining era that the entire town has been classified by the National Trust. There is also a gorge and waterfall to see nearby.

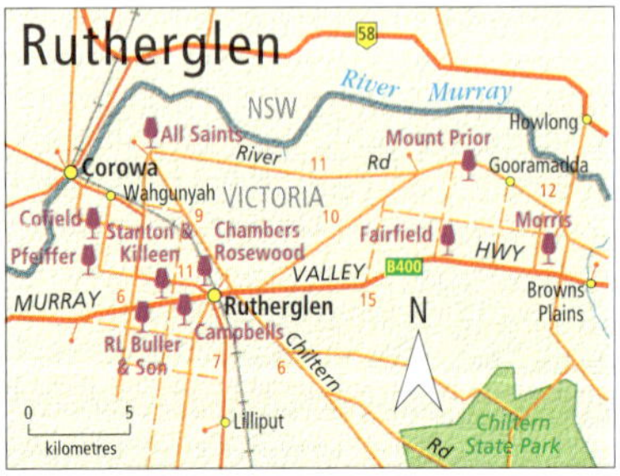

Kelly Country

You could easily spend a week checking out the highlights of Kelly country. Certainly Beechworth, with its museum, has an extensive collection of artefacts. The other main place to visit in the area is Glenrowan, where the 'Big Ned' statue

One of Australia's oldest wine regions and famous for its fortified wines, the picturesque, gently rolling countryside of the Rutherglen area enjoys a continental climate—perfect for viticulture.

VIC

Below: *Undoubtedly Australia's most famous outlaw, Ned Kelly and his homemade armour have been immortalised in this 6-m statue at Glenrowan, scene of his final shootout and subsequent arrest.*

stands beside the road. The reason for this important connection is that it was at Glenrowan that Kelly's gang forced two railway workers to tear up a section of track just to the east of town. They cut the telegraph wires and took over the Glenrowan Inn, detaining about 60 people while they waited to rob the train. It was here that Kelly, wearing his famous armour, tried to hold up the train. He was eventually shot and captured.

If you look carefully, you can search out the original places associated with Ned Kelly around Glenrowan. For those people with children who are quickly bored by historic sites, Kellyland is the place to go. Kellyland is a multi-million dollar cinematic and theatrical depiction of the Kelly gang's last stand, re-enacted by computerised robots. There are four different sets which each relate an important part of the story: the waiting room of Glenrowan railway station, the shootout, the burning hotel and Ned Kelly's execution at Melbourne Gaol. Visitors sit within these settings like first-hand participants, soaking up the atmosphere. Original props include the bar of McDonell's Tavern, an authentic hand-gun owned by Ned, Sergeant Kennedy's hitching post and a rare surviving copy of the findings of the Royal Commission into the Kelly manhunt. It is definitely something which will entertain the children—and many adults too.

Map: Vic 3 K6

Central Victoria

Central Victoria, because of the relative smallness of the state, is within easy reach of Melbourne. Halls Gap in the Grampians is only 251 km north-west of Melbourne, Ballarat is a short 110 km west of Melbourne and Daylesford is 111 km from Melbourne and 45 km from Ballarat. The region is famous for its delightful goldmining towns and for the spa towns where much of Australia's finest mineral water is bottled.

It is an area of rolling hills and historic towns. The visitor will be surprised by the diversity of accommodation and eateries, with nearly all the towns—partly because they are so close to Melbourne—boasting superior B&B and guesthouse accommodation and excellent restaurants well stocked with good quality local and interstate wines. This is a region where the visitor can relax in comfort, go on a number of bushwalks, enjoy good food and visit interesting historic destinations.

The Mackenzie River, named by explorer Major Thomas Mitchell, cascades spectacularly at Mackenzie Falls in the Grampians National Park.

Geographically it is the region which lies to the north-west of Melbourne.

The Grampians

The Grampians consist of four mountain ranges. Halls Gap is located between the southern tip of the Mount Difficult Range and the northern tip of the Mount William Range. The Serra Range runs adjacent to the Mount William Range, along its western side, and the Victoria Range is in the south-west of Grampians National Park.

Left: *The pied currawong* (Strepera graculina) *is just one of over 200 bird species which inhabit the Grampians National Park. Their diet includes small lizards, snails, caterpillars, berries and insects.*

Grampians National Park

Covering an area of 167 000 hectares, Grampians National Park is noted for its diverse range of Aboriginal art sites and a rich variety of flora and fauna which includes 200 bird species, koalas, kangaroos, possums, gliders and echidnas. So rich is the park in flora that it is said to contain a third of Victoria's native plant species.

The best time to visit the park is in spring when the wildflowers bloom and the waterfalls flow. There are numerous scenic drives and more than 90 different walking tracks. Other popular activities are picnicking, camping, rock climbing, fishing (in the reservoirs), cycling, horseriding, photography and nature studies.

There are many camping grounds in the park—all accessible by car and all with fireplaces, picnic tables and toilets (though not all have water). Bush camping is permitted in some areas and under certain conditions.

A sensible place to start your exploration of the Grampians National Park is the visitor centre which is located 2.5 km south of Halls Gap. It has useful information on all aspects of the park: phone (03) 5356 4381. Nearby, and not to be missed, is the Brambuk Aboriginal Cultural Centre (03 5356 4452) where there are displays of art, clothing, tools and weapons relating to the history and culture of the local Australian Aboriginals. There are a couple of interesting walks from the Cultural Centre.

If you want to start on some of the easier walks in the park it is sensible to return to Halls Gap, where three walks leave from the shopping centre. There's the easy Venus Baths Loop Walk (2.3 km) which follows a track along Stony Creek to the natural waterhole known as Venus Baths. Then there is the Bullaces Glen Loop Walk (1.7 km) which goes up to the waterfall and fern gully at Bullaces Glen. For those who are feeling a little more fit and full of energy, there is the superb 12.4-km return walk to Boroka Lookout as well as the medium-grade 9.6-km Wonderland Loop Track.

don't miss

Situated close to the Grampians, Stawell is an ideal jumping-off point for bushwalking and rock climbing. Since 1878, the famous Stawell Gift foot race—Australia's richest running race—has been held each Easter.

Of course this is to merely touch the surface. The national park has in excess of 90 walking tracks and such diversity ensures that everyone is catered for, from the daytripper to the person who wants to spend a fortnight exploring the area. There is also a circular drive from Halls Gap which passes the famous Elephants Hide (a huge rock formation which looks like the back of an elephant) and which runs along the ridge above the town. At various points the non-walker can alight from the car, walk a few hundred metres, and reach lookouts which offer breathtaking views across the whole valley.

Map: Vic 5 G3

The rugged peaks around Halls Gap are ideal for rock climbing and hang gliding. In spring, the mountains are covered in colourful wildflowers.

Halls Gap

The emotional, and practical, heart of The Grampians is the tourist town of Halls Gap, which is located on the floor of the Fyans Valley, 251 km north-west of Melbourne via Ararat. It is situated at the eastern edge of Grampians National Park, and it offers the visitor a wide range of bushwalking options and cultural experiences.

A vast number of organisations in Halls Gap conduct a variety of tours (by foot, bicycle, mountain bike, 4WD, hot-air balloon, aeroplane, canoe, camel, horse and horse-drawn vehicle) into or over the Grampians as well as the district generally. There are also abseiling and fishing tours. Nearby Lake Bellfield is an ideal spot for sailing and fishing.

Halls Gap offers a wide range of accommodation, from B&Bs to motels. The camping in the region is particularly good. While there are a number of local restaurants and cafés, they are pitched more at holidaymakers than at eaters of fine cuisine.

Map: Vic 5 G2

Established in 1858, Ballarat Botanical Gardens has a wonderful collection of statuary, including this sculpture of Scottish poet Robert Burns.

Ballarat

Ballarat is one of Australia's major inland cities. Located 110 km west of Melbourne, it is a thriving city relying on tourism, retail, manufacturing and community services as its economic mainstays. So why visit this large city? Well, it is an exceptionally grand old city. The first impression you are left with is one of stateliness and grandeur produced by the magnificent wide thoroughfares, the Victorian and Edwardian architecture, tree-lined avenues, parks, gardens and statuary. Ballarat grew rich on the goldfields which surrounded it and it made sure the world knew how grand it was.

The visitor could usefully spend half a day just wandering through the city centre and enjoying the various vistas, where great buildings stand tall behind statues of Queen Victoria and various local dignitaries. In Lydiard Street, for example, there is the beautiful facade of Her Majesty's Theatre (1875) and the

Aboriginal arts, crafts and cultural displays, acknowledging the long Koori association with the Grampians region, can be seen at the Brambuk Living Cultural Centre near Halls Gap.

did you know?

The world's second-largest gold nugget, known as the 'Welcome Nugget', was found by 22 Cornish miners at Bakery Hill near Ballarat on 9 June, 1858. It weighed a massive 68 956 grams.

VIC

fascinating three-storey Craig's Hotel which evolved from Bath's Hotel, built in 1853 by Thomas Bath. It was subsequently used as the headquarters of the visiting Duke of Edinburgh in 1867. The Australian poet Adam Lindsay Gordon ran Craig's Livery Stables in 1867–68 and American writer Mark Twain stayed at the hotel during a visit in the 1890s.

But the real attraction in Ballarat is the remarkable Sovereign Hill theme park which is so good, and so interesting, that any visitor should really spend a day (and perhaps half the night) exploring all its buildings and enjoying its experiences. A non-profit organisation, Sovereign Hill re-creates Ballarat as it was during the goldmining heyday of the 1850s. There are over 60 buildings which replicate original buildings in the town and each day 250 actors in authentic costumes engage in activities appropriate to the era. Even the sounds are what you might expect to hear on a

Ballarat's Sovereign Hill features a number of buildings that would have been found in an 1850s gold-rush town, from a Chinese temple to a blacksmith's shop.

don't miss

Kryal Castle, south of Ballarat, features re-enactments of medieval life. Constructed in the style of a Gothic castle, and the third largest of its type in the world, this theme park is a popular tourist attraction.

goldfield during the nineteenth century—steam engines, stamper batteries, horses' hooves and passenger coaches.

At night a sound-and-light show called 'Blood on the Southern Cross' re-creates the sights and sounds associated with the Eureka Stockade Rebellion, including the burning of the Eureka Hotel. Phone (03) 5333 5777 for bookings.

Map: Vic 5 M4

Bendigo

Bendigo is another gracious city made rich by the profits of goldmining. It has one of the finest collections of Victorian buildings of any inland city in Australia. Many of the streets are characterised by huge granite public buildings and, in the centre of the city, there is a fountain dedicated to Queen Victoria's daughter-in-law, Princess Alexandra, which sits in the middle of the main street. Located just 150 km north-west of Melbourne, the appeal of Bendigo lies largely in enjoying the unusual and fascinating history of the city.

Bendigo's Sacred Heart Cathedral, the largest in Victoria outside Melbourne, is said to be the last Gothic-style cathedral built in the world.

No trip to Bendigo can be considered complete unless the visitor has taken a quiet stroll through Rosalind Park on Pall Mall; admired the marvellously complementary architectural style of the Post Office (1883–87) and the Law Courts (1892–96); taken a guided tour of the Deborah Mine (phone 03 5443 8070 for details); visited the Chinese Joss House (1860) at Emu Point (03 5442 1685); or visited the Golden Dragon Museum to see the world's oldest imperial dragon and the world's longest imperial dragon (at over 100 m long, the dragon requires 52 men to carry it).

The outstanding Bendigo Art Gallery is an essential place to visit as it contains works by Alfred Sisley, Gustave Courbet and Theodore Rousseau plus Australian artists Arthur Streeton, George Lambert, Rupert Bunny, Grace Cossington Smith, Lloyd Rees, Jeffrey Smart, Clifton Pugh, Fred Williams, John Olson and Kwementwary Kngwarreye. It is also worth spending some time investigating Bendigo's excellent potteries and the fine vineyards that lie just outside the city, including Chateau Leamon and Jasper Hill.

Map: Vic 3 C7

Right: *Built in 1897 and still operating, the historic Shamrock Hotel in Bendigo, with its magnificent Victorian architecture, reflects the wealth of the town during the goldmining years.*

Daylesford and Hepburn Springs

The area around Daylesford and Hepburn Springs is known as the 'Spa Capital of Australia'. Daylesford is located at a point where waters trapped within subterranean basins have slowly leached minerals from 450-million-year-old rocks. These minerals are believed to have a curative effect, and both Daylesford and Hepburn Springs are sitting on 50 per cent of the country's known and active mineral water outlets and another 30 per cent is located nearby.

In conjunction with all the springs and spas (where you can bask in the rejuvenating waters), there are many 'alternative' services including massage, reiki, shiatsu, acupuncture, aromatherapy, reflexology, spiritual healing, tarot and psychic readings that operate in the area. They are listed in a brochure that is available from the Daylesford Visitor Centre (03 5348 1339). If all that sounds too healthy, there are several wineries and many excellent restaurants in the region.

For those who are happy just to relax within the local area, Lake Daylesford is a delightful retreat with a pleasant teahouse on the water's edge. It is also a popular fishing spot with picnic and barbecue facilities. There is a peaceful walking track around the lake and rowboats, aquabikes, paddleboats, canoes and surf skis can be hired on the foreshore.

Map: Vic 3 B9

The Boathouse Café on Lake Daylesford is a tranquil place to relax and watch the world go by. The man-made lake was created in 1929 where the Wombat Flat gold diggings once stood.

The South-Western Coast and Hinterland

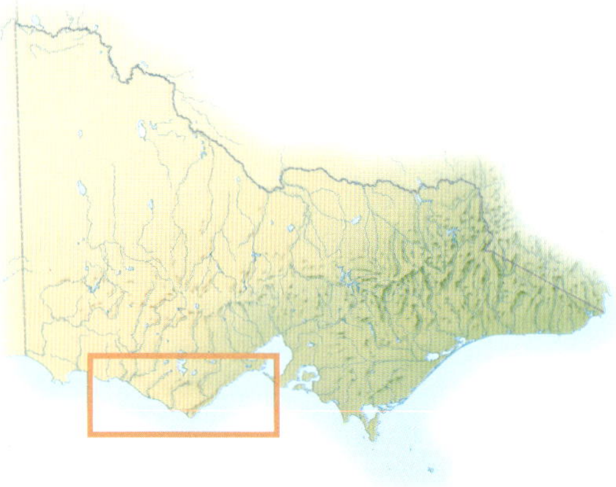

There may be more famous and popular stretches of coastline—the Gold Coast, the Sunshine Coast, the Whitsundays—but there is an argument that the Victorian coast from Port Phillip Bay to the South Australian border is the most beautiful stretch of coast anywhere in Australia.

The elegant beauty of Queenscliff, the delightful wineries and vineyards of the Bellarine Peninsula, the glorious views and vantage points of the Great Ocean Road culminating in the Twelve Apostles and the remnants of London Bridge, the historic charm of Port Fairy and Portland all add up to a region that is very special and which is an ideal destination for people eager to gaze and relax.

Queenscliff

If you are looking for pure sophistication and charm—a real escape from Melbourne but with all the city's attractions—it is hard to look beyond Queenscliff and the Bellarine Peninsula. Queenscliff is located on an isthmus at the south-eastern tip of the Bellarine Peninsula. The town sits just inside the entrance to Port Phillip Bay, 103 km south of Melbourne and 30 km east of Geelong. The real appeal of Queenscliff is that it combines fascinating maritime history with plenty of classy restaurants and a wide range of weekender-style accommodation. This attraction has been going on since the 1880s. At that time the town became a fashionable weekend getaway for the wealthier classes of Melbourne society who made their way across Port Phillip Bay in paddle-steamers.

Warning shipping traffic and pleasure craft alike of the treacherous waters, Point Lonsdale Lighthouse has stood guard on Port Phillip Bay since 1902.

Today visitors often start their exploration of the town at the Queenscliff Historical Centre and Museum which houses about 10 000 items, including historical artefacts, photographs, documents, lace, textiles and relics from local shipwrecks. They then move on to the Queenscliff Hotel (1887–88), a symbol of the town's gracious past which, although carefully restored, has not been modernised at all. It offers excellent lunches in a genteel ambience. After lunch they would move on to Fort Queenscliff which was built on Shortlands Bluff, overlooking the commercial shipping lanes to Melbourne and Geelong. The fort is open for inspection on the weekends.

For more active people, the town also offers trips on the old Bellarine Railway, dolphin-watching tours, diving, cycling, walking and fishing—including fishing boat chartering.

Nearby there are a number of excellent wineries including the well-known Scotchmans Hill Winery near Drysdale.

Map: Vic 6 B5

Ocean Grove and Barwon Heads boast over 6 km of pristine sandy beaches—the most popular of which is Smiths Beach. The local waters attract surfers, divers, water-skiers and sailors.

Ocean Grove and Barwon Heads

There is always an argument for doing nothing but enjoying the sea air and lying on a beach. The most popular place in the entire South-West has to be the twin towns of Ocean Grove and Barwon Heads (made famous by their appearance in the ABC-TV series 'SeaChange'). They seem to have endless caravan parks and

Scotchmans Hill Vineyard was the first winery on the beautiful Bellarine Peninsula. Its pinot noir is especially good, with a rich cherry and plum fruit aroma and a taste that hints at strawberry.

don't miss

Portarlington on the Bellarine Peninsula is a popular getaway destination. This picturesque small town offers sandy beaches, sailing, surfing, snorkelling, fishing, historic buildings and several vineyards close by.

camping facilities, plenty of fast-food eateries beside the beach and lots of areas (with many options) where families and groups can gather and enjoy themselves.

Ocean Grove is located only 25 km south-west of Geelong and 98 km south of Melbourne. It lies on the eastern bank of the Barwon River estuary, which separates it from its twin town of Barwon Heads. The two towns have the closest ocean beaches to Geelong, and there are safe family beaches along the banks of the river. The place to go in Ocean Grove is Smiths Beach, which is very popular for swimming, surfing and fishing.

There are also good walking trails in the area. Try the Ocean Grove Nature Reserve, which is located at the northern edge of town. The reserve has two enjoyable 3-km walking tracks and two birdhides for birdwatching enthusiasts.

Being a popular tourist destination, the area hasn't totally escaped from the high-profile fun parks. Adventure Park has just about every imaginable activity including a 100-m tube waterslide, go-karts, a nine-hole golf course, jumping castles, an archery range, a merry-go-round, paddleboats, Adventure Island mini-golf, aqua bikes, canoes, mountain-bike riding, the Adventure Express Train and the Adventure Playground.

At nearby Barwon Heads, which is only 22 km south-east of Geelong, the major attractions are walking around 'The Bluff' (also known as Barwon Head) which has a delightful ocean-viewing point (it extends out from the south-eastern corner of town beyond the river mouth and out into Bass Strait) and the Jirrahlinga Koala and Wildlife Sanctuary which is home to a range of native animals. There is a hospital where sick, injured or orphaned animals are nursed back to health. Contact (03) 5254 2484 for details.

Map: Vic 6 B5

Right: *As well as koalas* (Phascolarctos cinereus), *the Jirrahlinga Koala and Wildlife Sanctuary cares for possums, kangaroos, seals and an abundance of native birds such as owls and cockatoos.*

The Great Ocean Road

The Great Ocean Road starts at the Memorial Arch north of Lorne and continues for nearly 200 km until it reaches the town of Warrnambool. It is considered by many to be the finest coastal road in Australia. Built after World War I, it was initially conceived as a memorial to those who had fought in the war and all road builders were ex-servicemen. The section as far as Lorne was opened in 1922 and the roadworks continued for the next decade. The road to Warrnambool was not completed until 1933. Today some people like to stretch the Great Ocean Road, arguing that it

There are many lookouts along the Great Ocean Road, offering breathtaking views of pretty bays, sandy beaches and unpredictable Bass Strait, often with a dramatic backdrop of cliffs.

really starts at Geelong and continues to the South Australian border, also including the charming Port Fairy and Portland. However, this is not technically correct.

The appeal of the Great Ocean Road is that it is largely untouched. There are no high-rise tourist developments, no commercialised fun parks, no evidence of excesses of fast-food shops. It is an area of cliffs, rivers, forests and beautiful vistas across the Southern Ocean. It is sleepy and charming with an emphasis on both B&B and guesthouse accommodation and lazy eating—preferably fish and chips—in the parks and gardens that lie beside the ocean. People come here for a variety of reasons. Some come to marvel at the natural wonder of the Twelve Apostles. Others just want a quiet beach holiday and still others seek the cool comfort of the bushwalks through the picturesque Otway National Park.

Triplet Falls cascades past lush rainforest vegetation within the cool-temperate climate of Otway National Park, on the Great Ocean Road near Apollo Bay.

The Twelve Apostles were once part of a limestone cave system. Ocean waves have worn the outer limestone away, leaving these stacks. There are now just eight stacks left standing above the water line.

Port Campbell and the Twelve Apostles

No journey along the beautiful Great Ocean Road is complete without spending at least a day going from one vantage point to the next as you make your way from just east of Port Campbell along the coast to the township of Peterborough. Everyone has seen photographs of the Twelve Apostles—they do not disappoint in real life. The 'stacks', as they are known, are vertically jointed and flat-bedded limestone, with some standing 65 m above sea-level. There are excellent viewing platforms.

Loch Ard Gorge is only 7 km east of Port Campbell and was named after the iron clipper *Loch Ard* which was shipwrecked here on 1 June, 1878. London Bridge is another impressive formation which once looked like a bridge but now looks like another stack because it collapsed on 15 January, 1990, and became a bridge without a middle. Two people were on the bridge at the time but no one was injured.

This is a stretch of coastline which is all about driving and viewing. It is quite difficult to stay in Port Campbell because of the limited accommodation, but the township does have a number of good restaurants which are happy to serve the excellent local seafood.

Map: Vic 5 J8

don't miss

With a canopy of eucalypts and myrtle beech—including a 200-year-old specimen known as 'Big Tree'—and a light show provided by glow worms, Melba Gully State Forest (about 40 km east of Port Campbell) is a delight.

Port Fairy

Port Fairy is a charming old fishing village which is located about 290 km west of Melbourne, on the eastern headland of Portland Bay. The town is one of those delightful places where there is so much to see and do—not to mention just wandering around and enjoying the salty seaside ambience. There are museums to visit, historic walks, pleasant stretches of coastline, a fascinating harbour and charming old-world cottages. The Port Fairy Folk Festival (held annually in March) is recognised as the best of its kind in Australia, and each year tens of thousands of people flock to it.

There are over 50 historic buildings in Port Fairy, ranging from gracious public buildings (the ANZ Bank, for example, was originally known as The Colonial Bank and opened its doors to the public in 1856) to enchanting old homes such as Mott's Cottage, which was built some time in the 1830s or 1840s. The local Visitor Information Centre has a useful brochure listing all the buildings.

For those looking for activities, Port Fairy is ideal for fishing, and there is an unusual 2.1-km Shipwreck Walk which starts at the local surf club and runs to

the mouth of the Moyne River. The shipwrecks along this short stretch of coastline include the barque *Socrates*, which was battered and finally destroyed by huge seas in 1843; the barque *Lydia*, which was wrecked off the coast in 1847; the schooner *Thistle*, which broke her anchor chain and was wrecked on the coast in 1837 and the brig *Essington*, which sank while moored at Port Fairy in 1852.

The town also has an excellent Botanic Gardens and, for those who are interested in discovering the local flora and fauna, there are trips out to Lady Julia Percy Island, situated 17 km from Port Fairy, which is home to rookeries of muttonbirds, swamp harriers, sooty oystercatchers, kestrels and blue penguins. There are also seals which can sometimes be found on the ledges around the shoreline, eating squid and crabs. These trips depend entirely on the suitability of the weather.

Map: Vic 5 F7

The natural harbour of Port Fairy is an ideal place to cast a line. The town supplies a major share of Victoria's abalone and crayfish catch.

The rugged coastline and treacherous waters between Port Fairy and the headlands of Otway National Park are known as 'The Shipwreck Coast', as many vessels have foundered here.

Map 1

NSW 5
VIC 2
SA 4
NORTH
A
B
C
D
E
F
G
1
2
3
4
5
6
7
8
9
10
141°
142°
34°
35°
Danggali Cons Park
Chowilla Regional Reserve
Chowilla Game Reserve
Border Cliffs
Lake Victoria
Cal Lal
Rufus River
Lindsay Point
Lindsay Island
Lindsay
Murray River
Lake Wallawalla
Murray-Sunset National Park
Warrananga
SILVER CITY HWY
Tapio
Fletcher Lake
Wamberra
Wentworth
Curlwaa
Dareton
Lake Gol Gol
Buronga
Gol Gol
Merbein
Mildura
Birdwoodton
Merbein South
Irymple
Trentham Cliffs
Wallpolla Is
Wallpolla Creek
NSW
VIC
Kulnine
Neds Corner
Lake Cullulleraine
STURT HWY
Meringur North
Cullulleraine
Merrinee North
Lake Benetook
Cardross
Red Cliffs
Monak
Karadoc
Karadoc Swamp
Morkalla
Karween
Meringur
Yarrara
Bambill
Werrimull
Karawinna
Merrinee
Pirlta
Benetook
Thurla
Yatpool
Tarrango
Carwarp
Tunart
Kurnwill
Nangiloc
Colignan
CALDER
Taldra
SOUTH AUSTRALIA
VICTORIA
Taplan
SUNSET COUNTRY
Rocket Lake
Raak Plain
Nowingi
Hattah-Kulkyne National Park
Kulkyne
Murray-Kulkyne National Park
Lake Hattah
Lake Kramen
Hattah
Meribah
Millewa South Bore
Murray-Sunset National Park
Mt Cowra
Mt Crozier
Cramenton
Trinita
Peebinga
Bellbird Bore
Berrook
Peebinga Cons Pk
Pink Lakes
Mt Gnarr
Mt Gray
Kiamal
Ouyen
MALLEE
Wagant
Boltons Bore
Goongee
Pallarang
Paignie
Galah
Booroongie
Manya
Sunset
Torrita
Walpeup
Nunga
CALDER
Linga
Underbool
Bronzewing
Panitya
Tutye
Boinka
Timberoo South
Pinnaroo
Carina
MALLEE
Danyo
Murrayville
Cowangie
HWY
SUNRAYSIA
Gypsum
Kelley Lookout
Mt Observatory
Dering
Wirrengren Plain
Mt Jenkins
Patchewollock
Tempy
BIG DESERT
Baring
Speed
Scorpion Springs Cons Park
Pine Plains
Lake Agnes
Willa
Turriff West
Turriff
Big Billy
Wyperfeld National Park
Yarto
HWY
Gama
Mt Mattingley
Big Desert Wilderness Park
Lascelles
Ngarkat Conservation Park
Hopetoun West
Nypo
Lake Albacutya
Hopetoun
Lake Coorong
Moonlight Tank
A20
A79
B12
B220
B200
C252
79
12
20
147
73
35
139
67
87
26

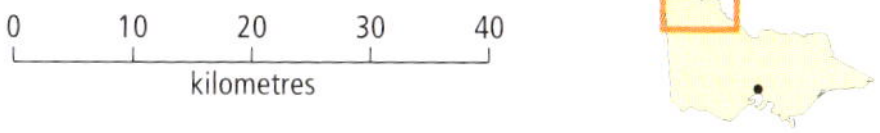

NSW 5

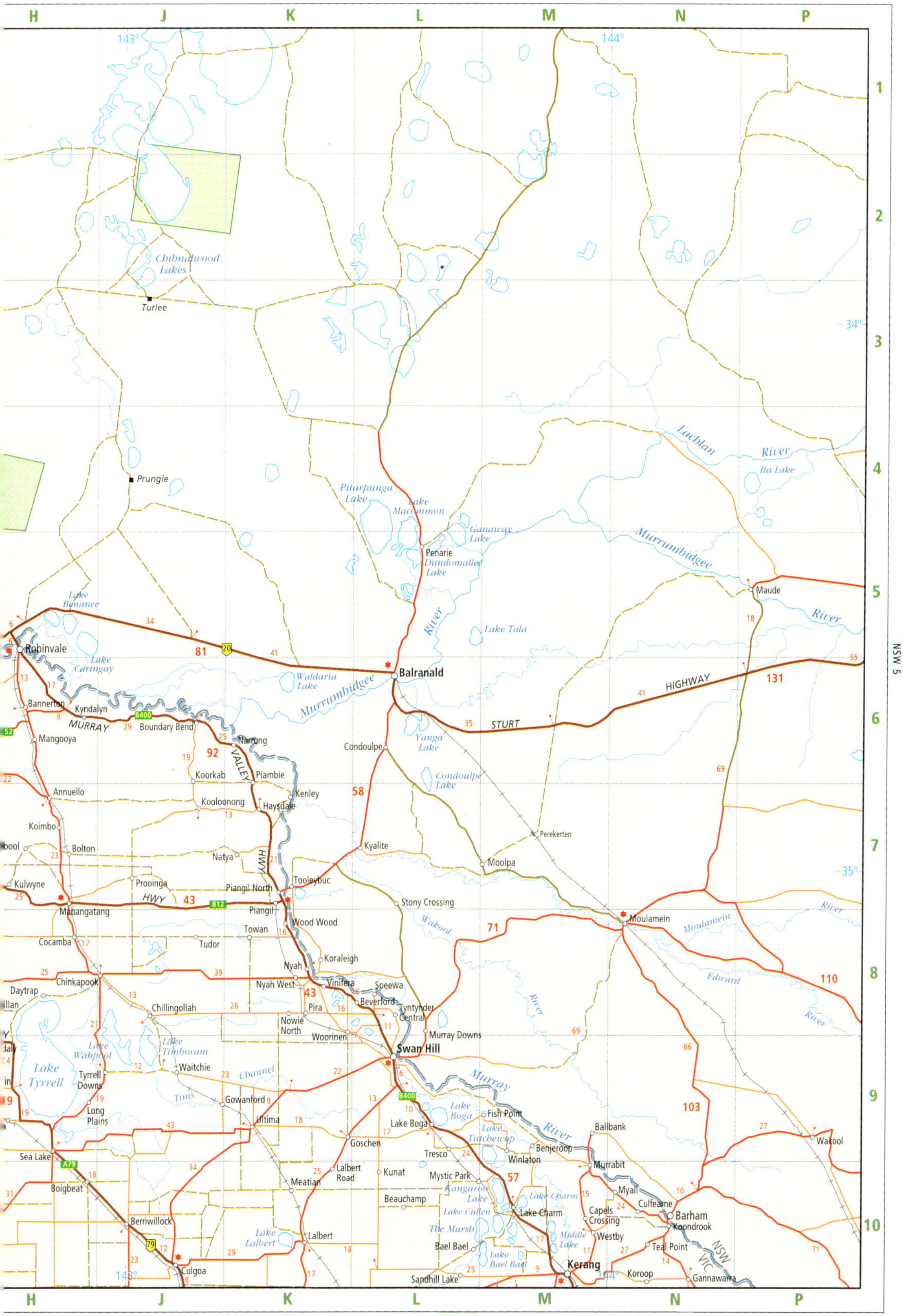

VIC 2

VIC

Map 2

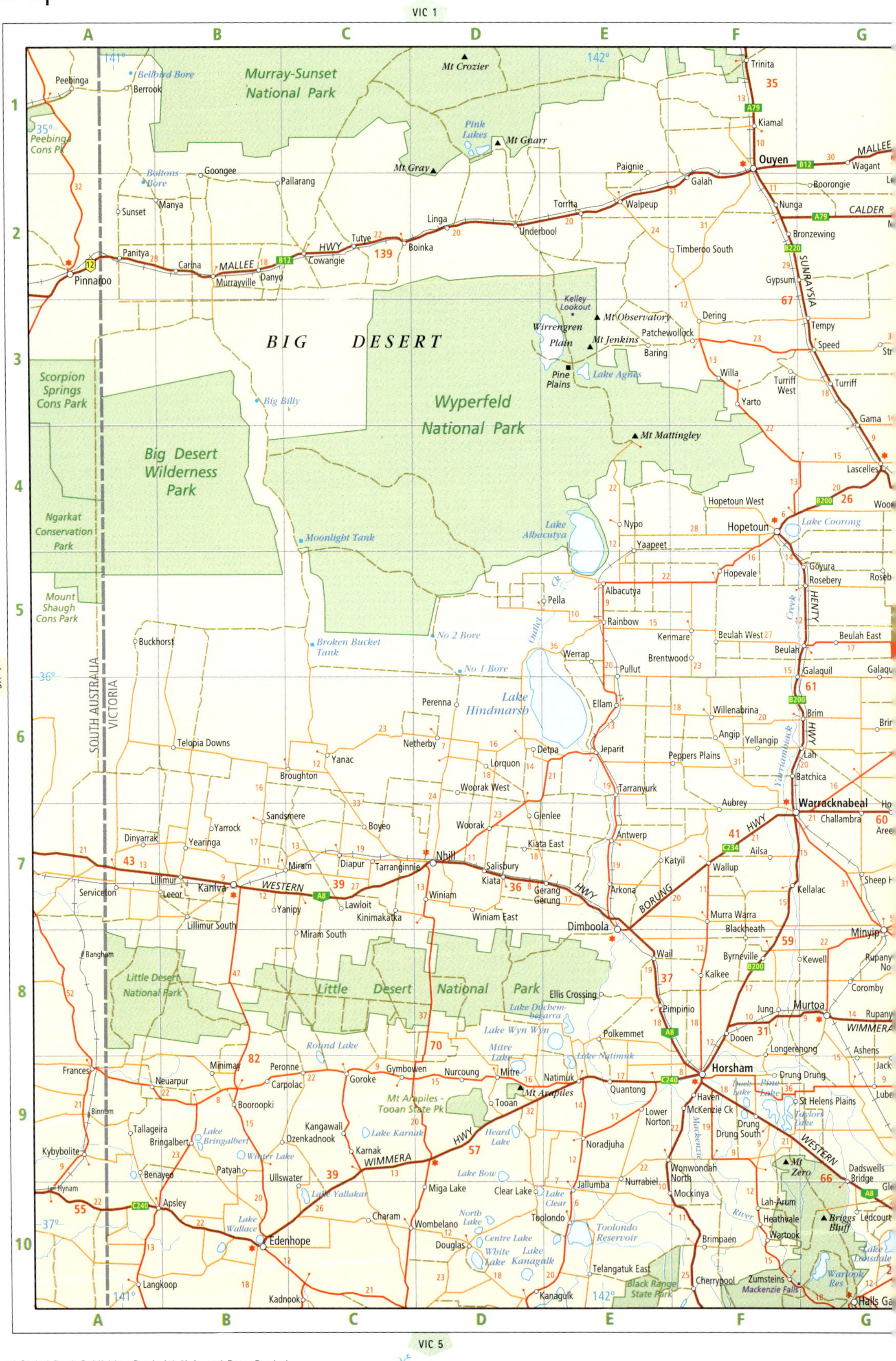
VIC 1
A
B
C
D
E
F
G
1
2
3
4
5
6
7
8
9
10
SA 4
VIC 5
141°
142°
35°
36°
37°
SOUTH AUSTRALIA
VICTORIA
Murray-Sunset National Park
Mt Crozier
Pink Lakes
Mt Gnarr
Mt Gray
Peebinga
Bellbird Bore
Berrook
Peebinga Cons Pk
Boltons Bore
Goongee
Pallarang
Manya
Sunset
Panitya
Pinnaroo
Carina
MALLEE
Murrayville
Danyo
HWY
Cowangie
Tutye
Boinka
Linga
Underbool
Torrita
Walpeup
Paignie
Galah
Trinita
Kiamal
Ouyen
Wagant
Boorongie
Nunga
CALDER
Bronzewing
Timberoo South
Gypsum
SUNRAYSIA
BIG DESERT
Kelley Lookout
Mt Observatory
Wirrengren Plain
Mt Jenkins
Pine Plains
Lake Agnes
Patchewollock
Baring
Dering
Tempy
Speed
Willa
Turriff West
Turriff
Yarto
Gama
Lascelles
Scorpion Springs Cons Park
Big Billy
Wyperfeld National Park
Mt Mattingley
Big Desert Wilderness Park
Ngarkat Conservation Park
Moonlight Tank
Lake Albacutya
Nypo
Hopetoun West
Hopetoun
Lake Coorong
Yaapeet
Hopevale
Goyura
Rosebery
HENTY
Mount Shaugh Cons Park
Pella
Albacutya
Rainbow
Kenmare
Beulah West
Beulah East
Beulah
Brentwood
Galaquil
Buckhorst
Broken Bucket Tank
No 2 Bore
No 1 Bore
Outlet Ck
Werrap
Pullut
Creek
Lake Hindmarsh
Perenna
Ellam
Willenabrina
Brim
HWY
Angip
Yellangip
Yarriambiack
Telopia Downs
Netherby
Yanac
Lorquon
Detpa
Jeparit
Peppers Plains
Lah
Broughton
Woorak West
Tarranyurk
Batchica
Aubrey
Warracknabeal
Challambra
Sandsmere
Boyeo
Woorak
Glenlee
Yarrock
Dinyarrak
Yearinga
Antwerp
Kiata East
Katyil
Ailsa
Wallup
Nhill
Diapur
Tarranginnie
Miram
Salisbury
Kiata
Lillimur
Kaniva
Leeor
Serviceton
WESTERN
Yanipy
Lawloit
Kinimakatka
Winiam
Winiam East
Gerang Gerung
Arkona
BORUNG
HWY
Kellalac
Sheep Hills
Murra Warra
Blackheath
Dimboola
Minyip
Lillimur South
Miram South
Bangham
Wail
Byrneville
Kewell
Kalkee
Rupanyup North
Corombry
Little Desert National Park
Little Desert National Park
Ellis Crossing
Lake Duchembegarra
Pimpinio
Jung
Murtoa
Rupanyup
WIMMERA
Lake Wyn Wyn
Polkemmet
Dooen
Longerenong
Ashens
Round Lake
Mitre Lake
Lake Natimuk
Frances
Minimay
Peronne
Gymbowen
Nurcoung
Mitre
Natimuk
Horsham
Drung Drung
Neuarpur
Carpolac
Goroke
Quantong
Haven
Duck Lake
Pine Lake
St Helens Plains
Mt Arapiles
Tooan
Binnum
Booroopki
Mt Arapiles-Tooan State Pk
McKenzie Ck
Taylors Lake
Tallageira
Bringalbert
Lake Bringalbert
Kangawall
Ozenkadnook
Lake Karnak
Heard Lake
Lower Norton
Drung
Drung South
Mackenzie
Kybybolite
Winter Lake
Karnak
WIMMERA
HWY
Noradjuha
Benayeo
Patyah
Ullswater
WESTERN
Mt Zero
Dadswells Bridge
Wonwondah North
Hynam
Lake Bow
Nurrabiel
Apsley
Lake Yallakar
Miga Lake
Clear Lake
Lake Clear
Jallumba
Mockinya
Lah-Arum
River
Heathvale
Briggs Bluff
Ledcourt
Lake Wallace
Charam
North Lake
Toolondo
Toolondo Reservoir
Wartook
Edenhope
Wombelano
Centre Lake
Douglas
White Lake
Lake Kanagulk
Brimpaen
Lake Lonsdale
Telangatuk East
Black Range State Park
Cherrypool
Zumsteins
Mackenzie Falls
Wartook Res
Langkoop
Kadnook
Kanagulk
Halls Gap

VIC 1

VIC 3

VIC 5

Map 3

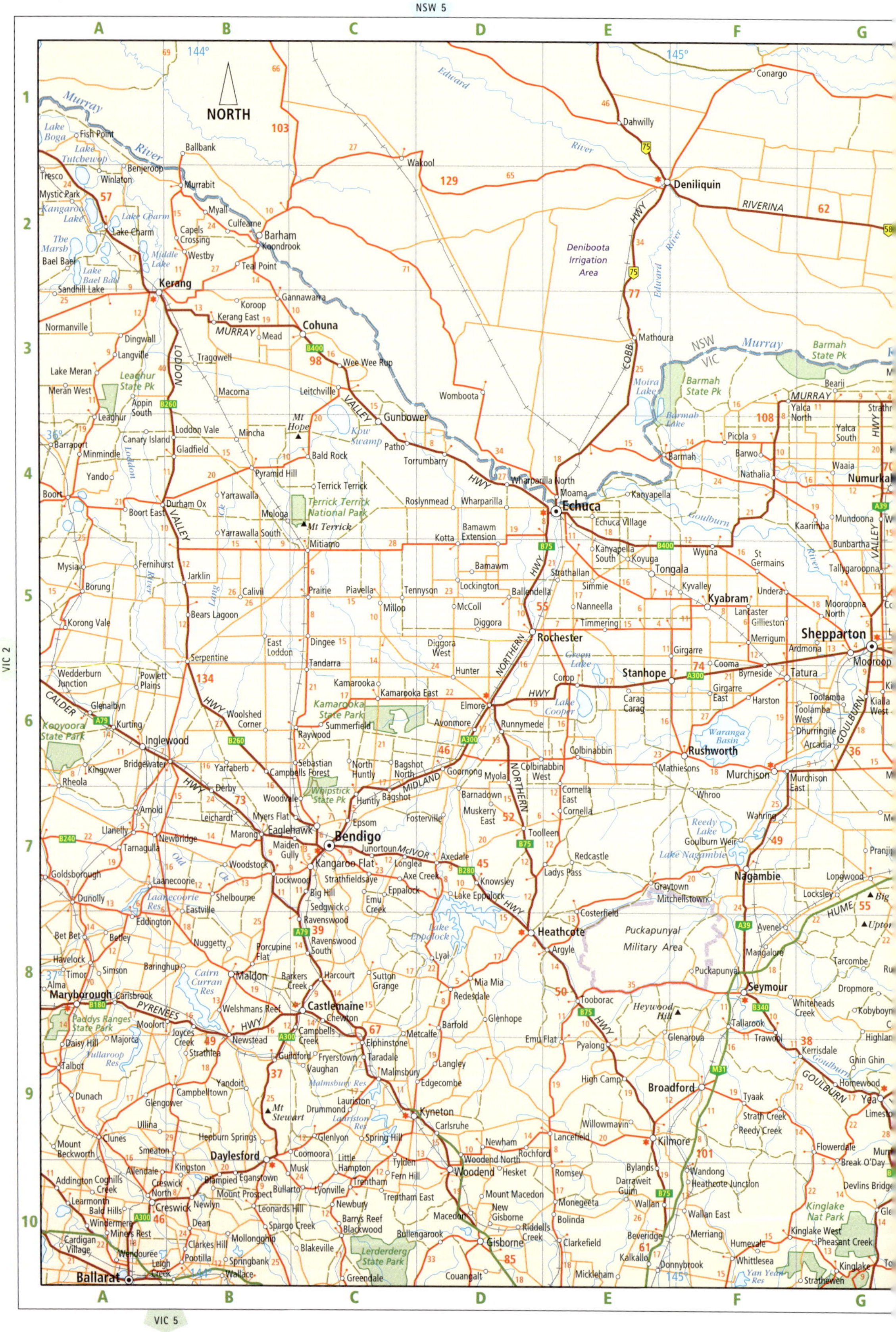
NSW 5
VIC 2
VIC 5
A
B
C
D
E
F
G
1
2
3
4
5
6
7
8
9
10
144°
145°
36°
37°
NORTH
Murray River
Lake Boga
Fish Point
Lake Tutchewop
Tresco
Benjeroop
Winlaton
Mystic Park
Kangaroo Lake
Lake Charm
The Marsh
Bael Bael
Lake Bael Bael
Sandhill Lake
Middle Lake
Ballbank
Murrabit
Myall
Capels Crossing
Westby
Culfearne
Barham
Koondrook
Teal Point
Kerang
Gannawarra
Koroop
Kerang East
Cohuna
MURRAY
Mead
Normanville
Dingwall
Langville
Tragowel
Wee Wee Rup
Lake Meran
Meran West
Leaghur State Pk
LODDON
Macorna
Leitchville
VALLEY
Appin South
Leaghur
Loddon Vale
Mincha
Mt Hope
Gunbower
Kow Swamp
Patho
Torrumbarry
Barraport
Minmindie
Canary Island
Gladfield
Bald Rock
Pyramid Hill
Yando
Loddon
Terrick Terrick
Terrick Terrick National Park
Mt Terrick
Boort
Durham Ox
Boort East
Yarrawalla
Yarrawalla South
Mologa
Mitiamo
Roslynmead
Wharparilla
Wharparilla North
HWY
Moama
Echuca
Echuca Village
Kanyapella
Kotta
Bamawm Extension
Bamawm
Lockington
Mysia
Fernihurst
Jarklin
Borung
Calivil
Prairie
Piavella
Tennyson
Millop
McColl
Diggora
Ballendella
Strathallan
Simmie
Nanneella
Timmering
Kanyapella South
Koyuga
Tonga la
Kyvalley
Kyabram
Lancaster
Gillieston
Merrigum
Korong Vale
Bears Lagoon
Dingee
East Loddon
Diggora West
Rochester
Green Lake
Serpentine
Tandarra
Hunter
Corop
Stanhope
Girgarre
Cooma
Byrneside
Tatura
Wedderburn Junction
Powlett Plains
Kamarooka
Kamarooka East
NORTHERN
Lake Cooper
Carag Carag
Girgarre East
Harston
Glenalbyn
CALDER
Kurting
Kooyoora State Park
Woolshed Corner
Kamarooka State Park
Summerfield
Elmore
Avonmore
Runnymede
Waranga Basin
Inglewood
Raywood
Rushworth
Kingower
Bridgewater
Rheola
Yarraberb
Sebastian
Campbells Forest
North Huntly
Bagshot North
Goornong
Myola
Colbinabbin
Colbinabbin West
Mathiesons
Murchison
Murchison East
Derby
Whipstick State Pk
MIDLAND
Barnadown
Cornella
Cornella East
Whroo
Arnold
Leichardt
Woodvale
Huntly
Bagshot
Muskerry East
Fosterville
Tooleen
Reedy Lake
Wahring
Llanelly
Myers Flat
Eaglehawk
Epsom
Marong
Bendigo
Junortoun
McIVOR
Goulburn Weir
Tarnagulla
Newbridge
Maiden Gully
Axedale
Redcastle
Lake Nagambie
Nagambie
Goldsborough
Woodstock
Kangaroo Flat
Longlea
Axe Creek
Knowsley
Ladys Pass
Laanecoorie
Lockwood
Strathfieldsaye
Graytown
Mitchellstown
Longwood
Locksley
Dunolly
Laanecoorie Res
Shelbourne
Big Hill
Emu Creek
Eppalock
Lake Eppalock
Costerfield
HUME
Eastville
Sedgwick
Ravenswood
Heathcote
Puckapunyal Military Area
Avenel
Eddington
Nuggetty
Porcupine Flat
Ravenswood South
Argyle
Mangalore
Bet Bet
Betley
Havelock
Simson
Baringhup
Cairn Curran Res
Maldon
Barkers Creek
Harcourt
Sutton Grange
Lyal
Mia Mia
Redesdale
Puckapunyal
Tarcombe
Timor
Alma
Maryborough
Carisbrook
Welshmans Reef
Castlemaine
Chewton
Tooborac
Seymour
Whiteheads Creek
Dropmore
Kobyboyn
Paddys Ranges State Park
PYRENEES
Moolort
Joyces Creek
Newstead
Campbells Creek
Metcalfe
Elphinstone
Barfold
Glenhope
Emu Flat
Heywood Hill
Tallarook
Trawool
Highlands
Daisy Hill
Majorca
Strathlea
Guildford
Fryerstown
Taradale
Pyalong
Glenaroua
Kerrisdale
Talbot
Tullaroop Res
Vaughan
Malmsbury
Langley
Ghin Ghin
Goulburn River
Yandoit
Malmsbury Res
Edgecombe
High Camp
Broadford
Homewood
Dunach
Campbelltown
Mt Stewart
Drummond
Lauriston
Tyaak
Yea
Glengower
Kyneton
Carlsruhe
Strath Creek
Limestone
Ullina
Lauriston Res
Willowmavin
Reedy Creek
Mount Beckworth
Clunes
Hepburn Springs
Glenlyon
Spring Hill
Newham
Lancefield
Kilmore
Flowerdale
Smeaton
Daylesford
Coomoora
Little Hampton
Tylden
Woodend North
Rochford
Murrindindi
Allendale
Kingston
Musk
Woodend
Hesket
Romsey
Bylands
Wandong
Break O'Day
Addington
Coghills Creek
Creswick North
Blampied
Eganstown
Mount Prospect
Bullarto
Trentham
Fern Hill
Darraweit Guim
Heathcote Junction
Devlins Bridge
Learmonth
Creswick
Newlyn
Lyonville
Trentham East
Mount Macedon
Monegeeta
Wallan
Wallan East
Glenburn
Bald Hills
Windermere
Leonards Hill
Newbury
New Gisborne
Bolinda
Kinglake Nat Park
Dean
Spargo Creek
Barrys Reef
Blackwood
Macedon
Riddells Creek
Beveridge
Merriang
Kinglake West
Cardigan Village
Miners Rest
Clarkes Hill
Mollongghip
Bullengarook
Gisborne
Clarkefield
Humevale
Pheasant Creek
Wendouree
Pootilla
Springbank
Blakeville
Lerderderg State Park
Kalkallo
Donnybrook
Whittlesea
Toolangi
Leigh Creek
Wallace
Ballarat
Greendale
Couangalt
Mickleham
Yan Yean Res
Kinglake
Strathewen
Wakool
Conargo
Dahwilly
Deniliquin
RIVERINA
Edward River
Deniboota Irrigation Area
COBB
Mathoura
NSW
VIC
Barmah State Pk
Moira Lake
Barmah Lake
Womboota
Bearii
Yalca North
Strathmerton
Yalca South
Picola
Barwo
Barmah
Nathalia
Waaia
Numurkah
Goulburn
Mundoona
Kaarimba
Bunbartha
Wyuna
St Germains
Tallygaroopna
Undera
Mooroopna North
Shepparton
Ardmona
Mooroopna
Toolamba
Toolamba West
Dhurringile
Arcadia
Kialla West
GOULBURN
Pranjip
Big Hill
Upton Hill
Rubicon
Murray
Loddon River
Lang Ck
Old Ck
Kow Swamp

0 10 20 30 40
kilometres

NSW 7

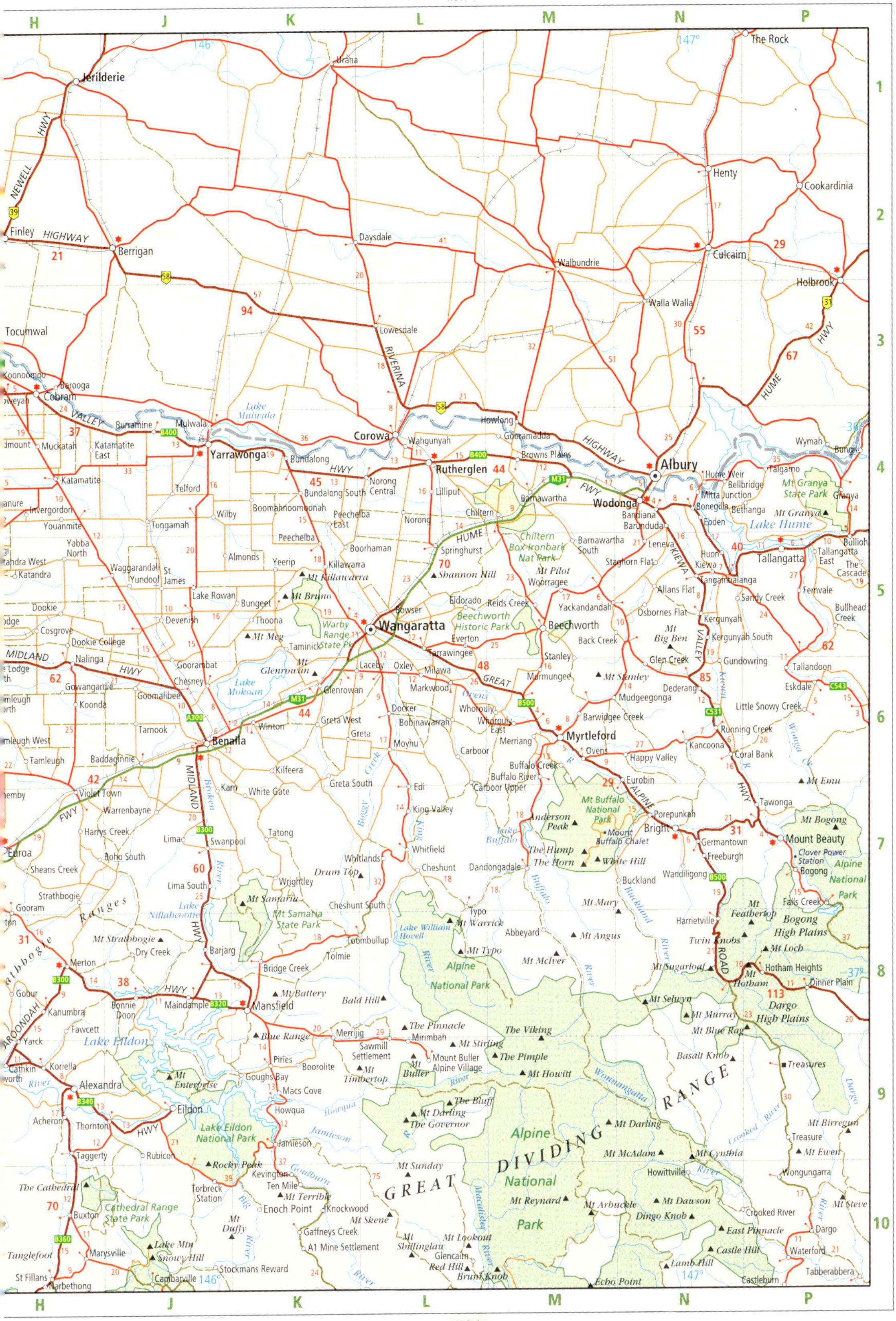

VIC 6

Map 4

NSW 7
VIC 3
VIC 6
A
B
C
D
E
F
G
1
2
3
4
5
6
7
8
9
10
147°
148°
36°
37°
38°
Kiandra
Cabramurra
Tumut Pond Reservoir
Albury
Wodonga
Hume Weir
Bellbridge
Mitta Junction
Bonegilla
Bethanga
Bandiana
Barunduda
Ebden
Leneva
Talgarno
Wymah
Bungil
Granya
Mt Granya
Mt Granya State Park
Lake Hume
HUME
HIGHWAY
MURRAY
KIEWA
VALLEY
Huon
Kiewa
Tangambalanga
Tallangatta
Tallangatta East
The Cascade
Tallangatta Valley
Staghorn Flat
Yackandandah
Allans Flat
Osbornes Flat
Sandy Creek
Fernvale
Kergunyah
Kergunyah South
Mt Big Ben
Glen Creek
Gundowring
Mt Stanley
Dederang
Mudgeegonga
Tallandoon
Eskdale
Little Snowy Creek
Running Creek
Kancoona
Coral Bank
Happy Valley
Eurobin
Mt Buffalo National Park
Porepunkah
Bright
Mount Buffalo Chalet
White Hill
Tawonga
Mount Beauty
Germantown
Freeburgh
Wandiligong
Buckland
Mt Mary
Harrietville
Twin Knobs
Mt Feathertop
Clover Power Station
Bogong
Falls Creek
Bogong High Plains
Rocky Valley Reservoir
Alpine National Park
Mt Bogong
Mt Loch
Hotham Heights
Mt Hotham
Mt Sugarloaf
Mt Selwyn
Mt Murray
Mt Blue Rag
Dargo High Plains
Dinner Plain
Cobungra
Basalt Knob
Treasures
GREAT DIVIDING
Wonnangatta
Mt Darling
Mt McAdam
Mt Cynthia
Howittville
Mt Dawson
Mt Arbuckle
Dingo Knob
Crooked River
East Pinnacle
Castle Hill
Lamb Hill
Freestone Creek
Avon Wilderness Park
Mt Blomford
Mt Hump
Mt Angus
Morgan
Wright Hill
Rocky Knob
Mt Margaret
Valencia Creek
Culloden
Maffra West Upper
Boisdale
Briagolong
Bushy Park
Newry
Maffra
Tinamba
Riverslea
Denison
Bundalaguah
Nambrok
Nambrok West
Kilmany
Fulham
Wurruk
Sale
Myrtlebank
Airly
Stratford
Munro
Cobains
RAAF Base East Sale
The Heart
Clydebank
Lake Wellington
Seacombe
Holland Landing
Loch Sport
Lake Victoria
The Lakes NP
Pelican Point
Perry Bridge
Meerlieu
Bengworden
Goon Nure
Delvine
Fernbank
PRINCES
Lindenow South
Stockdale
The Fingerboards
Glenaladale
Woodglen
Walpa
Lindenow
Iguana Creek
Bairnsdale
Eagle Point
Forge Creek
Paynesville
Raymond I
Pt Best
Point Wilson
Jones Bay
Lake King
Metung
Kalimna
Kalimna West
Lakes Entrance
Lake Tyers
Ninety Mile
Lake Corringle
Beach
Marlo
Newmerella
Orbost
Jarrahmond
Bete Bolong
Waygara
Tostaree
Wairewa
Colquhoun Hill
Lake Tyers State Park
Nowa Nowa
Swan Reach
Johnsonville
Tambo Upper
Mossiface
Bruthen
Sarsfield
Nicholson
Wy Yung
Lucknow
Wiseleigh
Clifton Creek
Mount Taylor
Bullumwaal
Mitchell River Nat Park
Davey Knob
Mt Ray
Cobbannah
Castleburn
Tabberabbera
Waterford
Dargo
Mt Steve
Wongungarra
Treasure
Mt Ewen
Mt Birregun
Dogs Grave
Mt Phipps
Morris Peak
Mt Hoad
Seldom Seen
Dawson City
Dogtown
Stirling
Forktown
Mt Sugarloaf
Deptford
Mt Little Dick
Pheasant Hill
Double Bridges
Tambo Crossing
Holstons
Ensay
Ensay North
Mt Delusion
Brookville
Cassilis
Tongio West
Tongio
Swifts Creek
Doctors Flat
Mt Livingstone
Omeo
Cobungra
Round Hill
GREAT ALPINE ROAD
Bingo Munjie North
Hinnomunjie
Mt Shanahan
Bindi
Mt Bindi
Mt Nugong
Benambra
Lake Omeo
The Brothers
Uplands
Mt Fraser
OMEO RANGE
Anglers Rest
Mt Battery
Glen Wills
Glen Valley
Christmas Creek
Lightning Creek
Bull Hill
Mt Emu
Mitta Mitta
Dartmouth
Granite Peak
Lake Dartmouth
Toke Gibbo
Mt Cooper
Mt Benambra
Connells Peak
Bucheen Creek
Henlow
Bullhead Creek
Wyeebo
Mt Cudgewa
Lucyvale
Beetoomba
Berringama
Shelley
Koetong
Darbyshire
Bullioh
Mt Lawson
Mt Lawson State Park
Mt Porcupine
Mount Alfred
Walwa
Burrowye
Burrowa - Pine Mtn Nat Park
Pine Mtn
Guys Forest
Mt Burrowa
Cudgewa
Cudgewa North
Corryong
Colac Colac
Mt Mitta Mitta
Tintaldra
Towong
Towong Upper
Thowgla
Biggara
Nariel Creek
Thowgla Upper
Wabba Wilderness Park
Mt St John
Nariel
Corryong Creek
Mt Morgan
Coleman Bend
Khancoban
Khancoban Pondage
Geehi
Geebi Reservoir
Alpine Way
Kosciuszko National Park
Mt Kosciuszko
Charlottes Pass
Jindabyne
Thredbo Village
Tom Groggin
Mt Pinnibar
Murray River
Mt Sassafras
Sassafras Gap
Mt Gibbo
Mt Anderson
Gibbo River
Buckwong Creek
Alpine National Park
Johnnies Top
Mt Murphy
The Pilot
Suggan
Mt Misery
Forest Hill
Moscow Peak
Mt Cobberas
Mt Pendergast
The Brothers
Big Hill
Mt Wombargo
Forlorn Hope
Brumby Hill
Mt Nunniong
Mt Seldom Seen
Wulgulmerang
Mt Statham
Suggan Buggan
Willis
NSW
Vic
Pinch Mtn
Kosciuszko National Park
Barry Way
Mt Hamilton
Deddick
Tubbut
Mt Deddick
Snowy River National Park
Campbell Knob
Gelantipy
Dingo Hill
Mt Joan
Butchers Ridge
Green Hills
Timbarra
Gillingall
Pretty Boy Saddle
Murrindal
Mt McLeod
Mt Victoria
Buchan Caves
Buchan
Buchan South
Mt Tara
Spanker Knob
Stringer Knob
Mt Sardine
Sardine Creek
Mt Watt
Fryingpan Hill
Brodribb River
Rodger River
Tambo River
Timbarra River
Nicholson
Crooked River
Dargo River
Mitchell
Snowy River

NSW 7

0
10
20
30
40
kilometres
NORTH
H
J
K
L
M
N
P
1
2
3
4
5
6
7
8
9
10
149°
150°
36°
37°
38°
SNOWY
MOUNTAINS
HWY
MONARO
HIGHWAY
GREAT
DIVIDING
RANGE
PRINCES
HWY
CANN
VALLEY
Adaminaby
Old Adaminaby
Cooma
Numeralla
Berridale
Dalgety
Snowy
River
Nimmitabel
Ando
Mt Rix
Deua
National Park
Moruya
Turlinjah
Bodalla
Tuross Lake
Narooma
Yowrie
Tilba Tilba
Cobargo
Bermagui
Wadbilliga
National Park
Biamanga
Nat Park
Brogo
Bemboka
Nat Park
Numbugga
Bega
Mimosa Rocks
National Park
Tathra
Tantawangalo
National Park
Candelo
Wallagoot Lake
Bournda
Nat Park
South East Forest
National Park
Cathcart
Merimbula
Bombala
Wyndham
Coolangubra
National Park
Delegate
Yowaka
National Park
Ben Boyd
National Park
Eden
Delegate
River
Craigie
Towamba
Dellicknora
Bendoc North
Pericoe
East Boyd
Haydens
Bog
Mt
Delegate
Bondi Gulf
Nat Pk
Genoa
National
Park
Mt Imlay
National Park
Ben Boyd
National
Park
Bonang
Bendoc
Mt Tennyson
Mt Poole
Mt Canterbury
Granite Mtn
Narrabarba
Brown Mtn
Buldah
Coopracambra
National
Park
Disaster
Bay
Green
Cape
Cobb Hill
NEW SOUTH WALES
VICTORIA
Goongerah
Errinundra
National Park
Chandlers Creek
Mealing
Hill
Wroxham
Combienbar
Weeragua
Wangarabell
Errinundra
Mt Ellery
Mt Kaye
Maramingo Hill
Nadgee
Nature
Reserve
Nadgee Point
Waldron Mtn
Noorinbee
North
Bee Tree
Hill
Pike Hill
Genoa
Gipsy Point
Fairhaven
Mt Carlyle
Lake
Barracoota
Cape Howe
Pyramid
Hill
Noorinbee
Puggaree
Tonghi
Creek
Club Terrace
Cann River
Alfred
Nat Park
Genoa Peak
Gabo Island
Lind
Nat Park
Mallacoota
Mallacoota
Inlet
Murrungowar
Mt Cann
Croajingolong
National Park
Bellbird
Creek
Little Rame Head
Lake
Furnell
Furnell
Mt
Everard
Croajingolong
National Park
Wingan Bay
Sandpatch Point
Cape Conran
Coastal Park
Swan
Lake
Tamboon
Bemm River
Wingan Point
Sydenham
Inlet
Tamboon
Inlet
Petrel
Point
Rame Head
East Cape
Pearl
Point
Cape
Everard
Cape
Conran

Map 5

VIC 2
SA 4
A
B
C
D
E
F
G
1
2
3
4
5
6
7
8
9
10
141°
142°
37°
38°
39°
NORTH
SOUTH AUSTRALIA
VICTORIA
Kybybolite
Hynam
Bringalbert
Benayeo
Apsley
Patyah
Winter Lake
Ozenkadnook
Ullswater
Lake Yallakar
Karnak
WIMMERA
HWY
Miga Lake
Lake Bow
Clear Lake
Lake Clear
Noradjuha
Wonwondah North
Jallumba
Nurrabiel
Mockinya
Mackenzie
WESTERN
Mt Zero
Wal Wal
Dadswells Bridge
Lah-Arum
Heathvale
Wartook
Briggs Bluff
Ledcourt
Lake Lonsdale
Lake Wallace
Edenhope
Charam
Wombelano
North Lake
Douglas
Centre Lake
White Lake
Lake Kanagulk
Toolondo
Toolondo Reservoir
Telangatuk East
Brimpaen
Cherrypool
Zumsteins
Mackenzie Falls
Wartook Res
Halls Gap
Langkoop
Wrattonbully
Kadnook
Powers Creek
Connewirrecoo
Harrow
River
Kanagulk
Black Range State Park
Mt Byron
Glenisla
Red Rock
Moora Moora Res
Lake Bellfield
Coonawarra
Poolaijelo
Glenelg
Dergholm State Park
Moree
Culla
Balmoral
Rocklands Reservoir
Pigeon Ponds
Chetwynd
Grampians National Park
Dorodong
Tarrayoukyan
Englefield
Glendinning
Woohlpooer
Chimney Pots
Green Hill
Penola
Dergholm
Brimboal
Nareen
Coojar
Caddens Flat
Vasey
Mooralla
Mirranatwa
Gatum
Gringegalgona
Roseneath
Red Cap Creek
Mt Dundas
Wannon
Lake Mundi
Wando Bridge
Wando Vale
Nangeela
Dunrobin
Brit Brit
HENTY
Lake Muirhead
Lake Mundi
Konong Wootong
Melville Forest
Cavendish
Gritjurk
Mt Cavendish
Victoria Valley
Carapook
Bulart
Cassidy Gap
Casterton
Coleraine
Karabeal
Lindsay
GLENELG
Sandford
Nigretta Falls
Moutajup
Dunkeld
Glenthompson
Bahgallah
Henty
Paschendale
Wannon
Kanawalla
Tarrenlea
Wannon Falls
Strathkellar
Warrayure
Strathdownie
Merino
Tahara West
Tahara
Hamilton
Yulecart
Tarrington
Lake Linlithgow
Ardno
Myaring
HAMILTON
Yatchaw
Tabor
Puralka
Digby
Grassdale
Miakite
Branxholme
Buckley Swamp
Glenburnie
Rennick
PRINCES
Yahl
Byaduk North
Mt Napier
Mt Napier State Pk
Penshurst
Chatsworth
Dartmoor
Hotspur
Mumbannar
Winnap
Wallacedale
Byaduk
Warrabkook
Caramut
Princess Margaret Rose Caves
Greenwald
Condah
Weerangourt
Wanwin
Drik Drik
Lyons
Myamyn
Knebsworth
Minhamite
Donovans
Nelson
Milltown
Lake Condah
Mt Eccles
Macarthur
Ripponhurst
Minjah
Merri
Piccaninnie Ponds CP
Lower Glenelg National Park
Sinclair
Drumborg
Fitzroy
Mt Eccles Nat Pk
Hawkesdale West
Hawkesdale
Lake Condah
Heywood
Broadwater
Dunmore
Discovery Bay Coastal Park
Kentbruck
Bessiebelle
Willatook
Mount Richmond
Mt Richmond Nat Park
Gorae
Heathmere
Tyrendarra
Tyrendarra East
Orford
Moyne
Woolsthorpe
Warrong
Winslow
Discovery Bay
Gorae West
Mt Richmond
Bolwarra
Narrawong
Codrington
St Helens
Kirkstall
Tower Hill Lake
Koroit
Mailors Flat
Woodford
Tarragal
Cashmore
Portland North
Portland
Portland Bay
Yambuk
Toolong
Crossley
Illowa
Killarney
Rosebrook
Tower Hill
Dennington
Allansford
Descartes Bay
Cape Duquesne
Trewalla
Point Danger
Port Fairy Bay
Cape Bridgewater
Bridgewater Bay
Nelson Bay
Cape Nelson
Cape Nelson State Pk
Lady Julia Percy Island
Point Percy
Port Fairy
Griffiths Island
Warrnambool
Logans Beach
SOUTHERN OCEAN
C240
B160
A1
A200
A8
B140

VIC 2

VIC 6

VIC

Map 6

VIC 3
VIC 5
A
B
C
D
E
F
G
1
2
3
4
5
6
7
8
9
10
145°
38°
39°
NORTH
BASS STRAIT
Port Phillip
MELBOURNE
Geelong
Glenlyon
Spring Hill
Carlsruhe
Newham
Lancefield
Kilmore
Reedy Creek
Flowerdale
Break O'Day
Murrindindi
Taggerty
Rubicon
Lake Eildon National Park
Coomoora
Little Hampton
Tylden
Woodend North
Rochford
Romsey
Bylands
Wandong
Heathcote Junction
Musk
Lyonville
Trentham
Fern Hill
Woodend
Hesket
Darraweit Guim
Wallan
Wallan East
Bullarto
Trentham East
Mount Macedon
New Gisborne
Monegeeta
Devlins Bridge
The Cathedral
Cathedral Range State Park
Buxton
Newbury
Barrys Reef
Blackwood
Macedon
Riddells Creek
Bolinda
Glenburn
Kinglake National Park
Bullengarook
Gisborne
Clarkefield
Beveridge
Merriang
Humevale
Kinglake West
Pheasant Creek
Mt Tanglefoot
Marysville
Lake Mountain
Blakeville
Lerderderg State Park
Kalkallo
Whittlesea
Coimadai
Sunbury
Mickleham
Donnybrook
Yan Yean
Yan Yean Res
Kinglake
Toolangi
St Fillans
Greendale
Korobeit
Myrniong
Ballan
Werribee Gorge SP
Toolern Vale
Diggers Rest
Bulla
Oaklands Junction
Yuroke
Craigieburn
Somerton
Wollert
Arthurs Creek
Mernda
Strathewen
Dixons Creek
Healesville West
Narbethong
White Hill
Mt Ritchie
Cambarville
Mt Observation
Fernshaw
Bacchus Marsh
Melton
Sydenham
Tullamarine
Greenvale
Broadmeadows
Epping
Morang South
Hurstbridge
St Andrews
Panton Hill
Winneke Dam
Yarra Glen
Yering
Healesville
Yarra Ranges National Park
Somers Park
Acheron Gap
Fiskville
Mount Wallace
Brisbane Ranges NP
Rowsley
Parwan
Melton Sth
Melton Res
Rockbank
Exford
Sydenham West
Keilor
Campbellfield
Thomastown
Diamond Creek
Eltham
Watsons Creek
Wonga Park
Coldstream
Gruyere
Don Valley
Millgrove
Warburton
Warburton East
McMahons Creek
Beremboke
Durdidwarrah
Balliang East
Balliang
One Tree Hill
Chartwell
Truganina
Deer Park
Sunshine
Footscray
Brunswick
Coburg
Preston
Heidelberg
Templestowe
Doncaster
Box Hill
Ringwood
Croydon
Lilydale
Wandin
Mount Evelyn
Seville
Woori Yallock
Yarra Junction
Wesburn
Three Bridges
Hyde Hill
Powelltown
Steiglitz
Laverton
Hoppers Crossing
Werribee
Williamstown
Kew
Camberwell
Dandenong Ranges NP
Silvan
Silvan Res
Mount Dandenong
Yellingbo
Hoddles Creek
You Yangs Regional Park
Altona
Altona Bay
St Kilda
Brighton
Oakleigh
Glen Waverley
Belgrave
Monbulk
Avonsleigh
Cockatoo
Egg Rock
Gembrook
Bunyip State Park
Gentle Annie
Tarago Reservoir
Piedmont
Nayook
Maude
Anakie
Little River
Point Cook
Campbells Cove
Werribee South
Sandringham
Moorabbin
Springvale
Mentone
Lysterfield
Lysterfield Lake Park
Emerald
Rothwell
Lara
Mordialloc
Noble Park
Dandenong
Cardinia Res
Upper Beaconsfield
Pakenham
Upper Pakenham
Maryknoll
Mt Toun
Neerim South
Jindivick
Tarago
Bannockburn
Lovely Banks
Avalon Airport
Kirk Point
Chelsea
Hallam
Narre Warren
Berwick
Hampton Park
Beaconsfield
Officer
Batesford
Corio
Avalon
Point Wilson
Point Richards
Portarlington
Norlane
Corio Bay
Jetty
Carrum Downs
Skye
Cranbourne
Clyde
Tynong
Robin Hood
Bunyip
Garfield
Longwarry
Drouin
Warragul
Stonehaven
Fyansford
Bellarine
Point George
Indented Head
Seaford
Frankston
Langwarrin
Junction Village
Cardinia
Pakenham South
Vervale
Cora Lynn
Bayles
Highton
Ceres
Clifton Springs
Drysdale
St Leonards
Mount Eliza
Baxter
Pearcedale
Koo-Wee-Rup
Modella
Ripplebrook
Belmont
Grovedale
Marshall
Leopold
Wallington
Mannerim
Edwards Point
Swan Bay
Swan Island
Mornington
Moorooduc
Somerville
Tyabb
Tooradin
Warneet
Quail Is
Western Port
Caldermeade
Yannathan
Athlone
Mount Moriac
Waurn Ponds
Freshwater Creek
Connewarre
Lake Connewarre
Queenscliff
Balcombe Bay
Mount Martha
Devilbend Res
Hastings
French Island
French Island Nat Park
Lang Lang
Topiram
Bellbrae
Breamlea
Barwon Heads
Ocean Grove
Point Lonsdale
The Rip
Portsea
Sorrento
Dromana Bay
Safety Beach
Dromana
Blairgowrie
McCrae
Rye
Rosebud
Red Hill
Balnarring
Bittern
Crib Point
Stony Point
Mt Wellington
Tankerton
Corinella
The Gurdies
Nyora
Poowong
Torquay
Jan Juc
Bells Beach
Point Addis
Anglesea
Surf Coast Hwy
Mornington Peninsula Nat Park
The Cups
St Andrews Beach
Boneo
Main Ridge
Merricks
Somers
Sandy Pt
Grantville
Kernot
Loch
Woodleigh
Korumburra
Bena
Point Leo
Shoreham
Flinders Bight
Cape Schanck
Flinders
West Head
Cat Bay
Ventnor
Cowes
Rhyll
Coronet Bay
Stony Point
Newhaven
Bass
Glen Forbes
Kongwak
Glen Alvie
Woolamai
Cape Schanck
The Nobbies
Phillip Island
Woolamai Waters
San Remo
Cape Woolamai
Anderson
Kilcunda
Dalyston
Dudley South
Archies Creek
Powlett River
Wonthaggi
Wonthaggi North
Inverloch
Outtrim
Leongatha South
Leongatha
Ellerside
Honeysuckle Hill
Cape Paterson
Point Smythe
Venus Bay
Anderson Inlet
Tarwin Lower
Liptrap
Walkerville
Morgan Beach
Cape Liptrap
WESTERN FWY
PRINCES FWY
PRINCES HWY
SOUTH GIPPSLAND HWY
BASS HWY
M1
M8
M31
A1
A79
A420
B75
B100
B110
B300
B360
B380
B420
B440
B460
M420

0 10 20 30 40
kilometres
H J K L M N P
1 2 3 4 5 6 7 8 9 10
147°
38°
39°
Jamieson
Kevington
Ten Mile
Mt Terrible
Enoch Point
Knockwood
Gaffneys Creek
A1 Mine Settlement
Mt Sunday
Mt Skene
Alpine National Park
Mt Reynard
Mt McAdam
Mt Cynthia
Howittville
Mt Arbuckle
Mt Dawson
Dingo Knob
Crooked River
East Pinnacle
Castle Hill
Mt Lookout
Glencairn
Mt Shillinglaw
Red Hill
Bruni Knob
Echo Point
Lamb Hill
Macalister River
Freestone Creek
Woods Point
Mt Matlock
St Clair
The Oaks
Matlock
Fiddlers Green
Mt Ronald
Mt Hump
Licola
Avon Wilderness Park
Mt Blomford
The Green Hill
Mt Useful
Big Hill
Mt Angus
Wright Hill
Morgan
Montys Hut
Mt Gregory
Aberfeldy
Basalt Hill
Lake Thompson
Mt Whitelaw
Sullivans
Myrrhee
Tanjil Bren
Mt Baw Baw
Baw Baw Alpine Village
Beardmore
Murderers Hill
Glenmaggie
Rocky Knob
Mt Margaret
Valencia Creek
Culloden
Glenmaggie Reservoir
Maffra West Upper
Briagolong
Bushy Park
Icy Creek
Fumina
Baw Baw National Park
Tyers Junction
Walhalla
Rawson
Erica
Seaton
Cowwarr Weir
Coongulla
Boisdale
Newry
Heyfield
Maffra
Tinamba
Riverslea
Thomson River
Fumina South
Hill End
Moondarra
Mt Lookout
Moondarra State Pk
Cowwarr
Denison
Bundalaguah
Winnindoo
Toongabbie
Nambrook
Nambrook West
Myrtlebank
Kilmany
Fulham
Wurruk
Sale
Willow Grove
Blue Rock Lake
Moondarra Reservoir
Tanjil South
Tyers Park
Glengarry
Yallourn North
Tyers
Lake Narracan
Moe
Newborough
Traralgon
Morwell
Yarragon
Trafalgar
Coalville
Narracan
Rosedale
Kilmany South
Flynn
Flynns Creek
Holey Plains State Park
Willung
Traralgon South
Hazelwood Cooling Pond
Churchill
Thorpdale
Childers
Yinnar
Koornalla
Hiamdale
Gormandale
Willung South
Allambee South
Boolarra
Carrajung
Carrajung South
Morwell Nat Park
Mirboo North
Budgeree
Boolarra South
Blackwarry
Tarra-Bulga Nat Park
Balook
Mardan
Mirboo
Mirboo East
Tarra Valley
Macks Creek
Wonwron
Darriman
Dumbalk
Dumbalk North
Tarwin East
Hiawatha
Ryton
Staceys Bridge
Devon
Greenmount
Woodside
Woodside Beach
Yarram
Hunterson
Turtons Creek
Dollar
Wonyip
Binginwarri
Alberton West
Alberton
Mount Best
Woorarra
Hazel Park
Foster
Toora
Tarraville
McLoughlins Beach
St. Margaret Island
Manns Beach
Hedley
Welshpool
Bennison
Port Franklin
Agnes
Barry Beach
Port Welshpool
Port Albert
Shallow Inlet
Sunday Island
Kate Kearney Entrance
Clonmel Island
Port Albert Entrance
Fish Creek
Hoddle
Waratah North
Corner Inlet
Snake Island
Yanakie
Duck Point
Entrance Point
Townsend Point
Mt Hunter
Lighthouse Pt
Sandy Point
Waratah Bay
Chinaman Knob
Three Mile Point
Wilsons Promontory Nat Pk
Monkey Pt
Five Mile Beach
Cotters Beach
Tongue Point
Whisky Bay
Leonard Point
Sealers Cove
Refuge Cove
Tidal River
Mt Oberon
Cape Wellington
Great Glennie Island
Oberon Bay
Mt Norgate
Waterloo Bay
Mt Boulder
South West Point
Anser Island
South Point
South East Point
Rodondo Island
Hogan Island
Curtis Island
Kent Group
Erith Island
Dover Island
Deal Island
Treasure
Mt Ewen
Mt Birregun
Wongungarra
Mt Steve
Dargo
Waterford
Castleburn
Tabberabbera
Cobbannah
Davey Knob
Mitchell River Nat Park
Mt Ray
Glenaladale
Iguana Creek
The Fingerboards
Stockdale
Woodglen
Walpa
Lindenow
Lindenow South
Fernbank
Munro
Stratford
Airly
Delvine
Bengworden
Meerlieu
Perry Bridge
Clydebank
Cobains
RAAF Base East Sale
The Heart
Lake Wellington
Seacombe
Longford
Dutson
Lake Coleman
Deadman Hill
Stradbroke West
Stradbroke
Giffard West
Giffard
Seaspray
The Honeysuckles
Glomar Beach
Flamingo Beach
Delray Beach
Golden Beach
Paradise Beach
Ninety Mile Beach
Jack Smith Lake
Gippsland Lakes Coastal Park
Loch Sport
Holland Landing
Lake Victoria
Swifts Creek
Doctors Flat
Ensay North
Ensay
Mt Delusion
Brookville
Seldom Seen
Dawson City
Dogtown
Stirling
Tambo Crossing
Forktown
Morris Peak
Mt Sugarloaf
Mt Hoad
Pheasant Hill
Deptford
Bullumwaal
Mt Little Dick
Clifton Creek
Bruthen
Wiseleigh
Mt Taylor
Mossiface
Sarsfield
Tambo Upper
Wy Yung
Lucknow
Nicholson
Bairnsdale
Swan Reach
Metung
Eagle Point
Lake King
Paynesville
Raymond I
Forge Creek
Goon Nure
Pt Best
Point Wilson
The Lakes NP
Pelican Point
Nicholson River
Tambo River
Mitchell River
Avon River
Perry River
Merriman Creek
Toms Cap Creek
Latrobe River
Princes Hwy
South Gippsland Hwy
Hyland Hwy
Strzelecki Hwy
Sale–Longford Hwy
B500 B440 B460 C482 C444 A1
14 68 56 46 51 57 66 92

Vittoria
Coffee

Tasmania

You cannot help falling under the spell of Tasmania. From the World Heritage-listed Wilderness Area to the rich history of Port Arthur, from the scrumptious seafood to the delectable dairy produce of King Island, Tasmania has the amazing power to revitalise the body and feed the soul. Take a walk within the stunning Cradle Mountain–Lake St Clair National Park and drink in the refreshing clean air, or let the delightful serenity of Freycinet National Park envelop you. Immerse yourself in the romance of the past with a trip to the gorgeous Georgian town of Richmond, or indulge the palate with a spot of taste testing at the Cascade Brewery and Cadbury Chocolate Factory in Hobart. Visit Tasmania, and let the Natural State work its unique magic.

Hobart and Environs

The accepted image of Australia is of a continent which is hot and dry. Tasmania turns this idea upside down. While the east coast can be quite dry, and Hobart can go without rain for extended periods, the island as a whole is cool and moist. Therefore people enjoy a very different experience to that offered by the mainland. Here the landscape, certainly in the central section of the state between Hobart and Launceston, is intimate and European. The accommodation is old-world and cosy, and the visitor can soak up the history of an island which has been largely untouched by modernity and globalisation.

Central Hobart

Hobart is a beautiful historic city. It is small and manageable. It is possible, for example, to stay in Glebe or at Battery Point and walk to the city's docks in no more than a brisk five or ten minutes. It is very enjoyable to walk along the docks, checking out the numerous excellent fish restaurants and watching the yachts arrive—this is particularly exciting at the time of the Sydney–Hobart race. You can also visit the oldest theatre in Australia: the Theatre Royal at 29 Campbell Street which was built in 1837. This spectacular Georgian playhouse is a reminder of the sophistication which existed in the colonies in the 1830s.

The Tasmanian Museum and Art Gallery is situated opposite Hobart's famous Constitution Dock. The Colonial Gallery features many works of art by John Glover.

It is also possible to use the city as a starting point for the experiences which are offered close by. You can drive to the top of Mount Wellington and enjoy the views over the city and the Derwent valley. There are a number of cruises which ply the Derwent River and travel through the D'Entrecasteaux Channel.

The city is also a good place to book a range of unique adventure experiences. Peregrine Travel operates a five-day rafting expedition on the Franklin River that departs from Hobart on Sundays, and The Lower Franklin Wilderness Expedition offers a similar experience. They can be booked through the local travel agents or on the Internet.

Map: Tas 3 K6

Battery Point and Salamanca Place

The highlight of any visit to Hobart is a quiet walk around Battery Point. An even more desirable option is to stay in one of the many charming B&Bs and guesthouses which are hidden in the historic backstreets of the area. What is the appeal? Well, if you want to know what an Australian settlement was really like in the middle of the nineteenth century then Battery Point is an almost perfectly

Georgian buildings, like these on the corner of Murray and Macquarie Streets, are a common sight around Hobart. They contribute greatly to the old-world charm of the city.

preserved example. It is a fantastic collection of beautifully restored houses which were built during the 1800s, close to the centre of Hobart.

Start your tour from Salamanca Place. It is here each weekend that locals and visitors mingle at the excellent Salamanca Markets. The old Georgian warehouses (built between 1830 and 1850) have been converted into wonderful restaurants, galleries, craft shops and gift stores. Most architects acknowledge that the Salamanca Place warehouses are the finest dockside Georgian warehouses remaining in the whole of Australia.

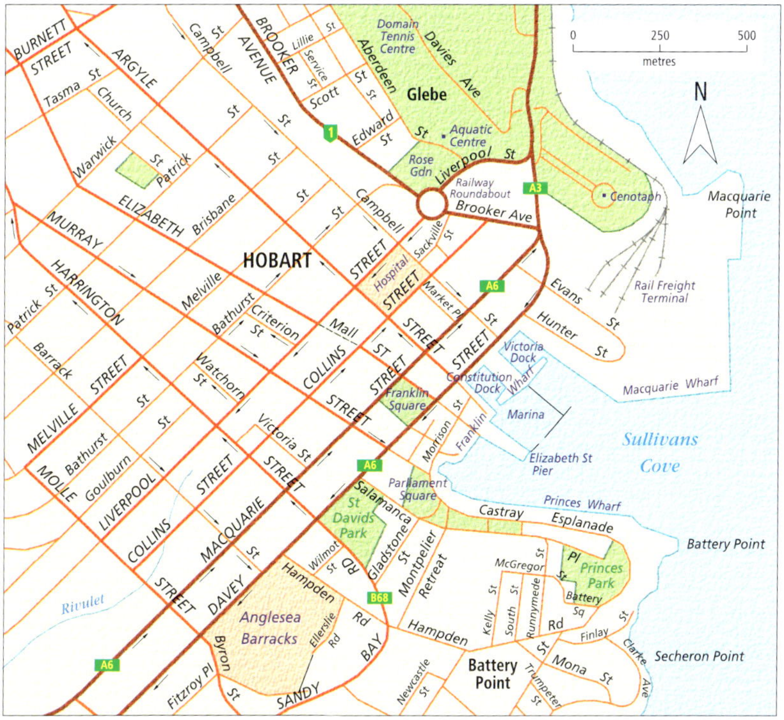

Arthur's Circus in Battery Point has 15 delightfully restored cottages that encircle a village green. Nearby there are old-style pubs and corner shops.

From Salamanca Place, walk up Kelly's Steps and start strolling through the winding streets of Battery Point.

Battery Point saw houses being constructed in the 1830s, and by the 1850s both Battery Point and Salamanca Place were the focal points of the city, attracting sailors from all over the world to the pubs and bawdy houses which were dotted around the area. At the same time, in a spirit of great egalitarianism, both workers' cottages and elegant Georgian mansions were built on the headland. Neat, tiny cottages owned by ordinary working people stand next to sumptuous mansions in a pretty streetscape which includes roads that wind around the point and even traditional 'village greens' designed to mimic those of rural and urban England.

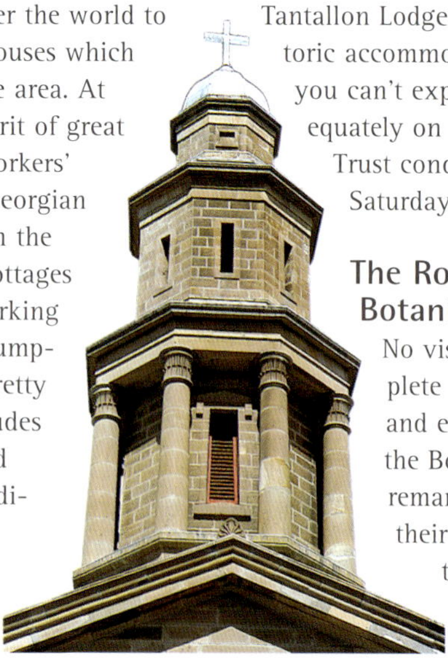

The tower of St George's Church is the dominant feature of Battery Point's skyline. It was designed by convict architect James Blackburn in the 1840s.

There are a number of particularly impressive buildings which should not escape the visitor's attention. St George's Church (1836–38) is regarded as the finest Greek Revival Church in Australia. Barton Cottage (1837), Colville Cottage (1877), Cromwell Cottage (1880) and Tantallon Lodge (1906) all provide historic accommodation. If you feel that you can't explore the headland adequately on your own, the National Trust conducts walking tours on Saturday mornings.

The Royal Tasmanian Botanic Gardens

No visit to Hobart is complete without a pleasant and extended walk through the Botanic Gardens. These remarkable gardens, with their excellent views across the Derwent River, were established as early as 1828. In 1806

a small parcel of land (approximately 20 hectares) was granted to a farmer named John Hangan. In 1826 the land was returned to the government because Van Diemen's Land's Governor Arthur had decided that Hobart Town would become the colony's capital. He had plans drawn up for both Government House (which still stands nearby) and the Botanic Gardens. An official gardener, William Davidson, was appointed, and in 1829 a house was built for him. Being a product of his age, Davidson immediately started importing plants from England. In fairness, he also collected 150 native species from nearby Mount Wellington. Over the years this sense of the importance of Tasmanian plants has grown, so that now the A. P. May section of the gardens displays over 300 Tasmanian natives.

There has never been a time since the 1820s when the botanic gardens have not been improved in some way. In the 1850s (between 1854 and 1856) the infamous bushranger, Martin Cash, was the overseer of the gardens. He was, coincidentally, a distant relative of the tennis player Pat Cash. The gardens are a true delight for those who are seeking a little relaxation. Walk around them and explore the historic Arthur Wall (built by Governor Arthur in 1829), the Rossbank Observatory site (the site of an observatory built by Governor Franklin in 1840), the Japanese garden, the cacti house, the Conservatory, Rosarium, Floral Clock, Fern House and Tropical Glasshouse. There is also a Discovery House offering hands-on exhibits which appeal to both adults and children.

don't miss

Open-air plays are often performed in Hobart's Royal Tasmanian Botanic Gardens over the warm summer period. The audience moves from one section of the gardens to another to view different scenes.

Accommodation

Completed in 1973, the Wrest Point Hotel Casino is now Hobart's most recognisable landmark. It offers a range of accommodation, from deluxe suites to economical motel rooms. It also has a revolving restaurant which provides panoramic views of the city and the Derwent River. For more information contact 1800 030 611.

For a more intimate experience, try some of the many B&Bs and guesthouses at Battery Point.

Tasmanian oysters are considered among the world's best and can be sampled at Barilla Bay Oysters, across the Derwent River from Hobart.

Eating and Drinking

Hobart is justifiably famous the world over for its exceptional fresh fish and crustaceans. Tasmanian lobsters are a true delight. The best places to sample this sensational seafood are all located around Constitution Dock. There are fish and chip shops, takeaways and classy restaurants to meet the needs of everyone, from the family wanting fast food to the foodie wanting some true culinary taste sensations. The answer is to wander and explore before you decide which of the restaurants meets your needs.

Left: *Native plants such as the Tasmanian laurel* (Anopterus glandulosus) *are an important feature of the Royal Tasmanian Botanic Gardens.*

Right: *The Cadbury Chocolate Factory is Australia's largest confectionery factory, at nearly 15 hectares in area. Popular tours reveal the manufacturing process and offer visitors delicious samples.*

Lovers of fine beer should visit the Cascade Brewery and museum in South Hobart—it is open to the public on weekdays. Phone (03) 6221 8300. If chocolate is more to your liking, the Cadbury Chocolate Factory in Claremont (phone 03 6249 0333) also conducts guided tours. Bookings are essential for both.

don't miss

Taste of Tasmania is a festival held from the end of December to the beginning of January in warehouses along the Hobart waterfront. You can sample a variety of products, from seafood to wine and chocolate.

North of Hobart

There are a number of interesting historic towns north of Hobart. Each has its own charm. For those eager to get to the essence of historic Tasmania, the towns of Richmond and Ross offer fine comparisons. Richmond is the tourist-orientated destination. Ross, while it has gift shops, is really quite untouched by tourism.

Richmond

Of course with Richmond being only 27 km from Hobart it is not surprising that this charming town, set in gently undulating country on the banks of the Coal River, has become so popular. It has no fewer than 45 buildings listed by the National Estate and many of these historic Georgian stone houses, buildings and hotels have been converted into gift shops, Devonshire tea cafés, restaurants, craft shops and museums.

The town's greatest appeal, and certainly its most photographed building, is the beautiful Richmond Bridge. Also of importance is the Richmond Gaol (1825) in Bathurst Street with its cookhouse, women's quarters and impressive gaoler's house; the Court House (1825–26); St John's Church; Ivy Cottage; St Luke's Church of England (1834–36); Bellevue House; Oak Lodge; and the Richmond Arms. All are listed by the National Estate and are well worth a visit.

Staying in Richmond can be quite fun. There is a large and interesting range of historic accommodation offered in and around the town. Of particular note are three buildings erected in the 1830s: Prospect House, Laurel Cottage and the Old Dispensary in Edward Street.

Map: Tas 3 K5

Nestled in the foothills of Mount Wellington, alongside a mountain stream, the Cascade Brewery is the oldest brewery in Australia. It was founded by Peter Degraves in 1824.

Ross

By comparison, Ross is a sleepy settlement. Located 117 km north of Hobart and 78 km south of Launceston, Ross is about as British as any Australian town could ever get. Warm sandstone buildings remind the traveller of the villages that are dotted through the Cotswolds.

The main crossroads within the town are known as Temptation, Recreation, Salvation and Damnation because there was once a hotel (Temptation), a church (Salvation), the Town Hall (Recreation) and a gaol (Damnation) on each corner.

The town's premier attraction is the Ross Bridge, which was built by convicts in 1836. It is characterised by exceptionally fine carvings on the side of the bridge. Other places of interest are concentrated on the remarkable main street, which is edged by elm trees. Along the street there is a grand collection of 40 colonial buildings, including the Scotch Thistle Inn (1840), the Ross Memorial Library and Recreation Room (1830s), St John's Church of England (1868) and the Macquarie House and Store (1840s).

Map: Tas 3 K1

Richmond Bridge is the oldest complete freestone bridge in Australia. Built by convicts between 1823 and 1825, it provided access from Hobart to the east coast and the Tasman Peninsula.

The North

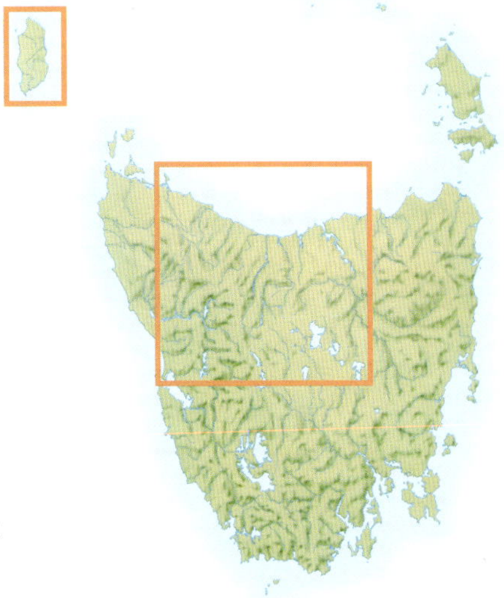

Most travellers arrive on the north coast of Tasmania. The *Devil Cat*, a wonderful way of experiencing the wildness of Bass Strait, arrives at George Town and the slower *Spirit of Tasmania*, a pleasant overnight voyage, arrives at Devonport. This means that for most visitors their exploration of Tasmania starts with the north coast. It is therefore sensible to decide how you are going to experience the island. Are you going to drive to Stanley and then back and down the centre of the island?

Or are you going to drive to Launceston and then go to Hobart before returning to explore the north? There are no rules. However you really do have to plan.

Launceston

Launceston's primary appeal is its history. Many people believe strongly that the city has the largest number of elegant nineteenth-century buildings of any substantial centre in Australia. Located 199 km north of Hobart on the Tamar River, Launceston is an easy point of departure for people wanting to see some of northern Tasmania's most beautiful houses and important Georgian buildings. Make sure you don't miss the fabulous Queen Victoria Museum and Art Gallery, which offers an insight into the history of Launceston, including both its Aboriginal and convict heritage. It is considered one of the best regional museums in Australia. There is also Prince's Square which has a number of particularly handsome Georgian and Victorian buildings. And Batman Faulkner Inn, once known as the Cornwall Hotel, is important in Australian history, for it was here that John Batman met with a group of friends to plan the colony on Port Phillip Bay which eventually became the city of Melbourne.

One of Launceston's real highlights is Cataract Gorge. This attractive recreation park seems to have just about everything. There are pleasant nature walks through the bush, excellent views and a range of facilities including a kiosk, restaurant and swimming pool. There is also a chairlift across part of the park and a pleasant walk across a suspension bridge. The area was developed in 1899, with the first suspension bridge being built in 1904.

Map: Tas 2 C7

Penny Royal Village is located in Cataract Gorge Reserve and includes a reproduction of a gunpowder mill, as well as a restaurant and tearooms.

Around Launceston

Within an easy drive of the city are the historic attractions of 'Woolmers' and 'Brickendon' (1831), near the town of Longford—both were built by the Archer family and both offer excellent and unusual accommodation for those interested in staying in historic homes. For more information, phone 1300 653 633.

And another particularly impressive place is Campbell Town, located 67 km south of Launceston. It is an almost perfectly preserved example of an early nineteenth-century town.

Stanley

Located 231 km west of Launceston, Stanley is the last major township on the north-west coast of Tasmania. It is an exceptionally interesting town, noted for the large number of historic homes and buildings. These include the Van Diemen's Land Company Store (1843–44) which is constructed of bluestone and came to the town as ballast in ships, and the famous Lyons Cottage, where J. A. Lyons, Tasmania's first Prime Minister of Australia (1932–9), was born in 1879.

As you approach Stanley you see 'The Nut'—it dominates the bay. The outcrop was first seen when Bass and Flinders sailed along the coast in 1798. The Nut is actually the stump of an old volcano. Everyone who goes to Stanley feels the need to climb this strange outcrop. Be warned: it is really quite steep and difficult. A much easier option is to take the chairlift to the top.

Map: Tas 1 G3

Above: *Red Bridge, built by convicts in 1836, spans the tranquil waters of Elizabeth River at historic Campbell Town, an old garrison settlement.*

Cradle Mountain

If you just want to go and experience the wildness of inland Tasmania, you can make your way to Cradle Mountain and book into the Cradle Mountain Lodge (03 6492 1303). For those who want relaxation the lodge is warm, comfortable and inviting. The Spa Suites are the ultimate luxury.

Below: *Cataract Gorge, only a short drive from Launceston, is an ideal place for a picnic. Thrill-seekers can try white-water rafting.*

If you are energetic, you can avail yourself of the many different activities that the lodge has to offer (such as horse-riding and canoeing) and reward yourself with a sauna or massage afterwards.

Located 144 km from Launceston, Cradle Mountain is the central feature of Cradle Mountain–Lake St Clair National Park. The park covers a total area of 124 942 hectares, and is dominated by glaciated landscape. There are over 25 major peaks, as well as glacial formations like tarns, lakes, moraine deposits, U-shaped valleys and waterfalls.

A familiar sight at night around the camp sites of Cradle Mountain–Lake St Clair National Park is the brush-tail possum (Trichosurus vulpecula).

Visitors who decide to stay at the Cradle Mountain Lodge can enjoy the short Enchanted Walk along the Pencil Pine River. At night-time the nocturnal animals that inhabit the park—such as Tasmanian devils, ring-tail possums and eastern quolls—come to the lodge to be fed. There are also pademelons and Bennett's wallabies in the area, plus birds ranging from black cockatoos to rosellas, honeyeaters and robins.

It is possible to take day walks to Cradle Mountain and Crater Lake, to go alpine skiing (although there are no lifts or ski facilities), to swim in the lakes (which are very cold), to climb Cradle Mountain or to take a number of interesting walks including Mount Campbell (about 3 hours), Hansons Peak (about

3 hours), Twisted Lakes (3–4 hours), Lake Rodway (5 hours), Lake Lilla (1 hour) and the Ballroom Forest (3 hours).

Map: Tas 1 J9

The crystal clear lakes and streams of Tasmania's Highlands draw anglers from around the world, who seek the freshwater trout found here.

King Island

Do you want to go somewhere that is really unusual? There is a regular ferry service from Stanley to King Island—and King Island, famous for its excellent dairy produce, is an ideal place for those people who want a holiday with a real difference. Here

The windswept highlands of Cradle Mountain–Lake St Clair National Park are renowned for their rugged beauty and are popular with photographers.

you really get away from everything and enjoy a little simple island hospitality.

Located approximately 80 km north-west of Tasmania and about 90 km south-east of Cape Otway on the Victorian coast, King Island is some 58 km long and 21 km wide and has a total area of 126 000 hectares. Given its location, it can often be wind-swept and rainy but it is also rugged and attractive, with a beautiful coastline which is 145 km long and certainly worth exploring. With a population of over 2500 people, it is one of Australia's undiscovered island retreats. The island has an estimated 57 offshore wrecks and a wide variety of seabirds and wildlife. Every visitor should go to see Reid Rocks Nature Reserve, a breeding ground for seals.

Left: *King Island is a haven for a number of native bird species, such as the protected Cape Barren goose* (Cereopsis novaehollandiae).

If you are looking to escape the often-inclement weather, visit King Island Dairy to taste the island's well-known and award-winning produce, including delicious cheddar, brie and clotted cream.

Accommodation on King Island ranges from motels and hotels to an extensive range of cottages and apartments.

Map: Tas 1 B8

The South

Tasmania is, as the advertisements enjoy depicting, shaped like an apple. The south, therefore, covers a huge range of diverse regions. People wanting to relax and explore the south of the island can head south-east to the bushwalking wonderland of Freycinet National Park (an area so beautiful Queen Elizabeth II once stopped there for a picnic) or the historic ruins at Port Arthur. Alternatively, they could head south-west into the Huon Valley where the apples and hops grow and where peace and tranquillity reign.

Or they can head due west across the central mountains and reach Macquarie Harbour—the loneliest convict settlement on Earth—which is now a superb region of untouched temperate rainforest.

Freycinet National Park

If you are looking for an eco-tourism experience it is hard to beat Freycinet Lodge in the Freycinet National Park. This is an area of dramatic granite outcrops (the Hazards rise beyond the lodge which looks across Coles Bay, located 202 km north-east of Hobart and 218 km south-east of Launceston). The park also offers superb bushwalks ranging in length from one hour to several days, and extensive habitats for possums, wallabies and a rich variety of birdlife. The most impressive attraction is the isolated and remarkable Wineglass Bay where, years ago, the royal yacht *Britannia* anchored to allow

don't miss

The Coles Bay Game Fishing Classic is held every March; it attracts entrants from the mainland as well as from overseas. Deep-sea fishing is one of the main activities of the towns dotted along the east coast.

Looking across Coles Bay to Freycinet National Park on Tasmania's east coast. This picturesque park is only a 2-hour drive north-east of Hobart.

the Queen ashore for an Australian-style beach barbecue. If this sounds a little strange, you will understand when you walk down onto this perfectly peaceful and secluded beach of impossibly white sand. This is the kind of destination that sets high standards for eco-tourism. It is peaceful, unspoilt and extraordinarily beautiful. It is fair to say that when the weather is perfect it is hard to imagine a more serene and awe-inspiring piece of coastline in Australia.

Freycinet Lodge is a masterpiece of eco-integrated accommodation featuring all-wood cabins, with a wealth of style and class, nestling within the bushland above Richardson's Beach on Coles Bay. There is a range of accommodation, from the basic Freycinet Cabin to the more expensive Wineglass Deluxe Cabin. There are a number of packages available, to suit all budgets. Contact Freycinet Lodge on (03) 6257 0101. If your budget is limited, there are some great waterfront camp sites, as well as youth hostels and moderately priced B&Bs.

Map: Tas 3 P1

Pirates Bay forms the eastern side of Eaglehawk Neck, which is the thin isthmus—only just wide enough for a road—that connects the historic Tasman Peninsula to the rest of Tasmania.

Port Arthur

If you are interested in early Australian history, there is no better way to spend a day than to visit the ruins at Port Arthur. This magnificently preserved penal colony is a powerful reminder of Australia's convict heritage. Here, in what is now a lovely area running down to the water's edge, there are mature English trees, neat paths and manicured lawns. From 1830 to 1877 this was a very harsh penal colony where the criminals of England and Ireland—people who had often committed only minor crimes by today's standards—ended up serving seven years. The scale of the punishment now seems out of proportion to the crimes that were committed. It is extraordinary to contemplate that 12 500 convicts served their time at Port Arthur between 1830 and 1877.

Located 100 km from Hobart, on the Tasman Peninsula, Port Arthur is isolated from the rest of the island state by a narrow sliver of land known as Eaglehawk Neck. Port Arthur was established in 1830 by Lieutenant-Governor Arthur to deal with the worst criminals. And, just to make the situation even worse, from 1834–1849 a special prison for juveniles was established across the bay at Port Puer.

Historic Port Arthur is Tasmania's pre-eminent tourist attraction. For an unusual experience, take a tour of the old buildings and ruins at night, when convict tales come to life by lantern light.

TAS

Close by, approximately 2000 convicts and townspeople are buried in the cemetery known as The Isle of the Dead.

Today the area is full of interest. The visitor can wander around the ruins of Port Arthur; there are over 30 buildings to inspect, from the prison chapel to the commandant's residence. You can then go to Eaglehawk Neck and, after visiting the tesselated pavement rock platform and marvelling at how easy it must have been to have dogs patrolling the 'neck' to prevent escapes, then move on through Doo Town (where the residents have named their homes Gunadoo, Doodle Doo, Love Me Doo, Doo Us, Doo Me, Doo Nix, Wee Doo, Xanadu, Rum Doo and Doo Little) to the impressive natural features at Tasman Arch and the Devil's Kitchen. Also of interest in the area is Saltwater River (located 106 km southeast of Hobart and 23 km from Port Arthur), a penal colony which is rarely visited and yet, in its own way, is as interesting as Port Arthur.

Map: Tas 3 M7

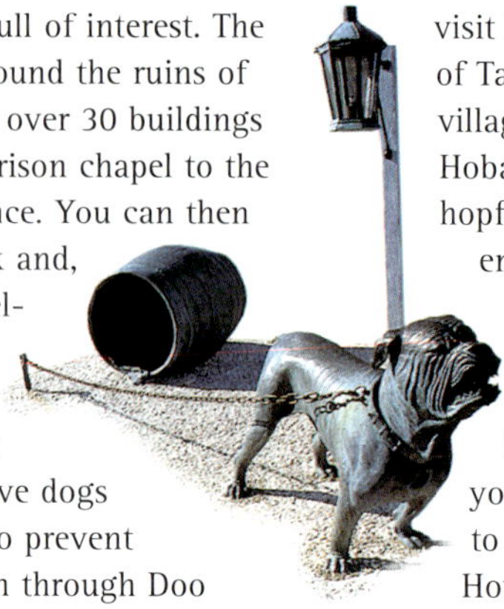

Right: *The Dog Line memorial at Eaglehawk Neck is a reminder of the brutality of Port Arthur. In the mid-1800s, 18 vicious dogs were kept on this narrow strip of land to prevent convict escapes.*

Cygnet and the Huon Valley

Driving directly south from Hobart the traveller encounters the beautiful Huon Valley which is famous for its hops and apples. This is the agricultural heartland of the state. Cygnet is located only 56 km south of Hobart. The valley has expanded its range of industries and as well as hops and apples, it has also turned to alternative-lifestyle activities. Consequently the visitor can now stop and inspect woodturning gift shops, wholefoods shops, craft shops and places involved with vintage car restoration—among many others. It is also a great place for holiday cottage accommodation and B&Bs. When in the area make sure you visit Bushy Park—the hop capital of Tasmania. This delightful little village is located just 58 km from Hobart. The area is awash with hopfields. Be sure that you also enjoy the drive around the D'Entrecasteaux Channel through the tiny townships of Woodbridge and Kettering. If you have time, you can make a daytrip across to Bruny Island from Kettering. However, the distances on the island are much longer than you initially think and the roads are far from perfect—so it is best to spend a few days here.

Map: Tas 3 J7

Doo Town is located near Tasman National Park on the Tasman Peninsula. It is famous for its quaint houses, which all feature 'Doo' in their names.

Strahan and Macquarie Harbour

It is worth remembering that when you stand on the beach at Strahan the waves have arrived uninterrupted from South America. In other words you are further south than Cape Town in South Africa, and when the Roaring Forties are blowing the experience is amazing. Strahan is a fishing port and it is necessary, if you care about food and arrive at the right time of the year, to have some of the excellent lobster caught by the local fishing fleet. It is also necessary to take one of the many boat trips up Macquarie Harbour. There are a number of cruises which leave Strahan and travel to the lower reaches of the Gordon River. Some will take visitors to Hells Gate, others go to Sarah Island (a convict settlement) and others simply pass those attractions and let passengers explore the rainforest on the edge of the Gordon River. The *James Kelly* travels most days of the year. Contact (03) 6471 7187.

Map: Tas 3 B2

The Tessellated Pavement near Eaglehawk Neck looks man-made, but it is the combined result of earth movements and erosion by sea water.

TAS

Situated on Macquarie Harbour, Strahan is the major port for Tasmania's west coast. Within the harbour lies Sarah Island, on which Tasmania's first penal settlement was established in 1822.

did you know?

James Kelly and his crew were the first Europeans to explore Macquarie Harbour, in 1815. They noted that the harbour was lined with large forests of Huon pine, which soon drew piners (timber-getters) to the area.

Map 1

A
B
C
D
E
F
G
1
2
3
4
5
6
7
8
9
10
NORTH
144°
144°30′
145°
40°30′
41°
41°30′
42°
40°
Cape Keraudren
Coulomb Bay
Lighthouse
Three Hummock Island
Cape Adamson
South Hummock
Hope Channel
Cuvier Bay
Lighthouse
Hunter Island
Goodwill Point
Walker Channel
Walker Island
Hunter Passage
Trefoil Island
Woolnorth Point
Woolnorth
Cape Grim
Valley Bay
Kangaroo Island
Robbins Island
Ransonnet Bay
Guyton Point
Flat Topped Bluff
Bluff Point
Studland Bay
Cape Elie
Robbins Passage
Montagu I
Stony Pt
Highfield Historic Site
North Point
Half Moon Bay
Lighthouse
The Nut Chairlift
Stanley
Circular Head
Perkins Island
Perkins Bay
Montagu
C215
Duck Bay
Sawyer Bay
Smithton
Wiltshire
Port Latta
Mella
Mt Cameron West
Ann Bay
Welcome River
Montagu River
Christmas Hills
BASS HWY
Smokers Bank
Forest
Crayfish Creek
South Forest
Mengha
Rocky
Green Point
Marrawah
Redpa
Bond Tier
Togari
Irishtown
Brittons Swamp
Alcomie
West Pt
A2
B22
Lileah
Mawson Bay
Sherstons Hill
Arthur Pieman Conservation Area
52
Duck River
Edith Creek
Nabageena
Mawbar
C225
Dip River
Bluff Hill Point
Lighthouse
Roger River
C218
Trowutta
Wedge Plains
Dip Fall
Arthur River
Gardiner Point
Arthur River
Arthur River
Kanunnah Bridge
Milkshakes Hills Forest Reserve
Frankland River
Nelson Bay
C214
Lake Chisholm Forest Reserve
Neasey Plains
Nelson Bay
Julius River Forest Res
Blue Peak
Couta Rocks
Rapid River
Temma
Richardson Point
Eel Ck
Horton
Hazard Bay
Balfour
Mt Balfour
Mt Frankland
Lyons
Keith
Mt Bertha
Thornton R
Lindsay
Leigh
Savage River National Park
Mt Hazelton
Kenneth Bay
Sandy Cape
Lighthouse
Pedder R
C249
Mt Norfolk
Mt Cleveland
Luina
Lagoon R
Whyte
Savage River
Arthur Pieman Conservation Area
Interview River
Donaldson
Mt Meredith
C247
Mt Ram
Blackguards Hill
Ford R
Mt Donaldson
Rupert Point
Pieman
Toll Punt
Corinna
Meredith Range
Whyte
Paradise
Hardwicke Bay
Pieman River State Reserve
Mt Livingstone
Conical Rocks Point
Yarrana Hill
Reece Dam
Stanley
Duck Ck
C249
Renison Bell
Granville Harbour
Lake Pieman
Mt Heemskirk
Mt Agnew
Zeehan
Mt Zeehan
Trial Harbour
Little Henty R
Glacial
B27
Henty
King Island
Scale same as main map
Cape Wickham
Lighthouse
Disappointment Bay
Cape Farewell
Phoques Bay
Lake Martha Lavinia
Egg Lagoon
Lavinia Point
New Year Island
Christmas Island
Whistler Point
Yambacoona
Lavinia Nature Reserve
Reekara
Counsel Hill
KING
B25
Cowper Point
Loorana
Sea Elephant R
Sea Elephant Bay
Currie Harbour
Lighthouse
Currie
ISLAND
Naracoopa
Fraser Bluff
Pegarah
Parenna
Ettrick R
B25
Yarrah Creek
Lymwood
Fitzmaurice Bay
Bold Head
Cataraqui Point
Grassy
Mt Stanley
Big Lake
Calcified Forest
Surprise Bay
Seal Bay
Lighthouse
Stokes Point

0 10 20 30
kilometres
H J K L M N P
1 2 3 4 5 6 7 8 9 10
146°
146°30′
147°
40°30′
41°
41°30′
42°
BASS STRAIT
Rocky Cape Nat Park
Sisters Beach
Boat Harbour Beach
Boat Harbour
Lighthouse
Table Cape
Sisters Creek
Flowerdale
Wynyard
Seabrook
Moorleah
Lapoinya
Somerset
Burnie
Emu Bay
Lower Mount Hicks
Oldina
Upper Mount Hicks
Calder
Preolenna
Elliott
Mooreville
Heybridge
Howth
Sulphur Creek
Penguin
Stowport
Upper Stowport
Cuprona
West Ridgley
Ridgley
Yolla
Henrietta
Guide Falls
Takone
Natone
Camena
West Pine
Mt Duncan
Highclere
Upper Natone
Riana
North Motton
Tewkesbury
South Riana
Hellyer Gorge State Res
Hampshire
Gunns Plains
Heka
Gunns Plains Cave
Preston
Ulverstone
Turners Beach
Leith
Gawler
Forth
Abbotsham
Don
Devonport
Bass Strait Ferry
Spalford
Sprent
Kindred
Central Castra
Paloona
Melrose
Eugenana
Spreyton
Tarleton
Latrobe
Wesley Vale
Moriarty
Northdown
Thirlstane
Port Sorell
Hawley Beach
Point Sorell
Badger Head
West Head
Bakers Beach
Asbestos Range Nat Park
Beaconsfield
Port Dalrymple
Five Mile Bluff
Low Head
Greens Beach
Kelso
Clarence Point
Beauty Point
George Town
Bell Bay
Stony Head
Beechford
Stony Head Military Area
Lulworth
Pipers River
Lefroy
Tippogoree Hills
Rowella
Kayena
Sidmouth
Deviot
Hillwood
Mount Direction
Paper Beach
Gravelly Beach
Exeter
Lanena
Blackwall
Windermere
Rosevears
Dilston
Glengarry
Legana
Bridgenorth
Winkleigh
Holwell
Frankford
West Frankford
The Dazzler Ra
Harford
East Sassafras
Sassafras
Warringa
Lower Wilmot
Upper Castra
Nietta
Paloona Power Stn
Lwr Barrington
Lake Paloona
Barrington
Nook
Devils Gate Power Station
Lake Barrington
Railton
Merseylea
Sheffield
Sunnyside
Kimberley
Parkham
Birralee
Rosevale
Selbourne
Lake Trevallyn
Westwood
Hadspen
Carrick
Hagley
Westbury
Deloraine
Lemana
Red Hills
Needles
Chudleigh
Mole Creek
Osmaston
Cluan
Glenore
Whitemore
Oaks
Toiberry
Bishopsbourne
Bracknell
Cressy
Quamby Brook
Golden Valley
Meander
Quamby Bluff
Liffey
Liffey Falls
Drys Bluff
Liffey Forest Res
Projection Bluff
Blackwood Creek
Poatina
Mt Blackwood
Central Plateau Conservation Area
Mother Lords Plains
Reynolds I
Reynolds Neck
Cramps
Great Lake
Liawenee
Tods
Flintstone
Wilburville
Arthurs Lake
Little Lake
Shannon Lagoon
Miena
Barren Tier
Wild Dog Tier
Breona
Bernacchi
Lake Augusta
Double Lagoon
Lake Fergus
Little Pine Lagoon
Meander Falls
Western Creek
Montana
Caveside
Elizabeth Town
Mole Creek
Weetah
Reedy Marsh
Dunorlan
Moltema
Weegena
Lower Beulah
Alum Cliffs State Res
Beulah
Paradise
West Kentish
Wilmot
South Nietta
Loongana
Leven Canyon
Roland
Claude Road
Mt Roland
Staverton
Gowrie Park
Mt Claude
Cethana Power Stn
Lake Cethana
Moina
Erriba
Winterbrook Falls
Black Bluff
Mt Cattley
Lake Lea
Lake Gairdner
Lorinna
Liena
King Solomon Cave
Mayberry
Marakoopa Cave
Emu Plains
Lemonthyme Power Station
Western Bluff
Devils Gullet Lookout
Lake Mackenzie
Ironstone Mtn
Blue Peaks
Forty Lakes Peak
Julian Lakes
Pillans Lake
Walls of Jerusalem National Park
Mt Jerusalem
Clumner Bluff
Fisher Bluff
Rowallan Power Stn
Lake Rowallan
February Plains
Borradaile Plains
Lake Parangana
Middlesex Plains
Pencil Pine Visitor Centre
Cradle Valley
Dove Lake
Cradle Mtn
Cradle Mountain
Mt Pelion West
Mt Ossa
Lake Will
Granite Tor
Granite Tor Cons Area
Lake Mackintosh
Mt Romulus
Mackintosh Dam
Tullah
Mt Black
Murchison Dam
Victoria Peak
Rosebery
Mt Charter
Mt Remus
Waratah
Mt Pearce
Guildford
Talbots Lagoon
St Valentines Peak
Lake St Clair National Park
Lake Murchison
Eldon Peak
Eldon Bluff
Mt Tyndall
Lake Plimsoll
Lake Margaret
Mt Lyell
Lake Louisa
Lake Myrtle
Lake Adelaide
Lake Meston
Lake Malbena
Lake Olive
Lake Rotull
Lake Naomi
Lake Fanny
Lake Ada
Lake Norman
Lake Ball
Lake Lenone
Travellers Rest Lake
Lake Petrarch
Overland Track
Mersey R
Forth R
Leven R
Wallace R
South Eldon River
Pine R
Nive R
Meander R
Brumby
Liffey R
Tamar R
BASS HWY
MURCHISON HWY
LAKE HWY
WESTERN TIERS
GREAT WESTERN TIERS
Rubicon R
Franklin R
Blythe R
Emu R
Guide R
Inglis R
Cam R
Wilmot R
Dasher R
Gog Ra
Vale R
Que R
Hatfield R
Fury River
Sophia R
Chalmers Ck
Campbell R
Iris R
Clayton R
Mt Remus
A10
B18
B26
B15
B16
B17
B14
B13
C132
C137
B12
A5
B71
B72
C515
C511
B51
B11
B28
A7

TAS
TAS 2

Map 2

TAS 1
TAS 3

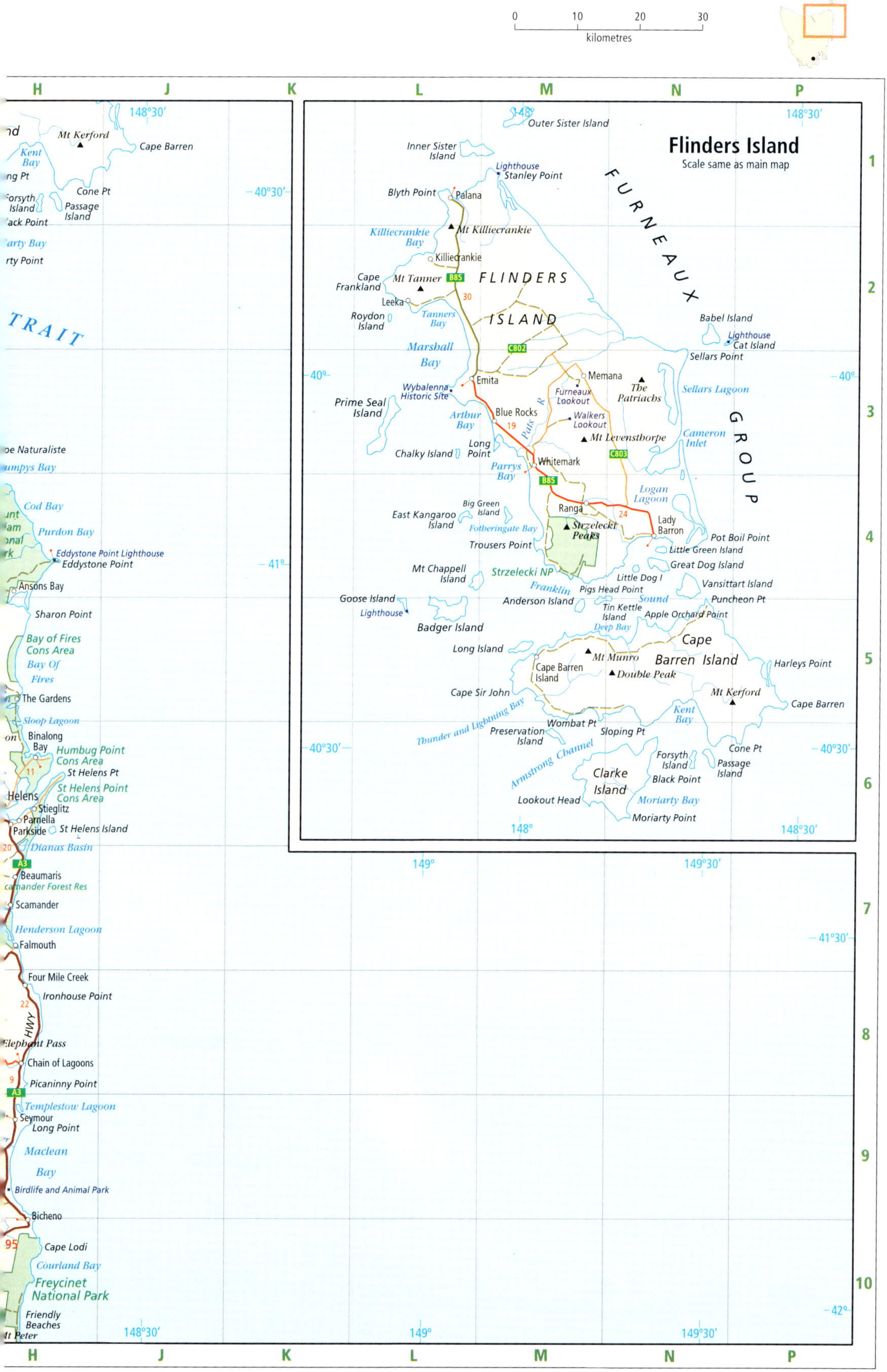
0 10 20 30
kilometres
Flinders Island
Scale same as main map
FURNEAUX
GROUP
FLINDERS
ISLAND
Outer Sister Island
Inner Sister Island
Lighthouse
Stanley Point
Blyth Point
Palana
Killiecrankie Bay
Mt Killiecrankie
Killiecrankie
Cape Frankland
Mt Tanner
B85
30
Leeka
Roydon Island
Tanners Bay
Marshall Bay
C802
Babel Island
Lighthouse
Cat Island
Sellars Point
Sellars Lagoon
Memana
The Patriarchs
Furneaux Lookout
Emita
Wybalenna Historic Site
Prime Seal Island
Arthur Bay
Blue Rocks
19
Pats R
Walkers Lookout
Mt Leventhorpe
Cameron Inlet
C803
Long Point
Chalky Island
Parrys Bay
Whitemark
Logan Lagoon
Big Green Island
East Kangaroo Island
Ranga
24
Lady Barron
Fotheringate Bay
Strzelecki Peaks
Trousers Point
Pot Boil Point
Little Green Island
Great Dog Island
Mt Chappell Island
Strzelecki NP
Little Dog I
Vansittart Island
Franklin
Pigs Head Point
Goose Island
Lighthouse
Anderson Island
Sound
Puncheon Pt
Tin Kettle Island
Apple Orchard Point
Badger Island
Deep Bay
Long Island
Cape Barren Island
Mt Munro
Double Peak
Harleys Point
Cape Barren Island
Cape Sir John
Mt Kerford
Cape Barren
Thunder and Lightning Bay
Kent Bay
Wombat Pt
Preservation Island
Sloping Pt
Cone Pt
Armstrong Channel
Forsyth Island
Passage Island
Clarke Island
Black Point
Lookout Head
Moriarty Bay
Moriarty Point
148°
148°30′
40°
40°30′
149°
149°30′
41°
41°30′
42°
H J K L M N P
1 2 3 4 5 6 7 8 9 10
Mt Kerford
Cape Barren
Kent Bay
Cone Pt
Passage Island
TRAIT
Cod Bay
Purdon Bay
Eddystone Point Lighthouse
Eddystone Point
Ansons Bay
Sharon Point
Bay of Fires Cons Area
Bay Of Fires
The Gardens
Sloop Lagoon
Binalong Bay
Humbug Point Cons Area
St Helens Pt
St Helens Point Cons Area
Stieglitz
Parnella
Parkside
St Helens Island
Dianas Basin
A3
Beaumaris
Scamander
Henderson Lagoon
Falmouth
Four Mile Creek
Ironhouse Point
22
Chain of Lagoons
Picaninny Point
Templestowe Lagoon
Seymour
Long Point
Maclean Bay
Birdlife and Animal Park
Bicheno
Cape Lodi
Courland Bay
Freycinet National Park
Friendly Beaches

Map 3

TAS 1
A
B
C
D
E
F
G
1
2
3
4
5
6
7
8
9
10
42°
42°30′
43°
43°30′
145°30′
146°
146°30′
Eldon Bluff
Cradle Mountain
Lake St Clair NP
Travellers Rest Lake
Lake Lenone
Little Pine Lagoon
Miena
Barren
Henty Glacial Moraine
Henty River
Yolande
Mt Lyell
Lake Burbury
South Eldon River
Pyramid Mtn
Mt Olympus
Lake St Clair
Lake Ina
Clarence Lagoon
Pine Tier Lagoon
Henty Dunes
Tully
Queenstown
Gormanston
Mt Owen
Lynchford
Balaclava
LYELL
Victoria Pass
Raglan Ra
A10
Alma
Cheyne Ra
Mt Rufus
Visitor Centre
Derwent Bridge
Bronte Park
Lake Big Jim
Wadda
Macquarie Heads
Ocean Beach
Strahan
Regatta Point
John Butters PS
Crotty Dam
Mt Alma
HWY
120
London Lakes
Lake Samuel
Lake Echo
Cape Sorell Lighthouse
Swan Basin Picnic Ground
King
Lake Burbury
Laughing Jack Lagoon
Lake King William
Bronte Lagoon
Bradys Lake
Teepookana Forest Res
Darwin Dam
Franklin
Loddon
Franklin River Nature Trail
Mt King William I
Butlers Gorge Power Station
Dee Lagoon
Lake Echo Power Station
Dee
Pine Cove
Sophia Pt
Braddon
Mt Sorell
Mt Darwin
Frenchmans Cap
Lake Binney
Tarraleah Power Station
Liberty Pt
Table Head
Gordon
Macquarie Harbour
Andrew
Engineer Range
Lake Rufus
Franklin-Gordon
Mt King William II
Tarraleah
Victoria Valley Falls
Sloop Point
Lake Richmond
Counsel
Derwent
Wild Rivers National Park
Gorge Point
Gould Pt
Kelly Basin
Cracroft
Mt McCall
Deception Range
Mt King William III
73
Strickland
Sarah Island Historic Site
Rum Pt
Heritage Landing
Hills
Western Plains
Jane
Norway Ra
Wayatinah
Wayatinah Lagoon
Wayatinah Power Station
Birthday Bay
Gulley Point
Modder River
Birch Inlet
Elliot Ra
Goodwins Peak
Prince of Wales Range
Wylds Craig
Lake Catagunya
Catagunya Power Station
Lake Repulse
Varna Bay
Repulse Power Station
Misery Plateau
Lake Curly
Denison Range
Dunrobin Bridge
Hibbs
Hibbs Bay
D'Aguilar Range
Sorell
Franklin
Princess Range
Mt Humboldt
Pleiades
Meadow
Point Hibbs
Mt Lee
Sprent
Smith River
Maxwell
Denison
Hamilton Range
Mount Field Nat Park
Lake Fenton
Ellendale
Spero Bay
Spero
Nicholls Ra
Clear Hill
Mt Field West
Skiing
National Park
Endeavour Bay
Southwest
Wanderer
Lake Gordon
Tiger Ra
Florentine
Lake Belton
Tim Shea
Hales
Moores Valley
Mt Lewis
Gordon Dam
Olga
Tyenna
Fitzgerald
Maydena
High Rocky Point
Conservation
Charles
Strathgordon
Serpentine Dam
Teds Beach
Mt Mueller
Ibsens Peak
Albert
Mt Sprent
B61
Frodshams Pass
Creepy Crawly Walk
Styx
Area
Mt Bowes
Mount Wedge Forest Res
Mt Osmund
Starfish Hill
McPartlan Pass
The Coronets
C607
Snowy Range
Hudson
Lawson
Range
Rookery Plain
Hardwood
Double Peak
Lake Pedder
Mt Eliza
Mt Anne
Weld
Lewis
Frankland Range
Mt Solitary
Lake Judd
Mt Weld
Low Rocky Point
Elliott Bay
Mt Giblin
Scotts Peak
Scotts Peak Dam
Gallagher Plateau
Giblin
Folded Range
Edgar Dam
Propsting Range
Piners Peak
White Monolith Range
Mt Frederick
Tahune Forest Res
Nye Bay
Elliot Point
Mt Hesperus
Huon
Arthur
Mt Orion
The Razorback
Mt Picton
Lake Picton
Lake Riveaux
Mulcaby Bay
Brier Holme Head
De Witt Range
Davey Gorge
Crossing
West Portal
Mt Hean
Lake Jupiter
Lost World Plateau
Spring River
Svenor Point
Wreck Bay
Settlement Point
Southwest
Cracroft Gorge
Picton Range
White Horse Plains
Mt Norold
Federation Peak
James Kelly Basin
Rugby Ra
Ripple Mtn
Lake Geeves
Pine Lake
Mt Bobs
Payne Bay
Erskine Ra
Rowitta Plains
Mt Pollux
Spiro Range
Davey Head
North Head
Point St Vincent
Port Davey
Mt Rugby
Bathurst Harbour
National Park
Bobs Knobs
SOUTHERN
Hilliard Head
Stephens Bay
South West Cape Range
Melaleuca Range
Melaleuca Ranger Station & Bird Observation
Ray Range
Mutton Bird Island
Mt Counsel
Mt Louisa
Mt Victoria Cross
Precipitous Bluff
Window Pane Bay
Mt Melaleuca
OCEAN
Doorstop Bay
Cox Bight
Red Point Hills
Louisa
Ironbound Range
New River Lagoon
Mt Karamu
New Harbour
Cox Bluff
Louisa Bay
Havelock Bluff
Prion Bay
Oval Lake
South West Cape
Telopea Point
Red Point
Louisa Island
Ile du Golfe
Point Cecil
Point Vivian
Wilson Bight
Surprise Bay
Shoemaker Point
NORTH
Maatsuyker Group
De Witt Island
Flat Witch Island
Walker Island
Maatsuyker I

0
10
20
30
kilometres
H
J
K
L
M
N
P
1
2
3
4
5
6
7
8
9
10
147°
147°30'
148°
42°
42°30'
43°
43°30'
Flintstone
Great Lake
Wilburville
Steppes
Lagoon of Islands
Woods Lake
Lake Sorell
Mt Franklin
Ross
Lake Leake
Lake Leake
Hobgoblin
Wyefield
Lost Falls Forest Res
Moulting Lagoon
Cranbrook
Freycinet Nat Park
Friendly Beaches
Mt Peter
Mt Paul
Alma Pass
Interlaken
Tunbridge
Woodbury
Antill Ponds
Old Mans Head
Lake Crescent
Table Mtn
Woods Quoin
Oatlands
Vincent Hill
York Plains
Callington Mill Historic Site
Pawtella
Lemont
Faddens Tier
Tooms Lake
Macquarie River
Meredith River
Buxton River
Mayfield Bay Cons Area
Nine Mile Beach
Hepburn Point
Coles Bay
Swansea
Great Oyster Bay
Spiky Bridge
Fleurieu Pt
Mt Dove
Lighthouse
Cape Tourville
Sleepy Bay
Wineglass Bay
Cape Forestier
Promise Bay
Mt Graham
Mt Freycinet
Weatherhead Point
Freycinet Pen
Mayfield Bay
Buxton Pt
Bryans Beach
Baldy Bluff
Cape Degerando
Schouten Passage
Schouten Island
Rooster Point
Cape Sonnerat
Little Swanport
Seaford Point
Little Swanport
Cape Faure
Freycinet National Park
Pt Bailly
Nicholas Sugarloaf
Thorpe Water Mill
Bothwell
Green Hill
Northumbria Hill
Jericho
Pike Hill
Lake Dulverton
Andover
Parattah
Mount Seymour
Stonor
Whitefoord
Spring Hill
Little Swanport Hill
Buckland Military Training Area
Boltons Beach Cons Area
Grindstone Point
Mt Murray
Mt Reid
Black Tier
Melton Mowbray
Lake Tiberias
Baden
Tunnack
Rhyndaston
Eldon
Woodsdale
Bluestone Tier
Triabunna
Cape Bougainville
Hamilton
Hollow Tree
Mt Spode
Pelham
Kempton
Colebrook
Quoin Mtn
Levendale
Mt Hobbs
Louisville
Lighthouse
Okehampton Bay
Craigbourne Dam
Prosser
Orford
Prosser Bay
Spring Beach
Cape Boullanger
Darlington
Maria Island National Park
Elderslie
Dysart
Bagdad
Mangalore Tier
Brown Mtn
Buckland
Thumbs Picnic Area
Rheban
Johnsons Pt
Return Pt
Maria Island
Mt Maria
Mistaken Cape
Broadmarsh
Mangalore
Lowdina
Tasman
Runnymede
Mt Morrison
Prossers Sugarloaf
Pt Lesueur
Booming Bay
Shoal Bay
Riedle Bay
Gretna
Glenora
Rosegarland
Pontville
Campania
Sandspit River Forest Res
Oyster Bay
Cape Maurouard
Bushy Park
Macquarie Plains
Mt Dromedary
Black Hills
Dromedary
Tea Tree
Brighton
Bridgewater
Richmond
Pawleena
Nugent
Mercury
Cape Bernier
Cape Peron
Plenty
Hayes
Magra
Salmon Ponds
Granton
Old Beach
Grasstree Hill
Orielton
Wattle Hill
Kellevie
Marion Bay
Moogara
Boyer
Claremont
Sorell
Bream Creek
New Norfolk
Feilton
Malbina
Molesworth
Otago
Risdon Vale
Midway Point
Forcett
Arthur
Copping
Glenfern
Glenlusk
Glenorchy
Cambridge
Pitt Water
Lewisham
Carlton
Cape Paul Lamanon
North Bay
Mount Lloyd
Lachlan
Collinsvale
Seven Mile Beach Protected Area
Mt Rumney
Dodges Ferry
Cape Frederick Hendrick
Collins Cap
Lookout
Seven Mile Beach
Carlton
Dunalley
Trestle Mtn
Mt Wellington
HOBART
Rokeby
Primrose Sands
Blue Hill
Fern Tree
Ridgeway
Lauderdale
Frederick Henry
Green Head
Dunalley Bay
Mt Forestier
Forestier
High Yellow Bluff
Mountain River
Neika
Taroona
Sandford
Sloping I
Lime Bay Nat Res
Smooth I
Murdunna
Lonnavale
Mt Misery
Crabtree
Grove
Leslie Vale
Shot Tower
Cremorne
Bay
Cape Surville
Judbury
Lucaston
Lower Longley
Longley
Kingston
Opossum Bay
Cape Deslacs
Clifton Beach
Chronicle Pt
Coal Mines Historic Site
Peninsula
Ranelagh
Sandfly
Blackmans Bay
Norfolk Bay
Eaglehawk Neck
Tessellated Pavement
Glen Huon
Huonville
Kaoota
Howden
South Arm
Saltwater River
Pirates Bay
Tasman Blowhole
Tasman Arch
Devils Kitchen
Waterfall Bay
Scotts Divide
Pelverata Falls
Pelverata
Margate
Tinderbox
Iron Pot Lighthouse
Betsey Island
Premaydena
Tasmanian Devil Park
Taranna
Electrona
Snug
North West Bay
Dennes Point
Outer North Head
Koonya
Woodstock
Snug Falls
Coningham
Killora
One Tree Point
O'Hara Bluff
Franklin
Cradoc
Oyster Cove
Kettering
Barnes Bay
Wedge Bay
Nubeena
Tasman Peninsula
Tasman Trail
South Franklin
Castle Forbes Bay
Port Huon
Glaziers Bay
Wattle Grove
Nicholls Rivulet
Ferry
The Yellow Bluff
White Beach
Fortescue Bay
Cape Huay
Geeveston
Cygnet
Woodbridge
Trumpeter Bay
Two Island Bay
Highcroft
Palmers Lookout
Port Arthur
Convict Ruins
Munro Bight
Petcheys Bay
Birchs Bay
Storm Bay
Remarkable Cave
Tasman National Park
Cairns Bay
Lymington
Gardners Bay
Great Bay
Variety Bay
Curio Bay
Waterloo
Surges Bay
North Bruny Island
Tasman National Park
Maingon Bay
Cape Pillar
Peak
Hartz Mts
Glendevie
Police Point
Middleton
Simpsons Pt
Cape Queen Elizabeth
Tasman I Lighthouse
Garden Island Creek
Channel
Isthmus Bay
Hideaway Bay
Surveyors Bay
Verona Sands
Gordon
Simpsons Bay
Raoul Bay
Cape Raoul
Esperance
Huon I
Adventure Bay
Dover
Maggot Pt
Esperance Pt
Ramines
Port Esperance
Alonnah
Fluted Cape
Strathblane
Venteman Point
D'Entrecasteaux
South Bruny Island
Adventure Bay
Hastings Caves
Partridge Island
Capt Cook's Landing Place
Bligh Museum
Lunawanna
Cape Connella
Thermal Pool
Great Taylors Bay
Hopwood Point
Bay of Islands
Lune River
Southport
Mangana Bluff
Ida Bay
South Bruny Nat Park
South Bruny National Park
Southport Lagoon
Historic Lighthouse
Cloudy Bay
Mt Bruny
Cape Bruny
Boreel Head
West Cloudy Head
East Cloudy Head
Tasman Head
The Friars
TASMAN SEA
Eliza Point
Recherche Bay
Catamaran
Whale Sculpture
Cockle Creek
Bare Hill
Whale Head
HWY
MIDLAND HWY
HUON HWY
TASMAN HWY
ARTHUR HWY
LAKE HWY
A3
A5
A6
A9
A10
B31
B32
B33
B34
B37
B64
B66
B68
B110
C305
C321
1
21
27
36
42
48
52
58
64
75
81
86

South Australia

South Australia could easily be called the 'Tranquil State'. The capital, Adelaide, is known as the 'City of Churches', and visitors often find themselves deeply moved by the stunning architecture of the cathedrals and other houses of worship here. Numerous wine regions—from the Barossa and Clare Valleys to McLaren Vale and Coonawarra—offer peaceful vistas dripping with vines, fine restaurants and, of course, taste testing. Further afield, the Eyre Peninsula provides magnificent views of southern right whales as they migrate north between June and October, and the spectacular sunsets over the Flinders Ranges have enchanted artists and authors for decades. So relax, unwind and let the wonders of South Australia wash your worries away.

Adelaide and Environs

There is no capital city in Australia quite like Adelaide. Where else can you drive for 20 minutes and be out of the city and in the bush? Where else can you still be in suburbia and checking out some of the world's greatest wines (the Penfolds Grange vineyard and winery is now surrounded by suburban homes)? Where else can you experience the contrasts of pleasant beachside suburbs and cool and pleasant hill station retreats so close together? And where else can you live far removed from the city centre and still be only a pleasant half-hour's walk away from the central business district?

Adelaide is a sublime mixture of old-fashioned country town and bustling city. It is accessible and private, cosmopolitan and rural, gracious and relaxed.

Adelaide Central

The city centre of Adelaide is so manageable that it is easy to walk from the Torrens River to the statue of John McDouall Stuart at the end of King William Street and from the markets at the end of Rundle Mall to the other end of Rundle Street. Anyone planning to visit should be prepared to walk and should be prepared to enjoy Adelaide's reputation as a 'city of churches'. They should also recognise that, by the standards of the eastern capitals, it is a very inexpensive city with good quality restaurants and accommodation often costing about half that in Sydney and Melbourne.

Adelaide is famous for beautiful churches such as Saint Necoles Parish Church in Greenhill Road, which features Russian-inspired domes.

Among the numerous churches worthy of inspection are the Anglican Holy Trinity Church located at 87 North Terrace for which building began as early as 1838, and St Francis Xavier's Cathedral situated in Wakefield Street (built progressively between 1856 and 1926).

Just down from the city centre is the arts complex on the banks of the Torrens River. The Festival Centre comprises a drama theatre, a lyric theatre, an open-air amphitheatre, an experimental theatre and a multipurpose concert hall. This is where the Adelaide Festival of Arts is held. Tours of the complex are offered: contact (08) 8216 8713.

Along the Torrens River is the excellent Adelaide Zoo, where the attractions include an Australian Wetlands Exhibit, a walk-through Australian Rainforest Exhibit and a re-creation of Seal Bay on Kangaroo Island. The zoo prides itself on its collection of endangered species, which include the golden-lion tamarin, red panda, scimitar-horned oryx and Persian leopard.

A good place to finish is the city's outstanding Botanic Gardens, which are located next to the zoo. It must be one of the most delightful botanic gardens in Australia. Established in 1855, it now has impressive displays of tropical rainforest, a magnificent wisteria arbour and an avenue of Moreton Bay figs which

were originally planted in 1866. There is also the State Herbarium, an institute for research which boasts an enormous collection of more than half a million dried plants from all over the world. From the Botanic Gardens go to the banks of the Torrens and enjoy a peaceful walk. There is a good cycleway here too. It is also possible to hire boats and go canoeing on the river.

A very desirable option for visitors is staying in North Adelaide. Excellent accommodation is available at the Lion Apartments (contact 08 8334 7799 or 1800 882 774), which are surrounded by a range of wonderful restaurants catering for every budget and style of cuisine. The walk from North Adelaide across the parks and along the Torrens River is delightful.

Map: SA 4 J3

Left: *Pretty pathways follow the Torrens River from the north-eastern suburbs of Adelaide to the coast. Cyclists and walkers will both enjoy the tranquil parklands that lie along the river.*

don't miss

Held biennially in March (in even-numbered years), the Adelaide Festival of Arts is one of the world's great cultural events. It features Australian and international musicians, writers, dancers, actors and other artists.

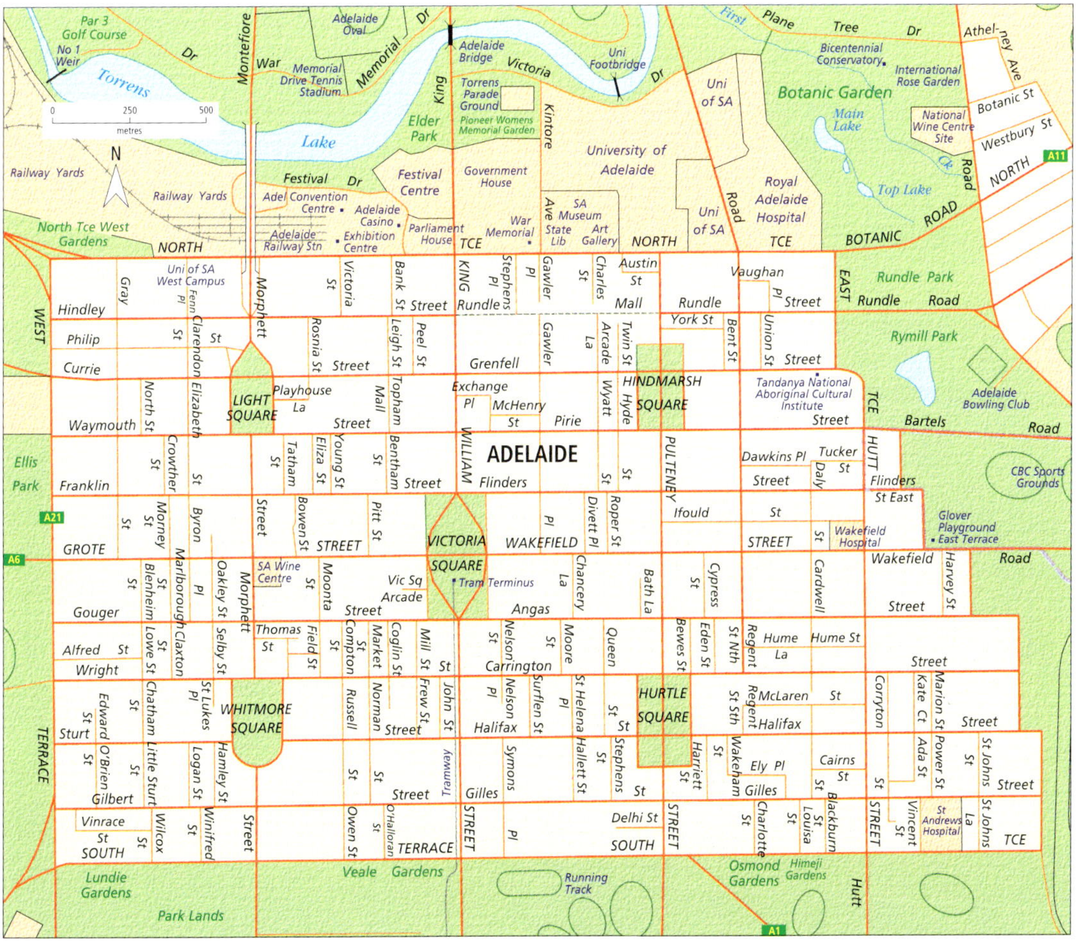

SA

don't miss

Dedicated in 1891, Belair National Park protects one of the few remaining areas of native bushland in the Adelaide Hills. A pleasant 1-km walking trail around the park's Playford Lake passes a variety of waterbirds.

Glenelg

Adelaide's most popular seafront swimming destination is the lovely suburb of Glenelg—which is just a 10-km tram ride from the end of King William Street. It is a typical seaside resort, an all-the-fun-of-the-fair place for Adelaide people to visit. A replica of the HMS *Buffalo*, the ship in which Governor Hindmarsh arrived, is located north of the centre of Glenelg. It is used as a restaurant. Contact (08) 8294 7000 for bookings.

Map: SA 4 J3

Adelaide Hills

The Adelaide Hills are a richly diverse area with a large number of interesting attractions. They are easily accessible from Adelaide, being only a 20-minute drive from the city centre.

This is one of the country's premier wine-making regions, with more than 30 wineries producing high-quality cool-climate wines. The Magill Estate is more than just a simple cellar with tastings. For a small fee you will get a tour of the Magill Estate where you can see the reds, whites and fortified wines and, like looking at a mound of diamonds and precious stones, you will be able to gaze in wonder on a complete set of single bottles of every vintage of Grange Hermitage. You will also learn the interesting history of Penfolds and Grange.

The new Mount Lofty Summit Lookout (the old one was burnt to the ground in the devastating bushfires of 1983) provides superb views across the city to Gulf St Vincent. As you travel to the summit you can see the rolling hills to the east with their vineyards, market gardens and orchards. You can have a coffee or tea while enjoying the view at the Summit Restaurant, which is also open for lunch from noon to 3.00 p.m. seven days a week.

Mount Lofty Botanic Garden is a gloriously and perpetually green parkland which is free to enter (although the parking has a small cost) and, regardless of the weather, is an ideal place for a quiet, reflective stroll. There is an arboretum amphitheatre, a woodland garden, a rhododendron trail (at its best from August to October), a Japanese cherry exhibition, vegetation from eastern Australia, a magnolia trail (August to September), a fern gully, a

Located just 25 minutes from Adelaide by tram, Glenelg has clean, white beaches and a superb selection of restaurants and shops on Jetty Road.

Left: *Owned by wine producer Petaluma, the Bridgewater Mill is an old flourmill that has been wonderfully restored. It features an award-winning restaurant and a cellar where you can buy a number of different Petaluma wines, including chardonnay, sauvignon blanc and shiraz.*

The cool, temperate climate found on the eastern side of the Mount Lofty Ranges is perfect for growing exotic plants such as rhododendrons.

rose collection (October to December), a number of sculptures and a nature trail.

Warrawong Earth Sanctuary at Mylor is run by Dr John Walmsley (he is well known as the man who designed a fur hat and a fur rug out of the skins of feral cats). It offers dawn and dusk tours when the native animals—eastern quolls, bandicoots, rufous bettongs, potoroos, red-necked pademelons, kangaroos and dozens of other creatures—are at their most active. Contact (08) 8370 9197.

Bridgewater is worth visiting because of the historic Bridgewater Mill, which features a huge water-driven mill wheel. The Bridgewater Mill Restaurant is a perfect place to enjoy lunch.

The famous Australian painter, Hans Heysen, had a home and studio near the town of Hahndorf. They are both open for inspection. Heysen's friend, Dame Nellie Melba, used to come to the home and entertain his family and acquaintances with her singing. It is also interesting to see Heysen's art, and his studio is well worth visiting.

Hahndorf is unusual because it is a little piece of Australia that will forever be a part of Germany. There is an eatery called Der Stumptisch, Otto's bakery offers Teutonic breads, a pub called The German Arms has the colours of the German flag emblazoned on its exterior, and traditional fare such as bratwurst and sauerkraut can be purchased in the main street.

There are lots of interesting accommodation options in the Adelaide Hills. The Orangerie, a B&B in the elegant and leafy village of Stirling, is located beside lily-covered pools in cool terrace gardens. It is just like staying in a Mediterranean villa. For more information contact (08) 8339 5458.

Map: SA 4 J3

SA

Established in 1839, the German Arms Hotel in Hahndorf—just 28 km from Adelaide—offers traditional German and international food, plus German lagers and South Australian wines.

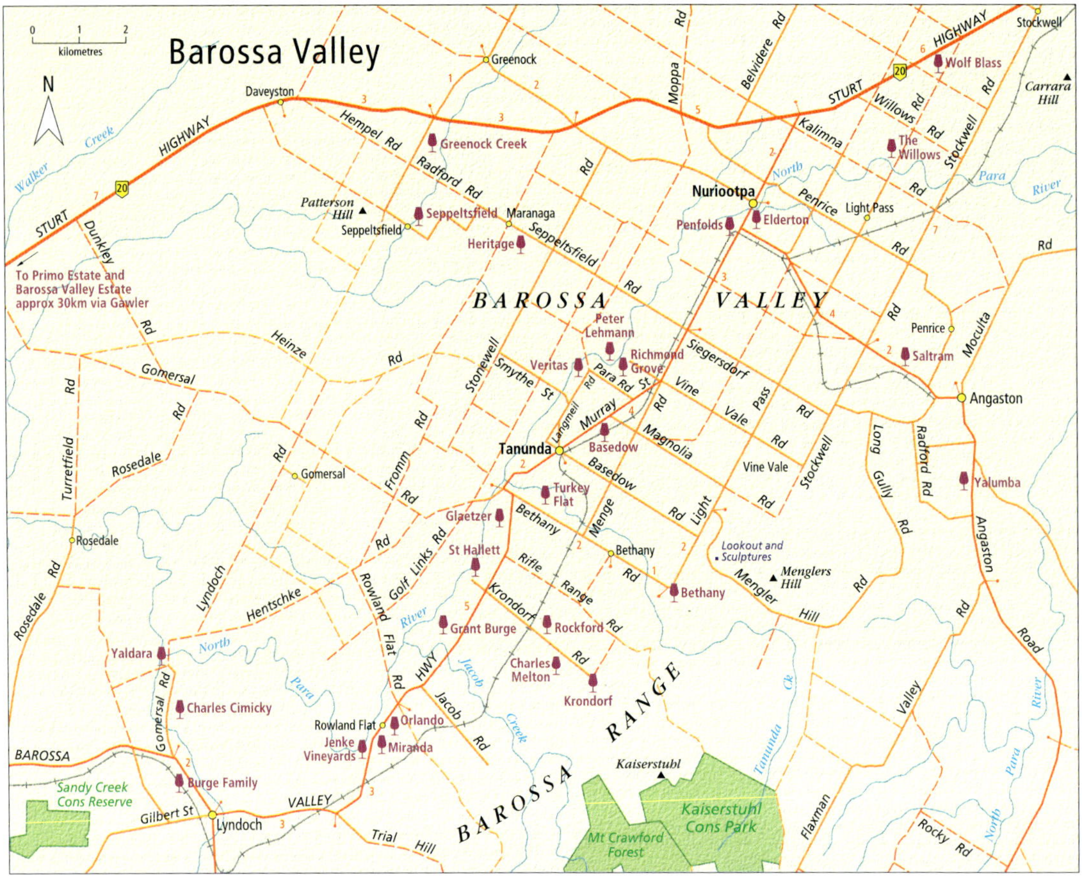

Barossa Valley

It was Colonel William Light, that sublime Surveyor General who laid out Adelaide with such geometric and aesthetic precision, who became the first European person to see the Barossa Valley. He had fought under a certain Lord Lynedoch at Barrosa in Spain during the Peninsula Wars and, wanting to honour both the man and the event, he called the valley Barossa (spelt Barrosa it would have meant 'hill of roses' in Spanish) and the first village Lyndoch (the 'e' somehow disappeared during the nineteenth century). Nowadays, the Barossa is only an hour's drive from Adelaide.

German Lutherans came to Tanunda in 1842. Their influence can be seen in the cottages and stone churches of the town.

The first Barossa wines were made in the 1840s, and many of today's producers are descendants of the original settlers. Johann Gramp planted grapes at Jacob's Creek by 1850, thus forming the basis for the mighty Orlando winery near Lyndoch, but it wasn't until 1867 that Joseph Seppelt made his first wine in his wife's small dairy at Seppeltsfield. Much more recently people like Wolf Blass have moved into the area.

The result is that there are now over 50 wineries in the Barossa Valley. With Lyndoch (the southernmost town) only 58 km from Adelaide and the valley's major town, Nuriootpa, only 76 km away, it is easy to hire a car, get hold of a good guide to the wineries, and weave your way from one winery to another engaging in tasting, buying and eating. The Barossa Valley is also full of excellent restaurants, many of which are attached to the wineries.

There are also many stone churches, a legacy of the early German Lutheran settlers, which are well worth a visit, and plenty of places to see and buy great arts, crafts and antiques.

Map: SA 4 K2

McLaren Vale

There are over 40 wineries in the immediate area around McLaren Vale. The appeal of McLaren Vale is that beyond the pleasant town (which is located only 39 km from Adelaide), and the interesting beaches to the west, there is really nothing more to do than head to the cellars and do a little wine tasting. The area is so suffused with good wineries that there are points where you stop at a crossroads (particularly if the road is either Olivers Road or Chalk Hill Road) and discover endless signposts directing the thirsty traveller to some delightful samples of cabernet sauvignon, pinot noir, chardonnay or shiraz.

The unique conditions found in McLaren Vale—including undulating terrain and a climate affected by the nearby ocean—mean that nearly all grape varieties flourish here.

Apart from the region's huge producers, notably Seaview (well worth a visit—there is an interesting Vat Gallery) and Hardy's Tintara (located in the centre of the town, it is a reminder of the importance of wine in the area—the vineyard dates from the 1850s) the roads around the town are awash with boutique wineries. Chapel Hill Winery on Chapel Hill Road has fantastic views across the endless fields of grapes.

Beyond the vineyards parts of the coastline are quite beautiful, particularly Aldinga Beach and Sellicks Beach. Excellent swimming, diving and surfing can be enjoyed.

Map: SA 4 J4

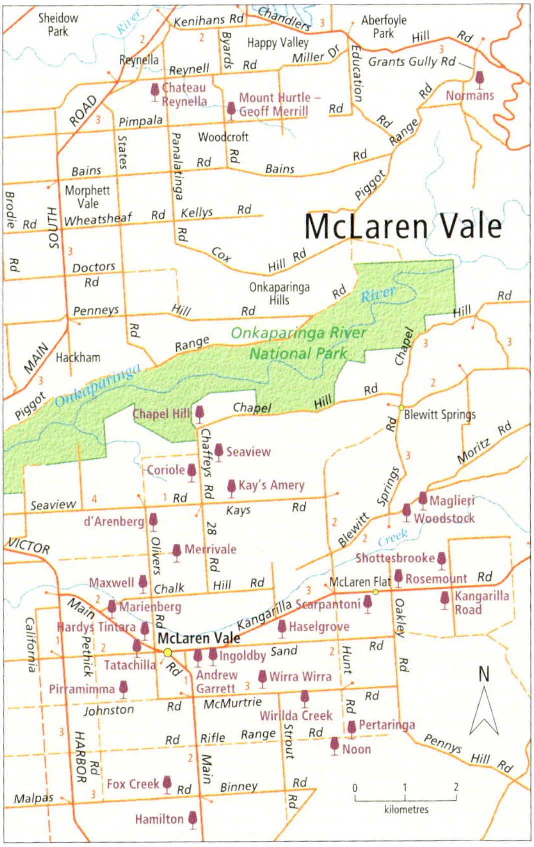

The Chapel Hill Winery offers attractive views across rows of vines from its hilltop position. Established in 1977, it produces chardonnay, verdelho, shiraz and tawny port.

South and South-East of Adelaide

If you look at a map of South Australia you will quickly realise that most of the state's population and farming is concentrated into the areas around the coast and a relatively small area in the south-east. The vast majority of the state is inhospitable desert which is inaccessible. However, the area south of Adelaide is a part of the state that has much to offer.

Kangaroo Island

Kangaroo Island is huge. It is the third-largest landmass found off the coast of Australia, stretching 155 km from east to west, 55 km from north to south at its widest point, and boasting more than 1600 km of sealed and unsealed roads. The island's major attractions are spread across its length and breadth, and a visit can become a week-long journey of surprises and exploration.

The major attractions on the island include the main township of Kingscote, the seals at Seal Bay, the beautiful rugged coastline around Vivonne Bay, the huge sand dunes at Little Sahara and the pretty beaches (particularly at Stokes Bay) along the northern coastline and around the Bay of Shoals. Flinders Chase National Park is located at the western end of the island, and contains the Remarkable Rocks, Admirals Arch and the Cape Borda lighthouse.

Vivonne Bay on Kangaroo Island is a great place to simply wander along the stunning sandy beach. There is a camp site with a picnic area, barbecues and toilet facilities.

The appeal of Kangaroo Island lies in its strange mixture of isolation and accessibility. Situated only 2½ hours from Adelaide, it is so isolated you could be on the sub-Antarctic Macquarie Island. While there are plenty of accommodation options on the island, the restaurants are not as plentiful. This is really an island best seen by people keen on camping and bushwalking.

Map: SA 4 F5

Victor Harbor

Victor Harbor is located 83 km south of Adelaide. It is now a successful and prosperous holiday destination, although it was once a main port of the South Australian coast and a vital access point for the paddle-steamers that took goods up and down the Murray River.

Before it became the most important port on the Fleurieu Peninsula, Victor Harbor was a stopover for the whalers and sealers who plied the waters of the Southern Ocean. As early as 1837 there was a whaling station on Granite Island, and a year later Victor Harbor (it had been named by a Captain R. Crozier after the HMS *Victor* which surveyed the harbour) was already being recognised as a port of some importance.

Today the town is one of the most popular holiday destinations on the Fleurieu Peninsula. Families come and book into the diverse range of accommodation on offer and then spend time on the beach, walk the beachside promenades and enjoy the usual range of activities offered by a typical seaside resort town.

The highlight of any visit to Victor Harbor is the horse-drawn tram service

Granite Island is linked to the mainland at Victor Harbor by a causeway. From June to October majestic southern right whales can sometimes be seen in the waters near this causeway.

did you know?

The word *goolwa* is thought to mean 'elbow' in the language of the Ngarrindjeri, the local Aboriginal people, and probably refers to the fact that the river bends here just before it meets the ocean.

SA

that travels along the causeway (it was constructed between 1878 and 1882) which links the town of Victor Harbor with Granite Island.

Another of the popular attractions are the penguin walks which are held on Granite Island every evening at dusk. Guides accompany small groups of walkers along the foreshore of the island to see the fairy penguins arrive home safely after a busy day at sea. Bookings can be made either at the Granite Island Shop or by phoning (08) 8552 7555.
Map: SA 4 J4

Goolwa

Recently Goolwa has become famous, or perhaps infamous, for the controversial Hindmarsh Island bridge. It not only polarised the local community (between those who wanted development and those who resisted development) but it also became a national issue when the complex 'secret women's business' was discussed and debated. Located 83 km from Adelaide, Goolwa is an interesting historic port which, because it is only an hour's drive from Adelaide, has become something of an upmarket holiday resort for Adelaide people. It boasts a rich assortment of interesting accommodation options—including great guesthouses and B&Bs—and there are a number of classy restaurants in the town.

Cruises from Goolwa on vessels like the paddle-steamer PS Mundoo *take visitors to Coorong National Park, Hindmarsh Island and Younghusband Peninsula, as well as along the Murray River.*

Right: *The remains of an extinct volcano form the base for the Blue Lake at Mount Gambier. It turns cobalt blue in November before changing back to grey in late summer.*

The town has been given a self-consciously 'historic' feel. Hotels like the Goolwa Hotel have been painted in heritage colours and genuinely old hotels like the Corio Hotel have been refurbished and revitalised. The best way to experience Goolwa is to walk around the streets and soak up the atmosphere.

One thing everyone should do while in Goolwa is go through the barrages (the walls which separate the seawater from the freshwater of the Murray) and cross the true mouth of the Murray River. There are a number of cruise options (up the Murray, along the Coorong) which are available from Goolwa. For more information contact Goolwa Cruises on (08) 8555 2203 or Coorong Experience on (08) 8555 1133.

Map: SA 4 K4

The Coonawarra and The Coorong

The south-east region also includes the stunning Blue Lake at Mount Gambier, the quaint seaside appeal of Robe, Adam Lindsay Gordon's charming 'Dingley Dell' cottage at Port MacDonnell, the bright red Big Lobster at Kingston S. E., the endless vineyards of the Coonawarra, the gracious Mary MacKillop Interpretive Centre in Penola, and the windswept beauty of The Coorong.

The Big Lobster—called Larry by the locals—is a startling introduction to one of the main sources of income for Kingston S. E.—rock-lobster fishing. At the base of the 18-m high crustacean you will find a gift shop and café.

Coonawarra is considered by many to be one of the best wine-growing regions found in Australia. That narrow strip of terra rossa soil, known affectionately to the locals as 'the Coonawarra cigar', has, over the years, produced fine red wines of such quality that wine connoisseur Len Evans once described the area as 'the Bordeaux of Australia', a claim that has been backed by an endless stream of national and international wine awards and honours.

The idea is to just wander through and taste the glories of the region. There is the Balnaves Winery with its garden of over 800 roses, the Rymill winery with an impressive equine statue in the forecourt, and dozens more. Nearby is the enchanting historic township of Penola, home to the Mary MacKillop Interpretive Centre. The town has a number of excellent restaurants which all offer the best of the local vintages. Particularly impressive is the Cobb & Co

Restaurant, which is located in the old Cobb & Co Booking Office.

The region offers some of the best B&B, cottage and guesthouse accommodation in the country. Visitors eager to experience the history of the region should ensure they spend time in these old, and beautifully restored, homes. Favourites include Lakeside Country House in Robe (08 8768 2042) and, to the north on the edge of The Coorong, the extraordinary Poltalloch Homestead complex (08 8574 0088).

Between Lakeside and Poltalloch lies The Coorong, a narrow spit of high sand dunes protecting a long channel of quiet water from the wildness of the Great Southern Ocean. It is one of Australia's coastal wonders. Most Australians know the region because they have either read the book or seen the movie of Colin Thiele's *Storm Boy*. They know about the pelican named Mr Percival and the harshness of life for Hide-Away Tom and his son. The best way to experience the area is to take a conducted tour with local experts. A wonderful and unusual experience awaits those who book into Camp Coorong (08 8575 1557), a unique Aboriginal tourism experiment where travellers can spend days living with the local community and experiencing their culture by learning about bush tucker and medicine, bushwalking and talking to the local elders.

Map: SA 4 M8

Below: *Pretty Leconfield Winery, situated in the Coonawarra wine region, produces a number of impressive drops including chardonnay, merlot, shiraz and cabernet.*

Bottom: *The chain of lagoons in The Coorong provides a rich habitat for thousands of birds, from pelicans and waders to Cape Barren geese and black swans.*

North of Adelaide

Northern South Australia is an area which very quickly changes from rich vineyards to dry desert. This is not a harsh judgement of the region. Every South Australian knows about Goyder's Line—a line drawn by the surveyor G. W. Goyder in 1865 which was the measure of land suitable for agriculture. Such is the accuracy of the line that the tiny town of Johnburg, 40 km north of the line, has experienced an average of only 272 mm of rainfall for 55 of the last 100 years.

Along with Mosel in Germany and Alsace in France, the Clare Valley is recognised as one of the world's top riesling producers. Less than 2 hours from Adelaide, the region is perfect for daytrips.

This has meant that in drought periods (one lasted for a decade between the 1920s and 1930s), cropping has been impossible and the farmers have been unable to make a living. There are really only four major areas of interest in this largely barren region. The Clare Valley is a verdant wine-growing area. The Flinders Ranges, and Wilpena Pound, have spectacular scenery and are ideal for bushwalking. Arkaroola is an isolated wildlife sanctuary and resort on the very edge of the desert. And the historic near-desert town of Burra is full of interesting artefacts which recall a time when the area was rich in copper.

The Clare Valley

The Clare Valley, located some 136 km from Adelaide, is the home of South Australia's boutique wine industry. A trip to the valley is about both wine tasting and exploring the quaint villages.

For those wanting to experience the region's wines, the smart starting point is Sevenhill's Cellars, the valley's oldest winery. An absolute joy to visit, the cellar was established by, and is still run by, the Jesuits. There are over 30 vineyards and wineries located throughout the Clare Valley, and with few exceptions they specialise in red and white table wines produced from grapes grown on relatively small holdings.

Right: *Wilpena Pound lies in the heart of the north Flinders Ranges. The word* wilpena *is said to mean 'a cupped hand' in the local Aboriginal dialect.*

No visit to the valley is complete without a stop at Mintaro, a delightful village which, because it is not on the Main North Road, has managed to avoid modernisation. There is an English feel to the place. The local pub, the Magpie & Stump, sits in the middle of the town and has a very British beer garden out the front. It was licensed in 1851 and quickly gained a reputation as one of the wildest pubs in South Australia, due to the fact that it was a popular overnight stop and watering hole for itinerant bullock and mule drivers moving copper from Burra to the coast. It has a charming winery, Reilly's Cottage Gallery and

Wines, across the road from the pub. Within a couple of blocks are the Teapot Inn; the Olde Devonshire House (which dates from 1856); The Old Manse; the Pay Office Cottage; Mintaro Mews; and Martindale Hall, a Georgian mansion that was used as the girls' school in the film *Picnic at Hanging Rock*.

Map: SA 4 J1

Flinders Ranges

The main attraction of the Flinders Ranges, particularly in spring, is the beautiful and dramatic Wilpena Pound, which is located 429 km north of Adelaide. Wilpena Pound is a remarkable natural amphitheatre nearly 5 km wide and 11 km long, covered in scrub and trees and totally surrounded by jagged hills that form a craggy rim. It is an ideal place for bushwalking and enjoying the quietness and peacefulness of the Australian bush. If you want to stay outside the pound and the park, the Rawnsley Park Station Tourist Park offers an excellent range of accommodation options. Contact (08) 8648 0030. The closer accommodation is the Wilpena Pound Resort. Contact (08) 8648 0004 or 1800 805 802.

Some of the countryside to the south, near the small town of Hawker, can be seen in the film *Holy Smoke*, while *The Shiralee*, *Gallipoli* and *Sunday Too Far Away* show the Quorn area.

Map: SA 3 J4

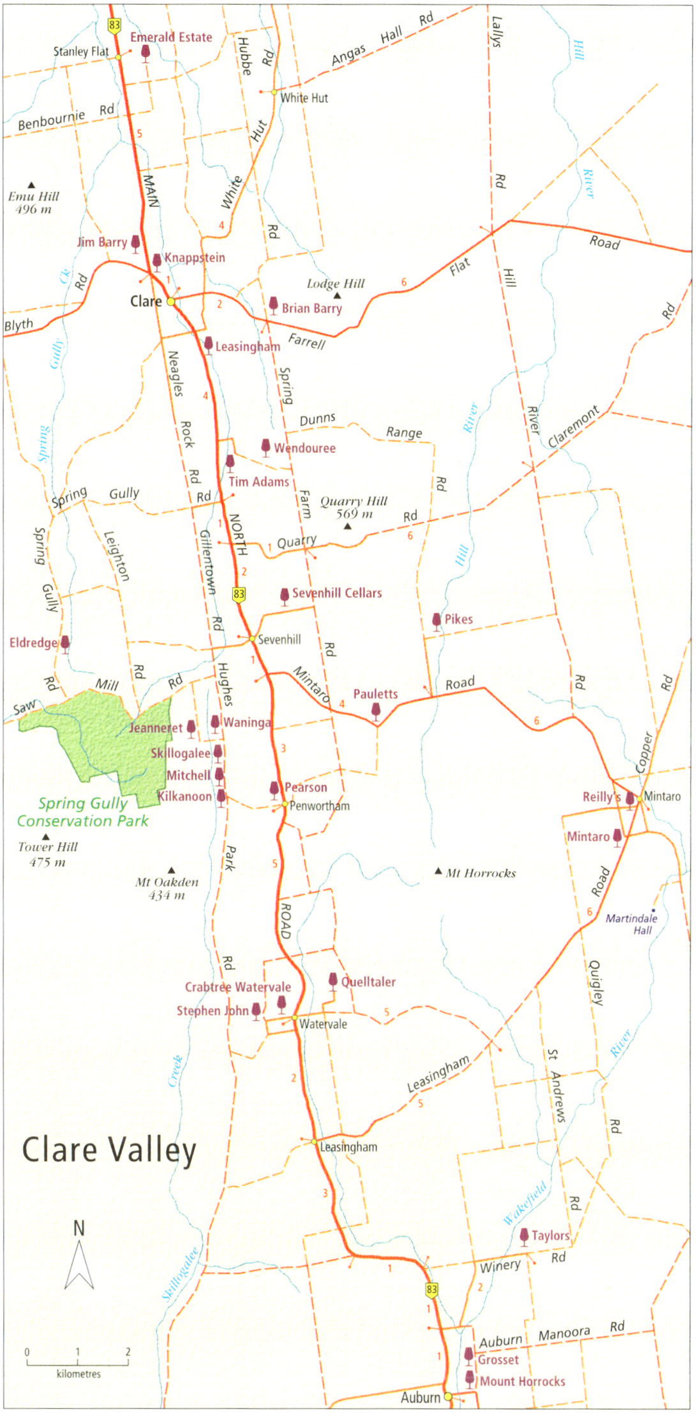

SA

Above: *Arkaroola offers visitors a truly rugged outback experience. It is located close to the Bolla Bollana smelter ruins and Paralana Hot Springs.*

Situated 176 km north of Adelaide, Burra became a State Heritage Town in 1994. Its historic charm makes it a popular place for weekend getaways.

Arkaroola

Located 660 km from Adelaide, Arkaroola is the personal vision of the geologist Dr Reg Sprigg (his son now runs the place), who purchased the 61 000-ha property in 1968 and slowly converted it into a wildlife sanctuary complete with a lodge and a marvellous astronomical observatory. Arkaroola is on the edge of the desert. It is a truly fascinating property with dramatic, ancient hills (some of the rocks are estimated to be older than 1000 million years), beautiful waterholes and a truly harsh and dry environment. People come to Arkaroola to experience the unique environment, to visit some of the outlying historic places, to marvel at a mountainous desert landscape and to be overwhelmed by the number of stars and planets which can be seen quite easily from the observatory when the desert skies are clear. For more information contact Arkaroola–Mount Painter Sanctuary Resort on (08) 8648 4848.

Map: SA 3 L2

Burra

Burra is a truly historic and fascinating copper town. It got the 'tourist' jump on the other South Australian copper towns when it was chosen as the site for the filming of the classic Australian movie *Breaker Morant*. Ever since, the locals have been tireless in the preservation and promotion of this extraordinary heritage town. They came up with the inspired idea of a 'passport' and key to the important sites in town. This means that you can go to the Burra Visitor Centre, purchase a passport and borrow a key and make your way around the town's 47 historic sites (some of which need a key to access) or, for a fee, you can have a guided tour of the town.

Copper was discovered in the Burra district in 1845. The area was so substantial that it was initially known as 'The Burra' and divided into a number of separate communities which reflected the origins of the miners. There was Redruth for the Cornish miners, Llychwr for Welsh miners, Aberdeen for Scottish miners and Hampton for the English miners. Remnants of these villages still exist and can be visited.

Today, with passport and key, you can explore the historic parts of the town and, if you want to experience the lives of the miners first hand, you can stay in the tiny cottages. For a good overview it's sensible to start at the Burra Mine Site (north of the town centre), which offers excellent views from the lookout. Vast amounts of interesting information about the mines is contained on photographic boards around the site. Nearby is Morphett Enginehouse Museum, which has been fully restored and features a number of displays.

But the most interesting places located in and around town are the Miners Dugouts, caves cut into the side of a creek bed where miners and their families lived until floods and disease drove them out; the Police Lock-up and Stables, built in 1847 and looking like something out of the Wild West; the Unicorn Brewery Cellars where, with the key, you can wander around the old cellars; Hampton, the ruins of the village which originally housed the English miners, and which sat on the hill overlooking the town; and Paxton Square, a delightful run of miners' cottages built between 1849 and 1852, which are now available as accommodation for visitors.

Map: SA 3 K9

don't miss

Just south of Arkaroola, Gammon Ranges National Park is perfect for 4WD enthusiasts. Make the trek to Grindells Hut to witness the breathtaking view towards the Illinawortinna Pound and the Gammon Ranges.

The Burra mine operated for over 30 years in the nineteenth century, and was one of the biggest mining operations in Australia at that time. Today, the site is a fascinating open-air museum.

SA

East and West of Adelaide

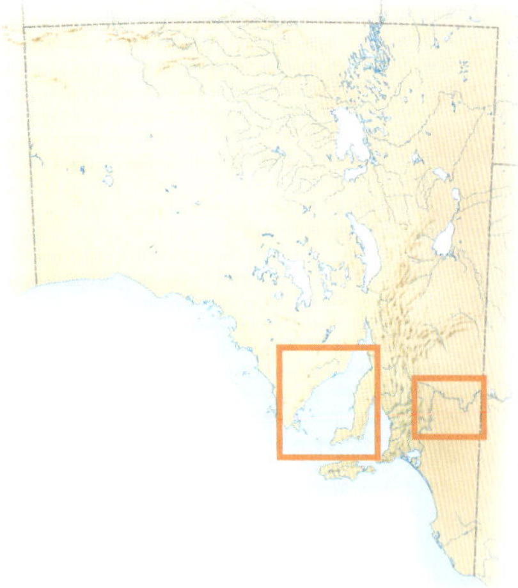

South Australia is a complex state. While most development occurred as people spread out from Adelaide, there were regions where other forces were at work. In the case of the Murray River, people settled along its banks in the nineteenth century because of the extensive river trade. Today the river's banks are a combination of holiday towns, historic paddle-steamer ports and agricultural regions.

The wide expanse of the Murray River near historic Blanchetown is a popular place for water sports, from sedate cruises to speedboat rides.

Many towns developed because the locals started pumping water and found that the region was ideal for orchards or vineyards. In the case of Port Lincoln, first a busy port serving the area's wheat and wool farmers and later adding both fishing and processing industries to its functions, it is the beaches and protected waterways of this magnificent coastline that attract visitors. And then there is the Yorke Peninsula, a place which is unmatched in any other state, where the people of Adelaide, overwhelmed by the intense summer heat (it is common for Adelaide to experience long spells when the temperature reaches over 40°C day after day) retreat to their beach huts and holiday homes to escape the oppressive conditions within the city. These are all places where people go to relax and enjoy themselves.

The Murray River

South Australians really know what a holiday shack is all about. If you go to the riverfront settlement of Blanchetown

Waikerie is Australia's biggest citrus-growing centre. From the Rotary cliff-top lookout there is a fine view of some of Waikerie's million-plus orange trees.

(located 133 km north-east of Adelaide) you will, in the first instance, experience an interesting historic town with a number of impressive buildings, all of which date from the 1850s and 1860s. But then if you drive down to the river and past the main river park you will find an entire riverside community of shacks. There is even a Blanchetown Shack Owner's Association. This is an extraordinary collection of shacks which have been built out of bits of corrugated iron, fibro and anything which came to hand. The way the houses have been built defies description. They have names like Dad's Den. It is the unique expression of the desire of all South Australians to have a home near the water. It is well worth seeing. Some of the blocks of land in Shack City have absolute water frontages.

Not all the towns situated along the Murray are like Blanchetown. Mannum, for example, which is further south, is a pleasant holiday town with extensive parks along the river. It caters for a wide variety of water sports, and there is both fishing and birdwatching (the birds range from seagulls—which have made their way to Mannum from the coast—to pelicans and swans). There is also a bird sanctuary next to the caravan park at the eastern end of town.

And when the visitor begins to travel upriver towards the towns of Waikerie, Berri and Renmark, they move into the rich riverlands region which features an abundance of flourishing orchards and successful vineyards.

Waikerie, for example, describes itself as 'The Citrus Centre of Australia'. It is in the heart of the rich Riverland district and is surrounded by orchards that cultivate citrus fruits as well as stone fruits such as apricots, peaches, pears and plums. Stopping off to buy fruit is a very obvious activity. Eating the fruit in a park beside the river is equally obvious.

Berri is famous for the Berri brand of fruit juices. It is also famous, certainly to all those who have driven through the town (it is situated 236 km north-east of Adelaide) for the Big Orange which not only sells local orange juice and oranges but also has a fascinating variety of displays covering classic motorcycles and cars, children's toys and dolls, models of fish found in the Murray River, indigenous culture and a lot more. Located across the road from the Big Orange is the Wilabalangaloo Nature Reserve, which is a pleasant retreat on the banks of the Murray River.

And the thriving township of Renmark is in the heart of an orchard area where garlic, limes, apricots, olives, grapes, plums and a wide range of other fruit are grown.

Left: *Situated on the Sturt Highway, just outside Berri, the Big Orange stands four storeys high. There is a souvenir shop and café, plus a viewing area at the top that overlooks the local area.*

For many, a houseboat is an idyllic way to travel the Murray River—there are many to choose from in Renmark. Fishing for golden perch and Murray cod from your houseboat is a great way to relax.

don't miss

Held biennially in May (in odd-numbered years), Kernewek Lowender—which means 'Cornish happiness'—is a cultural festival celebrating the Cornish heritage in the 'Copper Triangle' area of the Yorke Peninsula.

The river is the source of most of the local attractions, including river cruises on paddle-steamers, dinghies or something in between. There is also fishing and waterskiing, or just picnicking on the river banks.

Yorke Peninsula

Because it is so close to Adelaide (you can drive to Port Wakefield—it is 99 km north-west of Adelaide—in a little over an hour) the Yorke Peninsula is a popular holiday destination for Adelaide residents eager to escape from the city's heat and congestion. The tiny seaside villages—Port Clinton, Ardrossan, Port Vincent, Stansbury and Edithburgh—belong to a different era. They have a certain 1950s simplicity and charm. On the far side of the peninsula places like Port Victoria, Moonta and Wallaroo are all reminders that there was once a time when the Yorke Peninsula was a thriving centre of copper production and when the mighty clipper ships were seen at the jetties along the coast as they loaded up with wheat that was bound for England and the rest of continental Europe. Nowadays the waters are used for fishing, boating, diving, surfing and swimming. And on the shore there are plenty of walks to showcase the views, birdlife and native plants, as well as various historical attractions.

Map: SA 4 H1

Restored to its former glory, the PS Industry *is a floating museum and working paddle-steamer that still plies the waters of the Murray River near the town of Renmark.*

Port Lincoln

Port Lincoln is considered the jewel of the Eyre Peninsula. A substantial and prosperous city situated on Boston Bay and nestled in on the eastern side of the Eyre Peninsula, it is the most important grain and fishing port in the region. Port Lincoln is located 656 km west of Adelaide and enjoys a near-perfect Mediterranean climate. It is a large regional centre which is economically driven by the huge grain-handling facilities (the foreshore is dominated by the 47-m-high grain silos which have a total capacity of over 337 500 tonnes), the canning and fish processing works, fertiliser production and, in recent times, the vast wealth which has been made as a result of tuna fishing for the lucrative Japanese market.

Visitors to the area should ensure that they eat some of the locally caught fish at the restaurants in the city and that they go to the many national parks surrounding the town. The best include Lincoln National Park, 17 226 ha on the southernmost tip of the Eyre Peninsula, which is characterised by picturesque coastline. At the Flinders Monument on Stamford Hill there are magnificent views over the rugged coast, surrounding bays, off-shore islands, and across the water to Port Lincoln.

Then there is Memory Cove, which was named by Flinders as a reminder of the tragic accident which took the lives of his eight crewmen; it is possible to join pleasant day trips from Port Lincoln out to Boston Island.

Map: SA 4 D2

Above: *Looking towards Proper Bay and Lincoln National Park. There are many pleasant walks in this park along the secluded beaches, across the cliff-tops and inland to Flinders Monument.*

For divers, the coast off Troubridge Point on the Yorke Peninsula boasts a number of interesting shipwrecks. Anglers will find excellent fishing for whiting, snapper, snook and tommy ruff.

Map 1

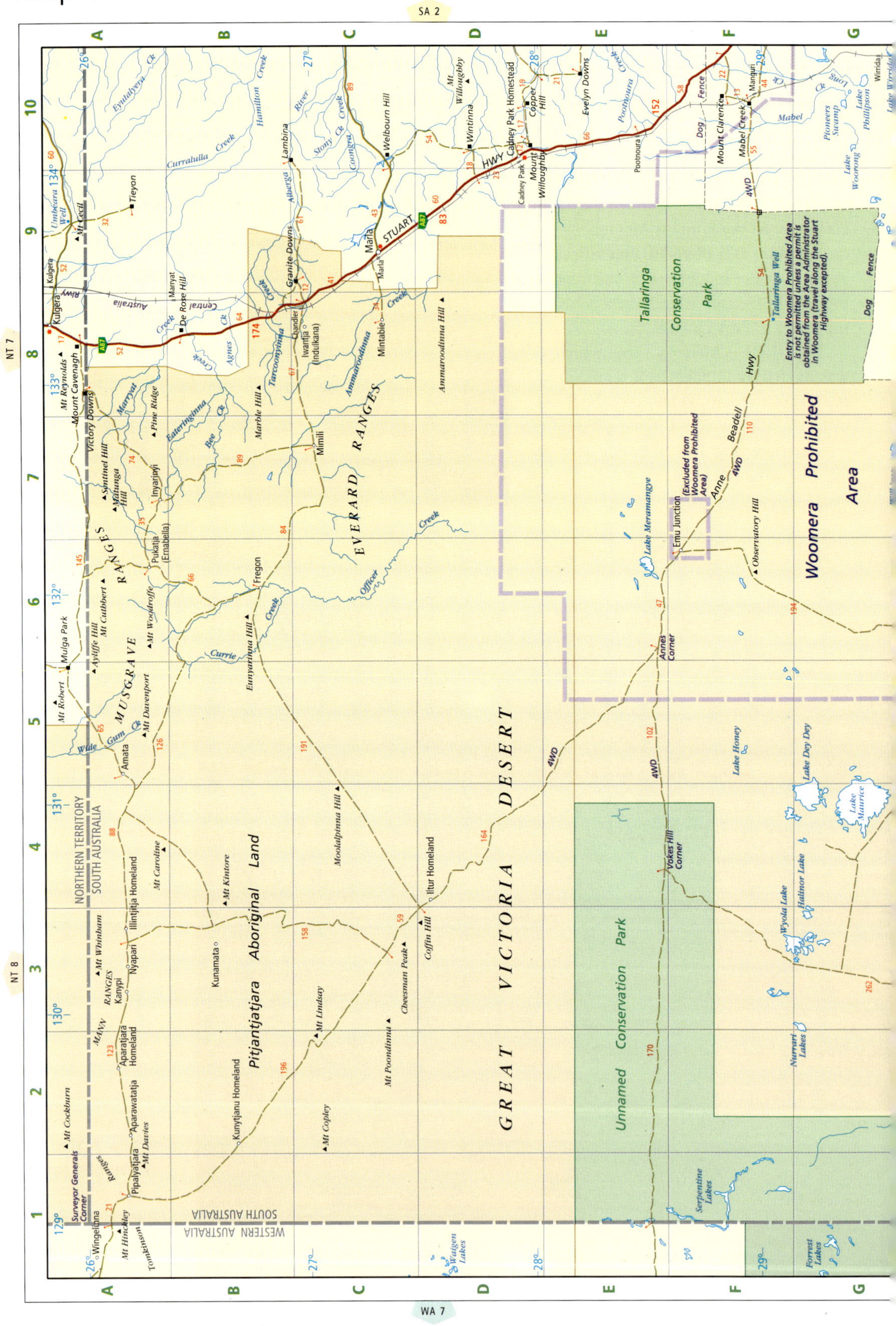
SA 2
WA 7
NT 7
NT 8
A
B
C
D
E
F
G
1
2
3
4
5
6
7
8
9
10
NORTHERN TERRITORY
SOUTH AUSTRALIA
WESTERN AUSTRALIA
Pitjantjatjara Aboriginal Land
GREAT VICTORIA DESERT
MUSGRAVE RANGES
EVERARD RANGES
MANN RANGES
Tallaringa Conservation Park
Unnamed Conservation Park
Woomera Prohibited Area
Entry to Woomera Prohibited Area is not permitted unless a permit is obtained from the Area Administrator in Woomera (travel along the Stuart Highway excepted).
(Excluded from Woomera Prohibited Area)
STUART HWY
A87
Anne Beadell Hwy
4WD
Dog Fence
Central Australia Rlwy
Kulgera
Mount Cavenagh
Victory Downs
Marla
Mintabie
Granite Downs
Iwantja (Indulkana)
Chandler
Mimili
Fregon
Pukatja (Ernabella)
Inyarinyi
Amata
Mulga Park
Nyapari
Kanypi
Illintjitja Homeland
Aparatjara Homeland
Aparawatatja
Pipalyatjara
Wingellina
Kunytjanu Homeland
Kunamata
Iltur Homeland
Emu Junction
Annes Corner
Vokes Hill Corner
Cadney Park Homestead
Cadney Park
Copper Hill
Mount Willoughby
Wintinna
Welbourn Hill
Lambina
Marryat
De Rose Hill
Tieyon
Evelyn Downs
Pootnoura
Mount Clarence
Mabel Creek
Manguri
Surveyor Generals Corner
Mt Cockburn
Mt Davies
Mt Hinckley
Tomkinson
Mt Whinham
Mt Caroline
Mt Kintore
Mt Lindsay
Mt Copley
Mt Poondinna
Cheesman Peak
Coffin Hill
Moolalpinna Hill
Eunyarinna Hill
Mt Robert
Mt Davenport
Ayliffe Hill
Mt Cuthbert
Mt Woodroffe
Malunga Hill
Sentinel Hill
Pine Ridge
Mt Reynolds
Marble Hill
Ammaroodinna Hill
Mt Willoughby
Mt Cecil
Umbeara Well
Observatory Hill
Tallaringa Well
Lake Meramangye
Lake Honey
Lake Dey Dey
Lake Maurice
Halinor Lake
Wyola Lake
Nurrari Lakes
Serpentine Lakes
Forrest Lakes
Waigen Lakes
Lake Wooroong
Pioneers Swamp
Lake Phillipson
Officer Creek
Currie Creek
Wide Gum Ck
Eyutalyera Ck
Hamilton Creek
Curralulla Creek
Alberga River
Stony Ck
Coongra Creek
Tarcoonyinna Creek
Ammaroodinna Creek
Agnes Creek
Marryat Creek
Eateringinna Creek
Bee Ck
Pootnoura Creek
Mabel Creek
Lora Ck
129°
130°
131°
132°
133°
134°
26°
27°
28°
29°

NULLARBOR PLAIN
Nullarbor Regional Reserve
Yellabinna Regional Reserve
Nullarbor National Park
GREAT AUSTRALIAN BIGHT
Maralinga Restricted Area
Maralinga
Ooldea Range
Yarle Lakes
Lake Bring
Lake Anthony
Half Moon Lake
Commonwealth Hill
Mulgathing
Carne Outstation
Mt Christie
Partridge Lakes
Trans Australian Railway
Dog Fence
Deakin
Hughes
Denman
Cook
Fisher
O'Malley
Watson
Ooldea
Bates
Barton
Mungala
Mount Christie
Wynbring
Lyons
Malbooma
Tarcoola
Ifould Lake
Lake Tallacootra
Mt Finke
Googs Track 4WD
WESTERN AUSTRALIA
SOUTH AUSTRALIA
Eucla
Border Village
Wilson Bluff
Eucla National Park
EYRE HIGHWAY
Koonalda
Nullarbor Roadhouse
Great Australian Bight Marine Park
Head of Bight
Great Australian Bight Whale Sanctuary
Yalata Swamp
Yalata Aboriginal Land
Yalata Roadhouse
Yalata
Black Hill
Wahgunyah Cons Res
Yumbarra Cons Res
Euria Well
Yumbarra Conservation Park
Radio Astronomy Station
Charoba Tank
Nundroo
Coorabie
Fowlers Bay Cons Res
Fowlers Bay
Cape Adieu
Nyuts Reef
Nuyts Reef Conservation Park
Bookabie
Bookabie Hill
Chadinga Cons Res
Penong
Cactus Beach
Point Sinclair
Point Bell
Lake MacDonnell
Woolshed Hill
Koonibba Community
Kalanbi
Pureba Cons Res
Pureba Cons Park
Wandana
Maltee
Denial Bay
Ceduna
Thevenard
Denial Bay
Mudamuckla
Puntabie
Chinbingina
Nunjikompita
Nunnyah CR
Laura Bay
Smoky Bay
Smoky Bay
St Peter I
Goat I
Evans I
Eyre I
Lacy Islands
Franklin Is
St Francis Island
Nuyts Archipelago Cons Park
Point Dillon
Pt Brown
Acraman Creek CP
Streaky Bay
Carawa
Wirrulla
Haslam
Petina
Courela
Chilpanunda
Eba I
Olive Island CP
Streaky Bay
Piednippie
Corvisart Bay
Point Westall
Yanerbie Beach
Calpatanna Waterhole CP
Sceale Bay
Sceale Bay
Searcy Bay
Calca
Witera
Point Labatt
Baird Bay
Cape Radstock
NORTH
0 20 40 60 80 100
kilometres
H J K L M N P
1 2 3 4 5 6 7 8 9 10
129° 130° 131° 132° 133° 134°
30° 31° 32° 33°
1 135 112 B100
SA

Map 2

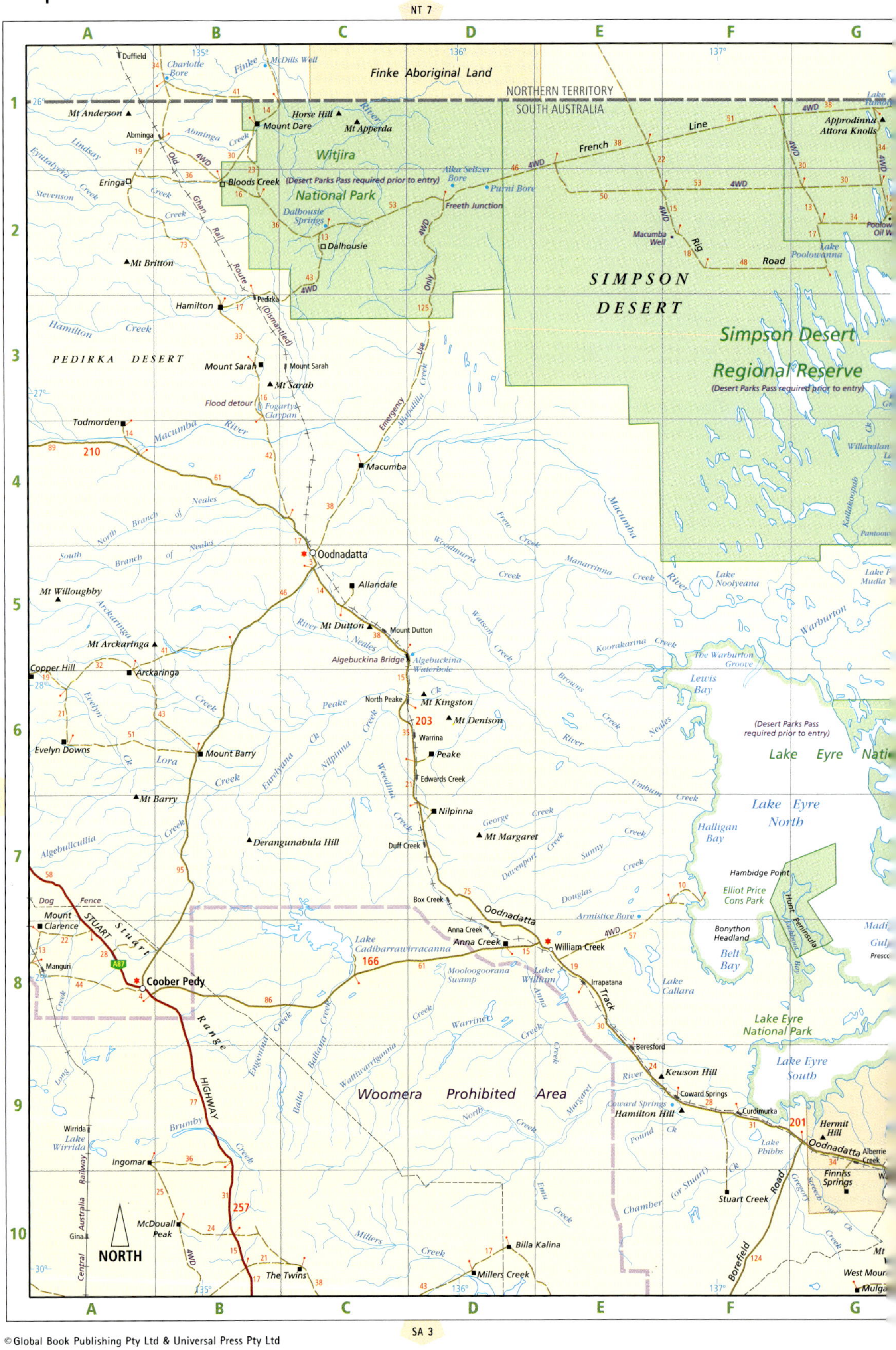
NT 7
SA 3
SA 1
A
B
C
D
E
F
G
1
2
3
4
5
6
7
8
9
10
NORTH
NORTHERN TERRITORY
SOUTH AUSTRALIA
Finke Aboriginal Land
Witjira
National Park
(Desert Parks Pass required prior to entry)
SIMPSON
DESERT
Simpson Desert
Regional Reserve
(Desert Parks Pass required prior to entry)
PEDIRKA DESERT
Woomera Prohibited Area
Lake Eyre
Lake Eyre North
Lake Eyre South
Lake Eyre
National Park
(Desert Parks Pass
required prior to entry)
Elliot Price
Cons Park
Duffield
Charlotte Bore
Finke
McDills Well
Mt Anderson
Mount Dare
Horse Hill
Mt Apperda
Abminga
Eringa
Bloods Creek
Dalhousie Springs
Dalhousie
Alka Seltzer Bore
Purni Bore
Freeth Junction
French
Line
Rig
Road
Macumba Well
Approdinna
Attora Knolls
Lake Poolowanna
Poolowanna Oil Well
Mt Britton
Hamilton
Pedirka
Ghan Rail Route (Dismantled)
Old
Mount Sarah
Mt Sarah
Flood detour
Fogarty's Claypan
Emergency Use Only
Todmorden
Macumba River
Macumba
Oodnadatta
Allandale
Mt Willoughby
Mt Dutton
Mount Dutton
Algebuckina Bridge
Algebuckina Waterhole
Mt Arckaringa
Arckaringa
Copper Hill
Evelyn Downs
Mount Barry
Mt Barry
North Peake
Mt Kingston
Mt Denison
Warrina
Peake
Edwards Creek
Nilpinna
Mt Margaret
Duff Creek
Derangunabula Hill
Box Creek
Anna Creek
William Creek
Oodnadatta Track
Lake Cadibarrawirracanna
Mooloogoorana Swamp
Lake William
Irrapatana
Lake Callara
Armistice Bore
Hambidge Point
Hunt Peninsula
Bonython Headland
Belt Bay
Halligan Bay
Lewis Bay
The Warburton Groove
Lake Noolyeana
Warburton
Dog Fence
Mount Clarence
Manguri
Coober Pedy
STUART HIGHWAY
A87
Stuart Range
Beresford
Kewson Hill
Coward Springs
Hamilton Hill
Curdimurka
Hermit Hill
Finniss Springs
Lake Phibbs
Stuart Creek
Borefield Road
Wirrida
Lake Wirrida
Ingomar
Central Australia Railway
Gina
McDouall Peak
The Twins
Billa Kalina
Millers Creek
West Mount
Mulga
Alberrie Creek
Neales
Arckaringa
Lora
Algebullcullia
Peake
Woodmurra
Frew
Manarrinna
Watson
Koorakarina
Browns
Umbum
George
Davenport
Sunny
Douglas
Warriner
Margaret
Eungana
Balta
Wattiwarriganna
Brumby
Chamber
Emu
North
Pound
Kallakoopah
Willawilan
Cadibarrawirracanna
210
203
166
201
257
135°
136°
137°
26°
27°
28°
29°
30°
4WD

QLD 6

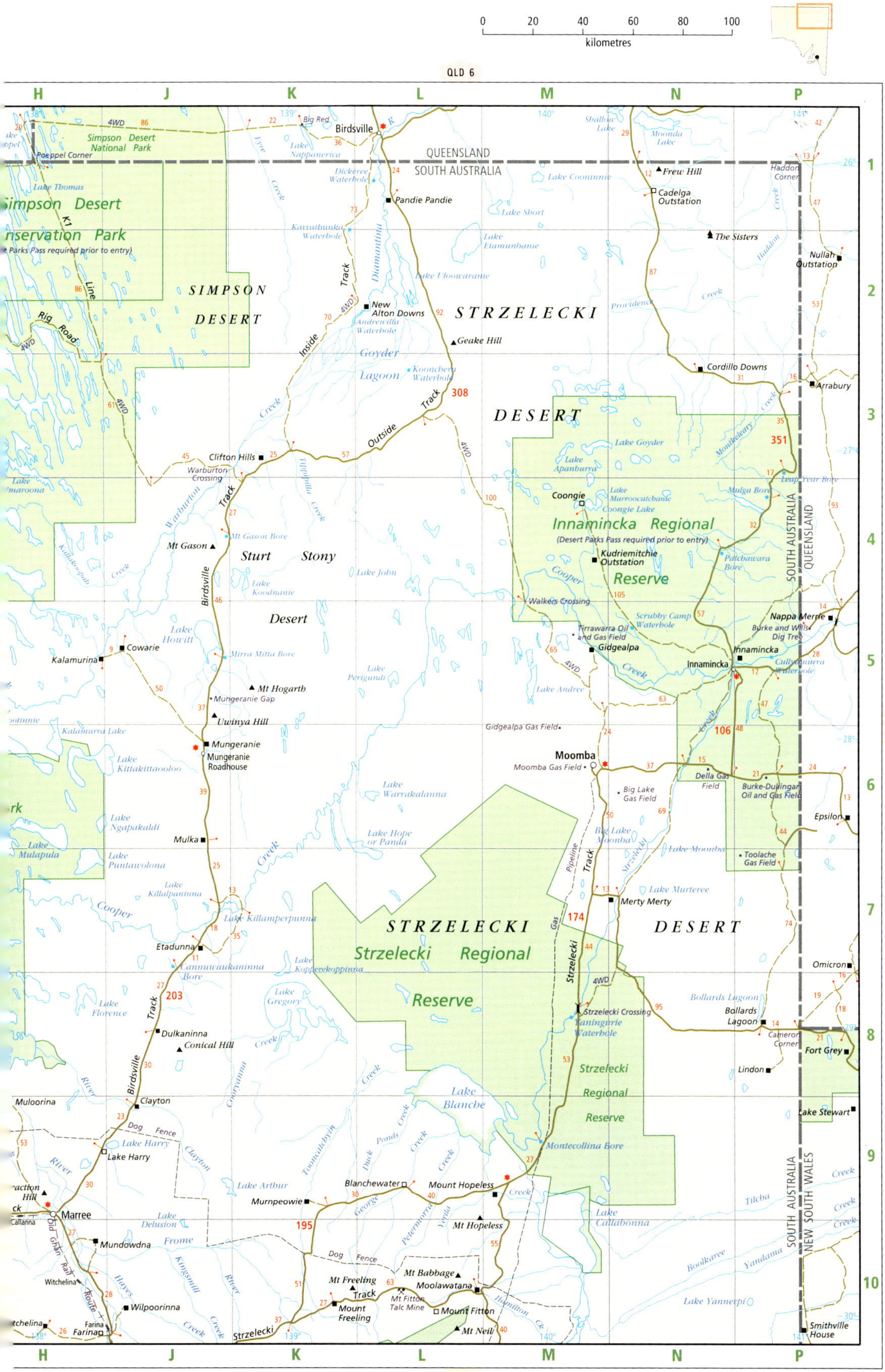

QLD 6

SA 3

Map 3

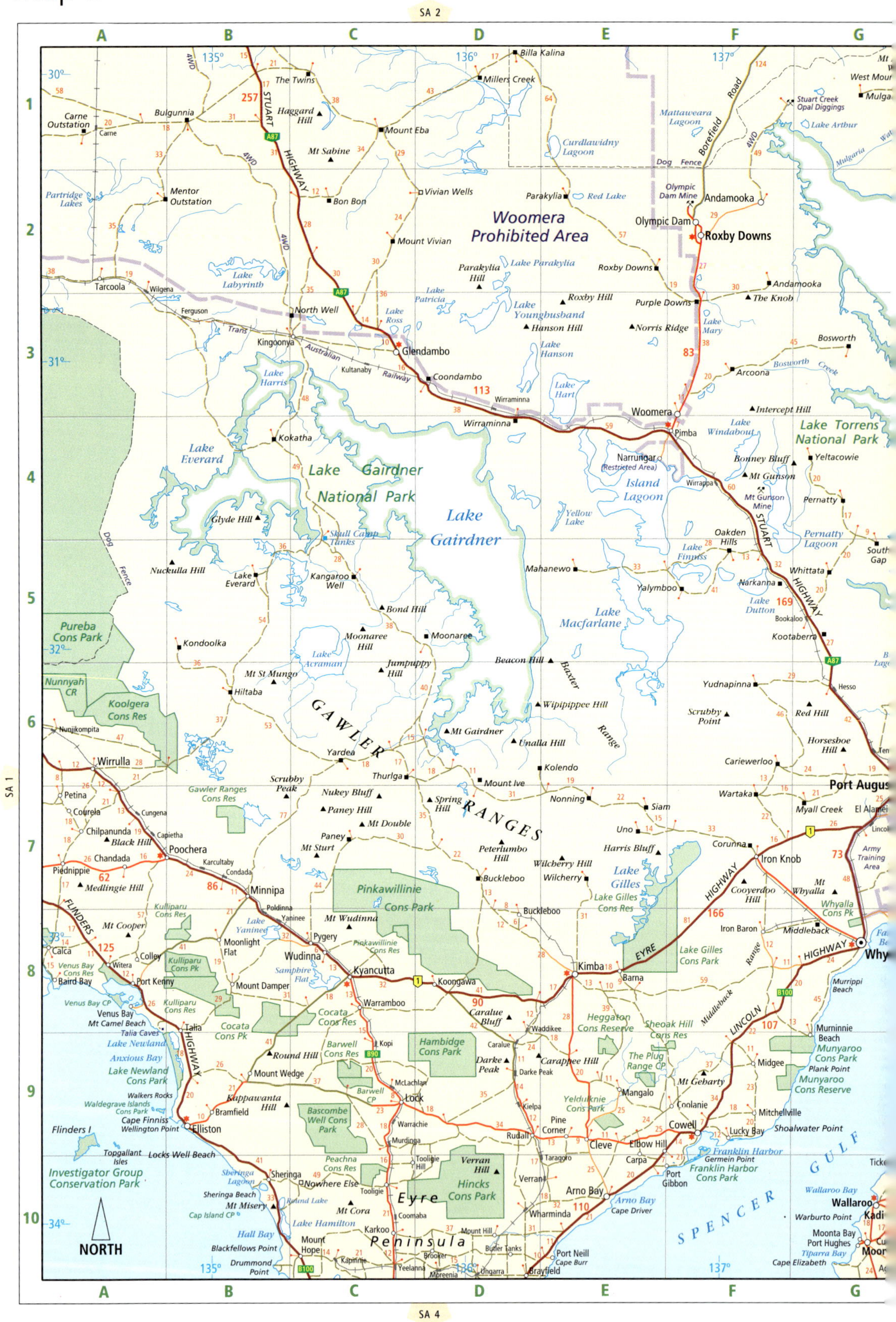
SA 2
SA 4
SA 1
A
B
C
D
E
F
G
1
2
3
4
5
6
7
8
9
10
NORTH
Woomera Prohibited Area
Lake Gairdner National Park
Lake Gairdner
GAWLER RANGES
Eyre Peninsula
SPENCER GULF
Lake Torrens National Park
Billa Kalina
Millers Creek
The Twins
Haggard Hill
Mount Eba
Mt Sabine
Bulgunnia
Carne Outstation
Carne
Curdlawidny Lagoon
Mattaweara Lagoon
Stuart Creek Opal Diggings
Lake Arthur
West Mount
Mulgaria
Partridge Lakes
Mentor Outstation
Vivian Wells
Bon Bon
Mount Vivian
Parakylia
Red Lake
Olympic Dam Mine
Andamooka
Olympic Dam
Roxby Downs
Dog Fence
Borefield Road
STUART HIGHWAY
Tarcoola
Wilgena
Ferguson
Lake Labyrinth
North Well
Kingoonya
Trans Australian Railway
Lake Ross
Lake Patricia
Parakylia Hill
Lake Parakylia
Lake Younghusband
Hanson Hill
Roxby Hill
Norris Ridge
Purple Downs
Lake Mary
The Knob
Bosworth
Bosworth Creek
Arcoona
Glendambo
Kultanaby
Coondambo
Lake Harris
Lake Hanson
Lake Hart
Wirraminna
Woomera
Pimba
Intercept Hill
Lake Windabout
Kokatha
Lake Everard
Narrungar (Restricted Area)
Island Lagoon
Wirrappa
Bonney Bluff
Mt Gunson
Mt Gunson Mine
Yeltacowie
Pernatty
Pernatty Lagoon
Glyde Hill
Skull Camp Tanks
Yellow Lake
Oakden Hills
Lake Finniss
South Gap
Nuckulla Hill
Dog Fence
Kangaroo Well
Mahanewo
Whittata
Narkanna
Yalymboo
Lake Dutton
Bookaloo
Bond Hill
Lake Macfarlane
Pureba Cons Park
Moonaree Hill
Moonaree
Kootaberra
Kondoolka
Lake Acraman
Jumpuppy Hill
Beacon Hill
Baxter Range
Mt St Mungo
Hiltaba
Yudnapinna
Hesso
Nunnyah CR
Koolgera Cons Res
Wipipippee Hill
Scrubby Point
Red Hill
Nunjikompita
Mt Gairdner
Unalla Hill
Horsesboe Hill
Wirrulla
Yardea
Cariewerloo
Thurlga
Mount Ive
Kolendo
Scrubby Peak
Gawler Ranges Cons Res
Nukey Bluff
Spring Hill
Nonning
Siam
Wartaka
Port Augusta
Myall Creek
Petina
Courela
Cungena
Paney Hill
Mt Double
Chilpanunda
Capietha
Black Hill
Paney
Uno
Corunna
Iron Knob
Army Training Area
Peterlumbo Hill
Harris Bluff
Poochera
Mt Sturt
Wilcherry Hill
Wilcherry
Lake Gilles
Lake Gilles Cons Res
Chandada
Piednippie
Karcultaby
Condada
Buckleboo
Cooyerdoo Hill
Mt Whyalla
Whyalla Cons Pk
Medlingie Hill
Minnipa
Pinkawillinie Cons Park
FLINDERS HIGHWAY
Kulliparu Cons Res
Poldinna
Yaninee
Lake Yaninee
Mt Wudinna
Mt Cooper
Iron Baron
Middleback
Moonlight Flat
Pygery
Pinkawillinie Cons Res
Calca
Colley
Wudinna
Kulliparu Cons Pk
Kimba
EYRE HIGHWAY
Lake Gilles Cons Park
Middleback Range
Whyalla
Venus Bay Cons Res
Witera
Baird Bay
Port Kenny
Mount Damper
Sampibre Flat
Kyancutta
Koongawa
Barna
Murrippi Beach
Venus Bay CP
Venus Bay
Mt Camel Beach
Warramboo
Caralue Bluff
Heggaton Cons Reserve
Sheoak Hill Cons Res
LINCOLN HIGHWAY
Murninnie Beach
Munyaroo Cons Park
Plank Point
Talia Caves
Talia
Lake Newland
Cocata Cons Pk
Cocata Cons Res
Waddikee
Kopi
Hambidge Cons Park
Caralue
Darke Peak
Anxious Bay
Round Hill
Barwell Cons Res
Carappee Hill
The Plug Range CP
Midgee
Munyaroo Cons Reserve
Lake Newland Cons Park
Mount Wedge
McLachlan
Barwell CP
Mt Gebarty
Walkers Rocks
Waldegrave Islands Cons Park
Kappawanta Hill
Lock
Kielpa
Mangalo
Yeldulknie Cons Park
Coolanie
Mitchellville
Cape Finniss
Wellington Point
Bramfield
Elliston
Bascombe Well Cons Park
Warrachie
Pine Corner
Cleve
Cowell
Lucky Bay
Shoalwater Point
Flinders I
Rudall
Murdinga
Elbow Hill
Franklin Harbor
Topgallant Isles
Locks Well Beach
Tooligie Hill
Verran Hill
Taragoro
Carpa
Germein Point
Franklin Harbor Cons Park
Port Gibbon
Investigator Group Conservation Park
Sheringa Lagoon
Sheringa
Peachna Cons Res
Hincks Cons Park
Verran
Nowhere Else
Tooligie
Arno Bay
Wallaroo Bay
Sheringa Beach
Mt Misery
Round Lake
Mt Cora
Arno Bay
Cape Driver
Wallaroo
Cap Island CP
Coomaba
Wharminda
Warburto Point
Lake Hamilton
Hall Bay
Karkoo
Mount Hill
Moonta Bay
Blackfellows Point
Mount Hope
Butler Tanks
Port Neill
Cape Burr
Port Hughes
Tiparra Bay
Cape Elizabeth
Drummond Point
Kapinnie
Brooker
Yeelanna
Moreenia
Ungarra
Brayfield
30°
31°
32°
33°
34°
135°
136°
137°

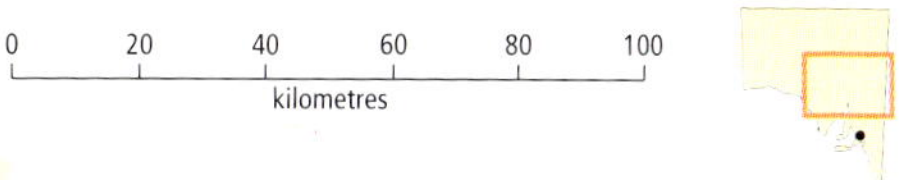

0
20
40
60
80
100
kilometres

SA 2

H J K L M N P
1 2 3 4 5 6 7 8 9 10
138°
139°
140°
141°
30°
31°
32°
33°
34°
Wilpoorinna
Farina
Termination Hill
Lyndhurst
Avondale
Strzelecki
Mount Lyndhurst
Track
Mount Freeling
Arkaroola-Mt Painter Sanctuary
Freeling Heights
Mt Fitton Talc Mine
Mount Fitton
Mt Neil
Paralana Hot Springs
Mt Painter
Arkaroola Village
Arkaroola
North Mulga
Hamilton Creek
Poontana Creek
Pipeline
Umberatana
Yankaninna
Benbonyathe Hill
Gammon Ranges National Park
Wooltana
Owieandana
Mount Serle
Mt McKinlay
Italowie Gorge
Balcanoona
Wertaloona
Nepabunna
Angepena
Maynards Well
North Moolooloo
Myrtle Springs
Telford
Leigh Creek Coalfield
Copley
Leigh Creek
Beltana Mine
NORTH FLINDERS
RANGES
Nantawarrina Aboriginal Land
Teatree Outstation
Big John Ck
Lake Frome
Lake Frome Regional Reserve
Ediacara Cons Reserve
Beltana Roadhouse
Beltana
Warraweena
Nantawarrina
Mulga View
Narrina
Nuccaleena Mine (ruin)
Patawarta Gap
Chambers Gorge
Mt Chambers
Moolooloo
Artimore
Glass Gorge
Nilpena
Parachilna Gorge
Parachilna
Blinman
Angorichina Village
Mt Emily
Wirrealpa
Balcoracana Creek
Bendieuta Creek
Motpena
Commodore
Brachina Gorge
Aroona
Wilkawillina Gorge
Flinders Ranges National Park
Oraparinna
Mt Caernarvon
Appealinna Station
Bunyeroo Gorge
Edeowie
Edeowie Gorge
St Mary Peak
Stokes Hill Lookout
Martins Well
Erudina
Erudina Woolshed
Upalinna
Wilpena
Wilpena Pound
Rawnsley Bluff
Rawnsley Park
Sacred Canyon
Wilpena Creek
Mt Neville
Mt Josephine
Curnamona
Mernmerna
Cotabena
Lake Torrens
Wonoka
Arkaba
Warcowie
Willippa
Mt Plantagenet
Holowilena
Willow Waters
Hawker
Warrakimbo
South
Flinders
Ranges
Wilson Historic Site
Holowilena South
Old Baratta
Baratta
Milang Well
Yednalue
Kanyaka
Cradock
Gordon
Witchitie
Belton
Willochra
Quorn
Price Hill
Minburra Plain
Oladdie Plain
Minburra
Carrieton
Johnburgh
Mt Brown Cons Pk
Mt Brown
Moockra
Hammond
Eurelia
Yalpara
Wilmington
Willowie
Morchard
Orroroo
Black Rock
Nectar Brook
Alligator Gorge
Melrose
Mt Remarkable Nat Park
Booleroo Centre
Pekina
Yatina
Oodla Wirra
Murray Town
Peterborough
Tarcowie
Wirrabara
Mannanarie
Appila
Hornsdale
Yongala
Belalie North
Mt Lock
Caltowie
Jamestown
Terowie
Laura
Gladstone
Crystal Brook
Georgetown
Campbell Hill
Belalie East
Whyte-Yarcowie
Pirie
Spotswood Hill
Melton
Waukaringa
Bonnie Brae
Chinamans Hat
Wabricoola
One Tree Hill
McCoys Well
Yunta
Paratoo
Mergenia
Black Rock
Dawson
Nackara
Hill Grange
Pandappa Hill
Franklyn
Pine Creek
Bendigo
Braemar
Pandappa Cons Pk
Mallett
Ketchowla
Collinsville
Mt Scrub
Hallett
The Bluff
Mt Bryan
Caroona
Hog Back
Glenora
Murkaby
Hallett Hill
Mount Bryan
Mt Cone
Poonunda
Koomooloo
Old Koomooloo
Thistlebeds
Grassville
Redcliffe
Burra
Burra Hill
Burra Creek Gorge
Hanson
Samson Well
Florieton
Black Springs
The Gums
Emu Downs
Apoinga
Robertstown
Clare
Sevenhill
Mintaro
Waterloo
Auburn
Saddleworth
Marrabel
Australia Plains
Eudunda
Riverton
Rhynie
Balaklava
Halbury
Blyth
Snowtown
Brinkworth
Koolunga
Redhill
Yacka
Narridy
Mundoora
Lake View
Wokurna
Andrews
Hilltown
Spalding
Booborowie
Rochester
Bald Hill Nth
Mt Tinline
Hart
Condowie
Bumbunga Lake
Kybunga
Penwortham
Watervale
Bowillia
Nantawarra
Whitwarta
Mount Mary
Bower
Morgan
Cadell
Qualco
Murbko
Ramco
Pooginook Cons Park
Frome Downs
Glenorchy
Mt Victor
Mount Victor
Koonamore
Plumbago
Four Brothers
Marialpa
Weekeroo
Florina
Mannahill
Oulnina Park
Panaramitee
Tiverton
Netley Gap
Manunda
Oak Park
Lilydale
Faraway Hill
Sturt Vale
Pine Valley
Kia Ora
Canegrass
Balah
Benda
Dlorah Downs
Wadnaminga
Devonborough Downs
Eringa
Olary
Waiwera
Bimbowrie
Outalpa
Wiperaminga Hill
Kalabity
Boolcoomata
Strathearn
Nancatee Hill
Kalkaroo
Mooleulooloo
Yarramba
Mulyungarie
Bulloo Creek
Mingary
Cockburn
Pine Creek
Corella
Ballara
Mutooroo
Burta
Kimberley
Oakvale
Loch Lilly
Oakbank
Quondong Vale
Morgan Vale
Danggali Conservation Park
Canopus (Park HQ)
Hypurna
Chowilla Regional Reserve
Belmore
Warrakoo
Ennisvale
Chowilla Game Reserve
Nelwood
Border Cliffs
Chowilla
Cal Lal
Calperum
Cooltong
Lindsay Point
Renmark
Paringa
Lake Yannerpi
Smithville House
Coonee
Lake Cootabarlow
Lake Muck
Rotten Swamp
McIntyre Bore
Border Downs
Lake Coontayunta
Starvation Lake
Lake Elder
Green Lake
Pine Dam
Lake Maljanapa
Quinyambie
Lake Kuturu
Lake Karpi
Lake Moko
Eurinilla
Lake Tarkarooloo
Billeroo Creek
Lake Namba
Dog Fence
Avenel
Silverton
Mingary Creek
White Ck
SOUTH AUSTRALIA
NEW SOUTH WALES
border follows Dog Fence
BARRIER HIGHWAY
MAIN NORTH ROAD
BARRIER HWY
NSW 1
NSW 5
SA
A32
B56
B64
B80
B82
A1

SA 4

Map 4

SA 3

NORTH
Mt Misery
Cap Island CP
Hall Bay
Blackfellows Point
Drummond Point
Mt Drummond
Convention Beach
Lake Greenly
Coles Point
Point Sir Isaac
Green Point
Reef Point
Coffin Bay
Coffin Bay National Park
Point Whidbey
Avoid Bay
Greenly Island Cons Park
Greenly Island
Point Avoid
Perforated Island
Four Hummocks
Whidbey Isles Conservation Park
Gunyah Beach
Shoal Point
Mt Cora
Lake Hamilton
Karkoo
Mount Hope
Kapinnie
Lake Malata
Cummins
Warrow
South Block
Coulta
Wangary
Lake Wangary
Coffin Bay
Kellidie Bay CP
Coomunga
Little Swamp
Port Lincoln
Tulka
D'Anville Bay
Cape Carnot
Liguanea Island
Cape Wiles
Jussieu Peninsula
West Point
Lincoln National Park
Cape Catastrophe
Williams I
Hincks Cons Park
Coomaba
Eyre Peninsula
Brooker
Yeelanna
Moreenia
Cockaleechie
Mount Hill
Wharminda
Butler Tanks
Brayfield
Ungarra
Yallunda Flat
Pillana
Edillilie
Koppio
White Flat
Wanilla
Pearlah
Green Patch
Poonindie
North Shields
Louth Bay
Boston Bay
Point Boston
Boston Island
Cape Donnington
Point Maclaren
Point Haselgrove
Dangerous Reef
Taylor I
Thistle Island
Observatory Point
Horny Point
Waterhouse Point
Gambier Islands Cons Park
Wedge Island
Neptune Islands
Port Neill
Cape Burr
Cape Hardy
Lipson Cove
Lipson
Tumby Bay
Cape Euler
Massena Bay
Red Point
Point Bolingbroke
Reevesby Island
Roxby Island
Sir Joseph Banks Group Conservation Park
Spilsby Island
Sir Joseph Banks Group
Arno Bay
Cape Driver
SPENCER GULF
Wallaroo
Warburto Point
Moonta Bay
Port Hughes
Tiparra Bay
Cape Elizabeth
The Gap
Weetulta
Balgowan
Chinaman Wells
Maitland
Reef Point
Point Pearce
Island Point
Wardang Island
Port Victoria
Wauraltee
Koolywurtie
Port Rickaby
Parsons Beach
Minlaton
Point Souttar
Port Minlacowie
Brentwood
Hardwicke Bay
Leven Beach CP
Corny Point
Point Turton
Gleesons Landing
Daly Head
Warooka
Yorketown
Edithburgh
White Hut
Formby Bay
Point Margaret
Browns Beach
Royston Head
Pondalowie Bay
West Cape
Inneston
Innes Nat Park
Marion Bay
Stenhouse Bay
Cape Spencer
Seal Island
Point Yorke
Butlers Beach
Foul Bay
Davenport CP
Sturt Bay
Althorpe Islands
Althorpe Islands Cons Park
Strait
Investigator
North Cape
Emu Bay
Stokes Bay
Cape Cassini
Cape Dutton
Snelling Beach
Western River Cove
Wilderness Protection Area
Cape Torrens
Harveys Return
Cape Borda Lighthouse
Cape Borda
Ravine des Casoars Wilderness Prot Area
Vennachar Point
West Bay
Cape Bedout
Maupertuis Bay
Cape du Couedic Lighthouse and Admirals Arch
Flinders Chase National Park
Rocky River
Remarkable Rocks
Karatta
Kelly Hill Caves
Western River WPA
Amen Corner
Cygnet River
Parndana
PLAYFORD HWY
American
Kangaroo Island
Vivonne Bay
Seal Bay CP
Cape Gantheaume Cons Pk
Cape Gantheaume
Weirs Cove
Cape du Couedic
Hanson Bay
Sanderson Bay
Cape Bouguer
Cape Kersaint
Point Ellen
Vivonne Bay CP
SOUTHERN OCEAN
34°
35°
36°
37°
38°
135°
136°
137°
A B C D E F G
1 2 3 4 5 6 7 8 9 10

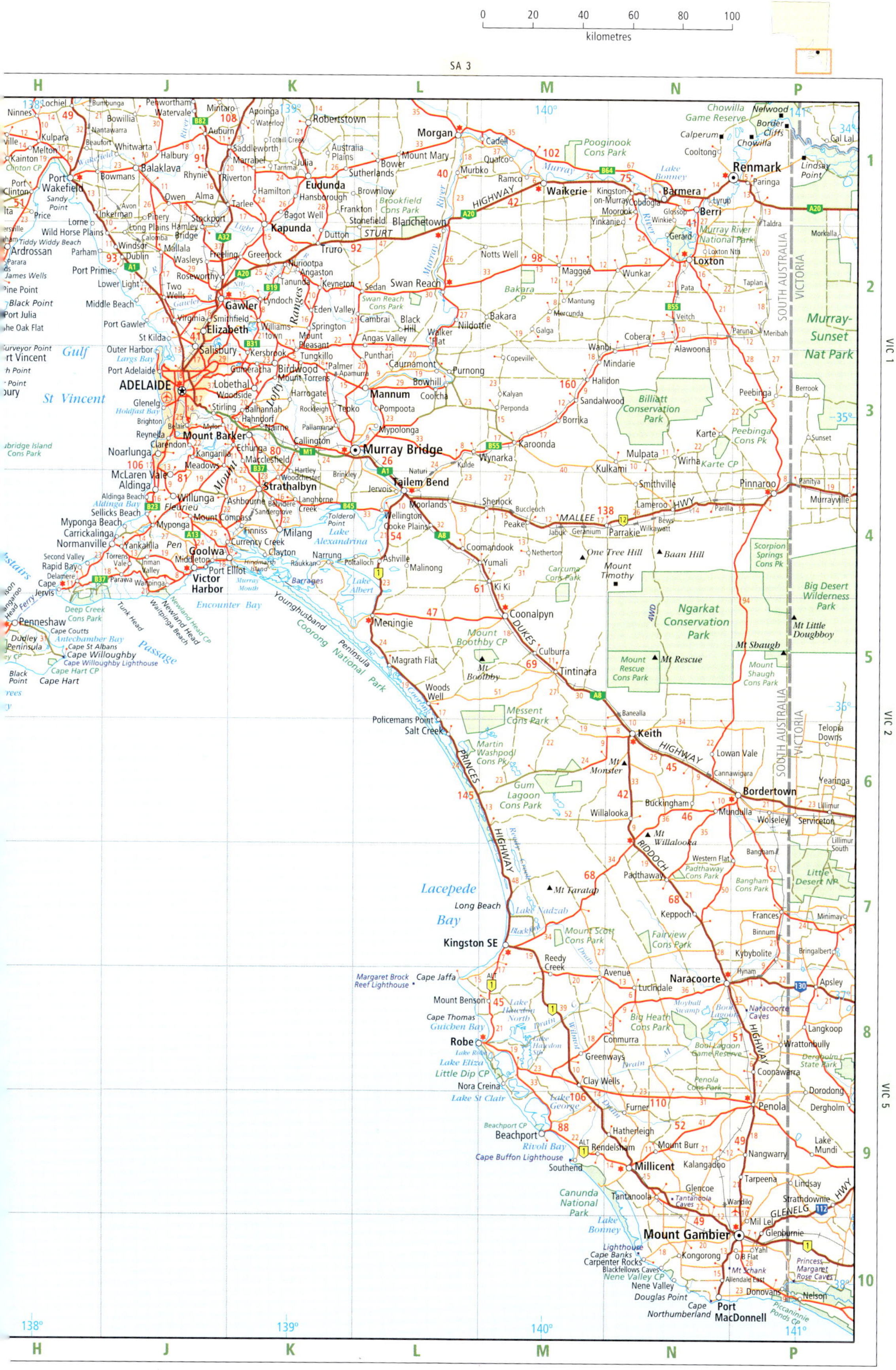

VIC 1
VIC 2
VIC 5

Western Australia

Western Australia is the nation's largest state, and this vast expanse of land affords the visitor many unique opportunities to seek isolation for quiet reflection and rejuvenation. Let the warm waters of the Indian Ocean wash over you as you snorkel along the coral reef of the Ningaloo Marine Park, or admire the grace and intelligence of the bottlenose dolphins that visit magical Monkey Mia. Beachcombers will enjoy wandering along Broome's beautiful Cable Beach, while the Pinnacles, silent sentinels of limestone in Nambung National Park, have long inspired poets and photographers. Colourful wildflowers carpet parts of the state in spring, cheering even the most jaded traveller—but you're sure to find Western Australia an absolute delight at any time of year.

Perth and Environs

Perth is, according to some geographic authorities, the most isolated city on Earth. While this may be true, it does not hint at the essence or the appeal of this particularly charming city on the Swan River. Perth is really a city of lovely parks and gardens. It is a place where, once you have managed to drag yourself away from the temptations of the Burswood Casino, you want to spend your days either wandering the parks or heading for the coast where the beaches are superb.

Perth

Perth is famous for its fine parks and gardens, many of which run along the banks of the Swan River, allowing both sightseers and joggers pleasant views across the river. A perfect place to start is Stirling Gardens in the heart of the city. In the right season these gardens are a glorious retreat from the high-rise buildings and the city's urgency. The flowerbeds are spectacular and the walkways offer a cool retreat. They are strategically located so that if you wish to explore the historic centre of the city, all the major buildings—Government House, the Supreme Court, the Old Court House, St Georges Cathedral, St Andrews Church and the Perth Town Hall—are within a few hundred metres. It is the simplest of walks to pass through Stirling Gardens into the adjacent Supreme Court Gardens (an ideal place to enjoy a little rest and recreation) before continuing on to the edge of the Swan River. Nearby is the Barrack Street wharf where ferries ply the river. It is possible from this wharf to catch a ferry across the river to the Perth Zoo (which has a great Australian animals display) or to book a cruise along the river. There are a number of operators and the range of tours includes an interesting journey downriver to Fremantle and a winery cruise.

Built in 1864, Government House is the home of the Western Australian governor. The architecture combines Jacobean and Gothic styles.

But when it comes to parks, there is really no substitute for magnificent Kings Park. This 4 sq km park offers the visitor a perspective on the whole of central Perth. There are outstanding views across the city from a number of vantage points. Part

On the northern bank of the Swan River, Perth is the fourth-largest city in Australia, with a population of over 1.2 million. Swimming and sailing are both popular activities on the river.

don't miss

If you are in Perth from the end of January to the middle of February, check out the action at the Perth International Arts Festival. The programme includes music, dance, visual arts, film, theatre and much more.

of the parklands is taken up with the Perth Botanic Gardens, which cover 17 hectares and combine a section of natural bushland with an impressive display of more than 2000 different plant species. It is possible to join free conducted tours of both Kings Park and the Botanic Gardens. The whole area is ideal for those who enjoy walking and cycling, and there are companies—notably Koala Bicycle Hire (08 9321 3061)—from whom bicycles can be hired.

Once you have visited some of the parks in the centre of the city, then it is time to check out the city's beaches. There are a number of beaches along the Swan River (at Peppermint Grove, Como and Crawley) but the real attractions are the surf beaches. The most famous is Cottesloe Beach where the city's workers go for

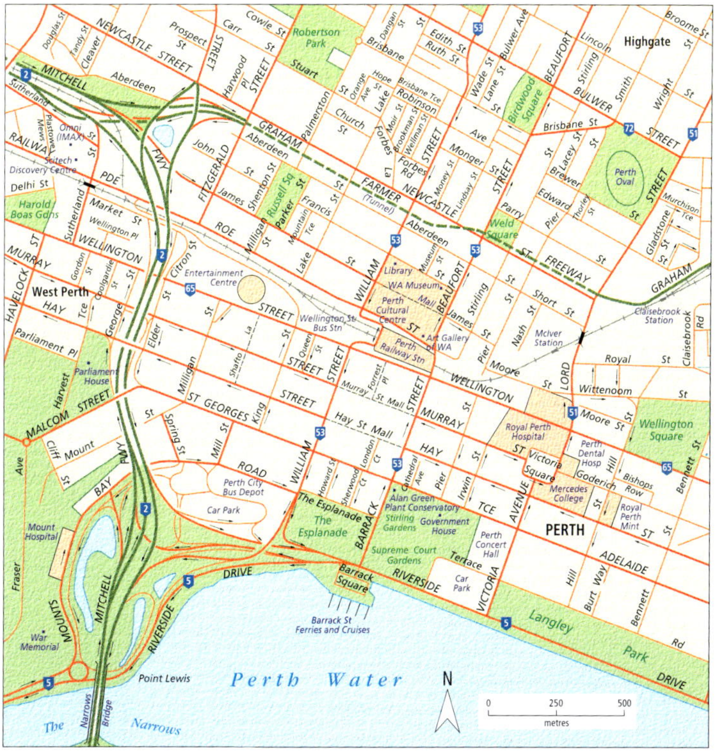

WA

Scarborough Beach has excellent surf, but strong currents along this part of the coast should deter inexperienced swimmers. Walking along the beach and sunbaking are safer, more relaxing options.

an early morning jog and dip. Other notable beaches include Swanbourne (a nude beach), Leighton and Scarborough.

The city has a number of good markets—at Subiaco, Wanneroo, Fremantle and Canning Vale—which are well worth visiting to find bargains and to inspect the range of local arts and crafts. Shopaholics can also spend many pleasant hours in the arcades and malls located in Hay and Murray Streets.

Perth's reputation as a place where a visitor can eat well and cheaply (particularly when it comes to seafood) is in evidence in areas like Northbridge in the city's north, which has a diverse ethnic influence and many excellent restaurants. Harry's Seafood Grill & Garden Restaurant and The Fishy Affair Seafood Garden Restaurant are highly recommended.

Accommodation in the city ranges widely. The Burswood Casino is set in sumptuous gardens only a few minutes from the city centre—if you can resist the lure of the gaming tables.

Map: WA 8 C4

One of the best reasons to visit Perth—especially in spring—is to see the colourful native flowers that grow in the city's parks and gardens.

Fremantle

There is an argument, probably put around by someone from Freo (as the locals like to call it) that Fremantle is actually more interesting and more exciting than Perth. This might not be entirely true but there is merit in the argument. Fremantle combines very interesting history with some superb local museums, some great swimming locations and lots of good bars and restaurants. It seems like a place where people go for a good time.

Fremantle is the ideal place to go for a Sunday outing. Have a delicious meal in one of the dozens of restaurants in the area, have a picnic, wander along the shoreline, visit the museums, gaze at the conspicuous wealth at the yacht club, wander the old streets, or visit the historic buildings—the choice is yours.

Of particular importance and interest is Fremantle Gaol (built between 1851 and 1859), with its 5-m high walls and its design based on Pentonville Gaol in

England; Fremantle Markets (first held in 1897), with their vast numbers of stalls—they are open on Fridays, Saturdays and Sundays; the Western Australian Maritime Museum, with its reconstruction of the Dutch ship *Batavia* which was wrecked off the Western Australian coast in 1629; the Sails of the Century Museum, with the most famous of contemporary boats—*Australia II*—which won the America's Cup; and the Fremantle Museum and Art Gallery, which often has concerts as well as free exhibitions.

Fremantle is also an ideal place for fishing. The seas always seem to have an abundance of skippy, salmon, pink snapper, herring, garfish and bonito, and there are a number of good locations—both beaches and seawalls—where these fish can be caught.

Map: WA 8 C4

Classified by the National Trust, the Esplanade Hotel in Fremantle was designed by J. H. Eales and erected in the 1890s during the gold rush.

Rottnest Island

Everyone in Perth seems to go to Rottnest Island. Located 19 km off the coast from Perth (12 minutes by air and 2 hours by water), it is the city's favourite holiday and daytripping destination. Over the

The Swan River near Fremantle. This city and port is home to a 500-strong fishing fleet and a vast number of yachts and pleasure craft. In 1987 it hosted the America's Cup sailing challenge.

Right: *Many visitors make the trip to Rottnest just to see the island's most famous inhabitants—the mischievous quokkas* (Setonix brachyurus).

The crystal-clear waters surrounding Rottnest Island draw swimmers, surfers and snorkellers. Sailing and windsurfing are also popular pastimes.

years Rottnest has changed dramatically. As early as 1848 it was a pilot station for Fremantle. There was a time when it was used as an internment camp and during World War II it became a military post. Since the late nineteenth century it has been a popular holiday resort for Perth people. There is a real sense of peacefulness about the island. This is greatly helped by the absence of cars. On the island everyone rides a pushbike, or walks. Apart from just enjoying 'getting away from it all', visitors to the island can take a look at its interesting historic buildings. There is also a charm about the huge Moreton Bay figs and the quiet waters around the island.

One of the joys of a visit to the island are the walks. There is the Vincent Way Heritage Trail—a 2-km walk which takes about 45 minutes. This is the most important of the Heritage Trails on the island as it includes all the buildings in the Rottnest Island Old Settlement which are listed by the National Estate. Then there is the Cape Vlamingh Heritage Trail—a short walk which takes a leisurely 30 minutes and includes opportunities to see the wreck of the *Kiryo Maru*, as well as to observe some of the island's fauna including the distinctive quokkas, dugites

The view of the vineyards at Talijancich Wines, with the Darling Range rising in the background. Established in 1932, this Swan Valley winery has won more than 120 national wine-show awards.

(poisonous snakes), fairy terns and dolphins. It also includes visits to Bridge Rock and the island's Blow Hole. Perhaps the most unusual Heritage Trail on the island is the Rottnest Wrecks Heritage Trail (make sure you wear a snorkel) which looks at all the shipwrecks around the coast of the island.

Accommodation and food on Rottnest Island tends to be focused on daytrippers who are more interested in exploring the island's features than staying and eating. A notable exception is the Rottnest Hotel (08 9292 5011) which was once used as the summer residence of the Governors of Western Australia. The Rottnest Island Authority's holiday accommodation is located in the Thomson, Geordie, Longreach and Fays Bay areas as well as at Kingstown.

Map: WA 8 B4

York

The township of York is located only 99 km from Perth (a perfect and easy daytrip) and, as the first settlement in the Avon Valley, it is full of really beautiful old buildings. It is one of the best preserved and restored nineteenth-century towns in Australia. There is real charm and interest here. No visit to the town is truly complete without inspecting and admiring the Court House and the Police Station (they both date from the 1840s), as well as the large number of impressive buildings in Avon Street. The York Heritage Trail lists 57 buildings and places of importance and the York Tourist Bureau, being more modest, lists 21 places. There is a lot to see in a relatively small town which gives the visitor a very clear idea of what life was really like in nineteenth-century Western Australia.

Map: WA 8 D4

Swan Valley

There are a number of charming trips up the Swan River Valley from Perth which are worth taking. This is an area of divine vineyards and early historic buildings. It is where Tranby House (1839), one of the oldest homes in Western Australia, is open for inspection and offers a view into the past.

Located at West Swan there is the interesting Caversham Wildlife Park which has an extensive collection of Australian wildlife. Nearby is Whiteman Park which not only has picnic and barbecue facilities but also contains an enchanting 'village' where local crafts and gift items are sold.

Map: WA 8 C4

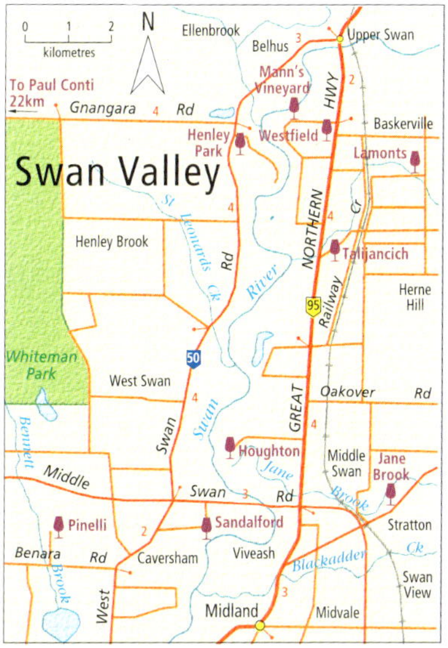

The South and the South-West

There is an argument for believing that people wanting to experience the real Western Australia need to escape from Perth and Fremantle, because the heart of this huge state lies in the abundance of rural riches and natural wonders found outside the cities. This is certainly the case when it comes to the South and the South-West, which is an area of unsurpassed loveliness that should not be missed.

While in the town of Margaret River, take a walk along the river and you will discover pristine hardwood forests and stunning waterfalls.

The coastal parks–particularly Leeuwin Naturaliste National Park–are known for their rugged beauty and excellent bushwalking. Regions like Margaret River are justifiably famous for their wineries, restaurants and accommodation. The towns along the coast–Bunbury, Busselton, Albany, Augusta and Esperance–are extraordinarily beautiful with superb beaches and dramatic rock formations. The forests, with the stands of karri and jarrah, are places of great beauty and tranquillity. And the inland sheep and wheat areas, like so much of the south and east of the state, are the true rural heartland.

People looking for rest and relaxation in this great area should be thinking in terms of bushwalking, swimming and surfing, fishing, having picnics in cool forests, checking out the wineries and marvelling at the beauty of the coastline. This is a very special part of Australia.

Established in 1972, Sandalford Wines was one of the first wineries in the Margaret River region. It has developed an impressive shiraz and cabernet, and its verdelho has an appealing tropical fruit taste.

Margaret River

The most famous part of southern Western Australia is the Margaret River region. This is because, over the past decade, the region has become famous for its fine wines. It is now considered the equal of the Hunter Valley in New South Wales, the Barossa in South Australia and the Yarra Valley in Victoria. Located 280 km south of Perth, Margaret River (the township) is a settlement of some substance with a number of quality motels and craft shops. It is a pleasant little town with an attractive upmarket feel, and it is in the heart of an area of limestone caves, vineyards, forests of hardwood and attractive coastlines. Its major industries include tourism, dairy cattle and timber.

For those wanting to enjoy the full range of activities of the area the focus will be on bushwalks and seaside pleasures. There are many bushwalks around Margaret River (including a walk from the town to Prevelly Beach). There are good-quality cycleways. And the beaches are known to be some of the best along the Western Australian coast.

There are more than 60 vineyards, all with tasting rooms and cellars,

Right: *The Margaret River region is responsible for just 1 per cent of Australia's overall wine production, but makes up 20 per cent of the premium market.*

Torndirrup National Park, just south of Albany, has a wealth of wildflowers in spring, which encourages native fauna such as possums and honeyeaters.

in the Margaret River area. Some of the most famous wineries include Amberley Estate (its chenin blanc is so successful it sells out before it has been bottled), Cullen, Driftwood Estate, Leeuwin Estate (famous for its concerts and marvellous gourmet picnic hampers), Sandalford, Brookland Valley, Vasse River, Ribbon Vale and Yungarra Estate. The first grape vines were planted as recently as 1967, but already the region is producing Rhine riesling, chardonnay, semillon, sauvignon blanc, cabernet sauvignon, pinot noir and shiraz.

Wine lovers usually start their explorations by visiting the Margaret River Regional Wine Centre which is located at 9 Bussell Highway in Cowaramup. Contact (08) 9755 5501.

Tours of the Margaret River region are available. They offer good quality B&B accommodation as well as visits to a number of the local wineries.

Apart from the surrounding wineries, the township of Margaret River has some interesting historical destinations. The superb Old Settlement Historical Museum is privately owned. It has a large number of farm buildings with farm machinery. It is a kind of monument to the Group Settlement farms which saw the early development of the area.

Eating in the district is a treat. Marron (a kind of freshwater lobster) is a local specialty, and the combination of fresh produce and the region's excellent wines ensures that some of the restaurants are quite outstanding. Chefs with international reputations have been attracted to working in the region.

Accommodation ranges from the delightful Geographe Bayview Resort situated on the Bussell Highway at Busselton (08 9755 4166) through to farmstays (most of which have large communities of animals to entertain the children), B&B destinations and camping. This is an area of major tourism. Some of the self-catering accommodation, although expensive, become very reasonable if you are travelling in a group. For example, the Karri Manor located in Margaret River (08 9758 7089) has room enough for four people and is centrally located in the town.

Margaret River really comes alive in November, when the Surf Classic and the Wine and Food Festival are held.

Map: WA 8 B8

Torndirrup National Park's most famous attraction is Natural Bridge, a granite rock formation carved out of the coastline by powerful Southern Ocean waves.

Albany

Located 406 km south of Perth, Albany is the major population centre on the Western Australian south coast and the oldest European settlement in the state. It is a special and unusual town. The main street seems to go straight into the Princess Royal Harbour. The town itself is steeped in history, but the real appeal is the coastline which has great walking trails and spectacular formations in the granite headlands that were carved out by the Southern Ocean. The highlight of any visit is a trip out to Torndirrup

National Park. Here the Natural Bridge, The Gap, the Blowholes and the Gorge, as well as Whale World (a whale museum), are all worth visiting.

In the town itself the local historical society recognises at least 40 places of genuine historic interest including the Old Gaol, the Government Residency and Stirling Terrace with the Penny Post Restaurant and the Old Post Office. The town has eight motels and over 20 B&Bs and guesthouses. It is worth visiting in spring for the wildflower displays.

Map: WA 8 F10

Bunbury

The trip down to the southern coast of Western Australia is nothing short of pure joy. Every town and village has its own charm. Stop off at Bunbury, which is only 173 km south of Perth, and check out the old lighthouse (which is an extraordinary combination—an earlier lighthouse has been placed on top of the present lighthouse), St Marks Church, King Cottage and the Regional Art Gallery Arts Complex. Located to the west of the city centre is Geographe Bay, which stretches south towards Busselton. Taking a drive along the coast, which is particularly beautiful, is

Situated 20 km south of Albany, within Torndirrup National Park, Misery Beach is great for swimming and fishing. Anglers are likely to catch herring, silver bream, skippy and sometimes salmon.

Left: *Bunbury is the major port in the south-west of Western Australia. Bays, beaches and inlets close to town offer safe swimming, and wild dolphins regularly visit the beach along Koombana Bay.*

interesting because of Rocky Point and the lighthouse.
Map: WA 8 C7

Busselton

Busselton is full of history and has an elegance which is uncharacteristic of many of the more modern holiday destinations. It is, by any measure, a delightful place with green parks, a wide range of interesting historical buildings (check out Wonnerup House which is run by the National Trust), a well-established town centre, a wide variety of accommodation ranging from the cheap to the sophisticated, and activities which reach far beyond the usual seaside attractions. There can be few more pleasant ways to relax than to walk along Busselton beach and make the long journey to the end of the town's jetty. The original jetty was built using jarrah and was 161 m long, but drifting sands and the shallowness of the bay resulted in the construction of an additional 131 m of jetty in 1875. A further stage was added so that today it is nearly 2 km long—one of the longest jetties in the world. It is used by anglers and holiday-makers and offers the hardy a pleasant 4 km walk.
Map: WA 8 B7

The striking lighthouse at Bunbury is 25-m high, and its light can be seen up to 27 km out to sea. The checkered section, built in 1959, has been placed above a newer section, erected in 1971.

Augusta

One of the highlights of a journey to the south-west of Western Australia is a visit to the town of Augusta. Located 317 km south of Perth, it is the third-oldest settlement in Western Australia. It is not the town's age but its location which makes it so essential to visit. Augusta is the access point for Cape Leeuwin—it is only 8 km away—which is located at the very edge of the Australian continent, so that the Southern Ocean lies to the south and the Indian Ocean lies to the west. Standing on Cape Leeuwin, you feel that you are at a point where two great systems meet. The walk to the headland is easy and pleasant but, as along so much of the Western Australian coastline, a gale is usually blowing. However, the walk up to the lighthouse, through an area which is often ablaze with wildflowers, is one of the great experiences on the Western Australian coast.

Myalup Beach, on the coast between Bunbury and Busselton, provides good fishing and hang-gliding. Beach fishing is at its most popular in the warmer months, when tailor are plentiful.

Cape Leeuwin is the point on the Western Australian coast where the Indian and the Southern Oceans meet. The historic Leeuwin Lighthouse was built in 1896; the view from the top is worth the climb.

did you know?

The limestone cave system in Leeuwin-Naturaliste National Park is among the oldest archaeological sites in Australia. Fossils of Tasmanian tigers, a shark, koalas and a huge wombat-like creature have been found here.

The major attraction in the town is the Augusta Historical Museum. It has a variety of displays covering the history of the construction of the Cape Leeuwin lighthouse, the importance of the local timber industry, and a photographic exhibition detailing the rescue of a school of whales which beached themselves near the town.

While you are visiting the Augusta region, make sure you stop at Leeuwin-Naturaliste National Park. This is one of the country's great coastal parks. Granite headlands jut out, separating beaches which are gloriously white. Offshore the sea changes from aquamarine to a dark Prussian blue.

Another particularly attractive destination is Hamelin Bay which was once a port for the sawmills at Karridale. Today it is a reminder of what a beautiful beach can be like when it is left untouched by tourism. Located just off the coast is the Hamelin Bay Wreck Trail which explores the numerous interesting shipwrecks that lie in Hamelin Bay.

Nearby is the magnificent Jewel Cave which was discovered in 1880 but not fully explored until 1958. It is an excellent limestone cave with an antechamber and two main caves. The fossil of a Tasmanian tiger which was carbon dated as being 25 000 years old was discovered in the cave.

Map: WA 8 B9

More than 360 caves have been discovered beneath Leeuwin-Naturaliste National Park. However, only four caves are open to the public: Yallingup, Mammoth, Lake and Jewel Caves.

WA

The Central Coast

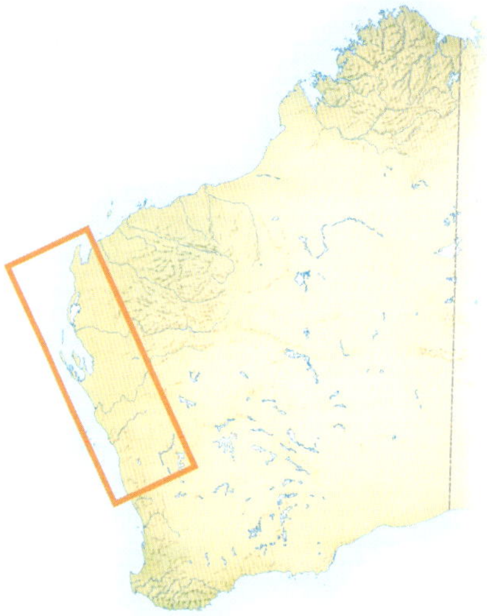

One of the great delights of Western Australia is to drive from Perth to Exmouth. There are so many pleasures and unique experiences along the way that, if you travel at the right time, you could easily spend a fortnight making the 1270 km journey. In the spring the wildflowers, almost beyond imagining if you have never experienced them, are in abundance on either side of the road. Then there are the famous Pinnacles (strange mounds of hardened limestone) near Cervantes.

There are the small fishing-port townships, each with its own special charm and attractions. There are, of course, the amazingly gregarious dolphins at Monkey Mia. And finally there's the remarkable Cape Range National Park and Ningaloo Marine Park where the reef, without a doubt, is actually much better than the Great Barrier Reef. Where else on earth can you snorkel with whale sharks?

When Dutch sailors first sighted the limestone columns of the Pinnacles in the seventeenth century, they believed these strange formations were the long-lost remains of an ancient city.

Cervantes and the Pinnacles

Located 245 km north of Perth, Cervantes is a pleasant fishing village and sleepy holiday destination. This is rock lobster fishing territory. All along the coast there are places selling lobster and, with very few exceptions, the locals know how to cook them to perfection.

But the best reason of all for visiting Cervantes is to make the 27-km journey from the town to the Pinnacle Desert in Nambung National Park. This is a photographer's delight. The strange pinnacles emerge out of the sand dunes and form amazing shapes, the result of a complex geological process. Although no one can say for sure how long ago this process occurred, the Western Australian Museum believes the pinnacles were formed some time in the last 80 000 years.

Map: WA 8 B1

Geraldton

Geraldton is the most substantial township on the north coast and is located 424 km north of Perth (via the Brand Highway). With an average of eight hours sunshine every day it is recognised as the state's most popular winter seaside resort town. If you go to the town looking for something more exciting than just lying on a beach and soaking up the sun, the obvious attractions include the excellent Geraldton Maritime Museum, a museum with a single theme: the exploration of the Western Australian coastline and the ships which were sunk off the coast during the seventeenth century.

Of similar interest is the Geraldton Museum, with its carefully designed displays on the history of local Australian Aboriginals plus the early European exploration and settlement of the area. There is also a fascinating exhibition of local animals prepared by a taxidermist.

The area around Geraldton is famous for its spring wildflower displays. These displays—which start around September and continue well into the early months of summer—are remarkable for their richness and diversity. Places like Eneabba and Kalbarri (the Kalbarri National Park not only has dramatic scenery, it also has some of the finest wildflower displays in the region) are of particular interest. Many people decide to take an organised tour of the wildflower region, and these tours are often arranged by travel agents outside Western Australia. There are also tours organised by special garden committees in cities such as Sydney, which spend a week or two exploring the area.

Map: WA 6 D7

Monkey Mia and Shark Bay

Shark Bay is a true jewel on the Western Australian coast. It features the largest sea grass meadows (3700 sq km) in the world. The meadows are home to an estimated 10 000 dugongs (about 10 per cent of the world's

Left: *St Francis Xavier Cathedral in Geraldton was designed by Monsignor John Hawes in the stunning Byzantine style, and completed in 1938.*

Below: *The stretch of coast between Geraldton and Dongara is popular with anglers, beachcombers, windsurfers and sailors.*

The Shark Bay region features over 700 species of wildflowers, with the longest flowering period in Western Australia. Some of the most common are golden lambstail and the Shark Bay daisy.

population), 6000 marine turtles (including the world's largest community of the endangered loggerhead turtle) and, as the name of the bay suggests, literally thousands of sharks.

Not surprisingly Shark Bay became World Heritage-listed in 1991. There are a number of attractions in the area. At Hamelin Pool, in the south-eastern corner of Shark Bay, there is a wooden walkway where the visitor can wander around and gaze down at hundreds of rocks which are shaped like solid cauliflowers. These 'rocks' are actually the end products of microscopic living organisms known as cyanobacteria. You are watching (although you can't really see it) a living process which is approximately 3 billion years older than the dinosaurs and which is being carried out by the oldest known living organisms on earth. Nearby is Shell Beach—which is made up of millions and millions of tiny white shells. At points along the coast the shells can reach a depth of up to 10 m.

A number of wild bottlenose dolphins visit the famous haven of Monkey Mia on a regular basis. The timing of their visits varies from day to day, but they are more likely to be seen in the morning.

Without a doubt, the tourist centrepiece of Shark Bay is Monkey Mia. It was here in the 1960s that a local angler's wife started feeding the dolphins. By the 1980s the area had become world famous for its friendly dolphins which came to the beach to nuzzle and frolic with visitors and eat fish provided by the local rangers. Today the dolphins are carefully monitored, the local caravan park has been turned into a good-quality but low-key eco-tourism resort, and there are two catamarans offering short trips around the bay where dolphins, turtles, dugongs and the occasional shark can be spotted and photographed by visitors.

Map: WA 6 B2

Many of the bottlenose dolphins (Tursiops truncatus) *that visit Monkey Mia are well known to the rangers—distinct markings on their dorsal fins are used to identity individual dolphins.*

Exmouth

Exmouth is an isolated township located 1272 km north of Perth. Although it is quite far from the capital city, it is the ideal starting point for excellent tours through Cape Range National Park and for snorkelling and exploring the beautiful Ningaloo Coral Reef which stretches from Exmouth, south for 260 km to Coral Bay. At Ningaloo you can literally walk in the water off the beach and be surrounded by a coral wonderland of soft and hard corals, huge and delicate formations, exotic and brightly coloured fish as well as turtles and reef sharks (a relatively harmless species). If you choose to go diving just south of Turquoise Bay, you don't even have to swim—all you've got to do is put your head down and let the current do the work. Between March and July it is possible to snorkel on Ningaloo Reef and watch whale sharks—friendly creatures which often measure more than 18 m in length and weigh up to 40 000 kg—drift by below you. Ningaloo Safari Tours and the Potshot Hotel Resort can be booked by contacting (08) 9949 1176.

Map: WA 5 C4

don't miss

Visit Cape Range National Park and take a relaxing boat cruise along Yardie Creek Gorge. As well as viewing spectacularly rugged scenery, you may be lucky enough to spot the rare black-striped rock wallaby.

WA

Snorkelling with gentle whale sharks (Rhincodon typus)*—the largest fish in the world—is an exhilarating experience. They come to Ningaloo Reef to feed on tiny marine creatures such as krill.*

The Kimberley

In recent times the unique Kimberley region has become an increasingly popular destination for those people—both Australians and international visitors—wanting to experience true isolation without sacrificing five-star comfort. The ethos of the Kimberley was really established by Lord McAlpine (a member of the British nobility who developed a love affair with Broome during the 1970s), who took the small pearling town of Broome and turned it into one of Australia's premier holiday destinations.

Once Broome, and particularly McAlpine's dream Cable Beach Resort, had been established, there was a movement to find more distant and more inaccessible resort locations. This has led to the Kimberley becoming one of Australia's best rest-and-recreation destinations.

While it's possible to drive from Perth to Broome via the Great Northern Highway, most people choose to arrive by plane. Roads to the north of Broome are unsealed and suitable for 4WD vehicles only.

Broome

Broome is located on Roebuck Bay, about 2200 km north of Perth. Historically it was a racially complex pearling town where peoples from the Indonesian archipelago, from the rest of south-east Asia and from Australia (Australian Aboriginals and Europeans) mixed within an environment which was both harsh and exciting. Today many of the old buildings—Matso's Store and Captain Gregory's House for example—have been restored (by Lord McAlpine) to their former glory. People eager to take advantage of the tourist boom have moved in, building good-quality shops, supermarkets, motels and hotels.

Of course, right at the heart of all this is Cable Beach Resort. It cost $55 million to build and it looks like it. With its manicured lawns, slightly oriental architecture and feeling of opulence, it has become an exclusive but popular tourist resort. It fronts onto Cable Beach which, it has been claimed, is the most beautiful beach in Western Australia. Some people fly in to Cable Beach and barely make contact with the township of Broome. It is that kind of resort. However, for those who want to experience Broome, there are certain vital spots to see. A visit to the Japanese Cemetery (it is the largest one of its kind in Australia) is a reminder of the huge toll in human lives taken by the early and very risky days of pearling. Hundreds of young Japanese divers died either from the bends (also known as diver's paralysis) or from drowning. It is worth noting that the cemetery has the graves of 33 men who died of diver's paralysis in 1914 alone.

If you have time, make sure you go to the movies at Sun Pictures in Carnarvon Street. It was built in 1916 and is thought to be the oldest open-air cinema in the world. Also everyone should stop for a drink at the historic Roebuck Inn—once the watering hole for sailors and pearlers, it still has a certain raffish air.

Map: WA 1 A9

Beyond Broome

There are a number of truly isolated destinations in the Kimberley which will ensure that every holiday is a very special experience. Kooljaman at Cape Leveque, for example, is 220 km north of Broome and has an idyllic coastal setting. It offers safari tents with glorious ocean views. There are also deluxe cabins with jarrah decking and ensuites. This is the perfect location for seaside activities such as beachcombing, fishing, island boat charters, swimming and snorkelling.

Off the coast is the Cockatoo Island Resort. It is the only island resort situated off the north-west of Australia. Cockatoo Island is one of over a thousand islands which make up the dramatic Buccaneer Archipelago wilderness. It has beautiful hidden beaches and the peacefulness of a true tropical paradise.

If you are looking for more creature comforts, then the King Sound Resort Hotel located in Derby offers accessible accommodation in easy reach of the Gibb River Road, which runs across the Kimberley and is suitable only for 4WD vehicles. If you go along the famous Gibb River Road you should stay at one of the excellent farmstays; the most famous is El Questro Wilderness Park which boasts accommodation styles for all budgets. Visitors can stay in the luxurious homestead, the El Questro bungalows or the wilderness retreat of Emma Gorge Resort. Set on a huge cattle station, the wilderness park offers a range of activities from

*At El Questro Wilderness Park, rangers lead horse-riding treks where you might come across a frill-necked lizard (*Chlamydosaurus kingi*).*

Gantheaume Point offers views of Cable Beach, and at low tide visitors can view dinosaur foot-prints that are more than 130 million years old.

WA

Above: *Layers of sediment from an ancient ocean are clearly seen in the Kimberley plateau.*

swimming in thermal pools to boat rides, scenic helicopter flights, bush and gorge walks, fishing and horseriding.

Also along the Gibb River Road is Mount Elizabeth Station, a fully operational cattle station, which invites the visitor to mix with the locals and to go on scenic flights and guided tours of the region, and the Diggers Rest Station, a cattle station located 30 km from the town of Wyndham, which offers chalets and a bunkhouse. Activities include fishing, horseriding and birdwatching.

All the resorts mentioned here can be booked by phoning the toll free number 1800 999 243.

The Kimberley region is a wild and isolated area where the distances are vast and the facilities can often be quite basic. It is also an area of great beauty. If you can make the difficult drive to the Bungle Bungle Range in Purnululu National Park it is well worth the effort. If not, see the 'little Bungle Bungles' of Hidden Valley National Park at the back of Kununurra. Equally, the views across Lake Argyle—a huge artificial lake in the middle of the desert—are surreal. It is like looking at a desert fjord. And the scenic views across Wyndham from the lookout above the town are truly remarkable. There can be few places on Earth where you can see five different rivers converging to form a mighty, muddy mass which heads towards the Timor Sea.

Right: *Helicopters allow anglers to explore otherwise inaccessible waterways in the Kimberley.*

Below: *Lake Argyle is a vast 1000 sq km in area. More than 60 bird species inhabit the region.*

Map 1

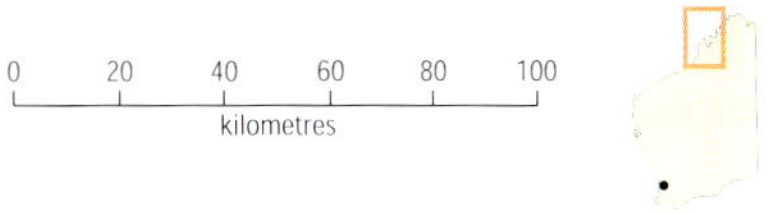
0
20
40
60
80
100
kilometres

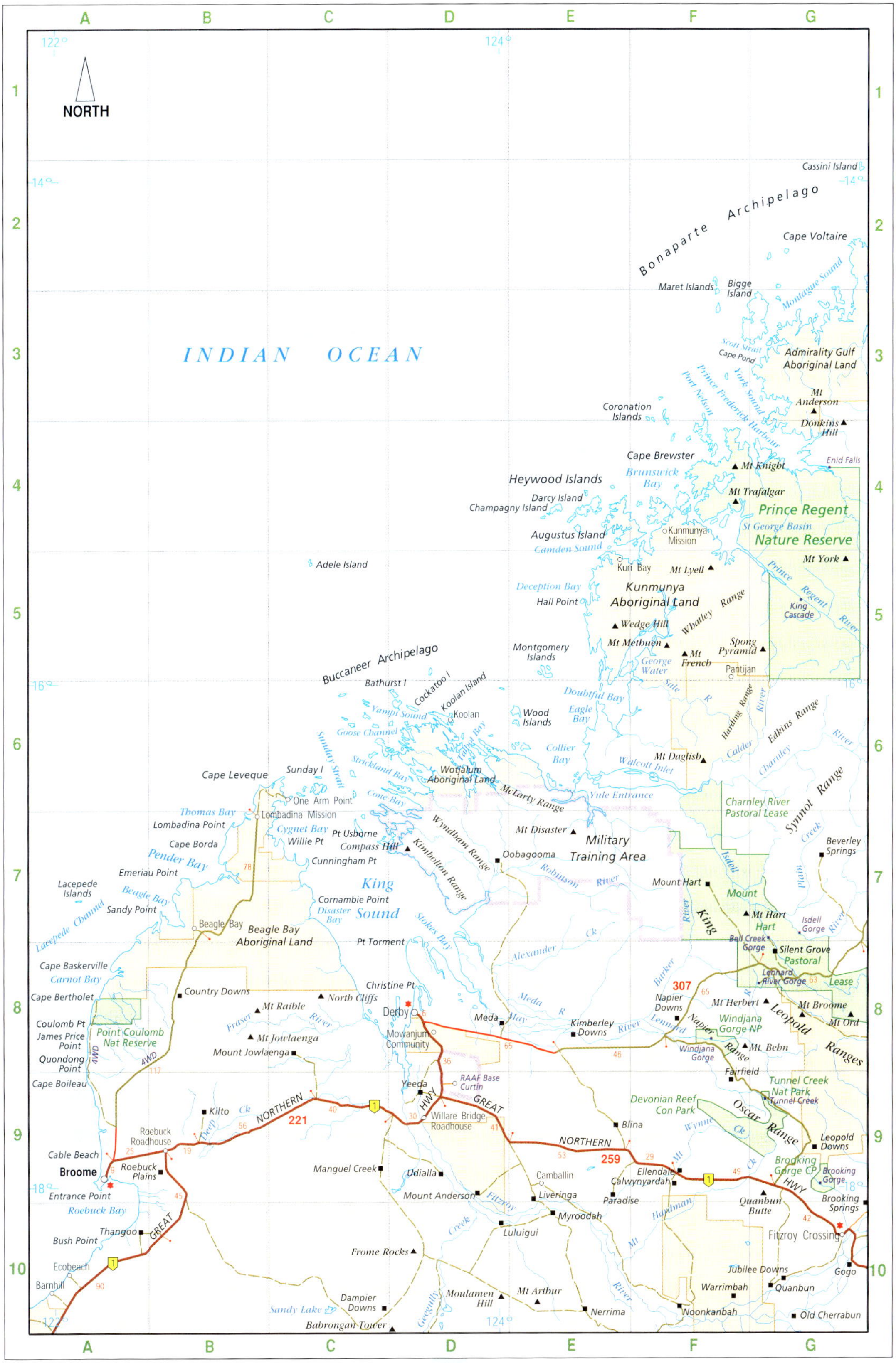
A
B
C
D
E
F
G
1
2
3
4
5
6
7
8
9
10
122°
124°
14°
16°
18°
NORTH
INDIAN OCEAN
Cassini Island
Bonaparte Archipelago
Cape Voltaire
Maret Islands
Bigge Island
Montague Sound
Scott Strait
Cape Pond
Admirality Gulf Aboriginal Land
York Sound
Prince Frederick Harbour
Port Nelson
Mt Anderson
Donkins Hill
Coronation Islands
Cape Brewster
Mt Knight
Enid Falls
Heywood Islands
Brunswick Bay
Mt Trafalgar
Darcy Island
Champagny Island
Prince Regent
St George Basin
Nature Reserve
Kunmunya Mission
Augustus Island
Camden Sound
Kuri Bay
Mt Lyell
Mt York
Adele Island
Deception Bay
Kunmunya Aboriginal Land
Hall Point
Prince Regent River
King Cascade
Whatley Range
Wedge Hill
Mt Methuen
Montgomery Islands
Mt French
Spong Pyramid
George Water
Pantijan
Buccaneer Archipelago
Bathurst I
Cockatoo I
Koolan Island
Koolan
Yampi Sound
Goose Channel
Sunday Strait
Doubtful Bay
Eagle Bay
Wood Islands
Sale R
Harding Range
Edkins Range
Calder
Charnley
River
Collier Bay
Walcott Inlet
Mt Daglish
Strickland Bay
Talbot Bay
Cape Leveque
Sunday I
Wotjalum Aboriginal Land
McLarty Range
Yule Entrance
One Arm Point
Cone Bay
Charnley River Pastoral Lease
Symont Range
Thomas Bay
Lombadina Mission
Lombadina Point
Cygnet Bay
Pt Usborne
Willie Pt
Compass Hill
Wyndham Range
Mt Disaster
Military Training Area
Creek
Beverley Springs
Cape Borda
Pender Bay
Cunningham Pt
Oobagooma
Robinson River
Isdell
Emeriau Point
Kimbolton Range
Plain
Lacepede Islands
King Sound
Mount Hart
Mount
Beagle Bay
Cornambie Point
Disaster Bay
Sandy Point
Lacepede Channel
River
King
Mt Hart
Hart
Isdell Gorge
Beagle Bay
Beagle Bay Aboriginal Land
Ck
Bell Creek Gorge
Silent Grove
Pastoral
Pt Torment
Stokes Bay
Alexander
Cape Baskerville
Carnot Bay
Barker
Lennard River Gorge
Lease
307
Country Downs
Christine Pt
Cape Bertholet
North Cliffs
Mt Raible
Meda
Napier Downs
Mt Herbert
Leopold
Mt Broome
Derby
Meda
May
R
Coulomb Pt
Fraser
River
Mowanjum Community
Kimberley Downs
River
Lennard
Napier
Windjana Gorge NP
Mt Ord
James Price Point
Point Coulomb Nat Reserve
Mt Jowlaenga
Windjana Gorge
Range
Mt Behn
Ranges
Quondong Point
4WD
Mount Jowlaenga
Fairfield
Cape Boileau
RAAF Base Curtin
Tunnel Creek Nat Park
Yeeda
HWY
Devonian Reef Con Park
Tunnel Creek
Oscar
Kilto
Ck
NORTHERN
221
GREAT
Willare Bridge Roadhouse
Blina
Wynne
Ck
Range
Leopold Downs
Roebuck Roadhouse
Deep
NORTHERN
259
Cable Beach
Fitt
Brooking Gorge CP
Brooking Gorge
Broome
Roebuck Plains
Manguel Creek
Udialla
Camballin
Ellendale
Calwynyardah
HWY
Entrance Point
Mount Anderson
Fitzroy
Liveringa
Paradise
Quanbun Butte
Brooking Springs
Roebuck Bay
Myroodah
Hardman
Thangoo
GREAT
Creek
Luluigui
Fitzroy Crossing
Bush Point
Mt
Frome Rocks
Ecobeach
Jubilee Downs
Gogo
Barnhill
Warrimbah
Quanbun
Dampier Downs
Moulamen Hill
Mt Arthur
River
Sandy Lake
Geegully
Nerrima
Noonkanbah
Old Cherrabun
Babrongan Tower
WA 2
WA

WA 4

Map 4

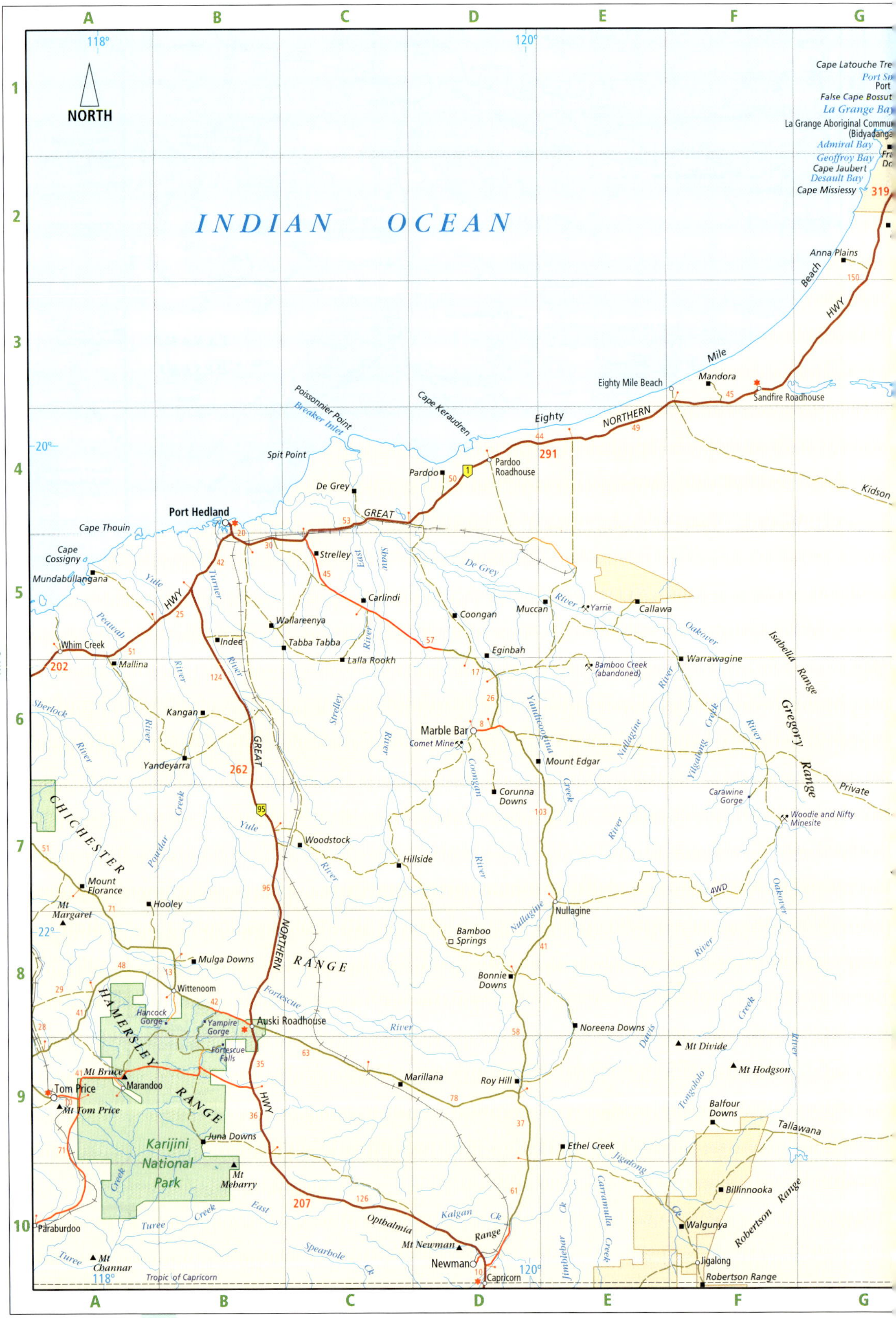

A
B
C
D
E
F
G
1
2
3
4
5
6
7
8
9
10
118°
120°
NORTH
INDIAN OCEAN
Cape Latouche Tre
Port Sr
Port
False Cape Bossut
La Grange Bay
La Grange Aboriginal Commu
(Bidyadanga
Admiral Bay
Geoffroy Bay
Cape Jaubert
Desault Bay
Cape Missiessy
319
Anna Plains
Beach
HWY
Mile
Eighty Mile Beach
Mandora
Sandfire Roadhouse
Eighty
NORTHERN
Kidson
Poissonnier Point
Breaker Inlet
Cape Keraudren
Spit Point
Pardoo
Pardoo Roadhouse
291
De Grey
GREAT
Port Hedland
Cape Thouin
Cape Cossigny
Mundabullangana
Strelley
Carlindi
Coongan
Muccan
Yarrie
Callawa
Wallareenya
Indee
Tabba Tabba
Lalla Rookh
Eginbah
Bamboo Creek (abandoned)
Warrawagine
Whim Creek
202
Mallina
Kangan
Yandeyarra
262
Marble Bar
Comet Mine
Mount Edgar
Corunna Downs
Isabella Range
Gregory Range
Private
Carawine Gorge
Woodie and Nifty Minesite
CHICHESTER
Woodstock
Hillside
Mount Florance
Mt Margaret
Hooley
Nullagine
4WD
Bamboo Springs
Mulga Downs
NORTHERN
RANGE
Bonnie Downs
Wittenoom
HAMERSLEY
RANGE
Hancock Gorge
Yampire Gorge
Auski Roadhouse
Fortescue Falls
Noreena Downs
Mt Divide
Mt Hodgson
Marillana
Roy Hill
Mt Bruce
Marandoo
Tom Price
Mt Tom Price
Juna Downs
Balfour Downs
Tallawana
Karijini National Park
Mt Mebarry
Ethel Creek
Billinnooka
207
Walgunya
Robertson Range
Paraburdoo
Ophthalmia
Range
Mt Newman
Newman
Capricorn
Jigalong
Mt Channar
Tropic of Capricorn
WA 5

0 20 40 60 80 100
kilometres
WA 1
WA 3
WA 7
H J K L M N P
1 2 3 4 5 6 7 8 9 10
22°
124°
126°
20°
22°
Ecobeach
Barnhill
Sandy Lake
Dampier Downs
Babrongan Tower
Mowla Bluff
Mt Collins
Geegully Creek
Moulamen Hill
Mt Arthur
Mt Jarlemai
Mowla Bluff
Nerrima
Noonkanbah
Kalyeeda
Mt James
Mt Tuckfield
Millajiddee
Jubilee Downs
Quanbun
Warrimbah
Gogo
Old Cherrabun
Dukes Dome
St George Ranges
Pillara Range
Cherrabun
Christmas Creek
Hicks Range
Jones Range
Barbwire Range
Worral Range
Edgar Range
Shovel Lake
McLarty Hills
Dragon Tree Soak Nature Reserve
GREAT SANDY DESERT
Track
Prescott Lakes
Gwenneth Lakes
Lake Waukarlycarly
Kidson
Percival Lakes
Tobin Lake
Route
Telfer Mine
Range
Mt Isdell
Creek
Lake Dora
Broadhurst Range
Rudall River National Park
River
Rudall
Eva Broadhurst Lake
Lake Blanche
Lake Auld
Lake George
Lake Winifred
Mt Connaughton
Cotton Ck
Track
Stock
Canning
Gary Junction
Highway
Harbutt Range
McKay Range
Tallawana
Track
Gary
Tropic of Capricorn

Map 5

NORTH
Montebello Islands CP
Montebello Islands
Dampier Archipe
Rosemary I
Enderby I
Cape Dupuy
Surf Point
Barrow Island Nature Reserve
Barrow Island
Wapet Camp
Boodie I
Mary Anne Passage
Cape Preston
Regnard Bay
Angle Point
Mardie
297
Fortescue Roadhouse
Great Sandy Island Nature Reserve
Thevenard Island
Mangrove Passage
Ashburton Road
Old Onslow Historic Ruins
Onslow
Yarraloola
NORTH WEST
Robe River
Pannawonica
Yallee
Mt Enid
Muiron Islands
Vlaming Head
North West Cape
Point Murat
False Island Pt
Exmouth
Tubridgi Point
Urala
Peedamulla
Mount Minnie
Mt Dempster
Red Hill
Exmouth Gulf
Low Point
Cape Range Nat Park
Cape Range
Minderoo
Cane River
Tulki Beach
Mt Hollister
Learmonth
Tent Island Nature Res
Ashburton
The Range
Mt Amy
PILB
Osprey Bay
Pt Lefroy
Exmouth Homestead
Koordarrie
Ningaloo Marine Park
Trealla Hill
Doole I
Mount Stuart
Lefroy Bay
Yanrey
Nanutarra
Nanutarra Roadhouse
Duck
Giralia
Norwegian Bay
Ningaloo
Bullara
Mt Alexander
Wyloo
Jane Bay
Uaroo
216
226
Glen Florrie
Kooline
Marrilla
Nyang
Deep Ck
Henry River
Barlee Range Nature Res
Ashburto
Chabjuwardoo Bay
Point Maud
Coral Bay
Cardabia
Giralia Range
Winning
Round Headed Hill
Round Knob
Yannarie
Ningaloo Marine Park
Lyndon
Mia Mia
Tropic of Capricorn
Warroora
Maroonah
Ullawarra
Bulbarli Point
Marsh Hill
Cape Farquhar
Lyndon
Gooch Range
High Range
Gnarraloo Bay
Minilya Roadhouse
Minilya
Wandagee
Edmund
Barlee Range
Gnaraloo
Minilya
Williambury
Middalya
Mangaroon
Lyons River
Minnie Creek
Gifford Creek
146
Manberry
Red Bluff
Lake MacLeod
Minilya River Sth
Kennedy Range
Cape Cuvier
Boologooro
Hill Springs
Red Ck
Mt Phillip
Mount Phillip
Cooralya
Mount Sandiman
Eudamullah
Quobba
Point Quobba Blowholes
Boolan Hill
Mardathuna
Lyons River
Lockier Range
Yinnetharra
Miaboolya Beach
Rocky Pool
Cape Ronsard
Gascoyne
Kennedy Range National Park
Bernier Island
Carnarvon
Doorawarrah
Bernier and Dorre Islands NR
Red Cliff Point
Oyster Ck
McNeill Claypan
Meeragoolia
Lyons
Mt Gasc
Cape Boullanger
Disaster Cove
Mooka
Jimba Jimba
Bidgemia
Low Pt
Grey Point
Callagiddy
Ellavalla
Gascoyne Junction
287
Mooloo Downs
Mt Puckfor
Dorre Island
Castle Pt
Mt Dalgety
Dalgety Downs
Dalgety
Yalbalgo
Shark Bay Marine Park
Winderie
Dairy Creek
Brook
Edaggee
Marron
SHARK BAY
Long Point
Towrana
Glenburgh

WA 6

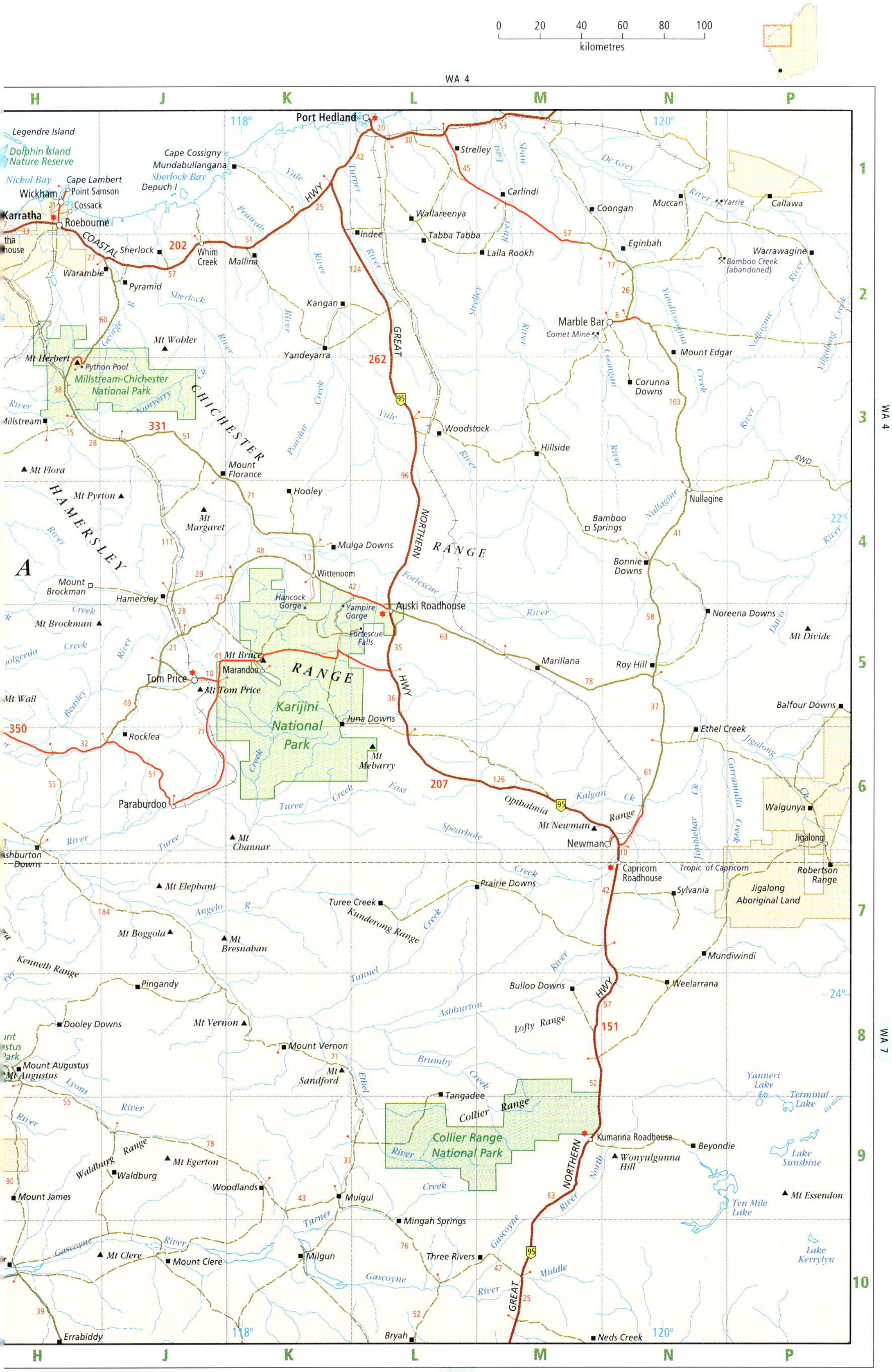
0 20 40 60 80 100
kilometres
WA 4
WA 6
WA 7
H J K L M N P
1 2 3 4 5 6 7 8 9 10
118°
120°
22°
24°
Port Hedland
Legendre Island
Dolphin Island Nature Reserve
Nickol Bay
Cape Lambert
Point Samson
Wickham
Cossack
Karratha
Roebourne
COASTAL HWY
Sherlock
Waramble
Pyramid
Cape Cossigny
Mundabullangana
Sherlock Bay
Depuch I
Whim Creek
Mallina
Strelley
Carlindi
Wallareenya
Indee
Tabba Tabba
Lalla Rookh
Coongan
Muccan
Yarrie
Callawa
Eginbah
Warrawagine
Bamboo Creek (abandoned)
Kangan
Yandeyarra
Marble Bar
Comet Mine
Mount Edgar
Corunna Downs
Mt Wobler
Mt Herbert
Python Pool
Millstream-Chichester National Park
Millstream
CHICHESTER
Mt Flora
Mount Florance
Woodstock
Hillside
Hooley
Mt Pyrton
Mt Margaret
HAMERSLEY
A
NORTHERN
RANGE
GREAT
Nullagine
Bamboo Springs
Bonnie Downs
Mulga Downs
Wittenoom
Mount Brockman
Hamersley
Hancock Gorge
Yampire Gorge
Auski Roadhouse
Fortescue Falls
Noreena Downs
Mt Divide
Mt Brockman
Mt Bruce
Marandoo
RANGE
Marillana
Roy Hill
Tom Price
Mt Tom Price
Karijini National Park
Mt Wall
Juna Downs
Balfour Downs
Ethel Creek
Rocklea
Mt Mebarry
Paraburdoo
Walgunya
Jigalong
Ophthalmia Range
Mt Newman
Newman
Capricorn Roadhouse
Tropic of Capricorn
Robertson Range
Jigalong Aboriginal Land
Mt Channar
Ashburton Downs
Mt Elephant
Prairie Downs
Sylvania
Turee Creek
Kunderong Range
Mt Boggola
Mt Bresnahan
Kenneth Range
Mundiwindi
Pingandy
Bulloo Downs
Weelarrana
Lofty Range
Dooley Downs
Mt Vernon
Mount Vernon
Mount Augustus
Mt Augustus
Mt Sandford
Yanneri Lake
Terminal Lake
Tangadee
Collier Range
Collier Range National Park
Kumarina Roadhouse
Beyondie
Lake Sunshine
Waldburg Range
Mt Egerton
Waldburg
Wonyulgunna Hill
Woodlands
Mount James
Mulgul
Mingah Springs
Ten Mile Lake
Mt Essendon
Mt Clere
Mount Clere
Milgun
Three Rivers
Lake Kerrylyn
Errabiddy
Bryah
Neds Creek
202 262 331 350 207 151 95

Map 6

WA 5
A
B
C
D
E
F
G
1
2
3
4
5
6
7
8
9
10
114°
116°
26°
28°
30°
Shark Bay
Marine Park
SHARK BAY
Cape Inscription
Cape Levillain
Dirk Hartog
Island
Quoin Head
Cape Lesueur
Cape Peron North
Herald Bight
Herald Bluff
Francois Peron
Nat Park
Peron Homestead (Historic Site)
Monkey Mia
Denham
Sound
Denham
Dubaut Point
Faure Island
Petit Pt
Gladstone
Cape Bellefin
Westernmost point of Australian mainland
Steep Point
Mt Direction
Useless Loop (No access)
Goulet Bluff
L'Haridon Bight
Hamelin Pool
Marine Nature
Reserve
Carbla
Nanga Bay
Cararang Pen
Garden Pt
Henri Freycinet Harbour
Zuytdorp Point
Carrarang
Tamala
Hamelin
Overlander Roadhouse
Long Point
Edaggee
Marron
Wahroonga
Pimbee
Winderie
Towrana
Meedo
Wooramel
Wooramel Roadhouse
Carlaweelban Hill
Yaringa
Woodleigh
NORTH
WEST
COASTAL
HWY
Gilroyd
Yalardy
Talisker
Carey Downs
Callytharra Springs
Dairy Creek
Dalgety Downs
Glenburgh
Erong Springs
Coordewandy
Yalbra
Innouendy
Daurie
Creek
River
Wooramel
Mt Nairn
Milly
Byro
Breberle Lake
Curbur
Manfred
Muggon
Mount Narryer
Mt Murchison
Coburn
Billabong Roadhouse
Toolonga
Nature Reserve
Zuytdorp Cliffs
Zuytdorp
Nature Reserve
Nerren Nerren
Murchison Roadhouse
Meeberrie
Murchison
Roderick
Wooleen
New Forest
Twin Peaks
Sanford
Murgoo
Yallalong
Billabalong
Eurardy
Coolcalalaya
Kalbarri
National Park
Gantheaume Bay
Murchison House
Kalbarri
Red Bluff
Shell House
Eagle Gorge
Natural Bridge
Hawks Head Lookout
Bluff Point
Mary Springs
Yandi
Galena
Woolgorong
Pinegrove
Bullardoo
Narloo
Wandina
Mallee
Wagoe Beach
Kulla Kulla Hill
Ajana
Yuin
Tardie
Half Way Bay
Shoal Point
Hutt Lagoon
Binnu
Wandana
Nature Res
Tallering Peak
Marlandy
Pindaring Rocks
Urawa Nat Res
Gabyon
Gregory
Broken Anchor Bay
North Island
Geelvink
Channel
Houtman Abrolhos
Wallabi Group
Easter Group
Mangrove Group
Pelsaert Group
Whaleboat Cove
Horrocks
Bowes Hill
Northampton
Yuna
Naraling
East Yuna Nature Res
Tallering
Wurarga
Nabawa
Nanson
Mullewa
Pindar
Greenough
Coronation Beach
Drummond Cove
Champion Bay
Geraldton
Point Moore
Moonyoonooka
Cape Burney
Burma Road NR
Barnong
Sullivan
Tardun
Canna
Gutha
Mellenbye
Greenough
Walkaway
Flat Rocks
BRAND
Yarragadee
Irwin
Pintharuka
Kadji Kadji
Seven Mile Beach
Dongara
Port Denison
Mingenew
Strawberry Hill
Morawa
Nullewa Lake
Bilieranga Hills
Koolanooka
Bowgada
Woolbumby Lake
White Point
Yardanogo Nature Res
Arrino
Perenjori
Three Springs
Cliff Head
Freshwater Point
Beekeepers Nature Res
Wotto Nat Res
Yarra Yarra Lakes
Carnamah
Bunjil
Illawong
Woodada Hill
Eneabba
Winchester
Latham
Coolimba
Tathra Nat Pk
Capamauro Nature Res
Coorow
Maya
Leeman
South Eneabba NR
Lake Logue NR
Alexander Morrison NP
Pinjarrega Nat Res
Green Head
Lesueur Nat Pk
Coomallo Nat Res
Pinjarrega Lake
Marchagee
Wubin
Salt Lakes
North Head
Jurien Bay
Jurien
Drovers Cave NP
Watheroo Nat Park
Watheroo
Dalwallinu
Badgingarra
INDIAN
OCEAN
NORTH
WA 8

WA 5

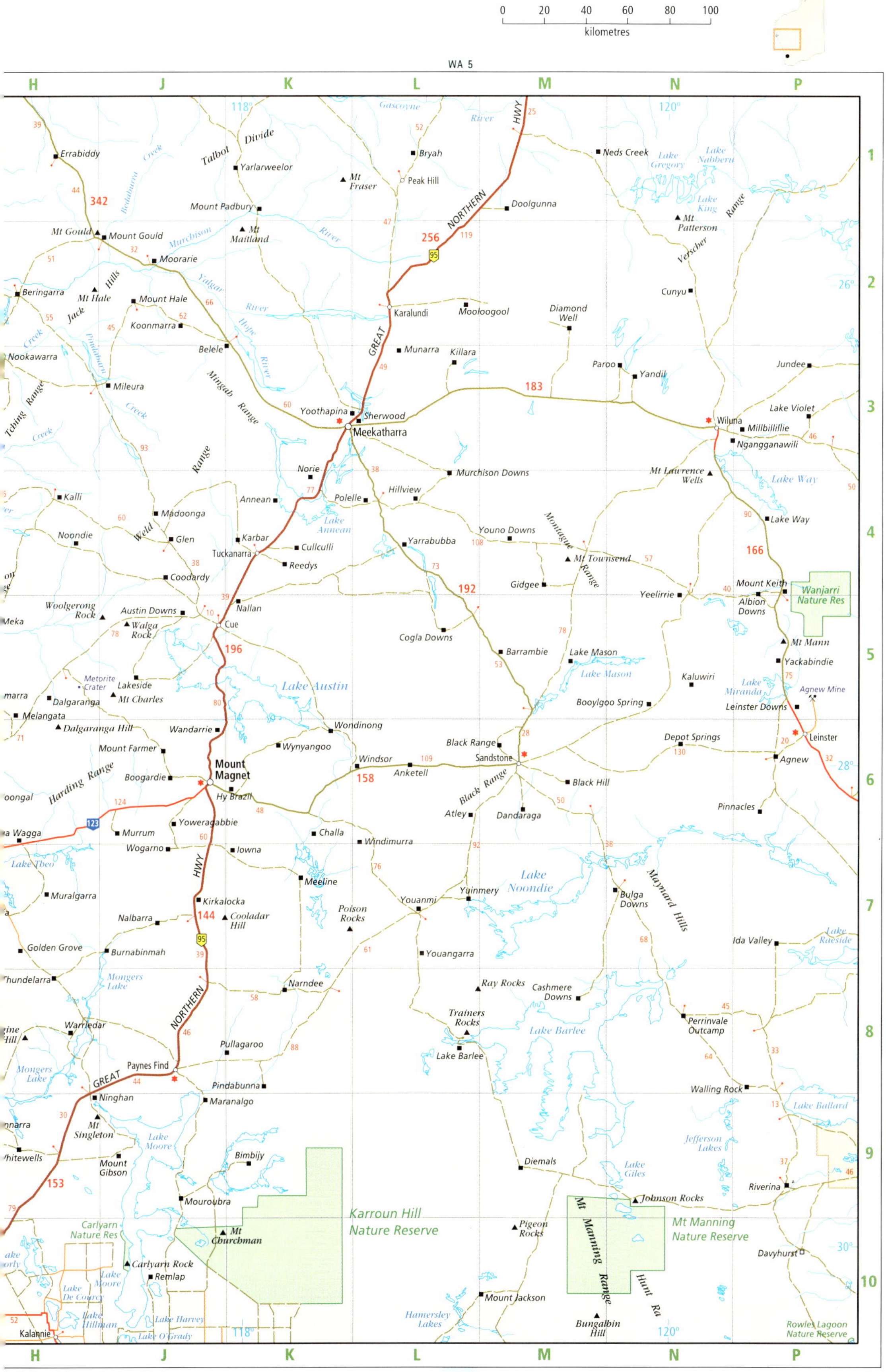

WA 7

WA 9

WA 8

Map 7

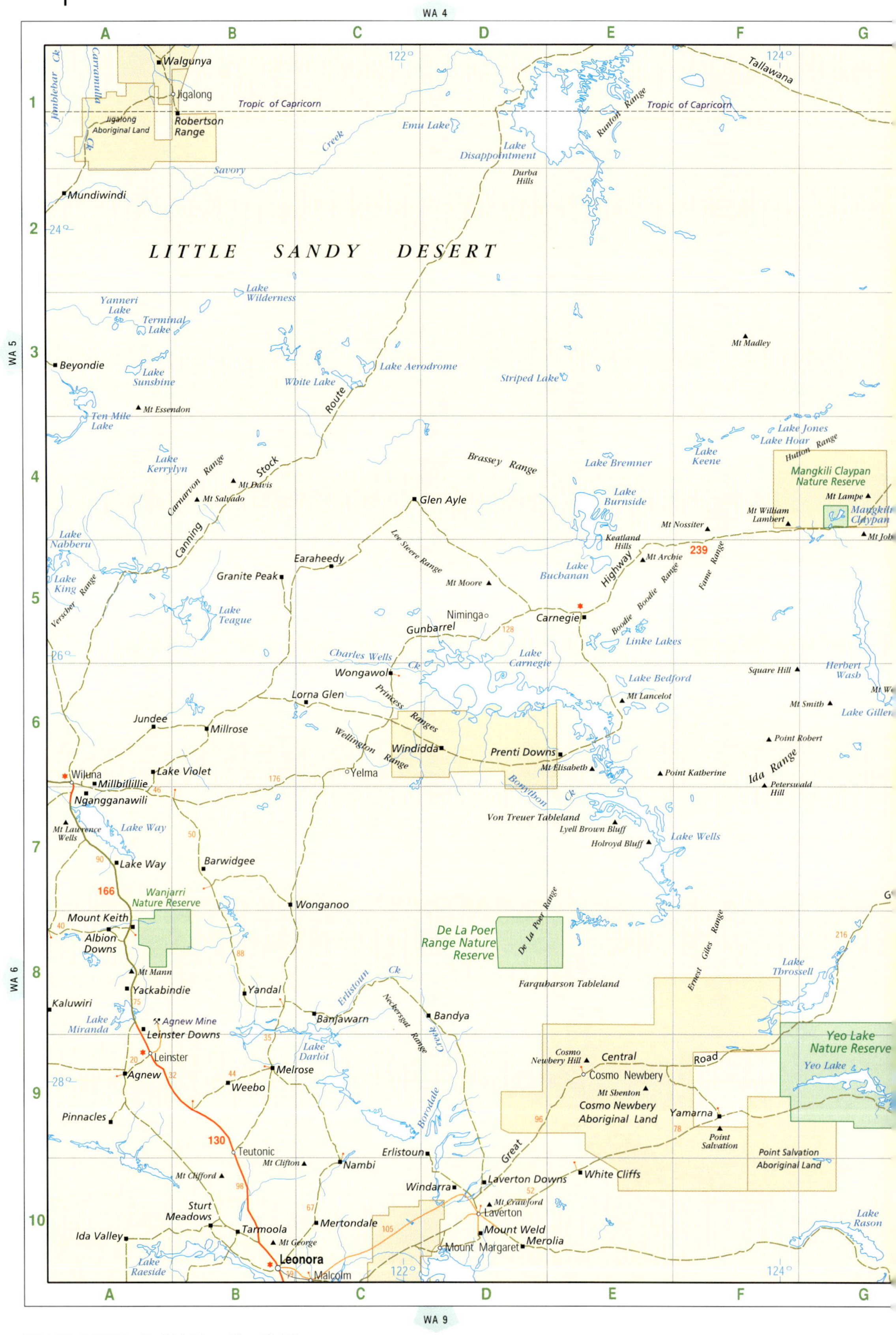
WA 4
WA 5
WA 6
WA 9
A
B
C
D
E
F
G
1
2
3
4
5
6
7
8
9
10
Walgunya
Jigalong
Jigalong Aboriginal Land
Robertson Range
Tropic of Capricorn
Emu Lake
Lake Disappointment
Runton Range
Tallawana
Durba Hills
Savory
Creek
Mundiwindi
LITTLE SANDY DESERT
Lake Wilderness
Yanneri Lake
Terminal Lake
Beyondie
Lake Sunshine
White Lake
Lake Aerodrome
Striped Lake
Mt Madley
Mt Essendon
Ten Mile Lake
Route
Stock
Lake Kerrylyn
Carnarvon Range
Mt Davis
Mt Salvado
Canning
Brassey Range
Lake Bremner
Lake Keene
Lake Jones
Lake Hoar
Hutton Range
Mangkili Claypan Nature Reserve
Mt Lampe
Mangkili Claypan
Mt William Lambert
Mt Nossiter
Lake Burnside
Glen Ayle
Lee Steere Range
Keatland Hills
Mt Archie
239
Fame Range
Lake Nabberu
Earaheedy
Granite Peak
Lake King
Verscher Range
Mt Moore
Lake Buchanan
Highway
Boodie Boodie Range
Lake Teague
Niminga
Carnegie
Gunbarrel
128
Linke Lakes
Charles Wells
Wongawol
Ck
Lake Carnegie
Lake Bedford
Square Hill
Herbert Wash
Lorna Glen
Princess Ranges
Mt Lancelot
Mt Smith
Lake Gillen
Jundee
Millrose
Wellington Range
Windidda
Prenti Downs
Point Robert
Wiluna
Lake Violet
Yelma
Mt Elisabeth
Point Katherine
Ida Range
Millbillillie
176
46
Bonython Ck
Peterswald Hill
Nganganawili
Mt Laurence Wells
Lake Way
Von Treuer Tableland
Lyell Brown Bluff
50
Lake Wells
Holroyd Bluff
90
Lake Way
Barwidgee
166
Wanjarri Nature Reserve
Wonganoo
Mount Keith
40
Albion Downs
De La Poer Range Nature Reserve
De La Poer Range
Ernest Giles Range
216
88
Mt Mann
Lake Throssell
Yackabindie
Yandal
Ck
Erlistoun
Farquharson Tableland
Kaluwiri
75
Neckersgat Range
Bandya
Lake Miranda
Agnew Mine
Banjawarn
Yeo Lake Nature Reserve
Leinster Downs
Creek
Cosmo Newbery Hill
Central
Road
Lake Darlot
Yeo Lake
20
Leinster
35
Cosmo Newbery
28°
Agnew
32
44
Melrose
Mt Shenton
Weebo
Cosmo Newbery Aboriginal Land
Yamarna
Pinnacles
Borodale
96
78
Point Salvation
130
Teutonic
Great
Point Salvation Aboriginal Land
Mt Clifton
Nambi
Erlistoun
Mt Clifford
98
Laverton Downs
White Cliffs
Windarra
52
Sturt Meadows
67
Mt Crawford
Laverton
Lake Rason
Mertondale
Ida Valley
Tarmoola
105
Mount Weld
Merolia
Mt George
Lake Raeside
Leonora
Mount Margaret
Malcolm
19
122°
124°
24°
26°

0 20 40 60 80 100
kilometres
WA 3
WA 9
NT 8
SA 1
WA
H J K L M N P
1 2 3 4 5 6 7 8 9 10
126°
128°
129°
24°
26°
28°
NORTH
Tropic of Capricorn
Walungurru
Lake MacDonald
Windy Corner
Track
Gary Highway
Ryan Buttes
Lake Anec
GIBSON DESERT
Lake Cobb
Lake Jones
Lake Coben
McPhersons Pillar
Gibson Desert Nature Reserve
Lake Blair
Alfred and Marie Range
Lake Newell
Mt Cox
Mt Colin
Young Range
Tsakalos Hills
Mt Gordon
Lake Gruszka
Brown Range
Gunbarrel Hwy
Mt Beadell
Lake Sprenger
Notabilis Hill
Lake Hopkins
Mt Destruction
Carnegie Range
Robert Range
Docker River
Rebecca Creek
Walter James Range
Christopher Lake
Rawlinson Range
Lake Farnham
Mt Buttfield
Gill Pinnacle
Kaltukatjara (Docker River)
Hull River
Giles Meteorological Station
Mt Russell
Giles Creek
Mt Deering
Range
Creek
Lassetters Cave
Hwy (abandoned)
Gunbarrel
Jamieson Range
Dean
Central Australia Aboriginal Land
WESTERN AUSTRALIA
NORTHERN TERRITORY
Mt Daisy Bates
Mt Fanny
Amy Giles Rocks
Mt Gosse
Mt Cockburn
Surveyor Generals Corner
Todd Range
Mt Charles
Sutherland Range
Lake Breaden
Heather Hwy
Boyd Lagoon
Mt Harvest
Bentley Hill
Barrow Range
Mt Rawlinson
Mt Clianthus
Warburton
Warburton Range
Mt Talbot
Mt Eveline
Mt Squires
Mt Jane
Wingellinna
Bell Rock
Mt Hinckley
Aparawatatja
Pipalyatjara
Tomkinson Ranges
Mt Davies
Cavenagh Range
Townsend Ridges
Point Read
Road
Lake Kadgo
Kunytjanu Homeland
WESTERN AUSTRALIA
SOUTH AUSTRALIA
Baker Lake
The Hann Breakaways
Central
Rowe Hills
Mt Copley
Hanns Tabletop Hill
Mt Irving
Lennis Hills
Ryans Bluff
GREAT VICTORIA DESERT
Point Lilian
Saunders Range
Saunders Point
Waigen Lakes
Lake Thistle
Neale Junction
Neale Junction Nature Reserve
Unnamed Conservation Park
Wanna Lakes
Serpentine Lakes
128
215
106
26
49
16
28
248
85
40
44
21

Map 8

WA 6
A
B
C
D
E
F
G
1
2
3
4
5
6
7
8
9
10
INDIAN
OCEAN
NORTH
116°
118°
32°
34°
North Head
Jurien Bay
Jurien
Drovers Cave NP
Watheroo Nat Park
Salt Lakes
Watheroo
Dalwallinu
Lake De Courcy
Lake Hillman
Lake Moore
Lake Harvey
Lake O'Grady
Southern Beekeepers NR
Badgingarra Nat Park
Badgingarra
Pithara
Kalannie
Jecundars Park
Bunketch
Beacon
Wialki
Bonnie
Ronsard Bay
Thirsty Point
Cervantes
Miling
Dalwallinu
Damboring
Kulja
Mollerin Lake
Mollerin Nat Res
Nambung Nat Pk
Pinnacles
Grey
Berkshire Valley
Bindi Bindi
Ballidu
Kokardine
Wanagarren Nature Res
Dandaragan
Moora
Walebing
Kondut
Cadoux
Narkal
Gabbin
Bencubbin
Welbungin
Chiddarcoo Nature Res
Wedge Island
Cataby
Koojan
Waddington
Piawaning
Yerecoin
Elphin
Wongan Hills
Manmanning
Cowcowing Lakes
Koorda
Lake Wallambin
Mukinbudin
Nilgen Nat Res
Namming NR
Gillingarra
New Norcia
Ejanding
Nalkain
Lake Campion Nature Reserve
Lake Brown
Lancelin
Moore River Nat Park
Mogumber
Calingiri
Konnongorring
Minnivale
Amery
Benjaberring
Wyalkatchem
Kununoppin
Ledge Point
Karakin Lakes
Wannamal
Trayning
Nungarin
Lake Campion
Breton Bay
Boonanarring Nat Res
Dowerin
Korrelocking
Yelbeni
Seabird
Bolgart
Goomalling
South Trayning
Guilderton
Gingin
Bindoon
Yorkrakine
Nukarni
Yeal Nat Res
Yorkrakine Hill
Burracoppin
Avon Valley Nat Park
Jennacubbine
Merredin
Two Rocks
Yanchep
Yanchep NP
Muchea
Toodyay
Northam
Cunderdin
Hines Hill
Doodlakine
Neerabup NP
Lake Pinjar
Bullsbrook
Clackline
Grass Valley
Meckering
Tammin
Bungalla
Kellerberrin
Korbel
Quinns Rocks
Wundowie
Wanneroo
Upper Swan
Wooroloo
Spencers Brook
Youndegin
Belka
Muntadgin
Marmion Marine Park
Mullaloo
Swan
Gidgegannup
Chidlow
Scarborough
Guildford
Midland
Mundaring
The Lakes
York
Green Hills
Kwolyin
Erikin
Bruce Rock
Rottnest Island
PERTH
Helena River Res
Mawson
Pantapin
Badjaling
Shackleton
Yalbarrin
Ardath
Gosnells
Pickering Brook
Quairading
Dangin
Fremantle
Kelmscott
Karragullen
Beverley
Morbining
Babakin
Narembeen
Woodman Point
Armadale
Mt Dale
Cockburn Sound
Byford
Garden Island
Kwinana
Baldivis
Rockingham
Mundijong
Monadnocks Cons Park
Yenyening Lakes NR
Bilbarin
Lake Kurrenkutten
Shoalwater Islands Marine Park
Warnbro Sound
Serpentine
Jarrahdale
Brookton
Bendering
Becher Point
Karnup
Serpentine NP
Serpentine Dam
Aldersyde
Bulyee
Kunjin
Corrigin
Gorge Rock
Mt Cooke
North Kalgarin
Keysbrook
Mandurah
North Dandalup
Moorumbine
Tutanning NR
Bullaring
Kondinin Lake
Kondinin
Peel Inlet
North Bannister
Pingelly
Newminster
Dawesville
Ravenswood
Yunderup
Pinjarra
Lake Banksiadale
Yealering
Cape Bouvard
Bannister
Wandering
Popanyinning
Cliffordville
Kulin
Yalgorup NP
Harvey Estuary
Coolup
Dwellingup
Yornaning
Lake Clifton
Crossman
Boddington
Wickepin
Jitarning
Cuballing
Waroona
Lane Poole Res
Marradong
Narrogin
Yilliminning
Dudinin
Preston Beach
Hamel
Mt William
Mt Saddleback
Toolibin
Harrismith
Yalgorup NP
Yarloop
Williams
Taarblin Lake
Walyurin Rocks
Lake Preston
Quindanning
Tarin Rock Nat Res
Lake Grace
Harvey
Highbury
Tarin Rock
Myalup Beach
Lane Poole Res
Binningup Beach
Harris Dam
Culbin
Kukerin
Piesseville
Australind
Brunswick Junction
Gundaring
Nippering
Moulyinning
Koombana Bay
Wagin
Bunbury
Picton
Collie
Darkan
Arthur River
Dumbleyung
Chinocup Nature Res
Dardanup
Wellington Dam
Bowelling
Dellyanine
Quanigallin
Dumbleyung Lake
Geographe Bay
Tuart Forest NP
Stratham
Boyanup
Cordering
Norring Lake
Lake Chinocup
Cape Naturaliste
Rocky Point
Capel
Duranillin
Woodanilling
Moojebing
Nyabing
Dunsborough
Yallingup
Donnybrook
Moodiarrup
Kwobrup
Badgebup
Coyrecup
Cape Clairault
Vasse
Busselton
Kirup
Boscabel
Katanning
Leeuwin-Naturaliste National Park
Murdong
Gracetown
Cowaramup
Balingup
Greenbushes
Boyup Brook
Muradup
Kojonup
Broomehill
Margaret River
Gnowangerup
Cape Mentelle
Rosa Brook
Nannup
Bridgetown
Ongerup
Prevelly
Witchcliffe
Blackwood
Tambellup
Leeuwin Naturaliste NP
Donnelly
Borden
Cape Freycinet
Tunney
Karridale
BROCKMAN
Manjimup
Gordon
Mungup
Hamelin Bay
Kudardup
Scott Nat Park
Unicup Nature Res
Camel Lake NR
Balicup Lake
Amelup
Cape Hamelin
Hardy Inlet
Augusta
Flinders Bay
Cranbrook
Cape Leeuwin
Lake Jasper
Beedelup Nat Park
Quindinup Nat Res
Frankland
Tenterden
Toolbrunup Peak
Ellen Peak
Stirling Range Nat Park
Black Pt
Eastbrook
Quinninup
MUIRS
Pemberton
Lake Muir
Rocky Gully
Kendenup
Two Mile Lake
Yeagarup Beach
Warren Nat Park
Shannon Nat Park
Lake Muir Nature Res
Table Hill
Mount Barker
Kamballup
Callcup Hill
Warren Beach
Northcliffe
Mt Frankland National Park
Mt Lindsay
Porongurup
Hassell Nat Pk
D'Entrecasteaux National Park
Porongurup NP
Mt Frankland
Narrikup
Windy Harbour
Point D'Entrecasteaux
Quarram Nat Res
Bow Bridge
Redmond
King River
Manypeaks
Broke Inlet
Walpole
Denmark
Wilson Inlet
Youngs
Albany
Two Peoples Bay
Two Peoples Bay Nat Res
Cliffy Head
Nornalup
Foul Bay
Owingup NR
Point Hillier
William Bay
William Bay NP
West Cape Howe NP
Torbay
Frenchman Bay
King George Sound
Point Nuyts
Walpole-Nornalup National Park
Point Irwin
West Cape Howe
Torndirrup Nat Pk
Bald Head
BRAND HWY
GREAT NORTHERN HWY
GREAT EASTERN HWY
GREAT SOUTHERN HWY
BROOKTON HWY
ALBANY HWY
VASSE HWY
BUSSELL HWY
SOUTH WESTERN HWY
MUIRS HWY
STH COAST HWY

0 20 40 60 80 100
kilometres
WA 9
H J K L M N P
1 2 3 4 5 6 7 8 9 10
Mount Jackson
Hamersley Lakes
Bungalbin Hill
Hunt Range
120°
122°
Rowles Lagoon Nature Reserve
Mt Carnage
Ora Banda
Mount Vetters
Yindi
Credo
Carbine
Broad Arrow
Kanowna
Jubilee Mine
Yangan Hill
Lake Penny
Woongaring Hills
3 Mile Rocks
Black Flag
White Flag Lake
Lake Deborah East
Watt Hills
Lake Roe
Lake Deborah West
Kangaroo Rock
Kalgoorlie
Boulder
West Kalgoorlie
Steeple Hill
Lake Yindarlgooda
Mount Colreavy
Baladjie Lake NR
Koolyanobbing
Timberfield
Mount Burges
Bonnie Vale
Hannan Lake
Stoneville
Curtin
Avoca Downs
Blamey
Karonie
Lake Seabrook
Coolgardie
HWY
Bullfinch
Bullabulling
Mount Monger
Cowarna Downs
Corinthia
Duladgin Rock
Woolibar
Keokanie Rock
Southern Cross
Yellowdine Nature Res
Boorabbin Nat Park
EASTERN
Boorabbin
COOLGARDIE
Nepean Nickel Mine
Kambalda NR
Kambalda
Kambalda West
Westonia
GREAT
Yellowdine
Karalee
Victoria Rock
Victoria Rock Nature Res
Lake Lefroy
Bodallin
Moorine Rock
Burra Rock Nat Reserve
Lefroy
Widgiemooltha
Strawberry Rocks
Marvel Loch
Lake Robin
Cockatoo Tank
Toomey Hills
Cave Hill NR
Cave Hill
Cowan Hill
Binyarinyinna Rock
Noombenberry Rock
Higginsville
Lake Cowan
Mt Hampton
Dulcie Jean Tank
Jilbadji Nature Reserve
Barker Lake
ESPERANCE
Hayes Hill
Skeleton Rock
Glenelg Rock
Sandalwood Rock
McDermid Rock
Killaloe Hill
EYRE
HWY
Mount Walker
Mt Holland
Disappointment Rock
Mt Thirsty
Norseman
Anderson Rocks
Mt Day
Lake Johnston
Mt Kirk
Lake Kirk
Woolyenyer Hill
King Rocks
North Ironcap
Lake Cronin
Dundas Nature Reserve
Wave Rock
Hyden
Lake Carmody
Lake Hope
Kerrigan Rocks
Marble Rocks
Lake Hurlstone NR
Lake Hurlstone
Bremer Range
Dragon Rocks NR
Middle Ironcap
Gilmore Rocks
Lake Dundas
Lake Varley NR
Holt Rock
Lake Varley
Lake Gilmore
Digger Rocks
Lake Gulson
Frank Hann National Park
Mt Vernon
Varley
Peak Charles
Kumari
Dragon Rocks
Lake King Nat Res
Lake Fox
Lake Ace Nature Res
Lake Ace
HWY
Lake Camm
Mt Gibbs
Lake Tay
Lake Sharpe
Peak Charles National Park
Salmon Gums
Nature Reserve
Lake Biddy
Pallarup Nature Res
Lake Mends
Circle Valley
Newdegate
Lake Bucban
Lake King
Lake King
Pyramid Lake
Red Lake
Mt Ridley
Breakaway Ridge Nature Reserve
Lake Pallarup
Lake Lockhart
Grass Patch
Mt Heywood
Lake Halbert
Mount Madden
Truslove
Truslove Townsite Nature Reserve
Kau Rock Nature Res
Lake Cobham
Dunn Rock Nature Res
Young
Griffiths Nature Res
Mt Short
Lake Magenta Nature Reserve
Lake Morris
Lake Magenta
Oldfield
Mt Burdett
Cascade
Scaddan
Jerdacuttup
Cheadanup Nature Res
River
Ravensthorpe
Speddingup
Beaumont Nat Res
COAST
Lort
Phillips
Kundip Nat Res
River
Burdett South Nature Res
Gibson
SOUTH
Munglinup
HWY
Hamersley
River
Lake Gore
Condingup
Fitzgerald River National Park
Lake Shaster
Pink Lake
Cape Le Grand National Park
Jerdacuttup Lakes
Stokes National Park
Esperance
Esperance Bay
Yarramungup
Perkins Rock
Hopetoun
Lake Shaster NR
Fanny Cove
Barker Inlet
11 Mile Beach
Yungarup Hill
Culham Inlet
Starvation Boat Harbour
Shoal Cape
Stokes Inlet
Buttty Head
Mt Le Grand
Dunn Rocks
Twin Bays
Bat Cave Point
Powell Point
Mason Bay
Cape Le Grand
Rossiter Bay
Hammer Head
Fitzgerald Inlet
Point Charles
Twelve Mile Beach
Jerdacuttup Lakes NR
Lucky Bay
Mt Bland
Point Ann
Mondrain Island
Gairdner
Trigelow Beach
Gordon Inlet
Boxwood Hill
Beaufort Inlet
Bremer Bay
Bremer Bay
Wray Bay
Cheyne Bay
Point Henry
Dillon Bay
Cape Riche
Cape Knob
Ledge Point
SOUTHERN OCEAN
34°
32°
WA

Map 9

WA 7
WA 8
A
B
C
D
E
F
G
1
2
3
4
5
6
7
8
9
10
122°
124°
30°
32°
34°
Sturt Meadows
Tarmoola
Mertondale
Mount Weld
Merolia
Ida Valley
Mt George
Leonora
Mount Margaret
Lake Raeside
Malcolm
Minara
Melita
Glenorn
Lake Rason
Bartlett Bluff
Lake Carey
Hope Campbell Lake
Yundamindra
Mount Remarkable
Walling Rock
Kookynie
Jeedamya
Morapoi
Lake Ballard
Lake Raeside
Mount Celia
Lightfoot Lake
Jefferson Lakes
Mendleyarri
Menzies
Lake Marmion
Riverina
Edjudina
Lake Minigwal
Menangina
Ponton
Goongarrie
Davyhurst
Lake Goongarrie
Goongarrie National Park
Lake Owen
Lake Rebecca
Pinjin
Creek
Mount Vetters
Rowles Lagoon Nature Reserve
Mt Carnage
Ora Banda
Queen Victoria Spring Nature Reserve
Credo
Broad Arrow
Kanowna
Yindi
Carbine
Lake Penny
Jubilee Mine
Yangan Hill
Black Flag
White Flag Lake
Cundeelee Aboriginal Land
Lake Roe
Steeple Hill
Lake Yindana
Cundeelee Community
Kalgoorlie
West Kalgoorlie
Boulder
Lake Yindarlgooda
Timberfield
Mount Burges
Bonnie Vale
Hannan Lake
Stoneville
Curtin
Avoca Downs
Blamey
Karonie
Chifley
Coolgardie
Mount Monger
Cowarna Downs
Coonana
Zanthus
Trans
Australian
Kitchener
HWY
EASTERN
Bullabulling
COOLGARDIE
Woolibar
GREAT
Nepean Nickel Mine
Boorabbin
Kambalda
Kambalda NR
Kambalda West
Boorabbin Nat Park
Victoria Rock
Victoria Rock Nature Res
Lake Lefroy
Harris Lake
Burra Rock Nat Reserve
Lefroy
Widgiemooltha
Lake Robin
Cowan Hill
Binyarinyinna Rock
Cave Hill Nature Reserve
Cave Hill
Lake Cowan
Higginsville
ESPERANCE
Hayes Hill
McDermid Rock
Killaloe Hill
EYRE
HIGHWAY
Newman Rock
Fraser Range
Kilidwerinia Granite Rock
Mt Day
Disappointment Rock
Mt Thirsty
Lake Johnston
Norseman
Southern Hills
Mt Kirk
Woolyeenyer Hill
Lake Kirk
Noondoonia
Balladonia
Old Telegraph Station
Lake Hope
Dundas Nature Reserve
Lake Dundas
Bremer Range
Gilmore Rocks
Lake Gilmore
Wonberna Granite Rock
Mt Andrew
Frank Hann National Park
Booanya Rock
Nuytsland Nature Reserve
Peak Charles
Kumari
HWY
Coragina Rock
Lake Tay
Lake Sharpe
Peak Charles National Park
Nature Reserve
Salmon Gums
Rays Rock
Wylie Scarp
Lake Mends
Circle Valley
Pyramid Lake
Red Lake
Mt Ridley
Mt Heywood
Grass Patch
Truslove
Pine Hill
Ark Point
Kau Rock Nature Res
Mt Dean
Young
Griffiths Nature Res
Truslove Townsite Nature Reserve
Beaumont Nature Reserve
Oldfield
Cascade
Scaddan
Mt Burdett
Mt Symmons
Cheadanup Nature Res
River
Speddingup
Cape Arid National Park
Muntz Nature Reserve
SOUTH
Lort
Burdett South Nature Res
Israelite Bay
Point Dempster
Kundip Nature Reserve
River
Gibson
The Diamonds Hill
Munglinup
COAST
HWY
Boyatup Hill
Lake Gore
Condingup
Lake Shaster
Pink Lake
Cape Le Grand National Park
Point Malcolm
Jerdacuttup Lakes
Stokes National Park
Esperance
Yungarup Hill
Duke of Orleans Bay
Yokinup Bay
Mt Arid
Sandy Bight
Mt Pasley
Cape Pasley
Daw Island
Hopetoun
Barker Inlet
Mt Le Grand
Cape Arid
Middle Island
Twelve Mile Beach
Starvation Boat Harbour
Shoal Cape
11 Mile Beach
Dunn Rocks
Hammer Head
Recherche Archipelago Nature Reserve
Mason Bay
Lake Shaster NR
Fanny Cove
Butty Head
Cape Le Grand
Rossiter Bay
Powell Point
Jerdacuttup Lakes NR
Lucky Bay
Mondrain Island
Archipelago of the Recherche
Salisbury Island

0 20 40 60 80 100
kilometres
H J K L M N P
1 2 3 4 5 6 7 8 9 10
126° 128° 129°
30° 32° 34°
GREAT VICTORIA DESERT
Gidgi Lakes
Jubilee Lake
Carlisle Lakes
Wanna Lakes
Serpentine Lakes
Forrest Lakes
Plumridge Lakes
Great Victoria Desert Nature Reserve
WESTERN AUSTRALIA
SOUTH AUSTRALIA
Connie Sue Highway
Premier Downs
Dry Creek
Railway
Rawlinna
Haig
Nurina
Loongana
Mundrabilla
Forrest
Reid
Deakin
NULLARBOR PLAIN
Nullarbor National Park
TABLELAND
Border Village
89
Eucla
12
Wilson Bluff
Eucla National Park
Mundrabilla Motel
66
Mundrabilla
116
HWY
Madura Hotel
Madura
286
EYRE
92
Arubiddy
Cocklebiddy Cave
Cocklebiddy
66
Nuytsland Nature Reserve
HAMPTON
Roe Plains
Low Point
Red Rocks Point
Eyre Bird Observatory
Twilight Cove
Scorpion Bight
Caiguna
1
Baxter Cliffs
Point Dover
Toolinna Cove
GREAT AUSTRALIAN BIGHT
SOUTHERN OCEAN
NORTH

WA 7
SA 1

Northern Territory

If your idea of relaxing and unwinding is getting away from it all, then the Northern Territory is certainly the place to go. You can get lost in Kakadu, Australia's largest national park, and discover ancient Aboriginal art sites, spectacular waterfalls and peaceful lagoons. If the intense heat and humidity of the north becomes oppressive, take a quick dip in one of the many waterholes found throughout the MacDonnell Ranges—they are surprisingly cool and invigorating! Sunset at Uluru inspires a meditative mood, as the huge monolith changes colour from burnt orange through scarlet to deep purple, and the night sky in the desert seems to glitter with a billion stars unseen by people in the big cities. For those who want to escape the rat race, the Northern Territory is nirvana.

Darwin and Environs

There's a simple lesson to be learned about the Northern Territory. It covers a truly vast area—somc 1 346 200 sq km (only Western Australia and Queensland are larger) and it is larger than France, Germany and the United Kingdom combined—therefore it is impossible to generalise. In an area of that size it is possible to experience everything from a tropical cyclone (Darwin during the wet season is hot, humid and debilitating) to dry desert storms with temperatures soaring towards the 50°C mark.

Thus the traveller must first ask (a) where am I planning to visit and (b) when am I planning to visit. It would be hard to imagine two more different experiences than Darwin during the wet season and Alice Springs in the middle of winter.

Most people who visit the Northern Territory go to look at, and experience, the amazing and beautiful landscape. They go to Kakadu National Park to see the Jim Jim and Twin Falls, to watch the wildlife from the lookouts, to inspect the Aboriginal art works and to see the sun set over the wetlands. All of this is very difficult during 'the wet'. Similarly they go to 'The Alice' and Yulara to inspect the glories of the MacDonnell Ranges with their wonderful gorges and pools, and marvel at both Uluru and Kata Tjuta as they appear to change colour during the course of the day.

Until recently, the colourful fibre arts of Australian Aboriginals were mainly purchased by museums. Now they have become a popular souvenir.

Darwin

When visiting Darwin it is always worth remembering that the British government madc numerous attempts to settle this quite inhospitable stretch of coast—at Fort Dundas (1826), Raffles Bay (1827), Escape Cliffs (1865) and Port Essington (1838)—before they finally succeeded in persuading people to permanently live here. Since then, the city has been hit and severely damaged by cyclones three times since its creation in 1870. So, if you are thinking of relaxation, it is vital to time your visit carefully.

Most Darwin visitors make sure they go to see the famous Fannie Bay Gaol (which is now a fascinating museum) and make their way along Darwin's impressive shoreline where a number of interesting historic buildings and museums—the British Australian Telegraph Residence Museum, the Esplanade Gallery and the outstanding Northern Territory Museum of Arts and Natural Sciences—are open to the public. This is a relaxed city, and a walk through the central business district with a view to purchasing some genuine Aboriginal artefacts followed by a stopover at any one of the air-conditioned hotels with their excellent lounges is strongly recommended.

Above: *The houses in Darwin's Myilly Point Historic Precinct, at the end of Smith Street, were built during the 1930s. One of the buildings is now an art gallery.*

did you know?

Darwin, Australia's only tropical capital city, is closer to many parts of Asia than it is to much of southern Australia—Jakarta in Indonesia is closer than Brisbane, and the city of Singapore is closer than Hobart.

The impressive shoreline of Darwin Harbour at sunset. The Wharf Precinct has been redeveloped and now boasts shops, cafés and an aquarium.

NT

But the real attractions for those visiting Darwin are the region's excellent parks. Start with a visit to Darwin's Botanic Gardens. This 42-hectare garden is located only 2 km north of the city and is a kind of symbol for Darwin's uniqueness. It emphasises both native Australian and South-east Asian plants and species. Wander around the different landscapes: escarpment, rainforest, woodland, wetland, coastal plain and mangroves. There are over 400 varieties of palm trees planted in the gardens as well as collections of tropical orchids, ferns, bromeliads and other exotic plants. Examples of all the world's baobab species can also be seen. There is an Aboriginal plant-use trail to follow and a well-established rainforest gully. This is certainly no ordinary city botanic garden. Visitors are advised to carry water and to wear a hat. Try to go on a cool day.

Map: NT 1 E4

Doctor's Gully, at the western end of Darwin's Bicentennial Park, is a popular place at high tide when catfish, mullet and other fish come to be hand-fed titbits of bread.

Beyond the City

The area around Darwin is famous for its parks. These are interesting tropical destinations where visitors can experience the pleasures of Darwin and its environs. For example Berry Springs Nature Park, which is located 57 km south of Darwin, is a combination of springs which form small creeks and, in turn, reach Darwin Harbour. The Nature Park is an ideal place for snorkelling, as the clear pools abound in native fish and interesting aquatic life. Nearby is the exceptional Territory Wildlife Park which showcases the rich variety of Northern Territory fauna. Here the visitor can see wallabies, wallaroos, kangaroos and other native animals as well as introduced species like the Northern Territory buffalo, banteng cattle and feral pigs. There is an aquarium which includes a number of saltwater crocodiles, and an aviary with Northern Territory exotics such as the

spangled drongo, the red-winged parrot and numerous birds of prey. It is very easy to spend a day in this fascinating 400-hectare Wildlife Park.

Equally interesting is the Casuarina Coastal Reserve, which lies in Darwin's northern suburbs and can be entered via Rapid Creek footbridge, Trower Road or Lee Point Road. In an area known for its mangrove swamps this reserve is characterised by a long, white, sandy beach fringed by casuarina trees and set against a backdrop of sandstone cliffs. There is a special nudist area but the beach is used primarily for picnics, cycling and walking. Visitors are advised not to swim at the beach because of the dangers of box jellyfish (which have been known in the area all year round) and crocodiles.

Left: *It is very relaxing to watch the sunset from the Dripstone Cliffs in the Casuarina Coastal Reserve. You can also see World War II observation posts and pockets of monsoon forest.*

Hot Springs

Particularly worthwhile for children (because there is a good paddling pool) is the Howard Springs Nature Park, which is located 35 km south of Darwin. With its extensive swamps, it boasts excellent wildlife habitats for magpie geese, whistling ducks and pygmy geese. There is a 1.8-km walking track and the adult swimming pool is clean and spring-fed.

If you are in the Darwin area in the dry season (May–September) it is worth driving the 200 km south to Tjuwaliyn (Douglas) Hot Springs Park where thermal pools exist like a strange oasis in the surrounding dry woodland of the park. These pools are owned by the Wagiman peoples but they are accessible to all visitors who can enjoy the curative properties of the waters. At the point where the Tjuwaliyn and the Douglas Rivers meet, the warm waters bubble to the surface. Be careful: these waters can be extremely hot. It is recommended that swimming take place 200 m either upstream or downstream from the hot springs. There is plenty of opportunity for bushwalking in the area and the park itself has good camping facilities including water, firewood, picnic tables and barbecues. There is, however, no power available at the site.

At the 400-ha Territory Wildlife Park, a 6-km path wanders through a range of habitats, passing native and feral animals found in the Northern Territory such as the water buffalo (Bubalus bubalis).

Adelaide River

Don't even think about swimming in the Adelaide River. There can be few more croc-infested rivers in the world and, with some of the local tour operators offering the crocs pieces of meat (arguing that they need to attract the animals to the sides of their boats), it has been suggested that even fishing in the river can be a dangerous activity. Still the crocodiles enjoy the free food and the visitors enjoy the sheer power and beauty of the animals. There are a number of good tours. It is always worth remembering that while the crocodiles are the premier attractions it is also common to see buffaloes, jabirus, sea eagles, kites, snakes and a variety of other wildlife during the tour. The Adelaide River Queen Wildlife River Tours run five times each day and have pickups from hotels in Darwin. Phone (08) 8988 8144.

Territorians are as serious about their beer as other Australians. This sign advertises the wares of a local pub in the township of Adelaide River.

It is worth remembering that there are two Adelaide Rivers: the river itself, and a small township which is on the Stuart Highway 114 km south of Darwin. The town is of interest to anyone wanting to know more about the Japanese bombing of Darwin. The Adelaide River War Cemetery is the only Australian war cemetery on Australian soil. There are 432 servicemen and 63 civilians, all of whom died as a result of Japanese bombing raids, buried in the cemetery. The cemetery, which is beautifully preserved and a place of great peace and tranquillity, can be reached by a road which runs along the north-east bank of the river.

Map: NT 1 E6

Litchfield National Park

There has been a tendency to see Kakadu National Park as the natural place for exploration and experiencing the real 'Top End' of the Northern Territory. This has occurred at the expense of the beautiful Litchfield National Park which boasts some of the most beautiful freshwater swimming destinations in the whole of the Northern Territory. It is located about 100 km south of Darwin (by sealed road) and is famous for its waterfalls which tumble from a sandstone plateau known as the Tabletop Range, forming attractive swimming pools at their base. The most famous and popular of all these falls are the Wangi Falls, which has both a picnic area and a kiosk to service the needs of people who decide to take a day off and enjoy the peacefulness of this area. It is worth noting that the falls are

The magnetic termite mounds in Litchfield National Park dot the landscape like headstones in a cemetery. They all face north–south, which may be a temperature-control mechanism.

often closed during the wet season. The appeal of Wangi Falls is the setting. The falls tumble down a cliff face which is adjacent to a palm-covered bank area. The water is cool and fresh and the pool is clean. The banks are ideal for picnics.

The national park has a number of pleasant walks and swimming is available at Wangi, Florence and Tjaynera Falls and Buley Rockholes. The walks are easy to locate. They are rarely more than 3 km in length and they all start from the various parking places which are spread throughout the park.

At Wangi Falls, Buley Rockhole and Florence Falls there are camping areas with toilet facilities and barbecues.

Map: NT 1 E6

Wangi Falls is one of the most popular sites in Litchfield National Park. There is a track that leads up to the escarpment at the top of the 80-m falls, where there is a great view of the area.

don't miss

If you have a 4WD you can reach remote areas of Litchfield National Park, such as the Lost City, with its spectacular freestanding sandstone formations. Note: most 4WD tracks are closed during the wet season.

The Red Centre

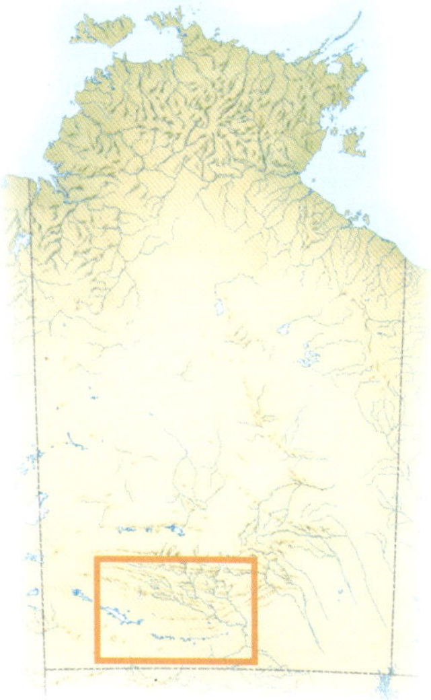

There was a time when all visitors to the Red Centre either drove into the area via the Stuart Highway or flew into Alice Springs. These days, with an airport located at Yulara that offers easy access to both Uluru and Kata Tjuta, it has become increasingly popular for people to fly into Yulara during the day, see the sun setting over Uluru in the evening, view the sun rising over Uluru the following morning, make a quick trip out to see the marvels of Kata Tjuta and then get back on the aeroplane. This is not the way to relax and unwind in the Red Centre.

Above: *There are many places in and around Alice Springs to buy genuine Aboriginal artwork.*

Below: *One of the more extraordinary ways you can explore the surrounds of Alice Springs!*

There are endless attractions in the Red Centre and if you are planning a journey of experience and adventure you would be short-changing yourself (and not experiencing the real magic of the Centre) if you did not take a camel ride, try a little outback wine, buy some unique Aboriginal art work, experience the local Aboriginal culture, drive to and swim in the beautiful waterholes that lie along the MacDonnell Ranges, and do the walk around Kings Canyon. Then, having done all of that, go and visit Uluru and Kata Tjuta.

Uluru and Kata Tjuta

There is something very special about Uluru (Ayers Rock). Everyone has seen it on photographs but, until you have seen it in all its vast reality, you cannot appreciate the special qualities of this huge monolith. There it sits in the middle of the desert, 862.5 m above sea level, 1395 km south of Darwin and 465 km south-west of Alice Springs. It is, as the vernacular would have it, 'the greatest stone on earth', rising 348 m above the surrounding countryside. It has an area of 3.33 sq km and a circumference of 9.4 km. It experiences an average of 200–250 mm of rainfall per annum and, with the viciousness of continentality, it experiences an amazing temperature range which can see the night-time temperature fall to –8°C

in winter and rise to a blistering 47°C during the middle of the day in summer.

So what do the visitors do at Uluru? There are three things that are special. Firstly go and watch the sun set over the rock. It is true that most of the year you will find yourself standing with hundreds of other people. Still, the experience is awe-inspiring as the rock surface really does change colour.

Secondly, and perhaps even more awe-inspiring, is the rock at dawn. As the sun's rays hit the rock, and as they rise and cover the surface, there is a superb changing of colour. It is just after dawn that most people climb the rock. There will always be arguments as to whether people should climb the rock. Let's just say that, unless you are very fit, you should be happy to stay on the ground and marvel at the grandeur. The climb is steep and coming down can be quite dangerous. If you want to unwind and relax try walking through Kata Tjuta or climbing Kings Canyon.

The real experiences of Uluru are to be had not by climbing up the rock (the traditional owners ask people not to do it) but by exploring the excellent Cultural Centre—the third special thing to do at Uluru. Visitors can learn about the sacredness of the rock from the Australian Aboriginal traditional owners (the Anangu people) and take one of the many walks around the base of the rock. There are four tracks which are particularly recommended.

The rock that makes up Uluru is quite fine in texture. It is mainly arkose, a smooth sandstone formed under immense pressure and rich in tiny grains of feldspar and quartz.

The Mala Walk is only 2 km long and is so easy that it is accessible to people in wheelchairs. It begins at the Mala Walk Carpark and ends at the Kantju Gorge.

The Base Walk is about 10 km long and goes around Uluru. It is a sensible alternative if you decide not to climb Uluru. There are sections of the track which have interpretative signs.

The Liru Track is only 2 km one-way and is an ideal way to walk from the Cultural Centre to the bottom of Uluru. The shady track winds through stands of wanari or mulga trees and links up at the end with the Base Walk track.

The Mutitjulu Walk is a short 1-km return walk from the Mutitjulu car park to a waterhole which is said to be the home of Wanampi, an ancestral watersnake.

Left: *It is thought that the 36 individual domes of Kata Tjuta may once have been a single dome many times the size of Uluru, which has slowly been weathered down by wind and rain.*

don't miss

Alice Springs has a surprisingly good range of restaurants and cuisines. You can find places to try a variety of local delicacies—including water buffalo, kangaroo, camel, crocodile, barramundi and emu—in the town.

No less impressive is the beautiful collection of rocks known as Kata Tjuta (The Olgas). Again this area can often be crowded with sightseers, but for anyone wanting to experience this remarkable area a walk through the Valley of the Winds is a necessity.

The Uluru–Kata Tjuta Cultural Centre is a perfect introduction to the national park and to the culture of the Anangu people. Phone the park information desk on (08) 8956 3138.

Perhaps one of the most appealing things about both Uluru and Kata Tjuta is the way the accommodation is structured to cater for a variety of tastes and budgets. The fantastic Ayers Rock Resort offers five different standards of accommodation, ranging from five-star hotel to clean, hostel-style, shared rooms with bunk beds. There is the Desert Gardens Hotel, the Emu Walk Apartments, the Outback Pioneer Lodge, Sails in the Desert and the Spinifex Lodge. Phone 1300 139 889. There are swimming pools, a general store and a range of eating places to suit all members of the family.
Map: NT 8 E8

Kings Canyon

To the north of Uluru and Kata Tjuta is Kings Canyon. This is really as important and interesting as Uluru. Located in the Watarrka National Park, the Canyon is characterised by sheer sandstone walls which have been carved by millions of years of erosion. Located 330 km southwest of Alice Springs, this is a stunning area where you can really feel the silence and beauty of the Australian outback. There are a number of walks up and around the canyon.

Over millions of years, floodwaters have eroded the soft sandstone at the base of Kings Canyon, causing huge slabs to shear from the walls.

The Kings Creek Walk is a fairly modest walk up the valley of Kings Creek. It is only 1.3 km long and offers excellent views of the cliffs which tower above the walker. Half of the walk is so easy and well laid out that it can be completed by people in wheelchairs.

The main walk is the Kings Canyon Walk, which is 6 km long and takes about 3 to 4 hours. It has been carefully designed to discourage the faint-hearted with a sharp climb at the very beginning. After the climb the walk moves around the canyon rim and passes such interesting features as the 'Lost City' and the 'Garden of Eden'.

The other walks include Kathleen Springs Walk, which is a 2.6-km, 1.5-hour return walk to a spring-fed waterhole, and the Giles Track, which is 22 km long.
Map: NT 7 B6

Around Alice Springs

There is so much to see around Alice Springs. Apart from the town's major tourist attractions (the Overland Telegraph Station, the Frontier Camel Park, the various memorials to Flynn of the Inland, the famous Chateau Hornsby winery—the only winery found in Central Australia—the Aboriginal Art and Cultural Centre and the remarkable Alice Springs Desert Park), the surrounding area offers so much. No visit to the Red Centre is really complete without

Left: *The town of Alice Springs began life as a repeater station on the Overland Telegraph line in 1871. The buildings and equipment have been restored and are now a tourist attraction.*

visiting Glen Helen and, if the water is flowing, going for a swim in the sometimes mighty (but more often very small) Finke River (which is known to the local Australian Aboriginals as the Larapinta). The idea is to hire a car and simply drive both east and west along the MacDonnell Ranges, stopping wherever there is a sign to a gorge or a waterhole. The age of this remarkable range is such that when it was first pushed up from the earth the mountains were higher than the Himalayas are today. It has been worn down by erosion so that all that is left are the very bones of the earth.

An equally important stop to make is at the Australian Aboriginal community of Hermannsburg, located about 125 km west of Alice Springs, which is famous as the home of the great Aboriginal artist, Albert Namatjira. It is possible to watch the local artists at work and to purchase samples of their work at the community.

Below: *Travelling by camel train is a great way to see the landscape of the ancient MacDonnell Ranges, which span some 400 km east to west and can reach heights of over 1500 m above sea level.*

The Top End

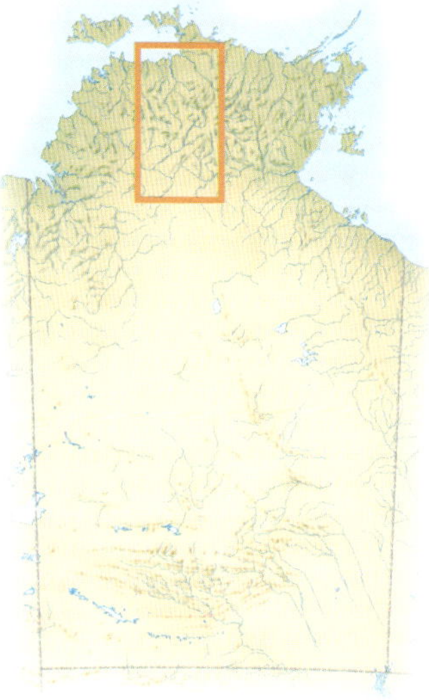

From Aboriginal art to unique wetlands, the Top End of the Northern Territory is an area of tremendous cultural and natural significance. Over 200 000 people a year visit Kakadu National Park, an internationally renowned World Heritage area, for its magnificent rock art sites and abundance of wildlife. The colourful sandstone walls of Katherine Gorge in Nitmiluk National Park form one of the greatest natural wonders of the north, while Mataranka's thermal pool has long been a shady oasis for travellers making their way through the Top End.

Kakadu National Park

The Northern Territory Visitor Centre describes Kakadu in the following terms: 'Kakadu National Park is just 257 km from Darwin along the sealed Arnhem Highway. In its 19 000 sq km, it is home to around 275 species of birds, 75 species of reptiles, 25 species of frogs, an estimated 10 000 species of insects and 1600 plant species.'

All this is true. What they don't tell anyone is that Kakadu is not tropical rainforest. It is predominantly tropical savannah, which led the Australian TV personality and naturalist Harry Butler to call it 'clapped-out buffalo country'. It is, of course, much more than that, but anyone expecting to enter a dense rainforest will be disappointed. This is dry, scrubby country which is magically

The best fishing for barramundi on the East Alligator River in Kakadu occurs as soon as the river becomes accessible after the wet season.

turned into wetlands when the Northern Territory's infamous 'Wet' hits and makes the roads impassible and the waterfalls dramatic and dangerous.

There are a number of good reasons for spending time in Kakadu. Firstly, it is not every day that you can go and stay in a motel designed to look like a giant crocodile. The Gagudju Crocodile Hotel at Jabiru (08 8979 2707) is definitely worth staying at—the hotel's 110 rooms are comfortable and the swimming pool is very necessary if you arrive when the humidity is unbearable. Secondly, the park has a truly marvellous array of attractions which are part of this country's unique cultural heritage.

The Yellow Waters Boat Cruise is a rare opportunity to get out on the wetlands and truly experience the early morning magic of the bird life on the lakes and billabongs.

Ubirr Rock is an important World Heritage-listed art site. The sign at the entrance explains 'Ubirr is an Aboriginal rock art site of international status. It's also of great significance to its Aboriginal owners with whose advice and approval material in this display has been prepared. We ask you to observe two simple rules: (i) follow directional signs and keep to defined walking paths and (ii) do not touch painted surfaces under any circumstances. Penalties may be imposed for interference with such sites.'

There are ranger talks at Ubirr Rock Main Gallery at 9.30, 12.00 and 4.00, at the Namarrkan Sisters at 10.30 and 5.30 and at the Rainbow Serpent at 11.30 and 4.00. There is nowhere else in Australia where such a vast gallery of rock art is so readily accessible to the general public. The work is amazing. Ubirr Rock also offers quite dramatic views over the surrounding countryside.

There are over 100 sacred sites in the Nourlangie Rock area, including a number of cave sites which include drawings of thylacines (Tasmanian tigers).

There are also a number of interesting walks which include visits to the lookouts at Gunwarrde and Nawurlandja, a walk around Anbangbang Billabong and a short walk to the Anbangbang Gallery where depictions of Namarrgon the Lightning Man and Nabulwinjbulwinj, a dangerous spirit who eats females after striking them with a yam, are fascinating.

The dramatic Twin Falls and Jim Jim Falls are possible to reach in the winter months because the waters are relatively low. In 'The Wet' the best anyone can hope for is a helicopter trip, because the falls are in flood. The view of the two falls is stunning and impressive.

Map: NT 2 D6

Mataranka

Driving in the Northern Territory really can be quite hard work. You can drive hundreds of kilometres in a day and seem to make very little progress towards your destination. The long drive from the Queensland border to Darwin is arduous, and its difficulty is compounded by the constant presence of huge road trains. The same applies to the Stuart Highway which cuts the Northern Territory from north to south.

Left: *The famous, crystal-clear thermal pool at Mataranka can become crowded during the day—for a more tranquil dip in the warm, soothing waters, try to visit in the early morning or evening.*

warning

When travelling through Kakadu, look out for the crocodile warning signs. Although some swimming holes are safe, estuarine (saltwater) crocodiles live in many of the waterways and are considered highly dangerous. If you are unsure as to whether a billabong is safe, check with the local ranger.

Left: *Found in Kakadu, the jabiru* (Ephippiorhynchus asiaticus) *is Australia's only species of stork. Their diet consists mainly of fish, but they also eat reptiles, frogs, rodents, crabs and carrion.*

Over millions of years the Katherine River has cut through the sandstone plateau to form the spectacular Katherine Gorge, which has cliff faces that can tower up to 100 m above the water.

Mataranka is known to many generations of Australians as 'The Never-Never' because it was here that Jeannie Gunn came with her husband to run the Elsey cattle station. She recorded her life story in the famous book *We of the Never-Never.* It is possible to visit both Elsey Station (known as Elsey National Park) and the cemetery which contains the remains of Aeneas James Gunn, who died on 16 March, 1902, only 13 months after the couple had moved to the area. The grave of Aeneas is located next to a memorial to Jeannie which reads 'In loving Memory of the "Little Missus"'. Jeannie died on 9 June, 1961.

Map: NT 3 E2

Consequently the idea of a break—and a really healthy one at that—is tantalising. Nothing can be more appealing than the spa waters at Mataranka. The violent monsoonal rains known as 'The Wet' are partially captured in the limestone beds of the Daly and Georgina Basins at 30–100 m below the surface and, at Mataranka, burst through to the surface at 30.5 million litres per day, at a temperature of 34–35°C. Whether you have been driving for long distances or not there can be nothing more pleasant than to stop at this small, 4-hectare park and have a healthy swim in its superb thermal pool which is surrounded by stands of cabbage tree palms and paperbarks. Owned and operated as the Mataranka Homestead Tourist Resort, this is a popular picnic spot for visitors to the area. For those interested in the technical aspects, the water is very slightly acidic (pH 6.9) and contains calcium, chloride, fluoride, iron, magnesium, potassium, silica, sodium, nitrate sulphate and bicarbonate.

Katherine

Further north is the thriving township of Katherine (it is worth remembering that the Northern Territory, for all its size, has only four major population centres—Darwin, Alice Springs, Tennant Creek and Katherine). No visit to Katherine is complete without a trip up the Katherine Gorge, which is actually 13 different gorges separated by rocky areas during the dry season. The national park offers swimming, bushwalking and boating.

Map: NT 2 C9

Right: *Take a break from driving in the Northern Territory and do a bit of sightseeing from the back of a horse. You can join a guided ride through the area around the thermal pool at Mataranka.*

Map 1

0 20 40 60 80
kilometres

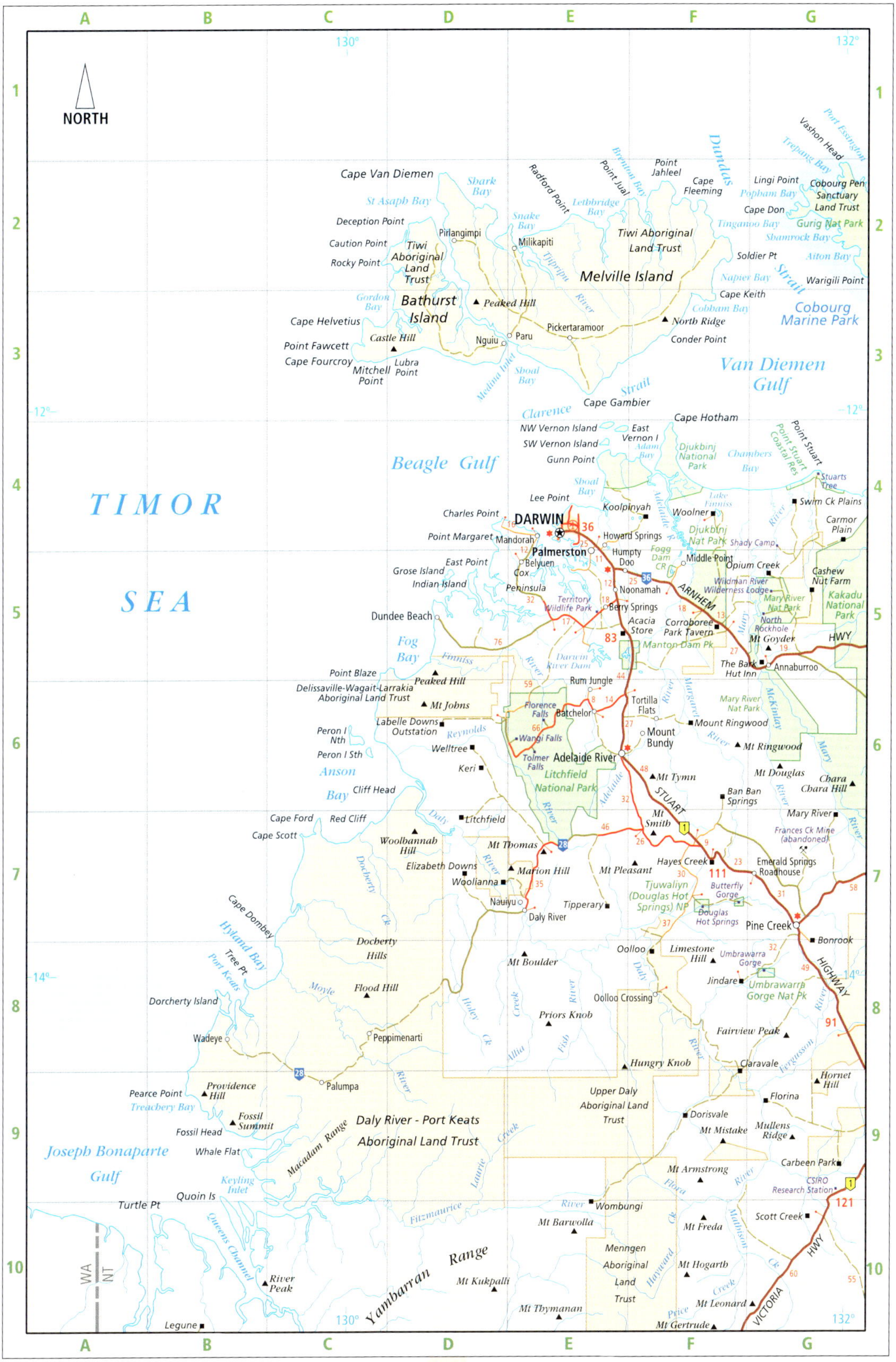

Map 2

A
B
C
D
E
F
G
1
2
3
4
5
6
7
8
9
10
132°
134°
12°
14°
Cobourg Marine Park
New Year Island
Cape Croker
Oxley Island
Somerville Bay
Croker Island
McCluer Island
Vashon Head
Port Essington
Smith Point
Port Bremer
Danger Pt
Minjilang
Mission Bay
Grant Island
Darch I
Trepang Bay
Dundas
Brenton Bay
Point Jahleel
Point Jual
Cape Fleeming
Lingi Point
High Pt
Bowen Strait
Popham Bay
Cobourg Peninsula Sanctuary Land Trust
Letbbridge Bay
Cape Don
Cape Cockburn
Cobourg Peninsula
Mountnorris Bay
De Courcy Head
ARAFURA
Tinganoo Bay
Tiwi Aboriginal Land Trust
Shamrock Bay
Gurig Nat Park
Valencia I
Gningarg Point
Goulburn Islands
Soldier Pt
Alton Bay
Wurgurlu Bay
Murgenella
Melville Island
Napier Bay
Strait
Warigili Point
Brogden Point
Cape Keith
Morse I
Aurari Bay
Warruwi
Turner Point
Cuthbert Point
Braithwaite Point
Cobbam Bay
Greenhill Island
Arrla Bay
Junction Bay
North Ridge
Endyalgout Island
Murgenella Creek
Conder Point
Salt Water Point
Rolling Bay
Van Diemen Gulf
Hawkesbury Point
Skirmish Point
Cape Gambier
Cooper Creek
King R
Jungle Creek
River
Cape Hotham
Field Island
East Vernon I
Adam Bay
Djukbinj National Park
Chambers Bay
Point Stuart Coastal Res
Point Stuart
West Alligator Head
Barron I
Finke Bay
Maningrida
Shoal Bay
Stuarts Tree
Mt Hooper
East
Nabarlek
Goomadeer
Koolpinyah
Lake Finniss
Swim Ck Plains
Kakadu National Park
Oenpelli
Woolner
Carmor Plain
Cahills Crossing
Djukbinj Nat Park
Shady Camp
Howard Springs
Palmerston
Middle Point
Opium Creek
Four Mile Hole
Jabiluka Mineral Lease
Mt Howship
Humpty Doo
Fogg Dam Cons Res
Mudginberri
Cadell
Noonamah
Wildman River Wilderness Lodge
Cashew Nut Farm
South Alligator
Ranger Mineral Lease
Mary River Nat Park
Two Mile Hole
Frontier Kakadu Village
Jabiru
Berry Springs
ARNHEM
Wildman
Mt Brockman
Territory Wildlife Park
North Rockhole
HWY
Alligator
Liverpool
Acacia Store
Corroboree Park Tavern
Mt Goyder
Park Entrance Stn
Koongarra Mineral Lease
Blyth
Manton Dam Park
Yellow Waters
Cooinda
Muirella Park
Nourlangie Rock
The Bark Hut Inn
Annaburroo
Spring Peak
Jim Jim Waterhole
Kub-o-wer Hill
Rum Jungle
Table Top
Tortilla Flats
Mary River Nat Park
Black Jungle Spring
Mt Gilruth
Batchelor
Mundogie Hill
Mt Partridge
Mann
Shadforth Hills
Mount Bundy
Mount Ringwood
Arnhem Land
Adelaide River
Mt Ringwood
Kakadu National Park
Jim Jim Falls
McKay Hills
Litchfield Nat Park
Mt Tymn
Mt Douglas
Goodparla
Chara
Chara Hill
Barramundie Gorge
Twin Falls
Wilton
Aboriginal Land Tru
Ban Ban Springs
Waterfall Creek Falls
McCaw
STUART
Mt Smith
Mary River
Frances Ck Mine (abandoned)
Mt Jean
Mt Evelyn
Hayes Creek
Emerald Springs Roadhouse
Mary River Roadhouse
Mt Pleasant
Coronation Hill
Mt Weir
Mt Marl
Bulman
Tjuwaliyn (Douglas Hot Springs) NP
Butterfly Gorge
KAKADU
Maimoru
McCarthy Hill
Coronet Hill
Mt Stretton
Tipperary
Douglas Hot Springs
Pine Creek
Black Mountain
Mt Stow
Bonrook
Oolloo
Limestone Hill
Umbrawarra Gorge
Mt Ebsworth
Road
Mt Catt
Mt Bridges
Jindare
Umbrawarra Gorge Nat Pk
HIGHWAY
Black Mountain
Mt Lambell
Flying Fox
Mountain Valley
Mainoru
Oolloo Crossing
Daly
Mt David
Mt Felix
Mt Bray
Nitmiluk (Katherine Gorge) National Park
Edith Falls
Manyallaluk Aboriginal Land Trust
Fairview Peak
O'Shea Hill
Whamelk Bluff
Arnhem
Eva Valley
Katherine Gorge
Mt Furner
Hungry Knob
Claravale
Fergusson
Beswick Aboriginal Land Trust
Mt Shepherd
Mt Karmain
Hornet Hill
Upper Daly Aboriginal Land Trust
Mt Bagste
Florina
Katherine
Black Cap
Dorisvale
Manbulloo
Barunga
Maranboy
Mt Mistake
Mullens Ridge
RAAF Base Tindal
Beswick
Cutta Cutta Caves
Mt James
Mt Armstrong
Carbeen Park
Flora
CSIRO Research Station
Roper B
Wombungi
Goondooloo
Mt Moray
Moroak
Mt Elanor
Yutpundji-Djindiwirritj Aboriginal Land Trust
Mt Barwolla
Mt Freda
Scott Creek
Butchers Hill
Mataranka Resort
Mt Price
Mataranka
ROPER
Elsey
Elsey Nat Park
Mt Forrest
Menngen Aboriginal Land Trust
Mt Hogarth
Mt Mueller
Mt Hughe
Elsey Cemetery
Mt Davidson
Warloch Ponds
Hodgson
Mt Kelly
Mt Leonard
VICTORIA
Mt Gertrude
Hodgson Downs
36
83
218
108
206
21
111
1
91
121
106
24
305
20
184
NT 1
NT 3

0 20 40 60 80
kilometres
NORTH
H J K L M N P
1 2 3 4 5 6 7 8 9 10
136°
138°
-12°
-14°
SEA
GULF OF CARPENTARIA
ARNHEM LAND
Rimbija I
Cape Wessel
Wessel Islands
Marchinbar Island
Cumberland Strait
Stevens Island
Guluwuru Island
Drysdale Island
Brown Strait
Raragala Island
Truant Island
The English Companys Islands
Nth West Crocodile Island
Cunningham Islands
Malay Road
Bromby Islands
Mooroongga Island
Elcho Island
Alger I
Cape Wilberforce
Cape Stewart
Galiwinku
Point Napier
Inglis Island
Rabuma I
Howard Island
Flinders Pt
Boney Point
Bremer Island
Milingimbi
Castlereagh Bay
Buckingham Bay
Probable I
Melville Bay
Nhulunbuy
Yirrkala
Mallison Island
Ramingining
Woolen River
Arnhem Bay
Cato River
Gove Peninsula
Cape Arnhem
Glyde River
Arafura Swamp
Gapuwiyak
Road
Port Bradshaw
Gulbuwangay River
416
191
Mt Alexander
Wanyanmera Point
Arnhem
Frederick Hills
Camburinga Village
Point Alexander
MITCHELL RANGE
Maidjunga River
Durabudboi R
Central
109
Caledon Bay
Mt Caledon
Goyder River
Cape Grey
Trial Bay
Bald Point
Koolatong River
116
Creek
Wardarlea Bay
Grindall Bay
Myaoola Bay
Point Arrowsmith
Jalma Bay
Cape Shield
Mt Fleming
Mt Ramsay
Parsons Range
Isle Woodah
Nicol Island
Morgan I
Walker River
Blue Mud Bay
Mt Ranken
Range
Burney I
Bartalumba Bay
North Point Island
Chasm I
Port Langdon
Thompson Bay
North East Isles
Hawk Island
Cape Barrow
Bath
Winchelsea Island
Zamia Ck
Galab Ck
Milyakburra
Bacchus Hill
Bickerton Island
Channel
Alyangula
Umbakumba
Groote Eylandt
Angurugu
Warwick
Bluff Hill
Mt Leane
Ilyungmadja Point
Arnhem Land Aboriginal Land Trust
Phelp River
Rose River
Dalumbu Bay
Ungwariba Point
Graces
Snowden Peak
Rantyirrity Point
Tasman Point
Sandy Hill
South Point
Numbulwar
157
Cape Beatrice
Boomerang Hill
Marangala Bay
Marangala Point
Inamalamandja Point
Nyinpinti Point
Edward Island
Downers Range
Warrakunta Point
Ngukurr
St Vidgeon
Port Roper
Roper River
18
44
Limmen Bight
Maria Island
Marra Aboriginal Land Trust
Towns River
107

NT

Map 3

NT 2
NT 4
NT 6
A
B
C
D
E
F
G
1
2
3
4
5
6
7
8
9
10
Hungry Knob
Claravale
Upper Daly Aboriginal Land Trust
Florina
Dorisvale
Mt Mistake
Mullens Ridge
Hornet Hill
Manbulloo
Katherine Gorge
Mt Shepherd
Katherine
RAAF Base Tindal
Cutta Cutta Caves
Barunga
Maranboy
Beswick
Beswick Aboriginal Land Trust
Black Cap
Mt Karmain
Mt Bagster
Mt James
Roper Bar
Mt Armstrong
Carbeen Park
CSIRO Research Station
Wombungi
Mt Barwolla
Mt Freda
Scott Creek
Butchers Hill
Goondooloo
Mt Moray
Mataranka Resort
Mataranka
Elsey Nat Park
Elsey
ROPER
Moroak
Mt Elanor
Mt Price
Yutpundji-Djindiwirritj Aboriginal Land Trust
Mennge Aboriginal Land Trust
Mt Hogarth
Mt Mueller
Mt Forrest
Mt Hughes
Mt Davidson
Mt Kelly
Elsey Cemetery
Warloch Ponds
Mt Leonard
Mt Gertrude
Innesvale
Willeroo
Mt Needham
Dry River
Alawa 1 Aboriginal Land Trust
Hodgson Downs
Mason Bluff
Wubalawun Aboriginal Land Trust
Coolibah
Fitzroy
Victoria River Wayside Inn
Illari Hill
Delamere
Mt Gregory
Old Delamere
Gorrie
Larrimah
Hodgson River
Western Creek
Gregory National Park
Mt Peake
Maryfield
Alexander Forrest Monument
Nutwood Downs
Mt Sandiman
Romula Knob
Dillinya Aboriginal Land Trust
Wambardi Aboriginal Land Trust
Mt Compton
Victoria River Research Station
Price Hills
Gallery Hill
Sunday Creek
Kalala
Killarney
Fraynes Knob
Mooloooloo Outstation
Daly Waters
Hi-Way Inn
CARPENTARIA
Two Mile Ck
Victoria River Downs
Mt Sullivan
Birrimba
Amungee Mungee
Top Springs
Hidden Valley
Mt Stevens
Montejinni
Dungowan
Dunmarra
Shenandoah
Yingawunarri Mudbura Aboriginal Land Trust
BUCHANAN
HWY
No. 11 Bore
Pigeon Hole
Mt Northcote
Lovell Hill
Murranji Aboriginal Land Trust
Sir Charles Todd Monument
Murranji
Camfield
Mt Williams
STUART
Newcastle
Beetaloo
Wave Hill
Newcastle Waters
Elliott
Cattle Creek
Wampana-Karlantijpa Aboriginal Land Trust
Ucharonidge
Barkly
Mungabroom
Lake Woods
HIGHWAY
Stock
Karlantijpa North Aboriginal Land Trust
Powell Creek
Renner Springs
Mt Willieray
Helen Springs
Nth Tomkinson Ck
Sth Tomkinson Ck
Muckaty Aboriginal Land Trust
Muckaty
TANAMI DESERT
Kuerschner
Banka Banka
Lotbari Hill
Brunchilly
VICTORIA
BUNTINE
HIGHWAY
HWY
132°
134°
16°
18°

NT 2

0
20
40
60
80
kilometres
NORTH
H
J
K
L
M
N
P
1
2
3
4
5
6
7
8
9
10
136°
138°
16°
18°
GULF OF
CARPENTARIA
Numbulwar
Boomerang Hill
Nyinpinti Point
Edward Island
Downers Range
Warrakunta Point
Ngukurr
St Vidgeon
Port Roper
Roper River
Limmen Bight
Maria Island
Marra Aboriginal Land Trust
Towns River
Cape Beatrice
Marangala Bay
Marangala Point
Inamalamandja Point
Nathan R
Limmen Bight River
The Four Archers
Nathan River
Rosie Ck
Alawa Aboriginal Land Trust
Cox
Sir Edward Pellew Group
Wurralibi Aboriginal Land Trust
Watson I
North Island
West Island
Cape Vanderlin
Bing Bong
Sth West Island
Centre I
Vanderlin Island
Wurralibi Aboriginal Land Trust
Batten Point
Port McArthur
King Ash Bay
Bing Bong Ck
Creek
Jandanku Aboriginal Land Trust
Tawallah Range
Batten
McArthur R
Fletcher
Manangoora
Borroloola
Mt Featherstop
Narwinbi Aboriginal Land Trust
Wearyan
Greenbank
Mt Joe
Bauhinia Downs
Tawallah
Bauhinia Ck
Limmen
McLeod Rd
Billengarrah
Seven Emu
Broadmere
McArthur River Mine
Eight Mile Waterhole
Robinson River
Kangaroo
Calvert
Settlement Creek
Sandy
Creek
October Ck
HIGHWAY
OT Downs
Cape Crawford
McArthur River
Cape Crawford
Balbirini
Glyde
Spring Creek
Foelsche
Pungalina
Bukalara Range
Robinson River
Running
Gold
Mambaliya Rrumburriya Wuyaliya Aboriginal Land Trust
Garawa Aboriginal Land Trust
TABLELANDS
Mallapunyah
Surprise
Calvert
Redbank Mine
Wollogorang
Calvert Hills
Little Calvert R
Bluey
Kiana
Lagoon
Puzzle
Creek
Road
Branch
China Wall
Waanyi-Garawa Aboriginal Land Trust
Nicholson River
HWY
Walhallow
Benmara
Cresswell Downs
Calvert
Route
Anthony Lagoon
Eva Downs
Creswell
Creek
Benmara
Ck
Buddycurrawa
Baubinia
Tarrabool Lake
TABLELANDS
Creek
Cleanskin
Nicholson
Fish Hole Ck
Corella
Corella Lake
Brunette Downs
Brunette
Creek
HWY
Mittiebah
Connells Lagoon Conservation Reserve
Carrara Range
Bluff Range
Little Range
Lake Sylvester
Mittebah
Carrara
Creek
Lawn Hill Ck
110
255
377
11
16
1
157
18
44
107
103
51
45
75
34
20
21
26
43
14
58
37
55
48
57
30
93
109
134
73
19
101
77
103

QLD 3

NT 6

Map 4

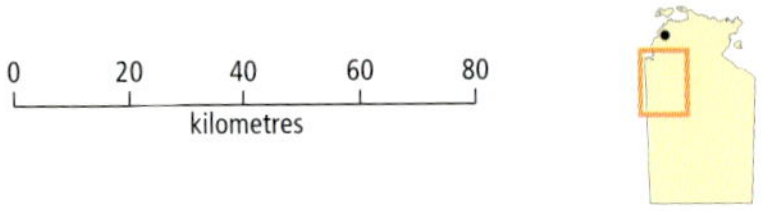
0
20
40
60
80
kilometres

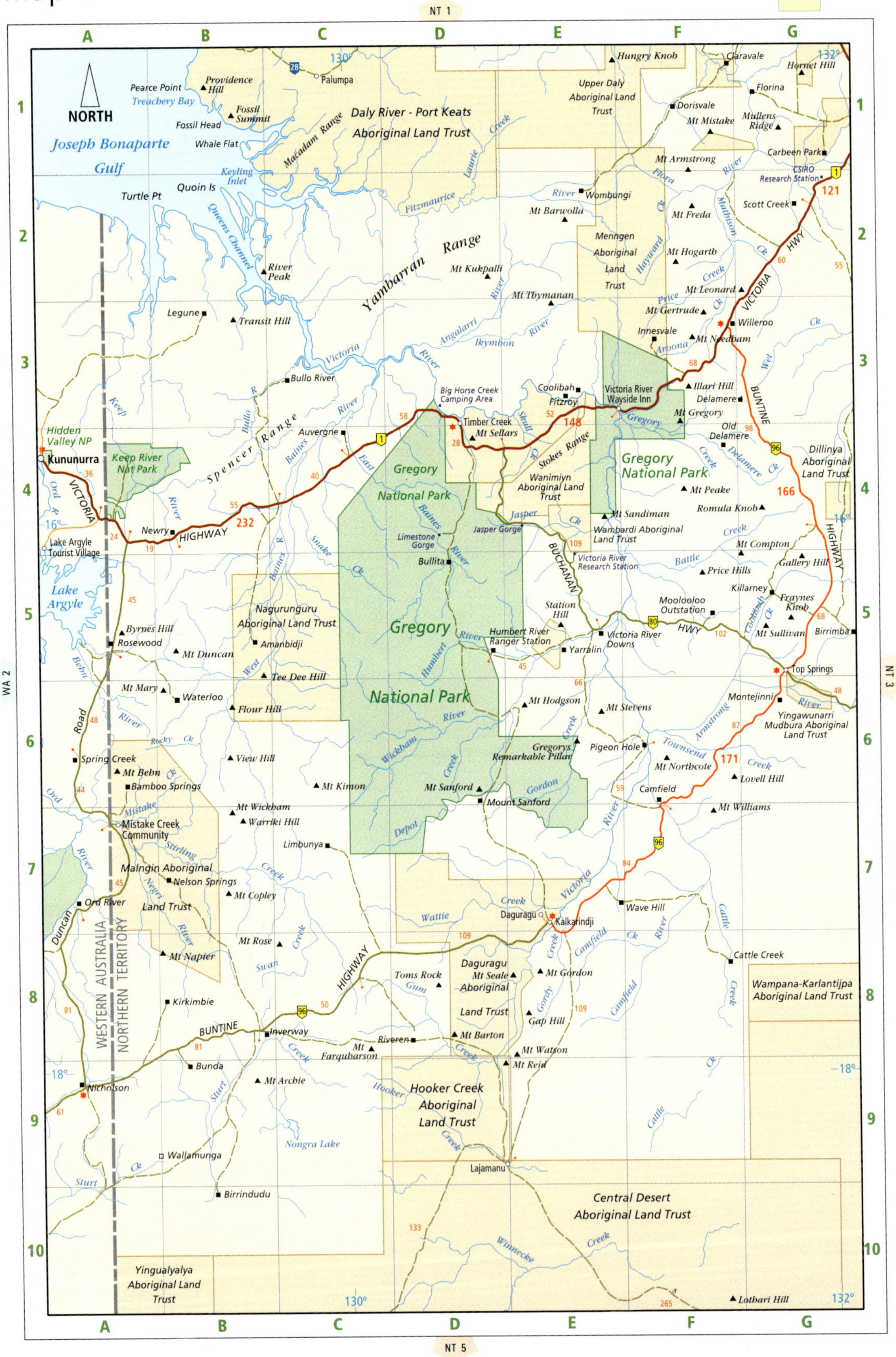
NT 1
NT 5
WA 2
NT 3
A
B
C
D
E
F
G
1
2
3
4
5
6
7
8
9
10
NORTH
130°
132°
16°
18°
Joseph Bonaparte Gulf
Pearce Point
Providence Hill
Treachery Bay
Fossil Summit
Fossil Head
Whale Flat
Keyling Inlet
Quoin Is
Turtle Pt
Queens Channel
Palumpa
Makadam Range
Daly River - Port Keats Aboriginal Land Trust
Hungry Knob
Upper Daly Aboriginal Land Trust
Claravale
Hornet Hill
Florina
Dorisvale
Mt Mistake
Mullens Ridge
Carbeen Park
Mt Armstrong
CSIRO Research Station
Laurie Creek
Fitzmaurice River
Wombungi
Mt Barwolla
Flora River
Mt Freda
Scott Creek
Mathison Ck
Menngen Aboriginal Land Trust
Hayward Ck
Mt Hogarth
River Peak
Yambarran Range
Mt Kukpalli
Mt Thymanan
Mt Leonard
Price Creek
Mt Gertrude
VICTORIA HWY
Willeroo
Innesvale
Arpona
Mt Needham
Legune
Transit Hill
Angalarri River
Ikymbon River
Victoria River
Bullo River
Bullo R
Keep River
Spencer Range
Big Horse Creek Camping Area
Coolibah
Fitzroy
Victoria River Wayside Inn
Illart Hill
Delamere
Mt Gregory
BUNTINE
Wet Ck
Hidden Valley NP
Kununurra
Keep River Nat Park
Auvergne
Timber Creek
Mt Sellars
Skull Ck
Stokes Range
Gregory
Old Delamere
Delamere Ck
Dillinya Aboriginal Land Trust
East Baines
Gregory National Park
Wanimiyn Aboriginal Land Trust
Mt Peake
Romula Knob
VICTORIA
Ord R
Newry
HIGHWAY
Jasper Ck
Jasper Gorge
Mt Sandiman
Wambardi Aboriginal Land Trust
Lake Argyle Tourist Village
Limestone Gorge
Baines River
Snake Ck
Bullita
BUCHANAN
Victoria River Research Station
Mt Compton
Battle Ck
Gallery Hill
Price Hills
Killarney
Lake Argyle
Baines R
Nagurunguru Aboriginal Land Trust
Mooloolo Outstation
Station Hill
Fraynes Knob
Birrimba
Byrnes Hill
Rosewood
Amanbidji
Humbert River Ranger Station
Victoria River Downs
HWY
Mt Sullivan
Mt Duncan
Humbert
Yarralin
Top Springs
Behn
West
Tee Dee Hill
Mt Mary
Waterloo
Flour Hill
National Park
Mt Hodgson
Mt Stevens
Montejinni
Armstrong River
Yingawunarri Mudbura Aboriginal Land Trust
Road
River
Rocky Ck
Spring Creek
View Hill
Wickham
Gregorys Remarkable Pillar
Pigeon Hole
Townsend
Mt Northcote
Mt Behn
Bamboo Springs
Mt Kimon
Mt Sanford
Mount Sanford
Gordon
Creek
Camfield
Lovell Hill
Mistake
Ord
Mt Wickham
Warriki Hill
Mt Williams
Mistake Creek Community
Stirling
Depot
Limbunya
Malngin Aboriginal Land Trust
Nelson Springs
Mt Copley
Ord River
Negri River
Wattie
Daguragu
Kalkarindji
Wave Hill
Cattle Creek
Duncan
WESTERN AUSTRALIA
NORTHERN TERRITORY
Mt Rose
Swan Ck
Mt Napier
Cattle Creek
Daguragu Aboriginal Land Trust
Mt Seale
Toms Rock
Gum
Mt Gordon
Camfield
Wampana-Karlantijpa Aboriginal Land Trust
Kirkimbie
Gordy Ck
Gap Hill
BUNTINE
Inverway
Riveren
Mt Farquharson
Mt Barton
Mt Watson
Mt Reid
Bunda
Hooker Creek Aboriginal Land Trust
Nicholson
Mt Archie
Sturt
Wallamunga
Nongra Lake
Lajamanu
Sturt Ck
Birrindudu
Central Desert Aboriginal Land Trust
Winnecke Creek
Yingualyalya Aboriginal Land Trust
Lotbari Hill
1
28
96
80
121
232
148
166
171

Map 5

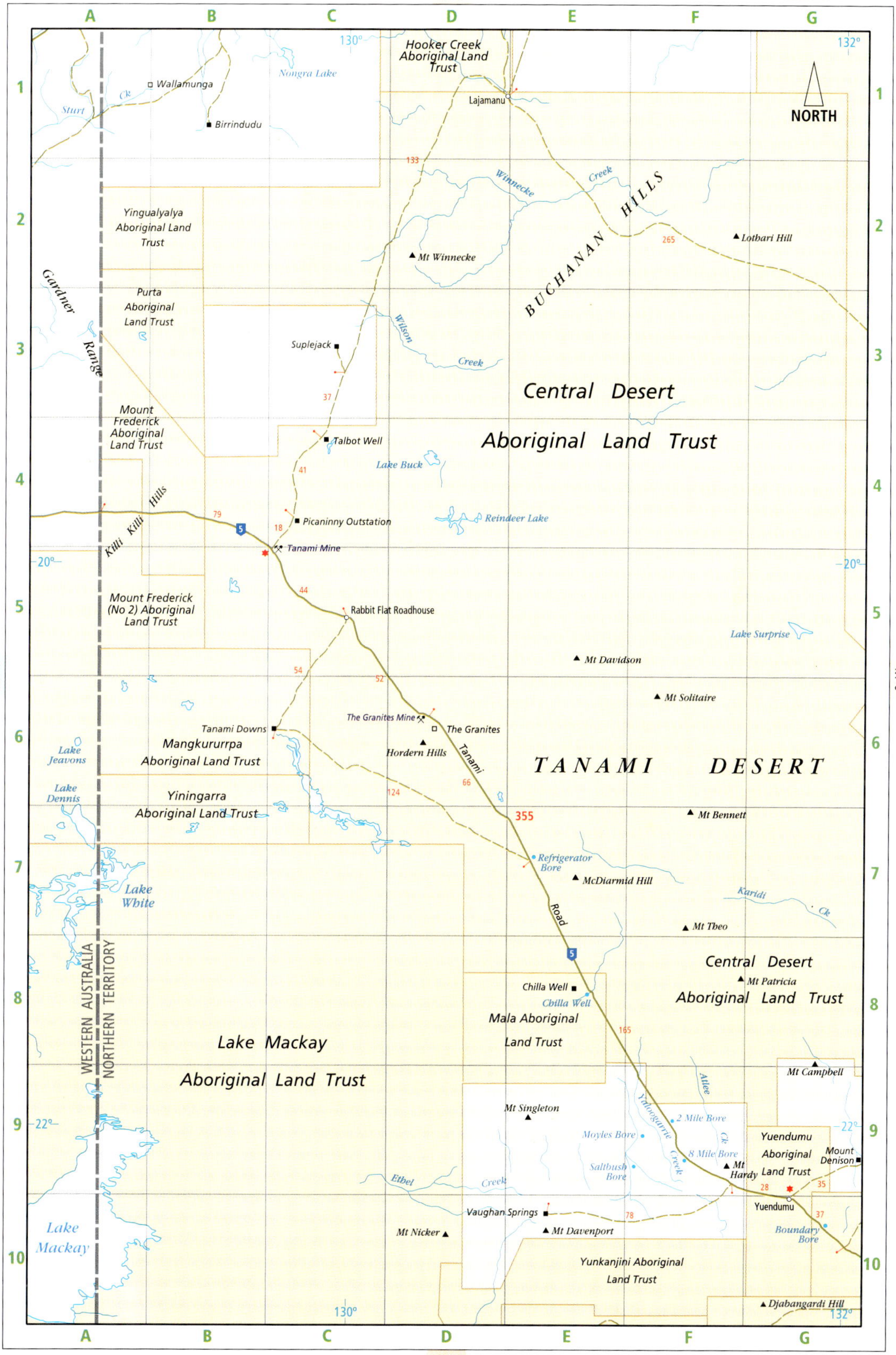
0 20 40 60 80
kilometres
NT 4
NT 6
NT 8
WA 3
NORTH
A B C D E F G
1 2 3 4 5 6 7 8 9 10
130°
132°
20°
22°
Hooker Creek Aboriginal Land Trust
Lajamanu
Wallamunga
Birrindudu
Nongra Lake
Sturt
Ck
Yingualyalya Aboriginal Land Trust
Purta Aboriginal Land Trust
Gardner
Range
Winnecke
Creek
BUCHANAN HILLS
Lothari Hill
Mt Winnecke
Suplejack
Wilson
Creek
Central Desert
Aboriginal Land Trust
Mount Frederick Aboriginal Land Trust
Talbot Well
Lake Buck
Killi Killi Hills
Picaninny Outstation
Reindeer Lake
Tanami Mine
Mount Frederick (No 2) Aboriginal Land Trust
Rabbit Flat Roadhouse
Lake Surprise
Mt Davidson
Mt Solitaire
Tanami Downs
The Granites Mine
The Granites
Hordern Hills
Mangkururrpa Aboriginal Land Trust
TANAMI DESERT
Lake Jeavons
Lake Dennis
Yiningarra Aboriginal Land Trust
Tanami
Road
Mt Bennett
Refrigerator Bore
McDiarmid Hill
Karidi
Ck
Lake White
Mt Theo
Central Desert
Mt Patricia
Aboriginal Land Trust
Chilla Well
Chilla Well
Mala Aboriginal Land Trust
WESTERN AUSTRALIA
NORTHERN TERRITORY
Lake Mackay
Aboriginal Land Trust
Mt Campbell
Mt Singleton
Yalyagarrie
Creek
Allee
2 Mile Bore
Moyles Bore
8 Mile Bore
Saltbush Bore
Mt Hardy
Yuendumu Aboriginal Land Trust
Mount Denison
Ethel
Creek
Vaughan Springs
Yuendumu
Mt Nicker
Mt Davenport
Boundary Bore
Lake Mackay
Yunkanjini Aboriginal Land Trust
Djabangardi Hill
5
133
37
41
79
18
44
54
52
124
66
355
165
78
265
28
35
37

Map 6

NT 3
A
B
C
D
E
F
G
132°
134°
1
2
3
4
5
6
7
8
9
10
NORTH
TANAMI DESERT
Karlantijpa North Aboriginal Land Trust
Central Desert Aboriginal Land Trust
Karlantijpa South Aboriginal Land Trust
Lotbari Hill
Green Swamp Well
Wiso Bore
Warrego Mine
Renner Springs
Mt Willieray
Helen Springs
Nth Tomkinson Ck
Muckaty Aboriginal Land Trust
Muckaty
Sth Tomkinson Ck
Kuerschner
Creek
Banka Banka
Churchills Head
Stuart Memorial
Hayward Creek
Gibson Ck
Short Range
Phillip Creek
John Flynn Memorial
Three Ways Road
Devils Pebbles
Mary Ann Dam
Tennant Creek
Lone Star
Mt Samuel
Nobles Nob
Warumungu Aboriginal Land Trust
Kanttaji Aboriginal Land Trust
STUART
HWY
Murchison
20°
Mungkarta Aboriginal Land Trust
Gilbert Bore
McLaren Creek
McLaren
Bonney
Bonney Well
Devils Marbles Conservation Reserve
Mt Fish
Lake Surprise
Mt Davidson
Mt Solitaire
Wauchope
Singleton
Wycliffe Well Roadhouse
Ali-Curung
Warrabri Aboriginal Land Trust
Nelson
Lander River
Wirliyajarrayi Aboriginal Land Trust
Mt Bennett
McDiarmid Hill
Karidi Ck
Mt Theo
Willowra
Crawford Range
Central Desert Aboriginal Land Trust
Mt Patricia
Chilla Well
Ingallan Creek
Mt Peake Ck
Mt Nelson
Taylor Ck
Barrow Creek
Neutral Junction
Pawu Aboriginal Land Trust
Mount Barkly
Bloodwood Ck
Murray Ck
Mt Stirling
Mt Gwynne
Stirling
Wilora
Mt Campbell
Mt Leichhardt
Anningie
Central Mt Stuart
Mt Tops
Central Mt Stuart Historical Reserve
Allee Ck
Yalooqarrie Creek
2 Mile Bore
22°
Moyles Bore
8 Mile Bore
Saltbush Bore
Mt Hardy
Tanami
Yuendumu Aboriginal Land Trust
Cockatoo Ck
Mt Treachery
Coniston
Mount Denison
Crown Ck
Nancy Hill
River
Ti-Tree
Ahakeye Aboriginal Land Trust
Mt Octy
Pmara Jutunta
Mount Skinner
Woolla Downs
Mt Harper
Yuendumu
Yuelamu
Tower Creek
Ti-Tree Farm
HWY
Boundary Bore
Yalpirakinu Aboriginal Land Trust
Hanson
Woodforde
Atartinga
Road
Napperby Ck
Napperby
SANDOVER
Waite River
Yunkanjini Aboriginal Land Trust
Prowse Gap
Mt Glaisher
Aileron
Ryan Well Historic Reserve
Djabangardi Hill
Mueller Ck
87
5
230
137
110
154
229
246
NT 5
NT 7

NT 3

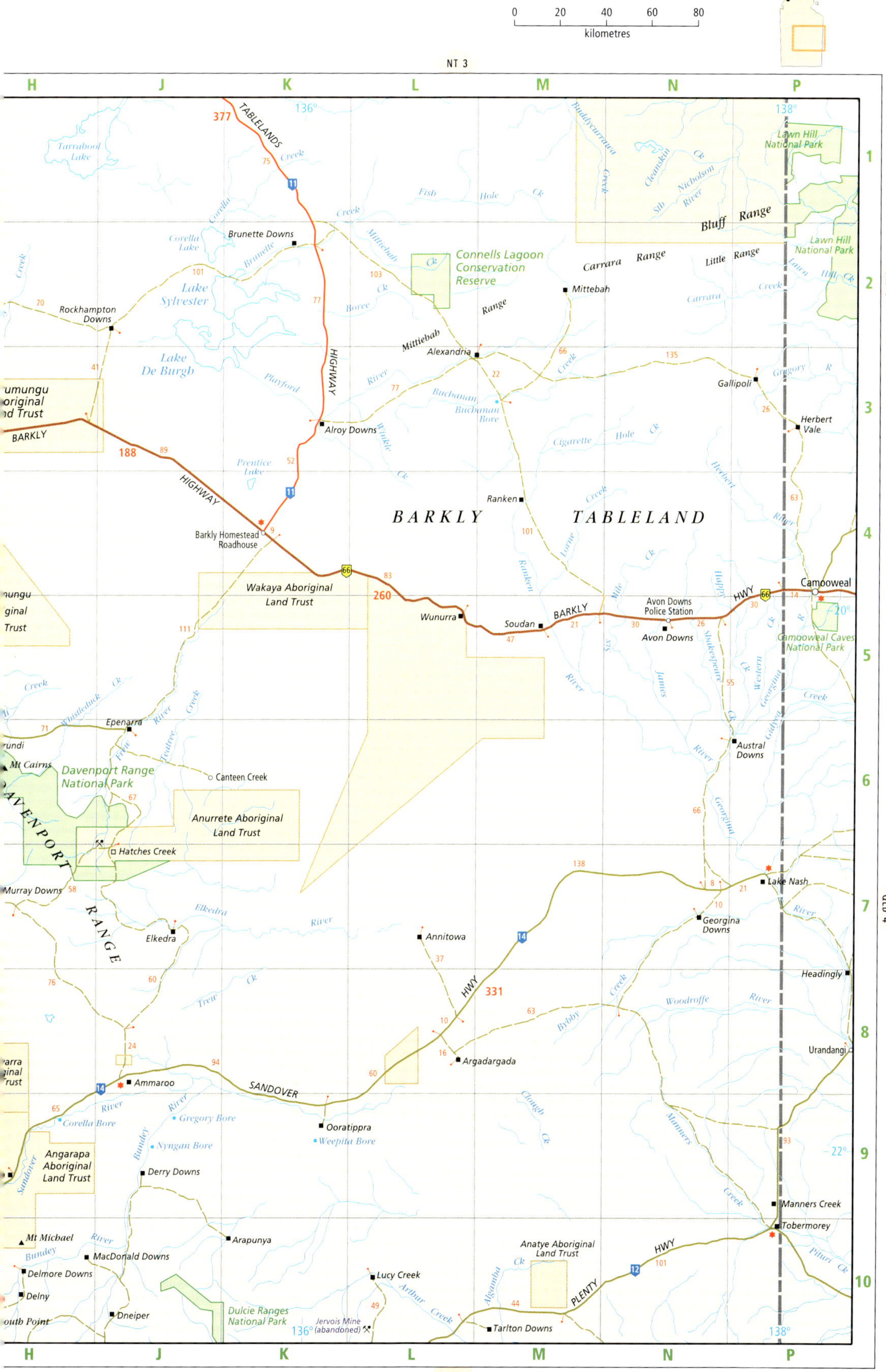

0 20 40 60 80
kilometres
H J K L M N P
1 2 3 4 5 6 7 8 9 10
136°
138°
20°
22°
QLD 3
QLD 4
Tarrabool Lake
TABLELANDS
377
Creek
Lawn Hill National Park
Buddycurrawa Creek
Cleanskin Ck
Nicholson River
Fish Hole Ck
Corella Creek
Corella Lake
Brunette Downs
Brunette
Bluff Range
Connells Lagoon Conservation Reserve
Carrara Range
Little Range
Mittebah
Carrara
Lake Sylvester
Rockhampton Downs
Boree
Range
Mittiebah
Alexandria
Lake De Burgh
Playford
River
HIGHWAY
Gallipoli
Gregory R
Buchanan
Buchanan Bore
Herbert Vale
Alroy Downs
Winkle
Cigarette Hole Ck
umungu original nd Trust
BARKLY
188
HIGHWAY
Prentice Lake
Ranken
BARKLY TABLELAND
Barkly Homestead Roadhouse
Lorne
Ranken
Camooweal
Wakaya Aboriginal Land Trust
260
Wunurra
Soudan
BARKLY
Avon Downs Police Station
Avon Downs
HWY
Camooweal Caves National Park
ungu ginal Trust
James
Shakespeare
Western
Georgina
Creek
Whistleduck Ck
Epenarra
River
Creek
Austral Downs
rundi
Mt Cairns
Frew
Teatree
Canteen Creek
Davenport Range National Park
DAVENPORT
Anurrete Aboriginal Land Trust
Hatches Creek
Lake Nash
Murray Downs
RANGE
Elkedra
River
Georgina Downs
Annitowa
331
HWY
Headingly
Tree Ck
Woodroffe
River
Bybby
Argadargada
Urandangi
arra inal rust
Ammaroo
SANDOVER
Clough Ck
Corella Bore
Gregory Bore
Ooratippra
Weepita Bore
Nyngan Bore
Bundey
Manners
Angarapa Aboriginal Land Trust
Sandover
Derry Downs
Manners Creek
Tobermorey
Mt Michael
Bundey River
Arapunya
Anatye Aboriginal Land Trust
HWY
MacDonald Downs
Delmore Downs
Lucy Creek
Arthur Creek
Algamba
PLENTY
Pituri Ck
Delny
Dneiper
Dulcie Ranges National Park
Jervois Mine (abandoned)
Tarlton Downs
outh Point
NT

NT 7

Map 7

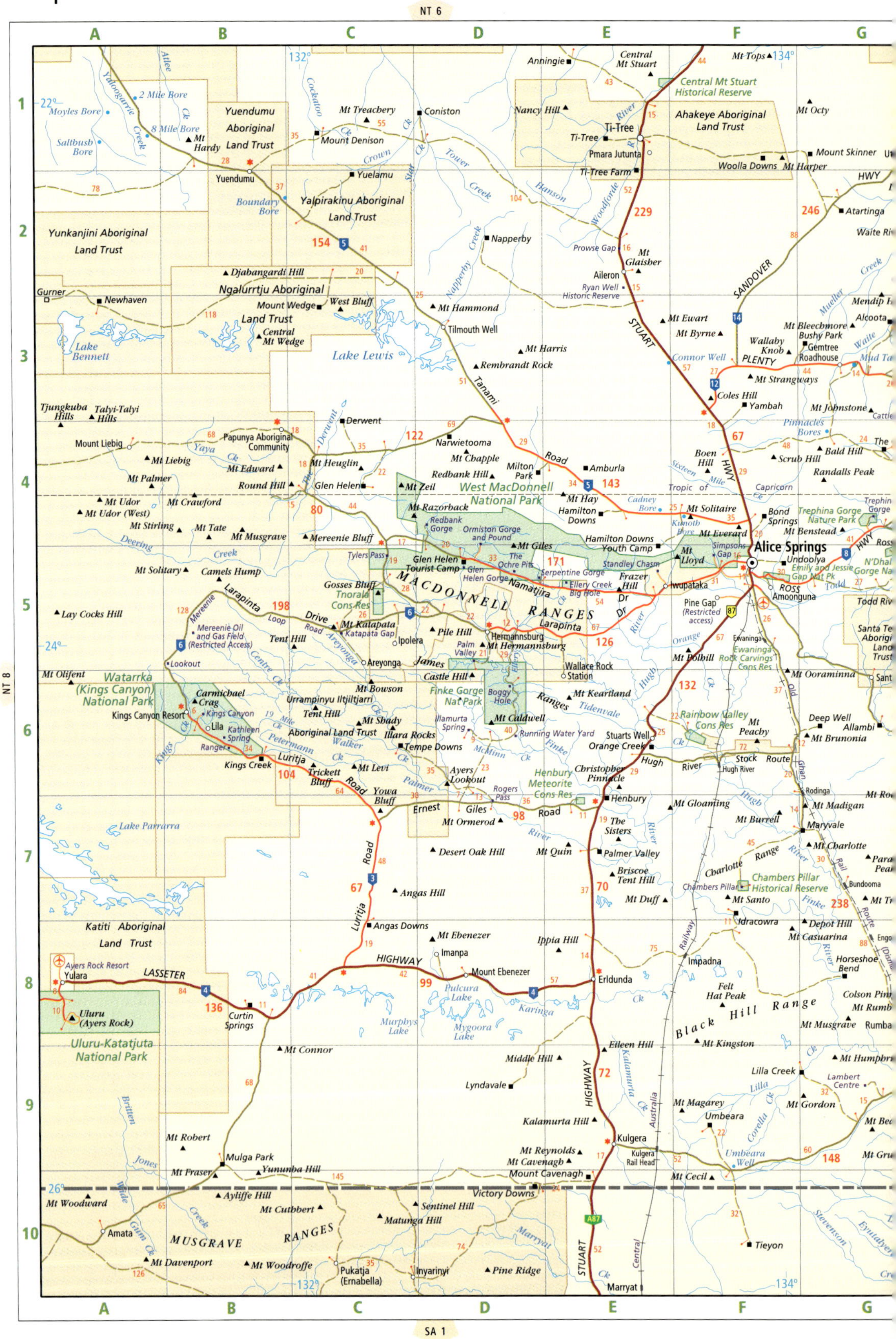
NT 6
A
B
C
D
E
F
G
1
2
3
4
5
6
7
8
9
10
NT 8
SA 1
132°
134°
22°
24°
26°
Yuendumu Aboriginal Land Trust
Yalpirakinu Aboriginal Land Trust
Yunkanjini Aboriginal Land Trust
Ngalurrtju Aboriginal Land Trust
Ahakeye Aboriginal Land Trust
Central Mt Stuart Historical Reserve
Katiti Aboriginal Land Trust
Uluru-Katatjuta National Park
Watarrka (Kings Canyon) National Park
West MacDonnell National Park
Finke Gorge Nat Park
Henbury Meteorite Cons Res
Chambers Pillar Historical Reserve
Rainbow Valley Cons Res
Trephina Gorge Nature Park
Ewaninga Rock Carvings Cons Res
Tnorala Cons Res
Emily and Jessie Gap Nat Pk
Papunya Aboriginal Community
Urrampinyu Iltjiltjarri Aboriginal Land Trust
MACDONNELL RANGES
MUSGRAVE RANGES
Black Hill Range
Alice Springs
Yuendumu
Ti-Tree
Pmara Jutunta
Ti-Tree Farm
Anningie
Central Mt Stuart
Nancy Hill
Mt Tops
Mt Octy
Mount Skinner
Woolla Downs
Mt Harper
Atartinga
Waite River
Mt Treachery
Coniston
Mount Denison
Yuelamu
Napperby
Mt Hardy
2 Mile Bore
8 Mile Bore
Moyles Bore
Saltbush Bore
Boundary Bore
Djabangardi Hill
Mount Wedge
West Bluff
Central Mt Wedge
Gurner
Newhaven
Lake Bennett
Lake Lewis
Mt Hammond
Tilmouth Well
Mt Harris
Rembrandt Rock
Aileron
Ryan Well Historic Reserve
Prowse Gap
Mt Glaisber
Mt Ewart
Mt Byrne
Connor Well
Coles Hill
Yambah
Mt Strangways
Wallaby Knob
Mt Bleechmore
Bushy Park
Gemtree Roadhouse
Alcoota
Mendip Hills
Mud Tank
Mt Johnstone
Pinnacles Bores
Bald Hill
Scrub Hill
Randalls Peak
Tjungkuba Hills
Talyi-Talyi Hills
Mount Liebig
Mt Liebig
Mt Palmer
Mt Edward
Round Hill
Mt Heuglin
Glen Helen
Derwent
Narwietooma
Mt Chapple
Redbank Hill
Milton Park
Amburla
Mt Hay
Hamilton Downs
Cadney Bore
Mt Solitaire
Boen Hill
Sixteen Mile Ck
Tropic of Capricorn
Bond Springs
Mt Benstead
Kunoth Bore
Mt Everard
Mt Udor
Mt Udor (West)
Mt Crawford
Mt Stirling
Mt Tate
Mt Musgrave
Mereenie Bluff
Mt Zeil
Mt Razorback
Redbank Gorge
Ormiston Gorge and Pound
Mt Giles
Hamilton Downs Youth Camp
Mt Lloyd
Simpsons Gap
Standley Chasm
Serpentine Gorge
Ellery Creek Big Hole
The Ochre Pits
Glen Helen Tourist Camp
Glen Helen Gorge
Tylers Pass
Mt Solitary
Camels Hump
Gosses Bluff
Undoolya
Ross
Amoonguna
Todd River
Frazer Hill
Iwupataka
Pine Gap (Restricted access)
Lay Cocks Hill
Mereenie Oil and Gas Field (Restricted Access)
Larapinta Drive
Mereenie Loop Road
Mt Katapata
Katapata Gap
Tent Hill
Areyonga
Ipolera
Pile Hill
Hermannsburg
Mt Hermannsburg
Palm Valley
Wallace Rock Station
Castle Hill
James Ranges
Mt Polhill
Ewaninga
Mt Ooraminna
Santa Teresa Aboriginal Land Trust
Mt Olifent
Lookout
Carmichael Crag
Kings Canyon Resort
Kings Canyon
Lila
Kathleen Spring
Ranger
Kings Creek
Mt Bowson
Tent Hill
Mt Shady
Illara Rocks
Tempe Downs
Illamurta Spring
Boggy Hole
Mt Caldwell
Running Water Yard
Mt Keartland
Stuarts Well
Orange Creek
Mt Peachy
Deep Well
Allambi
Mt Brunonia
Luritja Road
Trickett Bluff
Mt Levi
Yowa Bluff
Ayers Lookout
Rogers Pass
Ernest Giles Road
Mt Ormerod
Christopher Pinnacle
Henbury
Hugh River
Hugh River Stock Route
Rodinga
Mt Gloaming
Mt Madigan
Maryvale
Mt Burrell
Lake Parrarra
Desert Oak Hill
Mt Quin
The Sisters
Palmer Valley
Briscoe Tent Hill
Mt Duff
Charlotte Range
Mt Charlotte
Bundooma
Chambers Pillar
Mt Santo
Idracowra
Depot Hill
Mt Casuarina
Angas Hill
Angas Downs
Mt Ebenezer
Imanpa
Mount Ebenezer
Ippia Hill
Erldunda
Impadna
Horseshoe Bend
Felt Hat Peak
Colson Pinnacle
Mt Rumbalara
Ayers Rock Resort
Yulara
Uluru (Ayers Rock)
Lasseter Highway
Curtin Springs
Pulcura Lake
Mygoora Lake
Murphys Lake
Karinga Ck
Mt Connor
Middle Hill
Eileen Hill
Mt Kingston
Mt Musgrave
Mt Humphries
Lilla Creek
Lambert Centre
Lyndavale
Kalamurta Hill
Mt Magarey
Umbeara
Mt Gordon
Mt Robert
Mulga Park
Yunumba Hill
Mt Fraser
Mt Reynolds
Mt Cavenagh
Mount Cavenagh
Kulgera
Kulgera Rail Head
Umbeara Well
Mt Cecil
Mt Woodward
Ayliffe Hill
Mt Cutbert
Sentinel Hill
Victory Downs
Matunga Hill
Tieyon
Amata
Mt Davenport
Mt Woodroffe
Pukatja (Ernabella)
Inyarinyi
Pine Ridge
Marryat
Stuart Highway
Tanami Road
Namatjira Dr
Sandover Hwy
Plenty Hwy
Ross Hwy
Central Australia Railway
Old Ghan Route
Finke River
Palmer River
Hugh River
Woodforde River
Hanson River
Crown Ck
Tower Creek
Napperby Creek
Yaya Ck
Deering Creek
Walker Ck
Kings Ck
Britten Jones Ck
Gum Ck
Marryat Ck
Stevenson
Eyutalyeye
Kalamurta Ck
Lilla Ck
Coralla Ck
Finke River
Mueller Creek
Ross
Todd
A87
Britten Jones Creek
Wade Creek
154
229
246
122
143
198
80
171
126
132
104
98
70
67
99
136
72
238
148
145

0 20 40 60 80
kilometres

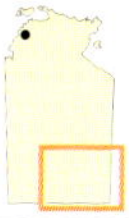

NT 6

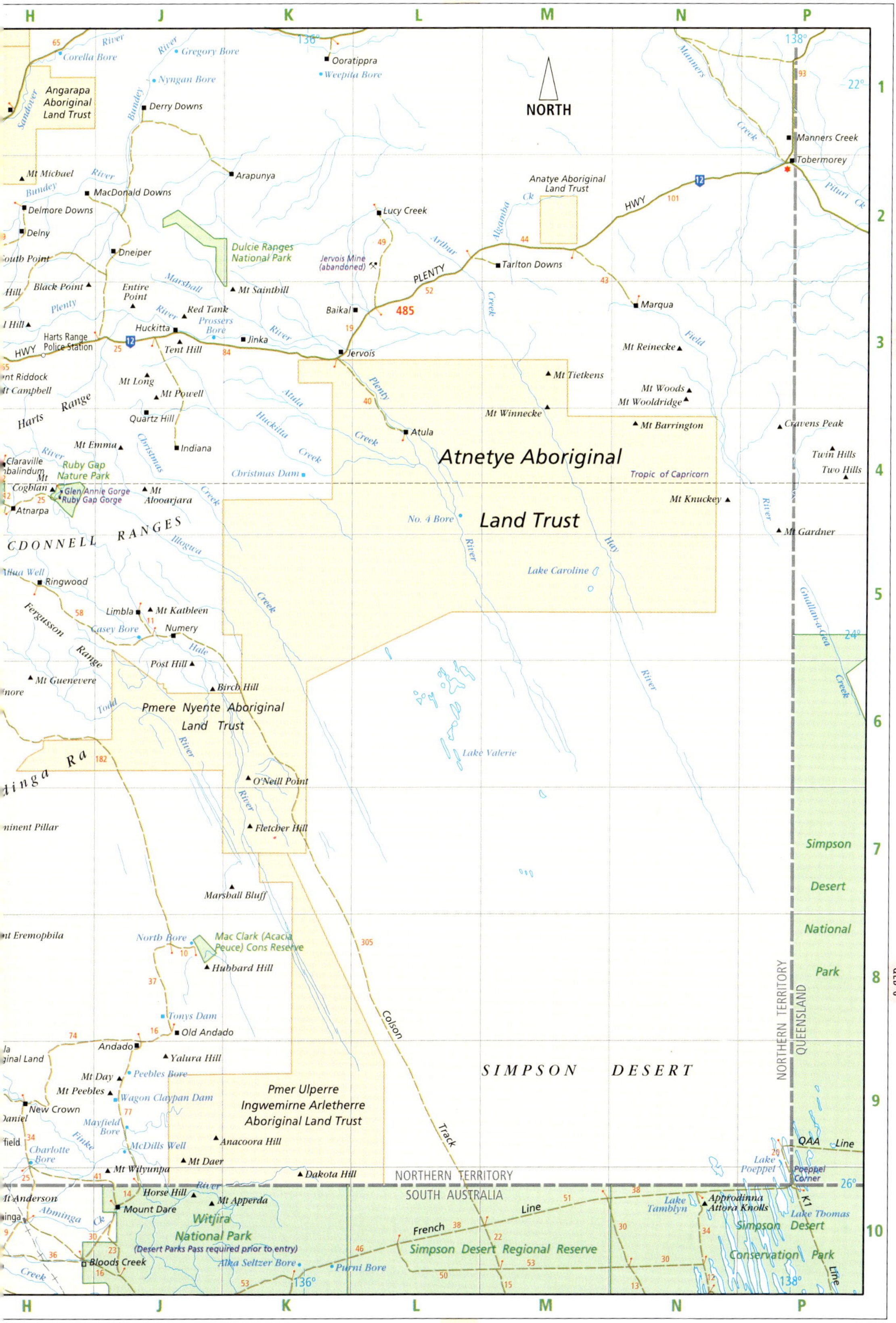

QLD 4
QLD 6

SA 2

Map 8

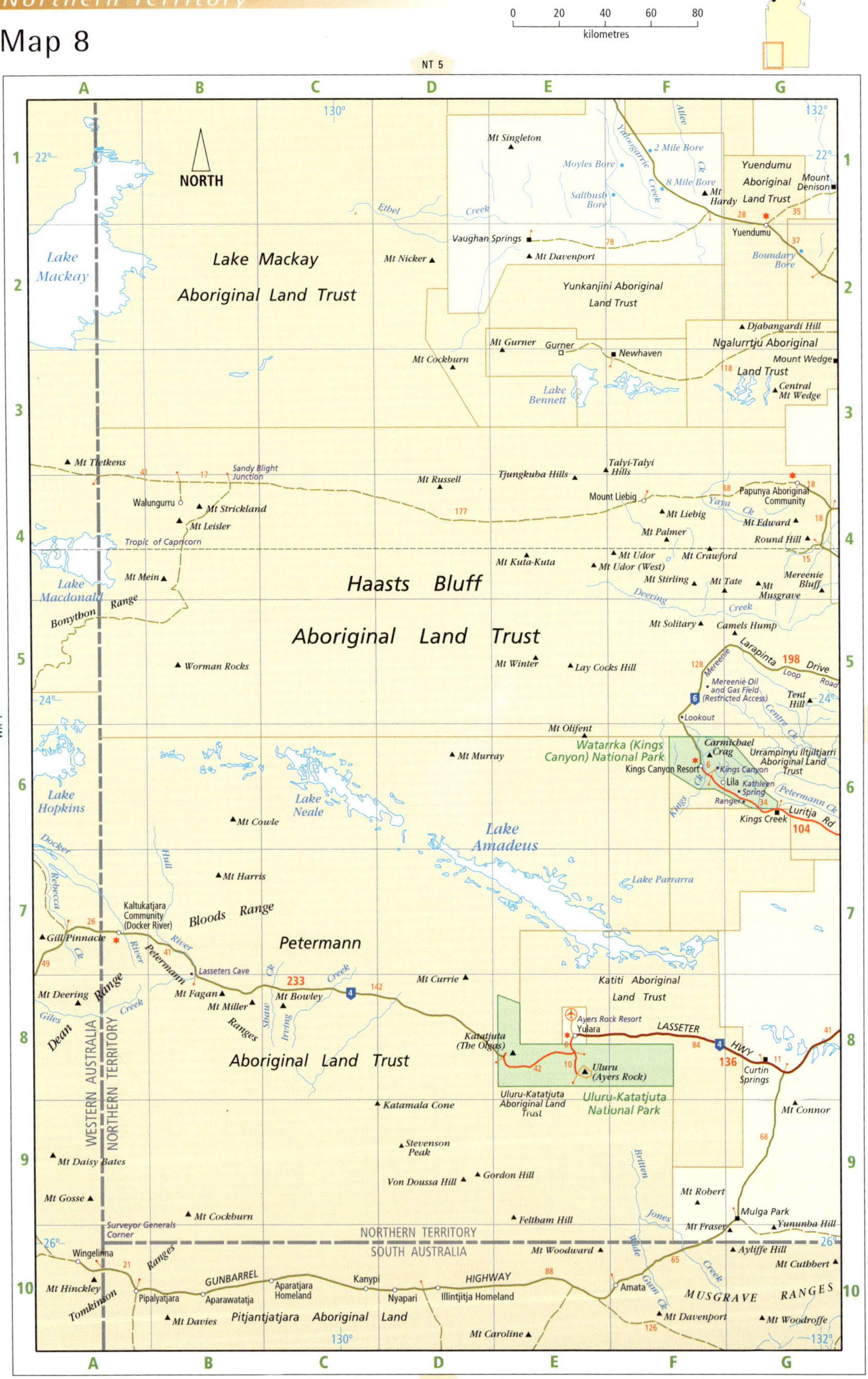
0 20 40 60 80
kilometres
NT 5
NORTH
Lake Mackay
Lake Mackay Aboriginal Land Trust
Yunkanjini Aboriginal Land Trust
Yuendumu Aboriginal Land Trust
Ngalurrtju Aboriginal Land Trust
Haasts Bluff Aboriginal Land Trust
Watarrka (Kings Canyon) National Park
Urrampinyu Iltjiltjarri Aboriginal Land Trust
Lake Amadeus
Lake Neale
Lake Hopkins
Lake Macdonald
Petermann Aboriginal Land Trust
Katiti Aboriginal Land Trust
Uluru-Katatjuta Aboriginal Land Trust
Uluru-Katatjuta National Park
Uluru (Ayers Rock)
Katatjuta (The Olgas)
Ayers Rock Resort
Yulara
LASSETER HWY
Curtin Springs
Kings Canyon Resort
Kings Creek
Luritja Rd
Larapinta Drive
Mereenie Loop Road
Mereenie Oil and Gas Field (Restricted Access)
Papunya Aboriginal Community
Mount Liebig
Walungurru
Kaltukatjara Community (Docker River)
Lasseters Cave
Tropic of Capricorn
Sandy Blight Junction
Surveyor Generals Corner
NORTHERN TERRITORY
SOUTH AUSTRALIA
WESTERN AUSTRALIA
GUNBARREL HIGHWAY
MUSGRAVE RANGES
Pitjantjatjara Aboriginal Land
Wingelinna
Pipalyatjara
Aparawatatja
Aparatjara Homeland
Kanypi
Nyapari
Illintjitja Homeland
Amata
Mulga Park
WA 7
NT 7
SA 1

Index to Attractions

Abbreviations

NP National Park
NR Nature Reserve

Index to Places

Text entries for places are shown in **bold**. Map references appear in the form of map title and grid reference, eg. WA 6 F2.

Abbreviations

CA	Conservation Area
CP	Conservation Park
NP	National Park
NR	Nature Reserve

Acknowledgements

The Publisher believes that permission for use of all images has been obtained from the copyright owners, however, if any errors or omissions have occurred Global Book Publishing would be pleased to hear from copyright owners.

Cover, inset: Image courtesy of Tourism Queensland Image Library
p. 1: Image courtesy of Tourism New South Wales
p. 2: Image courtesy of Tourism New South Wales
p. 11, middle: Image courtesy of Tourism Queensland Image Library
p. 11, bottom: Image courtesy of Tourism Queensland Image Library
pp. 12–13: Image courtesy of Tourism Queensland Image Library
pp. 16–17, top: Image courtesy of Tourism Queensland Image Library
p. 18, bottom: Image courtesy of Tourism Queensland Image Library
p. 20, bottom: Image courtesy of Tourism Queensland Image Library
p. 23, top: Image courtesy of O'Reilly's Guesthouse
p. 23, bottom: Image courtesy of Tourism Queensland Image Library
pp. 24–25, bottom: Image courtesy of Tourism Queensland Image Library
p. 30, top: Image courtesy of Tourism Queensland Image Library
pp. 36–37, top: Image courtesy of Tourism Queensland Image Library
p. 78: Image courtesy of Tourism New South Wales
p. 79, top: Image courtesy of Tourism New South Wales
p. 79, bottom: Image courtesy of Tourism New South Wales
p. 80, bottom: Image courtesy of Tourism New South Wales
p. 84, top: Image courtesy of National Museum of Australia
p. 84, bottom: Image courtesy of Australian War Memorial
p. 104, bottom: Image courtesy of Tourism Victoria
p. 109, top: Image courtesy of Tourism Victoria
p. 114, bottom: Image courtesy of Tourism Victoria
pp. 124–125, top: Image courtesy of Tourism Victoria
pp. 238–239, bottom: Image courtesy of Northern Territory Tourist Commission
p. 242, bottom: Image courtesy of Northern Territory Tourist Commission
p. 243, bottom: Image courtesy of Northern Territory Tourist Commission
p. 244, bottom: Image courtesy of Northern Territory Tourist Commission